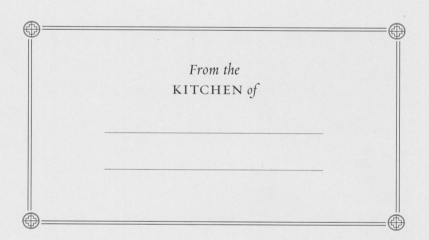

From the
KITCHEN *of*

_____

_____

THE

OF

IRELAND

THE

COUNTRY ✤ COOKING

of

IRELAND

by Colman Andrews

PHOTOGRAPHS BY
Christopher Hirsheimer

FOREWORD BY
Darina Allen

CHRONICLE BOOKS
SAN FRANCISCO

Do mo Érin féin, le grá mór

Text copyright © 2009 by Colman Andrews.
Photographs copyright © 2009 by Christopher Hirsheimer.

Library of Congress Cataloging-in-Publication Data available.
ISBN 978-0-8118-6670-5

Manufactured in China

Designed by Jacob T. Gardner
Typesetting by Janis Reed

Archival photography credits—Pages 43 and 375: courtesy of Tourism Ireland;
page 50 (top): copyright © Illustrated London News Ltd/Mary Evans;
pages 50 (bottom) and 153: courtesy of Waterford County Museum;
pages 75, 86, and 226: courtesy of National Photographic Archive, Dublin;
page 281: copyright © Pacemaker Press International;
page 289: courtesy Ulster Folk and Transport Museum.

10 9 8 7 6 5 4 3

Chronicle Books LLC
680 Second Street
San Francisco, California 94107
www.chroniclebooks.com

[O]ver it all—the white houses, the green fields with their stone walls, the long road winding, the slow herds coming along in the knee-deep dust, the sweet smell of turf burning, the little carts with coloured shafts, the soft Irish voices, the quick Irish smiles—over it all, and in it as if imprisoned in the stone and brick of this country, as if buried beneath the grass and hidden in the trees, is something that is half magic and half music.

—H. V. Morton, *In Search of Ireland* [1930]

We can feel the beauty of a magnificent landscape perhaps,
but we can describe a leg of mutton and turnips better.

—William Makepeace Thackeray, *The Irish Sketchbook* [1843]

TABLE·OF·CONTENTS

ACKNOWLEDGMENTS

Above all, I owe a great debt to Peter and Mary Ward, for showing me what Ireland was all about in the first place and making sure I fell in love with it; for countless meals and tastes of things and introductions and leads, and help with the Irish language; and in general for being so passionate about their native country and both its wonderful foods and its immense culinary potential. Next, I must thank Darina Allen, for all kinds of help and encouragement and a good many recipes, and of course Myrtle Allen, without whose efforts over the past half century it's very possible I wouldn't have found all that much to write about in Ireland today. (And thanks to Tim Allen for the bread lesson.) I have to express my gratitude as well to Enda and Marie Conneely, for hospitality and information galore; to Robert Ditty for baking advice, good company, and exposure to some of Northern Ireland's best artisanal foodstuffs; and to Margaret Jeffares of Good Food Ireland for bringing it all together and showing it to the world, and making my job easier along the way.

I must also sincerely thank the many restaurateurs, chefs, and hoteliers who have been generous with their time, their food and drink, their knowledge, and of course their recipes—chief among them Ross Lewis, Gerry Galvin, Maurice Keller, Catherine Fulvio, Noel McMeel, Peter MacCann, Kay Harte, Paul Flynn, Justin and Jenny Green, Seamus Hogan, Kevin Dundon, Ian Orr, Gerri Gilliland, Carmel Somers, Nancy Byrne and Anne Gernon, Elaine Murphy, Nick Price, and Ann De Piero. For recipes from their home kitchens, thanks go to Roselind Shaw and Kathleen McClintock, Anne Costelloe, Colm Finnegan, and Belle Casares. Liz Pearson, whose grandmother comes from County Clare, tested a number of the recipes and answered some basic food questions. Sarah Black of Fairway Markets was a font of information about baking, and Tod Bramble of King Arthur Flour gave me useful tips. Also, my sincere appreciation to those chefs and authors whose recipes I've adapted or drawn on for inspiration without them having realized it.

A number of writers, poets, and scholars generously shared their knowledge and insights with me, including Mairtin Mac Con Iomaire, Regina Sexton, Clodagh McKenna, Thomas McCarthy, Marjorie Quarton, Caiman O'Brien, and John and Sally McKenna.

Thanks, too, to the farmers and artisanal producers who welcomed me, let me sample their wares, and gave me an inside look into the heart of Ireland's food revolution. Key among these are Giana and Tom Ferguson, Fingal Ferguson, Frank Hederman and Caroline Workman, Frank Krawczyk, Norman and Veronica Steele, Sally Barnes, Anthony Creswell, Cait Curran, David Llewellyn, Anne Marie Mullen, Maurice Kettyle, Ed Hick, James McGeough, Jane Murphy, Esther Barron, Barbara Harding, Helen Finnegan, Gudrun and Frank Shinnick, Maya Binder and Olivier Beaujouan, Jeffa Gill, and Donal Creedon.

I'm grateful to Roger Dixon, Alan McCartney, and especially Fionnuala Carragher of the Ulster Folk and Transport Museum; to the staffs of Ireland's National Library and Photographic Archives in Dublin; to Desmond FitzGerald, the Knight of Glin; to Lady Alison Rosse and the Birr Castle Archives; and to Adrian Wisdom, Donal Moore, Pat Collum, and John O'Neill.

Ruth Moran and her colleagues at Tourism Ireland in New York City and Elaine Craig of Northern Ireland Tourism in Belfast have been a great help.

At Chronicle Books, I must thank Bill LeBlond for not laughing me out of that tapas bar when I suggested doing a major book on Irish cooking, Sarah Billingsley for shepherding the project through the system so ably, and Jacob T. Gardner for both his design skills and his flexibility. Thanks, too, to Deborah Kops, who offered many good suggestions. And many, many thanks to my agent, Michael Psaltis, of Regal Literary, Inc. and the Culinary Cooperative, for all his advice and support and, of course, for making the deal.

And finally, but also first and foremost, there's the A Team: Christopher Hirsheimer, whose delicious and evocative photographs don't just illustrate this volume but bring it alive, and her colleague Melissa Hamilton, who, with Christopher, made sense out of some of the most challenging recipes in this volume and elegantly refined some of the simplest. Couldn't have done it without you, guys.

⚫ FOREWORD ⚫

For many years, visitors to Ireland praised the quality of the produce but despaired when they tasted the end result on the plate. A lot has changed in Ireland. The produce is still beautiful, and becoming ever more so as people go back to organic farming, buying locally and seasonally, and living gently off the land. We've gone from a nation for whom "local" was a derogatory word to one in which farmers' markets are flourishing around the country. And you know, locally grown and prepared food never *really* went away, as Colman Andrews has discovered. The "local" that people talk about in yearning tones elsewhere is something we still have right under our noses. We spend a lot of time agitating for the preservation of our traditional food culture, and mourn keenly the loss of each small butcher or baker who shuts up shop. But Colman makes us see afresh the value of what we've managed to maintain—which is a lot, actually—and helps us understand the great urgency of fighting to preserve it.

I've been going to America for twenty years now, and I can't believe how many times I've had to emphasize that we don't just live on corned beef, potatoes, and cabbage in Ireland. Colman, more clearly than most, can see the evolution and the revolution that has taken place in Irish food and transmits that here in a clear and charming way.

Colman's tasteful curatorial eye is observant and eclectic, almost magpielike; he has chosen the best and most interesting sweetmeats to present. He's been extremely thorough in his research, too. But although I love the mixture of esoteric recipes with simple country dishes like prawns on brown bread and Mary Ward's secret recipe for Christmas pudding (reason alone to buy the book!), my favorite parts of this book are the delightfully interwoven snippets of country life he's captured in his historical research, interviews with artisans, and vignettes of country house hotels. Colman sees the potential of the new generation of Irish artisan food producers—farmhouse cheese and butter makers, meat curers, fish smokers, home bakers, and jam makers—to attract tourism. He recognizes the ways in which tradition and modernity have combined to form a progressive way forward for Ireland.

Colman, with his global perspective and vast knowledge of different food cultures, has looked in and seen how we are, and this book is an unprecedented celebration of what he's observed. I'm so glad that things have come full circle.

Darina Allen
BALLYMALOE COOKERY SCHOOL
SHANAGARRY, COUNTY CORK

ABOUT THE RECIPES

In selecting recipes for this book, I've defined "country cooking" broadly: Basically, I've considered as fair game anything from Ireland that isn't exclusive to or strongly associated with either of the island's two major cities, Dublin and Belfast (there is one exception to this; see page 150)—cities whose food is rich fodder for another kind of book entirely. Included are recipes for traditional dishes—among them all the basics, including several versions each of those definitive culinary creations, Irish stew and soda bread—but also for home cooking of the twentieth and twenty-first centuries, archaic dishes drawn from manuscripts dating back as far as the early eighteenth century, and modern Irish creations from contemporary country-house hotels and regional restaurants. Some of the recipes here are amalgams of several (or many), based on my own research and eating experiences in Ireland. Others come straight from a single source, whether cook or chef, manuscript or book, even the occasional Web site. I have always identified the source or inspiration where there is only one or where one predominates. To be fair to those sources and inspirations, though, I should note that there is not a single recipe herein that appears exactly as it did in the original material. I've adapted, streamlined, filled out, and rewritten as necessary. Any infelicities or inauthenticities that may appear—and I hope they are few—are thus mine alone.

A Note on Metric Conversions

For the convenience of readers who use metric measurements, quantity and temperature equivalents have been given in the recipes that follow. Please note that the conversions are approximate and have been rounded off for reasons of practicality (1 pound of weight, for instance, has been translated as 500 grams, not 454, which would be more accurate; an oven temperature of 400°F becomes 200°C, not the more precise 204°C). In one case, for butter, two different equivalents are used: 220 grams per cup for baking (close enough to the actual equivalent, 213 grams, to avoid changing the consistency of the baked item), 250 grams for cooking (an easier measure, for cases where precision is less important). Diameter and volume measurements for pots and baking dishes correspond to sizes that are actually available (e.g., a 2-quart vessel becomes a 2-liter one).

A Note on Ingredients

Bacon means conventional American bacon (which the Irish and British call "streaky bacon"), preferably a premium brand such as Nueske's, Niman Ranch, Applegate Farms, or Nodine's. *Irish bacon* means Irish or Irish-style back bacon, preferably Galtee's sliced cured pork loin, Tommy Mooney's mild-cured (not smoked or back rashers), or Donnelly's (see Sources, page 369). The word "bacon" in some recipe titles refers to cured pork loin; in those cases, pork loin is specified in the ingredients list.

Butter means unsalted butter, preferably Kerrygold from Ireland (now widely available in American supermarkets), which has a richness and elastic texture particularly suited to these recipes. Kerrygold is most often sold in the United States in ½-lb/220-g (16-Tbsp) bars. It is also available by mail order (see Sources, page 369).

Eggs are large (about 2 oz/60 g each) and should be fresh. Use organic eggs if possible.

Flour types are specified in ingredients lists. Whole wheat flour should be Irish or Irish-style if possible, and in any case, stone-ground flour (organic if possible) is preferred. White flour should also be Irish if possible, and unbleached and organic are always preferable. (See Sources on page 369 for information on where to get Irish flour.) Do not use self-rising flour unless specified. Soft unbleached pastry flour (not cake flour) is a workable substitute for Irish white flour in baking recipes. In recipes calling for a small amount of flour for thickening soups and stews, frying, dusting, etc., any good-quality white flour, preferably unbleached, may be used.

Fruit and vegetables are medium or standard size and are always washed, trimmed, and peeled, as necessary, before using, unless otherwise specified.

Herbs—in sprigs or chopped up—are always fresh unless otherwise specified. There is one exception: Bay leaves are dried but whole.

Milk means whole milk, unless buttermilk (which is by definition reduced in fat) is specified.

Pepper should be good quality coarse-ground black pepper, either packaged or freshly ground, unless otherwise specified.

Salt should be fine-ground sea salt or kosher salt.

Spices are always ground, unless otherwise specified, with the exception of cloves, which are whole.

Sugar is standard granulated sugar, unless powdered, super-fine (known in the United Kingdom as "castor sugar"), or brown sugar is specified. *Brown sugar* should be unrefined, like Demerara or turbinado.

Unless otherwise specified, all ingredients should be brought to room temperature before using.

Ireland

Bushmills

Londonderry/ Derry

NORTHERN

DONEGAL

Donegal

DERRY

Toomebridge

ANTRIM

Belfast

Castledawson

Lough Neagh

TYRONE

IRELAND

FERMANAGH

Enniskillen

ARMAGH

DOWN

Sligo

LEITRIM

CAVAN

MONAGHAN

MAYO

SLIGO

LOUTH

ROSCOMMON

LONGFORD

Lough Corrib

Connemara

GALWAY

WESTMEATH

MEATH

G

Galway

OFFALY

Galway Bay

Lough Derg

Birr

LAOIS

KILDARE

I RE L A N D

DUBLIN

Dublin

Dublin Bay

Ashford

Wicklow

WICKLOW

CLARE

Nenagh

TIPPERARY

KILKENNY

CARLOW

Limerick

Tipperary

Kilkenny

WEXFORD

KERRY

LIMERICK

Wexford

Dingle

Waterford

Killarney

CORK

WATERFORD

Arklow

Dungarven

Cork

Midleton

Cobh

Ballymaloe

Kinsale

Atlantic Ocean

Irish Sea

Gover '09

A NOTE ON GEOPOLITICS

As early as the sixth century A.D., Ireland was divided into five provinces, called *cúigí*, or "fifths." These were (to give them their English names) Ulster, Leinster, Connacht, Munster, and Mide, the last of which was later subsumed, mostly into Leinster. In the centuries following the Norman invasion of Ireland in the twelfth century, these provinces became divided, little by little, into counties—thirty-two of them eventually. Some boundaries and county names have changed over time, a few old counties have been grafted onto others, and in recent years, two counties—Tipperary and Dublin—have been further subdivided for administrative purposes. Thirty-two traditional names are still in common use, however, and most evoke strong cultural and historical associations. For that reason, in almost all cases in the pages that follow, when I mention a town or city, I link it to its county.

Those thirty-two counties, though, are divided between two countries: Ireland or Éire (sometimes incorrectly called the Republic of Ireland, which is its official description but not its name) and Northern Ireland, which is a part of the United Kingdom and has a large population of English and Scottish descent. The British Crown has exercised dominion over parts of the island, and at times the whole, for centuries. The division of Ireland into two parts came after Irish independence in 1921 and has been a matter of contention ever since—most tragically during the thirty-year period, beginning in the late 1960s, known as "the Troubles." During this time, internecine political and sectarian violence claimed the lives of more than three thousand people, mostly in Northern Ireland. The so-called Belfast or Good Friday Agreement, signed in 1998, began a healing process

that has greatly benefited the whole island. The spirit of cross-border cooperation since then has affected most aspects of Irish life, including the agricultural and touristic, and by extension the culinary.

Terminology remains tricky. In the pages that follow, when I refer simply to Ireland or to "the island," I am talking about the entire land mass as a cultural (and/or culinary) whole. "Northern Ireland," with the *n* capitalized, means the country that is part of the United Kingdom. Because Northern Ireland is not the northernmost entity on the island, though—Ireland's County Donegal reaches higher than Northern Ireland's northern edge—"northern Ireland" with a lowercase *n* means the northern part of the land mass, including portions of both countries. One of the terms of that historic 1998 agreement grants residents of Northern Ireland the right to describe themselves as British, Irish, or both. By including their county within "Ireland" in the broad sense of the word, I certainly mean no disrespect to those who have chosen the first of those alternatives.

A more difficult issue is how to refer to one of Northern Ireland's counties and major cities: It is Londonderry to the British and to many Northern Irelanders (mostly Protestants), and Derry in the south and to Catholic Northern Irelanders. The politically correct call it L'Derry or Derry/Londonderry, which has earned it the nickname Stroke City, the backward slash being the "stroke." For reasons of clarity, I've used Derry in these pages, at least partly because that's a direct Anglicization of its old Irish name, Daire, meaning "oak grove." Again, I mean no disrespect to those who prefer to give it its more recent (seventeenth-century) name.

INTRODUCTION

It is often said that the Irish do not have good food. This is not true. They just say that their food is not good so you won't get any of it!

——Colin Bladey, Irish food blogger

Nua gacha bid agus sean gacha dighe. ["Every food fresh, every drink mature."]

——Old Irish saying

There is a sense in which all Irish cooking—at least the good stuff, the real thing—is country cooking. It is almost inevitably straightforward, homey fare, based on first-rate raw materials whose identity shines through. Even in sophisticated urban restaurants, it tends to have an underlying earthiness and solidity that suggest honesty and respect for rural tradition. This is not surprising, since no other nation in Western Europe—not even Italy or Spain—remains as intimately and pervasively connected to the land as Ireland does. Almost any Irishman or Irishwoman you meet, including those Armani-suited business tycoons and Diesel-clad club kids you'll meet in Dublin or Belfast, will admit to some personal association with a farm: grew up on one, spent childhood summers on one, has a brother or an aunt or a good friend who owns one. At the very least, Grandma kept a cow for milk or Grandpa had a small potato patch or both. (The president of Ireland herself, Mary McAleese, has long maintained a vegetable garden and a chicken coop on the grounds of the Áras an Uachtaráin, the Irish White House.) Whether the average citizen realizes it or not, this close connection to the soil is one of the island's greatest cultural strengths, and it helps give great promise to the future of Irish cuisine.

At the same time, perhaps no other nation in Europe has heard its food so consistently maligned—often for good reason. More than one reader must have nodded in agreement when the Dublin physician F. R. Cruise observed, back in 1896, that "while God supplies the provisions, very often another, and unmentionable being, sends the cook!" Three generations later, in the 1960s, while attending a horse fair in Buttevant, County Cork, the County Tipperary writer and horse breeder Marjorie Quarton was subjected to a meal at a local hotel that was probably all too typical at the time: "[W]ashing-up-water soup . . . boiled whatever-it-is . . . raw potatoes . . . liquid grey cabbage and melting, onion-flavoured ice cream. . . . Even the tea was undrinkable, resembling liquid

brown boot polish." No sane person ever questioned the quality of Irish stout or whiskey, but what did people actually *eat* over there? Irish stew and soda bread, fine, and then what? An Irish seven-course dinner, went the old joke, was a potato and a six-pack of Guinness. Milton Berle once quipped that *Irish Gourmet Cooking* was one of the four shortest books in the world.

The truth is that the Irish used to eat very well indeed. Even back in the hunter-gatherer days, ten thousand years ago or so, inhabitants of the island enjoyed a varied diet, including salmon, eel, and trout (all of which they smoked), wild boar, hare, thrush, pigeon, wild apples, wild pears, hazelnuts, and possibly water lily seeds. Following the domestication of cattle, sheep, and goats and the first cultivation of cereal crops some millennia later, a variety of farm-raised meats and porridge and basic flatbreads were added to the diet. The Irish also developed an almost obsessive passion for what they called *bánbhianna*, or "white meats"—the collective name given to an immense range of milk products, including fresh milk, sour milk, buttermilk, butter (enjoyed both fresh and preserved), clabber, cheese curds, and numerous varieties of cheese.

Successive waves of invaders added to the larder: The Vikings, who first raided Ireland in A.D. 795 and went on to found Waterford, Wexford, Limerick, Cork, and Dublin, had a well-developed trade with the Mediterranean, and brought in olive oil and wine. In the twelfth century, the Anglo-Normans improved agricultural methods and introduced pulses and other vegetables previously unknown to the island, as well as spices and a taste for sweet-and-sour flavors. The English, who first settled in Ireland in significant numbers in the sixteenth century, gave the country still more new foods, everything from turkeys to (possibly) potatoes. The latter changed Irish life forever, in ways both positive and negative, and so did the English themselves. The history of the English in Ireland is a violent, complicated tale, controversial in interpretation even to this day, and this is not the place to attempt to retell it. Suffice it to say, in the words of the County Tipperary archeologist and food historian Caiman O'Brien, that "Ireland's indigenous food culture disappeared when the Irish lords lost their land."

Today, a new indigenous Irish food culture is being born.

There are countless Irish saints, kings, and mythological figures called Colman, and I can trace a branch of my father's family back to counties Tyrone and Donegal in the eighteenth and early nineteenth centuries (the names involved were mostly Scots-Irish or English ones like Hardy, Stewart, Craig, Creswell, Patton, Porter, and Whitehill). But my mother named me after Ronald Colman—she'd been an ingenue in a movie with him—and I visited Ireland for the first time only in 2002. I was invited that year by the Bord Bía, or Irish Food Board, to speak at a specialty food symposium in Kinsale, County Cork, the putative food capital of the country (see page 61). I didn't exactly have a culinary epiphany at the event, but I did get my first taste of some excellent artisanal Irish cheeses. More important, it was there that I met County Tipperary grocer Peter Ward (see page 301), who was to become my guide and mentor in all things Irish—above all those related to farming, cooking, and eating.

Encouraged by Ward, I returned to Ireland for another visit. Since then, I have been back more than a dozen times (I made six trips in 2008 alone, specifically to research this book). And on my third trip there—somewhere between nibbling Connemara lamb "prosciutto" at the innovative butcher James McGeough's shop in Oughterard, watching Barbara Harding slap her fresh-made country butter into slabs with two wooden paddles near Borrisokane, and devouring pig's trotter "boudin" and sautéed plaice with crushed potatoes and mushy peas at the stylish Chapter One in Dublin—the epiphany finally came. I saw the light, and tasted the full flavor of Irish culinary possibility. I came to the realization that Ireland—for its superlative raw materials, its immensely satisfying traditional home cooking, and its new wave of artisanal producers and imaginative but well-grounded chefs—was simply one of the most exciting food stories in the world today.

It all starts with that land that everyone's connected to: Ireland may be gray and rainy a lot of the time, but its climate is mild (the late-twelfth-century visitor Giraldus Cambrensis, or Gerald of Wales, called it "the most temperate of all countries"), and it boasts vast expanses of mineral-rich farmland conducive to growing things, above all grass and the animals that feed on it. Ireland also has more than 3,500 miles/5,600 kilometers of coastline, washed by unpolluted waters and teeming with fish and shellfish of the highest quality. (I've never before been in a country where so much freshly, locally landed seafood is available, in small towns as well as big cities—even though the Irish still take comparatively little advantage of it.) The island also has a living tradition of small farms, an increasing number of them organic or nearly so. (As the Irish-American author J. P. Donleavy once put it, the Irishman "has held up his hand to object to the poisonous residues which grant nations their badge of honor as they progress.") There is relatively little soulless agribusiness in Ireland, and there's an active campaign against genetically modified crops and livestock. The scale of production in much of the country makes sustainability and traceability endemic; "farm-to-table" isn't just a catch-phrase—it's a description of real distribution practices, at least in more enlightened quarters. Ireland is green in more ways than one.

It's also red-hot. All over Ireland, from the artisanal ateliers of West Cork to the lush market gardens of County Wicklow to bustling Galway and burgeoning County Antrim and stark but friendly County Donegal, a new culinary world is taking shape: Rural entrepreneurs are bucking food-unfriendly regulators to build little businesses around small-scale food production and distribution; established restaurants are revising their menus to take better advantage of the native bounty, while new ones are opening with a sense of Irish-based imagination and adventure; and scholars and lay writers are delving seriously into the lore and history of Irish cooking and eating, encouraging producers and chefs alike. Forget the jokes (remember how we used to laugh about quality of English cooking, before we dubbed London one of the best restaurant cities on earth?): Ireland has the potential to become, in the very near future, one of the most compelling gastronomic destinations in Europe—and it's already a darned good place to eat and, of course, to cook.

The Warmth of the Hearth

In the lavish days of old . . . it was believed that you couldn't have soup unless
you kept a perpetually-simmering cauldron in which legs of mutton and beef,
haunches of venison, flocks of fowl and game and entire market-gardens.
were coaxed into yielding up their succulence.

—Maura Laverty, *Maura Laverty's Cookbook* [1947]

Of all the things you cook in your kitchen, surely soup is the most
personal. It needn't have a name, it need never taste the same, and you may
never even remember how you made it.

—Monica Sheridan, *The Art of Irish Cooking* [1965]

Soup is the most basic of culinary preparations, precisely because, as the pioneering Irish food writer Monica Sheridan observed, it is the most personal. Another way of putting it is to say that it is the most forgiving: You can

throw almost anything into the pot—meat, seafood, fowl, game, offal, vegetables, herbs, even fruit—and then fiddle with it endlessly until it tastes right. The whole idea of soup is attractive; the very word sounds reassuring. It suggests warmth (the odd cold soup aside), seductive aromas, satisfaction. Soup comforts as it nourishes.

The earliest Irish soups were probably gruel-like mixtures of grains (most often oatmeal) and root vegetables or foraged plants, like the famous, ancient Brotchán Foltchep (facing page). But there was a cauldron on almost every open hearth in Ireland, and what went into it was whatever was available, maybe seaweed and wild berries, or dumplings made from leftover bread dough, or maybe, if you were lucky, bits of pig meat not otherwise employed, such as the cheeks and the tongue. Soup was a godsend to the rural poor—its main ingredient, after all, is water. But it could also be turned into a dish fit to be served at the finest tables, ladled out into bone china soup plates from a tureen of Georgian silver.

Vegetable soups remain common to this day in Ireland, even in dining rooms of great refinement; elegant purées are especially popular. Meat and poultry are used mostly as flavoring. In this seafood-rich country, fish and shellfish are surprisingly rare in traditional soups, except along the coast. Whatever they're made from, though, Irish soups tend to be serious business, distillations of the best of the land (and sometimes the sea).

Cottage Broth

Serves 6 to 8

Variously known as cottage broth, farm broth, or farmhouse soup, this basic restorative was typically constructed with odds and ends of whatever vegetables, dried or fresh, could be found in the house, and can be made with either beef or lamb. The early-twentieth-century Northern Irish cooking teacher Florence Irwin noted that "This used to be the peasants' Christmas dinner, perhaps the only day in the year on which fresh meat was eaten."

1/2 LB/250 G BONELESS BEEF SHANK, BRISKET, STEWING BEEF, OR STEWING LAMB, CUT INTO SMALL CUBES

1/4 CUP/50 G PEARL BARLEY

1/4 CUP/50 G DRIED GREEN SPLIT PEAS OR MARROWFAT PEAS [SEE SOURCES, PAGE 369], SOAKED OVERNIGHT

1 CARROT, CHOPPED

1 ONION, CHOPPED

1 SMALL RUTABAGA OR WHITE TURNIP, CHOPPED

1 STALK CELERY, CHOPPED

SALT AND PEPPER

1 TBSP MINCED FRESH PARSLEY

Combine the beef or lamb, barley, and split peas in a large pot with 6 cups/1.5 L of water. Bring to a boil over high heat, then reduce the heat to low, skim off any foam that rises to the surface, and simmer, covered, for 1 hour.

Add the carrot, onion, rutabaga or turnip, celery, and salt and pepper to taste. Continue cooking, partially covered, for 1½ hours or until the meat is very tender, the vegetables are very soft, and the liquid has reduced by about one-third.

Stir in the parsley and adjust the seasoning if necessary.

Brotchán Foltchep

[Leek and Oatmeal Soup]

Serves 4 to 6

This is a modern version of the famous soup, also called *brotchán (or brochan, or brothchán) roy*, or "the king's soup," that is said to have been the favorite dish of Ireland's celebrated sixth-century spiritual and literary icon, St. Columkille. (Some sources say that Columkille's version included nettle tops, and some scholars think that *foltchep* meant "onion" or "chive," not "leek"). It is in any case quite possibly the oldest traditional Irish dish for which it is possible to reconstruct a recipe.

2 TBSP BUTTER

3 TO 4 LEEKS, TRIMMED AND SLICED INTO VERY THIN RINGS

2 CUPS/475 ML CHICKEN STOCK [PAGE 356]

2 CUPS/475 ML MILK

1/2 CUP/80 G IRISH STEEL-CUT OATMEAL

1/2 TSP GROUND MACE

SALT AND PEPPER

Melt the butter in a medium saucepan over low heat, then add the leeks and cook, stirring occasionally, for 12 to 15 minutes, or until the leeks are very soft.

Add the stock and milk. Raise the heat to high and bring to a boil, then sprinkle in the oatmeal. Add the mace and salt and pepper to taste, and return the liquid to a boil, stirring occasionally.

Reduce the heat to low, cover, and simmer for about 45 minutes.

Cráibechán

Serves 8 *to* 10

One chronicler describes *cráibechán* as "[a] pottage or hash formed of meat chopped up small, mixed with vegetables," while a glossary of Irish food names compiled at Queens University in Belfast defines it as porridge or gruel. According to old Irish documents, *cráibechán* is what Esau, in the Old Testament, received from Jacob in return for his birthright. It is also almost certainly the kind of thing being referred to in the eleventh-century tale "The Vision of Mac Conglinne" (see page 175) as "sprouty meat-soup, with its purple berries." On the other hand, an American recipe website gives a recipe, from an Irishman living in Canada, for "cráibechán of the sea," a kind of minced seafood salad garnished with radish roses! The recipe given here involves no seafood; it's just a homey and filling (and vitamin-filled) pottage that would make a good winter supper.

I LB/500 G STEWING BEEF, FINELY DICED

3 ONIONS, MINCED

3 LEEKS, WHITE PART ONLY, MINCED

6 SHALLOTS, MINCED

3 CLOVES GARLIC, MINCED

4 CARROTS, DICED

I PARSNIP, DICED

I RUTABAGA, DICED

I HEAD KALE, FINELY CHOPPED

I BUNCH SORREL, FINELY CHOPPED

I BUNCH WATERCRESS, FINELY CHOPPED

I CUP/150 G FRESH OR I/2 CUP/70 G FREEZE-DRIED ELDERBERRIES [SEE SOURCES, PAGE 369]

I CUP/200 G PEARL BARLEY

I CUP/160 G IRISH STEEL-CUT OR STONE-GROUND OATMEAL

2 BAY LEAVES

SALT

BOILED POTATOES [PAGE 229] FOR SERVING [OPTIONAL]

Combine beef, onions, leeks, shallots, garlic, carrots, parsnip, rutabaga, kale, sorrel, watercress, elderberries, barley, oatmeal, and bay leaves in a large pot and add 4 qt/3.8 L of water. Bring to a boil over high heat, then reduce the heat to low, cover the pot, and simmer for about 3 hours, or until all the vegetables are very soft and the barley is cooked. Season to taste with salt.

To serve in the traditional manner, ladle into large bowls and pass a bowl of boiled potatoes, to be added to the *cráibechán* and broken up with a large spoon.

Watercress and Almond Soup

Serves 4

The late cookbook author Theodora FitzGibbon adapted the recipe for this unusual and delicious soup from "a handwritten recipe book, 1735"; she doesn't specify the family name or county. She does note, though, in her indispensable *Irish Traditional Food*, wherein her version appears, that "Almonds were immensely popular in richer homes in 18th-century Ireland. They were not only used for cakes and puddings, but also with meats, fish, vegetables and in soups." Watercress is a far more ancient food in Ireland, eaten since prehistoric times.

I CUP/240 ML MILK

I CUP/240 ML HEAVY CREAM

RIND OF I LEMON, IN I PIECE IF POSSIBLE, PITH REMOVED

I/2 CUP/40 G GROUND ALMONDS

2 TBSP BUTTER

2 CUPS/300 G MINCED CELERY HEART

2 TBSP WHITE FLOUR

2 I/2 CUPS/600 ML CHICKEN STOCK [PAGE 356]

SALT AND WHITE PEPPER

2 BUNCHES WATERCRESS, TRIMMED

Combine the milk and cream in a small saucepan over high heat. Add the lemon rind and almonds. Bring almost to a boil, then reduce the heat and simmer for 5 to 7 minutes.

WATERCRESS AND ALMOND SOUP

NETTLE SOUP

Remove from the heat, cover, and set aside to infuse for about 30 minutes.

Meanwhile, melt the butter in a medium pot over low heat, add the celery, and cook for 2 to 3 minutes. Sprinkle in the flour and cook for 2 to 3 minutes, stirring constantly with a wooden spoon. Add the stock in a slow, steady stream, stirring constantly, and cook for about 5 minutes, continuing to stir until the sauce thickens.

Strain the infused milk into the stock. Season to taste with salt and pepper. Add the watercress and continue to cook for 6 to 8 minutes more.

Purée the soup in a food processor or blender. Adjust the seasoning if necessary.

Serve hot or cold.

Nettle Soup

Serves 6 to 8

The most common Irish culinary use for nettles, which have a pleasant spinachy flavor, is in soup. This version comes from Giana Ferguson, the master cheese maker from Gubbeen in County Cork. To avoid the nettles' sting, she says, wear rubber gloves when handling them, and snip the tips and tender leaves with scissors (they lose their sharpness and toxicity completely when cooked). In America, unless you're an accomplished forager, look for nettles in farmers' markets in the spring and early summer.

2 TBSP BUTTER

1 ONION, CHOPPED

7 CUPS/1.7 L CHICKEN STOCK [PAGE 356]
OR DUCK STOCK

2 MEDIUM RUSSET POTATOES, CHOPPED

1 LEEK, WHITE AND LIGHT GREEN PARTS ONLY,
CHOPPED

3 TIGHTLY PACKED CUPS YOUNG NETTLE TIPS AND
TENDER LEAVES [ABOUT 1/4 LB/125 G]

SALT AND PEPPER

2 TBSP LEMON JUICE

1/2 CUP/120 ML HEAVY CREAM [OPTIONAL]

Melt the butter in a medium pot over medium heat. Add the onion and cook, stirring frequently, until it softens, 6 to 8 minutes. Add the stock, potatoes, and leek. Bring to a boil, then reduce the heat to medium-low and simmer for about 15 minutes, or until the potatoes are soft.

Add the nettles, season generously with salt and pepper, increase the heat to medium, and cook until the nettles are soft, 5 to 7 minutes.

Remove the soup from the heat and allow to cool slightly. Working in batches if necessary, purée in a food processor or blender, transferring to a bowl as each batch is done. Wipe out the pot and return the soup to it. Heat the soup through over medium heat, then stir in the lemon juice and (if using) cream.

Root Soup

Serves 6 to 8

Ellinor, Lady Bellew, née Ellinor Moore, married Sir Edward Bellew circa 1728 and lived with him at Barmeath Castle in Dunleer, County Louth. In introducing his privately published little volume of eighteenth- and nineteenth-century recipes collected by Lady Bellew, her great-great-great-great-grandson George Bellew advises that if the reader is tempted to try any of the formulae contained therein, "I must proffer a warning not to do so without at least consulting a qualified expert." In fact, some of the recipes are very straightforward and, once you get past archaic and eccentric punctuation, spelling, and abbreviations ("Season wth. Salt & peper to yre. teast"), the style often seems almost modern. This recipe for a hearty fall or winter soup is the first in the collection.

1 LB/500 G DRIED WHOLE WHITE OR YELLOW PEAS,
SOAKED OVERNIGHT

1 CUP/250 G BUTTER

5 CARROTS, THINLY SLICED

1 PARSNIP, THINLY SLICED

4 TURNIPS, THINLY SLICED

4 ONIONS, THINLY SLICED

2 LEEKS, WHITE PART ONLY, THINLY SLICED

1 BUNCH CELERY, THINLY SLICED

2 TBSP WHITE FLOUR

1/2 TSP GROUND MACE

3 TO 4 SALT-PACKED ANCHOVY FILLETS,
WELL RINSED

SALT AND PEPPER

Put the peas into a large pot with about twice as much water as it takes to cover them. Bring to a boil, then reduce the heat to low, cover tightly, and simmer for 2 to 3 hours or until the peas are very tender, adding more water if necessary to keep level constant.

Meanwhile, melt the butter in another large pot over low heat. Add the carrots, parsnip, turnips, onions, leeks, and celery, stir well, and cook for about 10 minutes, stirring frequently. Scatter the flour over the vegetables, stir in well, and continue cooking for about 20 minutes more.

Add the peas and their liquor to the pot with the vegetables and rinse out the pea pot and set aside. Bring the soup to a boil over high heat, then reduce the heat to low, cover, and simmer for 1 hour.

Strain the soup into the empty rinsed pot through a sieve or china cap, pushing down with the back of a wooden spoon to push some puréed solids through.

Add the mace and anchovies, bring the soup to a boil, and let boil for 3 to 4 minutes. Remove from the heat and season to taste with salt and pepper.

Lettuce, Potato, and Pea Soup

Serves 4 to 6

Northern Irish quilt preservationist and collector Roselind Shaw learned to make this soup when she studied cooking at the College of Business Studies in Belfast.

2 TBSP BUTTER

1 LARGE HEAD ROMAINE OR BUTTER LETTUCE,
JULIENNED

1 ONION, MINCED

1 TBSP WHITE FLOUR

2 CUPS/475 ML MILK

3 POTATOES, DICED

1 CUP SHELLED FRESH PEAS
[ABOUT 1 LB/500 G PEAS IN PODS]

SALT AND PEPPER

1 TO 2 CUPS/240 TO 475 ML CHICKEN STOCK
[PAGE 356]

Melt the butter in a Dutch oven or heavy-bottomed pot over low heat, then add the lettuce and onion, stir well, and cook for 2 to 3 minutes. Sprinkle in the flour and stir until it is well integrated.

Add the milk in a slow, steady stream, stirring constantly. Add the potatoes and peas and season to taste with salt and pepper.

Add as much stock as you need for the desired consistency, then raise the heat to high and bring to a boil. Reduce the heat to low, cover the Dutch oven, and cook for about 20 minutes, or until the peas and potatoes are done.

SHARP AND GOOD

Nettles—often called "stinging nettles" for the tiny, mildly toxic needlelike hairs that cover them—are wild plants of the genus *Urtica*. They have been foraged in Ireland for thousands of years and were mentioned often in old tales and folklore. The historian A. T. Lucas recounts the story of the hermit priest St. Kevin (circa 498–618), abbot of Glendalough, County Wicklow: According to tradition, he lived on a diet of nettles and sorrel (and slept in the open air on a dolmen) for seven years, and perhaps not coincidentally—since nettles are rich in Vitamin K and other salutary compounds—lived to be 120 years old.

Harvested when still tender, usually between February and April, nettles form the basis of a traditional spring tonic; it was said that three meals of nettles early in the season would prevent illness all year long. Some country folk believe that nettles will increase egg production when added to chicken feed and encourage milk to flow freely when fed to cows.

There's an old tradition that the best place to gather nettles—the place where they grow higher and better than anywhere else—is in a graveyard, supposedly because they like disturbed earth. In southern County Cork, May Eve, on April 30, was known as Nettlemas. For the occasion, youngsters would roam the streets holding bunches of nettles (if you grasp them tightly, they don't sting) and punishing each other with swipes of the leaves.

Robert Ditty, a baker of County Derry, says that nettles attract butterflies and bees.

Pea Soup

Serves 6

Peas are thought to have been brought to Ireland by the Normans in the late twelfth century, and are first mentioned there in a legal manuscript dating from 1374. Peas were eaten fresh in season and dried for soups and stews, and pea meal was used to make bread in times of grain shortage.

2 TBSP BUTTER

1 SMALL ONION, FINELY CHOPPED

1 SMALL CARROT, FINELY CHOPPED

1 SMALL PARSNIP, FINELY CHOPPED

1 SMALL TURNIP OR RUTABAGA, FINELY CHOPPED

4 CUPS/1 L CHICKEN STOCK [PAGE 356]

1 CUP/200 G DRIED SPLIT PEAS, SOAKED OVERNIGHT

1 HAM HOCK

SALT AND PEPPER

1 CUP/240 ML MILK

3 TBSP WHITE FLOUR

Melt the butter in a Dutch oven or heavy-bottomed pot over low heat, then add the onion, carrot, parsnip, and turnip or rutabaga. Cook, stirring frequently, for 10 to 12 minutes or until the vegetables soften.

Add the chicken stock, then drain the peas and add them. Bring to a boil, then reduce the heat to low, add the ham hock, and season to taste with salt and pepper. Cover the Dutch oven and simmer for 1 hour.

In a small saucepan, warm the milk to just below boiling, then whisk in the flour. Add the mixture to the Dutch oven, stir it in well, and raise the heat to high. Boil for 5 minutes, stirring constantly.

Celeriac Bisque with Thyme

Serves 8

Though wild celery was a popular food with the ancient Irish, its close relative, this so-called turnip-rooted celery, was little known on the island until the second half of the twentieth century. One modern-day Irish chef who uses it creatively is Catherine Fulvio of Ballyknocken House in Ashford, County Wicklow, who turns it into this Irish-style soup.

4 TBSP BUTTER

3 STALKS CELERY, CHOPPED

1 LARGE ONION, CHOPPED

1 LARGE CELERIAC, CUT INTO 3/4-IN/2-CM CUBES

1 LARGE POTATO, CUT INTO 3/4-IN/2-CM CUBES

4 1/2 CUPS/1 L CHICKEN STOCK [PAGE 356]

1 1/2 TSP MINCED THYME, PLUS MORE FOR GARNISH

1/2 CUP/120 ML HEAVY CREAM

SALT AND PEPPER

Melt the butter in a large pot over medium heat, then add the celery and onion, cover the pot, and cook for about 3 minutes. Add the celeriac, potato, chicken stock, and thyme. Increase the heat to high and bring to a boil, then reduce the heat and simmer, covered, for about 40 minutes or until the vegetables are very soft.

Remove the soup from the heat and allow to cool slightly. Working in batches, purée in a food processor or blender, transferring to a bowl as each batch is done. Wipe out the pot and return the soup to it. Stir in the cream, and warm the soup through over low heat, stirring occasionally. Season to taste with salt and pepper. Garnish with additional thyme.

Butternut Squash and Apple Soup

Serves 6

This is another soup served by Catherine Fulvio at Bally-knocken House.

2 TBSP BUTTER

I TSP CANOLA OR SUNFLOWER OIL

2 ONIONS, CHOPPED

I MEDIUM BUTTERNUT SQUASH, DICED

I COOKING APPLE, CORED AND DICED

I TBSP MINCED FRESH SAGE,
PLUS 6 SMALL WHOLE LEAVES

6 CUPS/1.5 L CHICKEN STOCK [PAGE 356],
PLUS EXTRA AS NEEDED

SALT AND PEPPER

2 TBSP CRÈME FRAÎCHE

Melt the butter with oil in a large pot over low heat. Add the onions and cook, stirring occasionally, for about 10 minutes. Add the butternut squash, stir well, and cook for about 10 minutes more.

Add the apple and chopped sage leaves, then add the chicken stock, raise the heat to high, and bring to a boil. Reduce the heat to medium-low and cook for about 15 minutes, or until the apple and squash are very soft. Season to taste with salt and pepper.

Remove the soup from the heat and allow to cool slightly. Working in batches if necessary, purée in a food processor or blender, transferring to a bowl as each batch is done. Wipe out the pot and return the soup to it, diluting it with a bit more chicken stock if it's too thick. Heat the soup through over medium heat, stirring occasionally. Adjust the seasoning.

To serve, garnish each bowl of soup with a dollop of crème fraîche and a sage leaf.

Curried Parsnip and Apple Soup

Serves 4 to 6

Curry powder has had a place in the Irish kitchen since the early nineteenth century, if not earlier. The recipe note-books of Anna Irvine of Rosebank, of Downpatrick, County Down, for instance, undated but written on paper water-marked 1822, contain several recipes for it, as well as one for the "Indian method of making chicken curry" and another for "a good curry," which calls for turmeric and coriander seed. Parsnips are an ancient Irish food, once harvested wild from the meadows. At least one Irish saint, the fifth-century St. Ciarnan, founder of Seir-Kieran, County Offaly, practically lived on them: It is said that "His evening meal was a small piece of barley cake and two parsnips from the garden and water from the spring well."

2 TBSP BUTTER

I LB/500 G PARSNIPS, THINLY SLICED

I LB/500 G APPLES, PEELED, CORED AND
THINLY SLICED

I ONION, MINCED

I TBSP CURRY POWDER

I TSP GROUND CUMIN

I TSP GROUND CORIANDER

I CLOVE GARLIC, CRUSHED

4 CUPS/1 L CHICKEN STOCK [PAGE 356]

SALT AND PEPPER

I/2 CUP/120 ML HEAVY CREAM

2 TSP CHOPPED FRESH CHIVES

Melt the butter over medium heat in a large pot, then add the parsnips, apples, and onion and cook, stirring frequently, until they soften but don't brown, 4 to 5 minutes. Add the curry powder, cumin, coriander, and garlic, stir well, and cook for about 1 minute more.

Reduce the heat to low. Add the chicken stock, stir well, cover the pot, and simmer for about 30 minutes, or until the parsnips and apples are very soft. Season to taste with salt and pepper.

Remove the soup from the heat and allow to cool slightly. Working in batches, purée in a food processor or blender, transferring to a bowl as each batch is done. Wipe out the pot and return the soup to it. Whisk in the cream and heat the soup through. Serve garnished with chives. (This soup is also very good served cold.)

Turnip and Rosemary Soup with Honey

Serves 6 to 8

Honey was an important food for the ancient Irish, used as a sweetener but also to flavor savory dishes, and as the raw material for mead. Later, on the grand Anglo-Irish estates, the beekeeper was a servant of particularly high status. At the superb Rathmullan House in Rathmullan, County Donegal, near Lough Swilly in the far northern reaches of Ireland, chef Ian Orr makes this soup with heather-scented honey from nearby Glenvar. As usual in Ireland, "turnip" means rutabaga, though white turnips may be used in this dish, too.

1/2 CUP/125 G BUTTER

2 LARGE RUTABAGAS OR 5 TO 6 WHITE TURNIPS [2 1/2 TO 3 LB/1 TO 1.5 KG TOTAL], CHOPPED

2 CUPS/475 ML CHICKEN STOCK [PAGE 356], PLUS EXTRA AS NEEDED

LEAVES FROM 4 SPRIGS ROSEMARY, CHOPPED

3/4 CUP/175 ML HEAVY CREAM

SALT AND PEPPER

1/2 CUP/120 ML HEATHER OR OTHER HONEY

Melt the butter in a large pot over medium-low heat, then add the rutabagas or turnips.

Cook for 10 minutes, stirring occasionally, then add the chicken stock. Raise the heat to high and bring to a boil. Reduce the heat to medium-high and cook for 20 to 30 minutes or until the rutabagas or turnips are very soft.

Remove the soup from the heat and allow to cool slightly. Working in batches, purée in a food processor or blender, transferring to a bowl as each batch is done. Wipe out the pot

and return the soup to it, diluting it with a bit more chicken stock if it's too thick.

Bring the soup to a boil, then reduce the heat to low, stir in the cream, and season to taste with salt and pepper.

Divide the soup evenly between 6 to 8 warm bowls or soup plates and drizzle honey into each bowl.

Turnip and Brown Bread Soup

Serves 8

This unusual soup is another specialty at Catherine Fulvio's Ballyknocken House in Ashford, County Wicklow.

4 TBSP BUTTER

1 ONION, CHOPPED

2 LB/1 KG RUTABAGAS OR TURNIPS, PEELED AND CUT INTO PIECES ABOUT 1/2 IN/1.25 CM SQUARE

7 CUPS/1.7 L CHICKEN STOCK [PAGE 356]

PINCH OF NUTMEG

THREE 1-IN/2.5-CM SLICES BROWN SODA BREAD [PAGE 272] OR ANOTHER DENSE BROWN BREAD [SEE PAGES 275 AND 282], CRUSTS REMOVED, CUT INTO 1-IN/2.5-CM PIECES

SALT AND PEPPER

1 TBSP EXTRA-VIRGIN OLIVE OIL

1/4 CUP/60 ML HEAVY CREAM

Melt 3 Tbsp of the butter in a large pot over medium-low heat. Add the onions and cook until soft, about 10 minutes, stirring occasionally. Add the rutabagas or turnips and cook for about 10 minutes more. Add the chicken stock, nutmeg, and half the bread pieces, and season to taste with salt and pepper. Stir well, cover, and simmer for 45 to 50 minutes or until the rutabagas or turnips are soft.

Set the soup aside to cool slightly, then purée in a blender or food processor until smooth, working in batches if necessary. Wipe out the pot and return the soup to it, keeping it warm over low heat.

Meanwhile, melt the remaining 1 Tbsp of butter in a large skillet over medium-high heat. Stir in the olive oil, then add the

TURNIP AND BROWN BREAD SOUP

remaining bread pieces. Toss them in the butter and oil and cook for 4 to 5 minutes, stirring constantly, until golden brown.

Put the soup into a warm tureen, drizzle the top with cream, and garnish with croutons.

Colcannon Cream Soup

Serves 6

More than one contemporary Irish chef has had the notion of turning colcannon, the island's emblematic kale and potato dish (see page 219), into soup. This version comes from Gerry Galvin (see page 79), proprietor of The Vintage in Kinsale, County Cork, and later of Drimcong House in Moycullen, County Galway. Giana Ferguson of Gubbeen in County Cork (see page 61) makes a similar soup, with her son Fingal's smoked bacon added, under the delightful name "yum, yum, pig's bum soup," from an old children's skipping song that goes "Yum, yum, pig's bum, cabbage and potataaaas."

6 TBSP BUTTER

1/2 LB/250 G KALE, FINELY CHOPPED

1 1/2 LB/750 G POTATOES, FINELY CHOPPED

2 LEEKS, WHITE PARTS ONLY, FINELY CHOPPED

5 CUPS/1.2 L CHICKEN STOCK [PAGE 356]

NUTMEG

SALT AND PEPPER

1 CUP/240 ML HEAVY CREAM

Melt the butter in a large pot, then add the kale, potatoes, and leeks, and cook over low heat for about 10 minutes, being careful not to let them brown.

Add the stock, raise the heat, and bring to a boil. Reduce the heat and simmer, uncovered, for about 20 minutes. Season to taste with nutmeg, salt, and pepper.

Remove the soup from the heat and allow to cool slightly. Working in batches, purée in a food processor or blender, transferring to a bowl as each batch is done. Wipe out the pot and return the soup to it. Whisk in the cream and heat the soup through before serving.

Enniscoe Celery and Blue Cheese Soup

Serves 6

This recipe comes from Enniscoe House, one of the exclusive Blue Book country house hotels, in Castlehill, Ballina, County Mayo—by way of Georgina Campbell's *Irish Country House Cooking: The Blue Book Recipe Collection*. Wild celery, or sollory (as it was once spelled), is an ancient food in Ireland, and the island's soil is said to be particularly good for growing it.

4 CUPS/1 L STRONG BEEF OR CHICKEN STOCK
[PAGE 357 OR 356]

8 TO 10 STALKS CELERY, CHOPPED, PLUS A HANDFUL
OF THE LEAVES FOR GARNISH

1 CUP/240 ML WHITE SAUCE [PAGE 360]

3 OZ/85 G BLUE CHEESE, PREFERABLY CASHEL BLUE
[SEE SOURCES, PAGE 369], CRUMBLED

SALT AND PEPPER

Bring the stock to a boil in a medium pot, add the chopped celery, reduce the heat, cover, and simmer for about 30 minutes.

Remove the soup from the heat and allow to cool slightly. Working in batches, purée in a food processor or blender, transferring to a large bowl as each batch is done. Strain the soup into another large bowl.

Warm the white sauce gently in a small saucepan, then add the cheese, whisking until it melts.

Whisk the cheese sauce into the soup and season to taste with salt and pepper. Serve garnished with a few celery leaves.

MR. SOYER'S SOUP

Ireland's most famous soup maker was, ironically, a Frenchman based in England. Alexis Soyer (1810–1858) was a native of Meaux who became head chef at the Reform Club in London, where he introduced such innovations as gas ranges and ovens with adjustable temperatures. He journeyed to Dublin in 1847, as famine raged in Ireland, to open the original "soup kitchen," dispensing liquid nourishment to the starving poor. The government soon copied his idea all over the country, as did Protestant landowners on their estates. (The latter were accused of using them to proselytize their Catholic workers, and subsequently, Protestants who bore names that were clearly Catholic in origin became known as "soupers.") Unfortunately, as Soyer's recipes got disseminated, his reputation suffered. A contemporary verse parodying the witches' scene in *Macbeth* suggested that his potions contained "Scale of codfish, spiders' tongues, / Tom-tit's gizzards, head and lungs / Of a famished French-fed frog." Soyer fled back to London in a hail of popular criticism.

In fact, Soyer's original basic soup included beef shin, drippings, onions and other vegetables, pearl barley, flour, and brown sugar—reasonable enough ingredients. He claimed that a daily serving of this concoction, together with a biscuit, could sustain the strength of a normal healthy man. Countless other formulas for "famine soup" were developed around Ireland. Their spirit may be divined by a recipe published as late as 1947, by Lady Pim in Belfast, for a soup to feed 200 (presumably indigent) people: It calls for 24 pounds of potatoes, 12 pounds of carrots, 3 large turnips, and 3 parsnips, seasoned with salt, pepper, and the concentrated beef extract Bovril, cooked until the vegetables are soft enough to be pushed through a sieve. "Result," reads the recipe, "should be thick enough for a wooden spoon to stand upright. This enables a large bulk to be easily transported. Take from this puree basis as much as is needed for the day and add water to make the soup the thickness required. Heat up, stirring constantly. Various tins of soup may be added at will to improve the taste."

Chicken Soup

Serves 8 to 10

Every culture seems to have its version of chicken soup. In Irish farmhouse kitchens, this dish was often made with aging fowl no longer giving eggs—birds that would have had much more flavor than the typical supermarket chicken today. Some markets do sell what they label as "stewing" or "boiling chicken," though, which are older than fryers or roasting chicken, and preferable for this recipe. Instead of the egg and cream called for here, Irish chicken soup is sometimes thickened with oatmeal (about ¾ cup/120 g uncooked, in this case).

2 EGG YOLKS

3 TBSP HEAVY CREAM

ONE 3- TO 3 1/2-LB/1.5-KG STEWING CHICKEN,
CUT INTO 8 PIECES

BOUQUET GARNI [2 SPRIGS PARSLEY,
2 SPRIGS THYME, AND 1 BAY LEAF, WRAPPED AND
TIED IN CHEESECLOTH]

1 ONION, SLICED

1 CARROT, SLICED

2 STALKS CELERY, CHOPPED

1 BAY LEAF

1/2 TSP GROUND MACE

6 TO 8 SPRIGS PARSLEY, TRIMMED AND MINCED

1/4 LB/125 G IRISH BACON
[SEE SOURCES, PAGE 369], COARSELY CHOPPED

SALT AND PEPPER

Put the egg yolks into a small bowl, then whisk in the cream and set aside.

Put the chicken and bouquet garni into a large pot and add water to cover. Cover the pot and bring to a boil over high heat, then reduce the heat to low and simmer, covered, for 30 minutes, occasionally skimming off any foam that rises to the surface.

Add the onion, carrot, celery, bay leaf, mace, parsley, and bacon. Return the soup to a boil, then reduce the heat to low and simmer, uncovered, for about 2 hours, or until the chicken is very tender.

Remove the chicken pieces from the soup and set aside to cool. When cool enough to handle, pull off and discard the skin, then pull the meat off the bones and chop it coarsely.

If the egg yolk mixture has separated, whisk it briefly, then stir it into the soup. Return the chopped chicken to the soup, return almost to a boil over high heat, then season to taste with salt and pepper.

Mulligatawny

Serves 4 to 6

This Anglo-Indian soup has long been popular in Ireland. The name, first recorded in English in 1784, is a corruption of the Tamil word *milakutanni*, meaning pepper water. In her *Irish Family Food*, Ruth Isabel Ross notes that it is "enjoyed especially by those who have lived in India," which would have meant a not inconsiderable number of Irish-born soldiers and administrators in the days of the British Raj. At the National Library in Dublin, I found a recipe for the dish, spelled "mulagatawny" (along with one for "Bengal chetney") in an early-nineteenth-century manuscript, "possibly compiled by members of the Pope family" of County Waterford. Florence Irwin, the early-twentieth-century "cookin' woman" of Northern Ireland, gives variations on mulligatawny using fish and rabbit, but lamb or chicken are more traditional.

2 TBSP BUTTER

1 LB/500 G LAMB NECKS OR STEWING MEAT
[WITH BONES] OR CHICKEN THIGHS [WITH BONES
AND SKIN]

1 ONION, MINCED

1 APPLE, CORED BUT NOT PEELED, MINCED

1/2 CARROT, MINCED

1 TBSP WHITE FLOUR

1 TBSP CURRY POWDER

4 CUPS/1 L CHICKEN STOCK [PAGE 356]

JUICE OF 1/2 LEMON

SALT AND WHITE PEPPER

MULLIGATAWNY

Melt the butter over medium heat in a large pot, then add the lamb or chicken and cook, stirring frequently, until nicely browned, 10 to 12 minutes. Remove the lamb or chicken from the pot and set aside. Add the onion, apple, and carrot and cook, stirring frequently, until they soften but don't brown, 4 to 5 minutes. Add the flour and curry powder and stir well, then cook for about 1 minute more.

Reduce the heat to low. Add the chicken stock and return the lamb or chicken to the pot. Stir well, bring almost to a boil over high heat, and reduce the heat to low. Cover the pot and simmer for about 2 hours.

Remove the lamb or chicken from the pot and set aside to cool. Strain the soup into a large bowl, discarding the solids. Rinse out the pot and return the soup to it. When the lamb or chicken is cool enough to handle, shred the meat with your hands, discarding the bones and skin (if any), and then add the meat to the soup.

Add the lemon juice and season to taste with salt and pepper.

West Cork Fish Soup

Serves 4

At her Good Things Café in Durrus, in West Cork, Carmel Somers brings a Mediterranean sensibility to the best products of the region and beyond. This is her interpretation of a popular Provençal-style dish, really more a main-dish stew than just a soup.

1/4 CUP / 60 ML EXTRA-VIRGIN OLIVE OIL

1 SMALL ONION, MINCED

1 STALK CELERY, MINCED

2 CLOVES GARLIC, MINCED

1/2 CUCUMBER, MINCED

2 OR 3 SPRIGS PARSLEY, TRIMMED AND CHOPPED

2 SPRIGS THYME

2 OR 3 SPRIGS DILL OR FENNEL

1/2 TSP SAFFRON THREADS

ONE 14-OZ / 397 G CAN ITALIAN TOMATOES
[PREFERABLY SAN MARZANO], CHOPPED,
WITH THEIR JUICES

3/4 CUP DRY WHITE WINE

2 CUPS / 475 ML FISH STOCK [PAGE 356]

JUICE OF 1/2 LEMON

SALT AND PEPPER

1 1/2 LB / 750 G ASSORTED FIRM-FLESH WHITE FISH
[SUCH AS HAKE, HADDOCK, COD, OR POLLACK],
CUT INTO 1/2-IN / 1.25-CM CUBES

GRATED IRISH CHEDDAR FOR SERVING

CROUTONS AND / OR GARLIC MAYONNAISE [PAGE 358]
FOR SERVING [OPTIONAL]

Heat the oil in a large pot over medium-low heat, then add the onion and celery and cook, stirring occasionally, for about 10 minutes, or until very soft and beginning to brown.

Add the garlic, cucumber, parsley, thyme, dill or fennel, saffron, tomatoes and their juices, and wine. Stir well and simmer for about 5 minutes. Stir in the fish stock and lemon juice, then season to taste with salt and pepper. Bring to a boil over high heat, then reduce the heat to low and simmer, uncovered, for about 20 minutes.

Return the soup to a boil over high heat and stir in the fish. Immediately remove the pot from the heat and set aside, uncovered. (The fish will cook in the hot soup.) Adjust the seasoning if necessary.

Serve with grated Irish cheddar. If you like, you can also offer croutons and/or a bowl of garlic mayonnaise.

Eel Soup with Saffron

Serves 4

Noel McMeel, who won praise as the chef at Castle Leslie in Glaslough, County Monaghan, and is now in charge of several restaurants at the Lough Erne Golf Club near Enniskillen, County Fermanagh, grew up in Toomebridge, on the shores of Lough Neagh—the site of Europe's largest eel fishery (see page 73). This is one of his favorite ways to prepare the slithery creature. Look for eel at Asian seafood markets.

2 SILVER EELS, SKINNED AND FILLETED
[RESERVE SKIN AND BONES], WITH MEAT CUT
INTO CUBES ABOUT 2 IN/5 CM SQUARE

2 MEDIUM ONIONS, CHOPPED

2 TBSP UNSALTED BUTTER

1 STALK CELERY, CHOPPED

1 LARGE CARROT, CHOPPED

2 CLOVES GARLIC

1 LARGE TOMATO, CHOPPED

ZEST OF 1 SMALL ORANGE

1 TSP SAFFRON THREADS

1/4 CUP/60 ML HEAVY CREAM

CAYENNE

SALT

Put the eel skin and bones into a large saucepan with half the onions and 4 cups/1 L of water. Bring to a boil, then reduce the heat and simmer, uncovered, for 20 minutes. Strain the stock into a bowl and set aside.

Melt the butter in a large saucepan, then add the celery, carrot, garlic, and the remaining onions. Cook over medium-low heat for 6 to 8 minutes or until the vegetables have softened but not browned. Add the tomato, orange zest, saffron, eel, and reserved eel stock. Bring almost to a boil over high heat, reduce the heat to low, and simmer for 20 minutes.

Pass soup through a strainer or china cap, pushing down on the ingredients with the back of a wooden spoon or wooden pestle to form a purée. Stir in the cream and season to taste with cayenne and salt.

Smoked Cockle Chowder

Serves 4 to 6

The Hook Peninsula in County Wexford, on the east side of Waterford Harbor, has a place in popular idiom: Half a dozen miles (about ten kilometers) to the north, on the Waterford side of the River Barrow, is the town of Crooke, and the twelfth-century Norman nobleman known as Strongbow once boasted that he would take Waterford "by Hook or by Crooke."

Today, the Hook Peninsula village of Arthurstown, just across from Crooke, is the home of Dunbrody House, a country house property famous for the cooking of one of Ireland's best (and best-known) young chefs, Kevin Dundon. This is one of Dundon's signature recipes. Cockles are small clams.

2 CUPS/475 ML FISH STOCK [PAGE 356]

3 TO 4 SPRIGS TARRAGON

2 TBSP BUTTER

1 SMALL ONION, FINELY CHOPPED

1 LARGE LEEK, WHITE PART ONLY, FINELY CHOPPED

1 SMALL CARROT, FINELY CHOPPED

1 SMALL POTATO, CUT INTO 1/2-IN/1.25-CM CUBES

2 OZ/60 G SMOKED SALMON, JULIENNED

1/2 CUP/120 ML DRY WHITE WINE

2 SMALL CANS SMOKED BABY CLAMS
[7 TO 9 OZ/200 TO 250 G TOTAL]

1 TBSP CHOPPED FRESH PARSLEY

3/4 CUP/175 ML HEAVY CREAM

SALT AND WHITE PEPPER

Bring the stock to a boil in a small pan over high heat, then reduce the heat to low and add the tarragon. Simmer for 15 minutes, then strain, reserving the stock and discarding the tarragon.

Melt the butter in a medium pot over medium heat, then add the onion, leek, carrot, potato, and smoked salmon. Cook for 2 to 3 minutes, stirring constantly.

Add the wine to the pot, increase the heat to medium-high, and cook for 3 or 4 minutes, or until the wine has reduced by half. Add the reserved fish stock, then reduce the heat to low and add the clams.

Stir in the parsley and cream and season to taste with salt and white pepper. Cover the pot and simmer for about 5 minutes more.

COOKING WITH A LID

Marjorie Quarton of Nenagh, County Tipperary, is a former farmer and breeder of both horses and border collies and the author of some thirteen books, ranging from how-tos to novels. In her charming memoir, *Saturday's Child*, she writes, "When I was growing up, we always had a cook: not necessarily a good one—some of them were appalling—but a person capable of putting some kind of meal on the table at stated intervals. By degrees, they disappeared. . . . I was sixteen when the last one departed. There followed an interval of hunger and indigestion. My mother could make only cakes, which she did excellently; my repertoire consisted of porridge and scrambled eggs; my father could make soup and curry. . . . For the purpose of cooking, he first put on his hat—I don't know why. As a rule it was a sign that he was going to do something fairly dramatic."

A REALLY BIG CAULDRON

Irish folklore is full of food. One famous character was the god Dagda, high king of the mythological Tuatha Dé Danann people. Dagda was famous for his magic club, which had the power to both slay men and bring them back to life, but also for his two pigs, one always growing fatter and the other always roasting—and for his bottomless cauldron, called the Undry, which could feed one and all to satiety. Before the battle of Magh Tuireadh, Dagda's enemies, the Fomor, knowing of his reputation as a trencherman, filled his cauldron with "four times twenty gallons of new milk, and the same of meal and fat, and they put in goats and sheep and pigs along with that, and boiled all together, and then they poured it all out into a great hole in the ground." He was challenged to eat it all or be slain. The Fomor had underestimated Dagda: He finished the soup neatly, even scraping up the bits from the gravel at the bottom of the pit—and went on to defeat his challengers on the battlefield.

THE CITY OF TRIBES

Galway is one of the most enchanting cities in Ireland, a lively but easygoing port town, refreshed by sea breezes and brightened by the colorful façades (pink, blue, yellow, green) of the shops and restaurants on the old streets in the heart of town. At times, it has an almost Mediterranean feeling to it, and indeed has a long history of trade with Spain, whose northern coast is, after all, a straight shot south. (Iberian merchants reportedly used to congregate by the sixteenth-century gateway near the harbor now known as the Spanish Arch.)

Built up around a twelfth-century fortress, the city is named for the River Gaillimh—the word itself supposedly means "stony," though the etymology is disputed— now called the River Corrib. (Flowing only about three and a half miles/five and a half kilometers, from Lough Corrib into Galway Bay, it is said to be the shortest river in Europe.) Galway became known as "the City of the Tribes" in the fifteenth century, after the fourteen mostly English merchant families (originally called "tribes" perjoratively), who ruled the city for generations. In fact, Galway became in effect an English town; a sixteenth-century bylaw stated that, without special permission, "neither O' nor Mac shall strutte nor swagger through the streets of Galway." Nonetheless, Galway thrived under the tribes, becoming the major conduit into Ireland for goods not only from Spain but from France as well. Even Christopher Columbus once put in here, in the years before he sailed off into history. (Oddball trivia: Che Guevara was descended from one of the Galway tribes, the Lynches.)

The waters of Galway Bay produce some of Ireland's best oysters, the flat-shelled native variety (see page 95), and today Galway is the site of a large annual oyster festival. The city is also the home base of Ireland's premier cheese shop, Sheridans. Though it frankly isn't the best restaurant town in the country, it does have some good seafood places, including first-rate "chippers"—fish-and-chips emporiums—both old and new, some pleasant cafes, and what may be the best Japanese restaurant in Ireland, Kappa-Ya. Galway is also the gateway to Connemara, a mountainous and ruggedly beautiful district that every visitor to Ireland should see.

MUSSEL AND OYSTER HOT POT

Dom Paul McDonnell's Mussel Soup

Serves 4 to 6

Dom Paul McDonnell, OSB, the chaplain at Kylemore Abbey in the Connemara hills in County Galway until shortly before his death in 2005, was an enthusiastic strander. "Stranding," he once explained, "is like beach-combing except that you are searching for seafood." Among the treasures he would find were "wild mussels encrusting the rocks." He continued, "You can reap a large harvest, and there is great satisfaction in cooking and eating the result of your labors. Mussels straight from the briny ocean retain the taste of the sea, and my favorite recipe is this one."

48 MUSSELS [ABOUT 2 LB/1 KG],
SCRUBBED AND DEBEARDED

2 ONIONS, CHOPPED

3 CLOVES GARLIC, CHOPPED

3/4 CUP/175 ML DRY WHITE WINE

4 TBSP BUTTER

1/2 CUP/50 G WHOLE WHEAT FLOUR

2 1/2 CUPS/600 ML MILK

2/3 CUP/160 ML HEAVY CREAM

SALT AND PEPPER

1 TBSP CHOPPED FRESH PARSLEY

Put the mussels into a large pot and add the onions, garlic, and wine. Cover the pot and bring the wine to a boil over high heat. Cook just until the mussels open, shaking the pot a few times. Remove the mussels from the pot, discarding any unopened ones and reserving the cooking liquid. Set the mussels aside to cool.

Melt the butter in another large pot over medium heat, then sprinkle in the flour, whisking constantly and cooking for about 1½ minutes, or until a roux forms. Slowly add the milk, stirring constantly, then strain the reserved mussel cooking liquid into the pot. Raise the heat to high and bring to a boil, then reduce the heat to low and simmer until the sauce thickens a little and becomes smooth and creamy.

Remove the mussels from their shells and add to the pot. Stir in the cream, then season to taste with salt and pepper, Increase the heat to medium and cook until the soup and mussels are hot (do not boil). Sprinkle with parsley before serving.

Mussel and Oyster Hot Pot

Serves 4

This dish was invented by Gerry Galvin, one of the pioneering chefs of the new Irish cuisine (see page 79). He sometimes flavors it with sweet cicely, an aniselike herb traditionally used as a sugar substitute, he told me when he cooked up a batch for me in a borrowed kitchen in Galway. Chervil makes a good substitute.

48 MUSSELS [ABOUT 2 LB/1 KG],
SCRUBBED AND DEBEARDED

1 CUP/240 ML DRY WHITE WINE

4 CUPS/1 L FISH STOCK [PAGE 356]

8 OYSTERS, SHUCKED

1 CUP [ABOUT 1 OZ/30 G] SHREDDED DULSE
[SEE PAGE 264], SOAKED IN COLD WATER FOR
2 MINUTES AND DRAINED

SALT AND PEPPER

3 TBSP SHREDDED IRISH CHEDDAR

1 TBSP MINCED FRESH SWEET CICELY OR CHERVIL

Put the mussels into a large pot with the wine, cover tightly, and bring to a boil over high heat. Reduce the heat to medium and let the mussels steam, shaking the pot occasionally, until the shells open, about 10 minutes. Remove the pot from the heat, uncover, and allow the mussels to cool slightly. When the mussels are cool enough to handle, remove them from their shells (discard any mussels that haven't opened). Set the mussels aside, discarding the shells and cooking liquid.

Bring the fish stock to a boil over high heat in a medium pot. Add the mussels, oysters, and dulse. Cook for 2 to 3 minutes or until the shellfish is heated through. Season to taste with salt and pepper.

Serve garnished with cheese and cicely or chervil.

EGGS

and

CHEESE

Farmhouse Basics

Normal things run deep, God knows
Like love in flat-land, eggs on toast.

—Thomas McCarthy, "Toast" [1987]

[T]o the present day cheese still remains an alien thing
to the Irish countryman.

—A. T. Lucas, *Irish Food Before the Potato* [1960]

The word for "egg" in Irish sounds almost primal—*ubh* [pronounced "oove," not far from the French *oeuf*]—and in fact eggs have been part of the Irish diet since prehistoric times.

At first these would have been the eggs of seabirds—auks and puffins—which may have been preserved in wood ash, and later the eggs of wild ducks and plovers. Chickens, and thus hen eggs, probably reached Ireland from Roman Britain in the first or second century A.D. Goose eggs were highly regarded; the fifth-century bishop Erc of Slane, County Meath, is said to have kept a flock of birds specifically to produce the eggs for his table, and accounts of ancient banquets often mention them.

Another old method of preserving eggs, especially in the Irish butter capital of Cork, was to swath them in butter; thus protected, they would stay "fresh" for as long as three months. (Buttered eggs are still sold at Moynihan's Poultry in Cork's English Market.) Eggs and butter have a natural affinity for each other, and in Irish homes, eggs were, and sometimes still are, served fried on toast with a buttery cream sauce on top or poached in milk and butter. Writer and artisanal publisher Malachi McCormick remembers his childhood breakfasts in Cobh, County Cork: "The eggs themselves . . . were magnificent: a burning Van Gogh sun would pale beside the intense deep orange of their yolks."

Cheese—*caís* in Irish (think *queso*)—formed a major part of the early Irish diet. Writer and folklorist Bríd Mahon enumerates some of the old varieties: "[T]anach, a hard-pressed skim-milk cheese [the legendary Queen Mebh's nephew is said to have slain her by hurling a round tanach at her with his sling]; *táth*, a soft cheese made from heated sour milk curds . . . ; *mulchán*, made of buttermilk beaten to form a soft cheese which was then pressed and moulded; and *milseán*, made from sweet milk curd."

Irish cheese making began to decline in the eighteenth century, perhaps because the potato supplanted cheese in the daily diet, perhaps because the world market for Irish butter (easier and quicker to make than cheese) demanded all the surplus milk, or perhaps simply because it was a farmhouse craft and the Irish for the most part no longer owned the land. Some kind of cheese industry did survive: Oliver St. John Gogarty, contributing to *Cheddar Gorge: A Book of English Cheeses*, reports that in 1922, when Ireland's minister of agriculture asked Danish authorities for the loan of an instructor to teach the Irish how to make better butter and cheese, they replied that they couldn't send their top expert, "because he had just gone back to Cork!" Gogarty adds that, after a period of producing cheeses with English names (Cheddar, Stilton, and so on), Irish cheese makers had begun calling them after their places of manufacture—Ardagh, Galtee, Whitethorn, Mitchelstown (the "greatest of all").

Nonetheless, by the 1950s, according to agricultural historian John Feehan, "the only cheeses on the farm table were foil-wrapped blocks of the two processed cheeses then available." This is probably an exaggeration: Nenagh grocer Peter Ward remembers an excellent Irish cheddar, packed in wooden boxes, that was widely sold around Ireland at the time, as well as a convent-made version of Pont-l'Évêque from Lough Rynn, County Leitrim—but these were exceptions to the rule. In any case, it wasn't until the mid-1970s, after Norman and Veronica Steele started to make cheese from the milk of a single cow on an isolated peninsula down in West Cork (see page 51), that the modern Irish cheese industry was born. Today, Ireland produces a wide range of extraordinary artisanal cheeses (see pages 62 and 64), and they end up on tables both in restaurants and at home either in their native glory or integrated into salads, savory pies, soufflés, and other good things.

Eggs Mayonnaise

Serves 4

This light appetizer was long a staple of country-house dinner menus and buffets around Ireland.

4 HARD-COOKED EGGS, HALVED LENGTHWISE

1/4 CUP/60 ML MAYONNAISE,
PREFERABLY HOMEMADE [PAGE 357]

1 TSP MINCED FRESH CHIVES

1/2 TSP MINCED FRESH CHERVIL [OPTIONAL]

SALT AND PEPPER

SHREDDED LETTUCE FOR SERVING [OPTIONAL]

Carefully scoop the yolks out of the egg halves and, with the back of a spoon, press them through a sieve into a small bowl.

Mix the mayonnaise, half the chives, and the chervil (if using) into the sieved yolks and season to taste with salt and pepper.

Put mixture into a pastry bag fitted with a decorating nozzle and pipe into the cavities of the egg whites. Garnish with the remaining chives.

Serve on a bed of shredded lettuce as a small appetizer, or as an accompaniment to smoked salmon.

Convent Eggs

Serves 2 to 4

Seven years after Alexis Soyer opened his soup kitchen in Dublin in 1847 to help feed famine victims (see page 37), he published a book called *A Shilling Cookery for the People*, meant for ordinary folk who lacked elaborate kitchens. It became very popular in Ireland, and much later Theodora FitzGibbon discovered a well-used copy that had belonged to her aunt in County Clare. She adapted this recipe from its pages.

2 TBSP BUTTER

1 ONION, SLICED

1 TBSP WHITE FLOUR

2 CUPS/475 ML MILK

1/2 TSP SALT

1/4 TSP PEPPER

4 HARD-COOKED EGGS, SLICED INTO 6 PIECES EACH

TOAST FOR SERVING

Melt the butter in a medium saucepan over medium-low heat, then cook the onions for 6 to 8 minutes, until they are soft but not browned. Add the flour and mix well, then add the milk, stirring until the mixture thickens into a sauce. Season with salt and pepper.

Add eggs to pan, toss in sauce, and cook for a minute or two until heated through. Serve on toast.

Eggs and Soldiers

Serves 4

This British nursery food classic is popular at breakfast time at country inns and B&Bs in Northern Ireland. Children sometimes call the toast fingers "dippies" instead of "soldiers."

4 EGGS

4 SLICES GOOD-QUALITY WHITE BREAD

2 TBSP BUTTER

SALT AND PEPPER

Bring a medium pot of water to a boil over high heat, then reduce the heat to medium to keep the water at a slow rolling boil. Carefully put the eggs into the pot and cook for 3 minutes.

Meanwhile, toast the bread lightly, then butter it generously and cut each slice into 4 "fingers" or "soldiers."

To serve, place the eggs in egg cups and tap the top of each shell gently with a dinner knife to crack the top. Remove the top and season the eggs with salt and pepper. Eat by dipping the toast fingers into the egg.

MILLEENS

In the mid-1970s, Veronica Steele and her husband, Norman, found themselves with a farm at Eyeries on the Beara Peninsula in West Cork and a single one-horned cow named Brisket. "She lost the other one gadding down a hill, tail-waving, full of the joys of Spring," Veronica has written. "Her brakes must have failed." Brisket gave at least three gallons/eleven liters of milk a day, more than the Steeles could drink. Remembering the great wheels of crumbling cheddar in an old shop in nearby Castletownbere—and remembering that when the shop closed and reopened as a modern store, all the cheese was precut and wrapped in plastic—Steele thought she might try to turn Brisket's milk into cheddar of her own. She collected all the available pamphlets about making cheese, and, maybe more important, acquired a book called *The Cheeses and Wines of England and France with Notes on Irish Whiskey* by novelist John Ehle. "The leaflets told you how to make cheese," says Steele, "but this book told you what cheese *was*."

Steele made cheddars for two years. "They were absolute flops," Steele says. "I suppose they were too small and salty." Then her husband suggested that she try making a soft cheese.

She did, and it turned out "wild, weird, and wonderful." It was all a question of the ambient mold, she says. "The mold was here already, and what happened was that the cheese just wanted to be here, too."

The Steeles used to sell vegetables from their garden to a restaurant called the Blue Bull, across the River Kenmare in Sneem, County Kerry. One day Steele stuck a twelve-ounce/four-hundred gram package of her cheese, which she'd named Milleens, after their farm, in among the peas and spinach. It went out on the cheese board, and one of the customers who sampled it was Declan Ryan, proprietor of the (now-defunct) Arbutus Lodge in Cork, Ireland's first Michelin-starred restaurant. He loved it. "Rumor has it," Steele has suggested, "that there was a full eclipse of the sun and earth tremors when the first Milleens was presented on an Irish cheese board."

Inspired by the Steeles' example, other fledgling cheese makers tried their luck. Today, there are at least fifty or sixty artisan producers, and they can be found in every corner of the country. The Steeles' son, Quinlan, meanwhile, now makes Milleens.

[TOP] The butter market in Cork City, 1859.

[BOTTOM] Eddie Dee and John Moore outside Coolnagour Dairy, County Waterford.

Eggs Messine

Serves 6 to 8

Sir Alfred Beit, a Conservative member of Parliament in England and the son of a South African diamond millionaire and art collector, married Clementine Mitford, a cousin of the famous Mitford sisters, in 1939. In 1952, the couple— and their inherited art collection, which included works by Vermeer, Rubens, and Goya—moved from homes in London and South Africa to Russborough House, a country estate in Blessington, County Wicklow. It became well known over the years for its hospitality—as well as for the fact that art thieves pilfered its treasures on three separate occasions. Clementine Beit gave this recipe to Rosie Tinne for her book *Irish Country-house Cooking*. Messine, in the recipe title, may refer to the Battle of Messine (in Belgium) during World War I, in which several Irish regiments fought. Beit notes that the same prepa-ration may be adapted to poached sole fillets, which can be substituted for the eggs.

2 CUPS/325 G HOT COOKED RICE

8 SOFT-COOKED EGGS

4 TBSP BUTTER, CUT INTO SMALL PIECES

1 TSP WHITE FLOUR

2 EGG YOLKS

1 TSP DIJON MUSTARD

1 TSP FRESH CHERVIL

1 TSP MINCED FRESH PARSLEY

1 TSP MINCED FRESH TARRAGON

2 SHALLOTS, MINCED

1 TSP GRATED LEMON ZEST

1 CUP/240 ML HEAVY CREAM

1 TBSP LEMON JUICE

SALT AND PEPPER

Spread the rice evenly over the bottom of a large serving dish, then gently nestle the eggs into the rice. Set the dish aside.

Pour enough water into the bottom half of a double boiler to reach a depth of about 2 in/5 cm and bring to a boil over high heat. Meanwhile, work the butter and flour together with your fingers in a medium bowl until a paste forms, then stir in the yolks and mustard. Add the chervil, parsley, tarragon, shallots, and lemon zest and mix well. Whisk in the cream.

Reduce the heat under the double boiler to medium-low so that the water simmers gently, then transfer the cream mixture to the top half of the double boiler. Cook, stirring constantly without letting the mixture boil, until thick and velvety, 8 to 10 minutes. Remove the sauce from the heat and stir in lemon juice and salt and pepper to taste. Pour the hot sauce over the eggs and rice and serve immediately.

St. Clerans Eggs

Serves 4 to 6

St. Clerans is the country house estate in Craughwell, County Galway, owned for years by the great American director and actor John Huston. It is now an elegant hotel. This recipe, credited to one Madge Creagh (a cook at St. Clerans), was given to Rosie Tinne, for her *Irish Countryhouse Cooking*, by "Mrs. John Huston." This Mrs. Huston was probably ballerina Enrica Soma, Anjelica Huston's mother, though by the time Tinne's book was published, Soma had perished in an auto-mobile accident and John Huston was married to Celeste Shane.

2 TBSP BUTTER, PLUS MORE FOR GREASING

2 TBSP CANOLA OIL

1/2 ONION, FINELY CHOPPED

6 MEDIUM MUSHROOMS [ABOUT 1/4 LB/125 G], FINELY CHOPPED

1 TBSP DIJON MUSTARD

1 TBSP MINCED FRESH PARSLEY

2 CLOVES GARLIC, MINCED

SALT AND WHITE PEPPER

4 SMALL TOMATOES, EACH CUT CROSSWISE INTO 4 SLICES

8 HARD-COOKED EGGS, HALVED LENGTHWISE

1 CUP/240 ML WHITE SAUCE [PAGE 360]

1 CUP/125 G SHREDDED IRISH CHEDDAR

Heat the butter and oil together over medium heat in a large skillet until the butter is melted. Add the onions and cook until softened, stirring occasionally, for about 5 minutes. Stir in the mushrooms and cook for 4 to 5 minutes more, then add the mustard, parsley, garlic, and salt and pepper to taste. Continue to cook, stirring often, for 3 to 4 minutes more, then transfer the mixture to a medium bowl.

Preheat the broiler.

Lightly grease a 9-x-13-in/23-x-32-cm baking dish with butter, then arrange the tomato slices in the bottom of the dish in a single layer. Scoop out the yolks from the eggs with a spoon and add to the mushroom mixture. Mash together until well combined. Fill each egg half with about 1 Tbsp of the mushroom mixture, then put one on top of each tomato slice.

Put the white sauce into a small pot and heat over medium-low heat until hot throughout. Add half of the cheese and stir until completely melted. Pour the sauce evenly over the eggs and tomatoes, then scatter the remaining cheese over the top. Broil until the cheese is golden brown, 2 to 3 minutes. Serve immediately.

Nested Eggs

Serves 4

Twentieth-century novelist and playwright Maura Laverty of Rathangan, County Kildare, ate this dish as a substitute for fish when it wasn't available on Fridays and other fast days.

1 TBSP BUTTER, PLUS MORE FOR GREASING

3 CUPS/640 G MASHED POTATOES [PAGE 223]

1/4 CUP/100 G COOKED PEAS

5 EGGS, 1 OF THEM BEATEN

SALT AND PEPPER

Preheat the oven to 375°F/190°C (Gas Mark 5).

Lightly grease a small baking sheet with butter. Form the potatoes into 4 mounds on the baking sheet, so they are not touching. Press a small cup or a large spoon into the middle of each mound to make a crater.

Put 1 Tbsp of peas in each crater, then break a whole egg over each "nest." Season the eggs with salt and pepper, then top each one with some of the 1 Tbsp butter.

Brush the exposed sides of the potato mounds with beaten egg, then bake for 20 minutes, or until potatoes are lightly browned.

Mum's Egg Specials

Serves 2 to 4

"If you think that chefs who spend their lives cooking up the most extravagant and eye-catching meals for their customers eat only stylish gourmet food themselves," Raymond Moran, former chef at Beech Hill Country House in Derry wrote in a recipe pamphlet he produced for the hotel, "you'd be very wrong. After hours being creative in the Beech Hill's kitchen I often long for something that's quick to make but full of goodness, energy, and taste. And for that I will very likely turn to a treat that my Mum used to make us for lunch or for a quick snack. Simple enough, but . . . what a mouth-watering treat they were for a bunch of hungry kids." Alas, these aren't on the Beech Hill menu, even at breakfastime—but they're certainly easy enough to make at home.

8 SLICES GOOD-QUALITY WHITE BREAD

4 THICK SLICES IRISH CHEDDAR

4 SLICES COUNTRY HAM

3 TBSP BUTTER

4 EGGS, BEATEN

Make 4 sandwiches with the bread, cheddar, and ham. Press them lightly together, then cut each into 4 pieces.

Melt the butter in a large skillet over medium heat. Working in batches, dip the sandwich quarters in the beaten egg, making sure that it coats both sides well. Fry the quarters for 2 to 3 minutes per side, or until golden brown.

WICKLOW PANCAKE

Wicklow Pancake

Serves 4

A specialty of County Wicklow (obviously), this dish was apparently first concocted in the early years of the twentieth century. Despite its name, it is really more of an omelette or frittata than a pancake.

4 EGGS

1 CUP/240 ML MILK

1 CUP/240 ML HEAVY CREAM

1 1/2 CUPS/90 G FRESH BREAD CRUMBS

4 SCALLIONS, TRIMMED AND MINCED

2 OR 3 SPRIGS PARSLEY, TRIMMED AND MINCED, PLUS 4 TO 6 LARGE LEAVES FOR GARNISH

1 TSP MINCED FRESH THYME

SALT AND PEPPER

4 TBSP BUTTER

Preheat the oven to 400°F/200°C (Gas Mark 6).

In a large bowl, beat the eggs lightly, then gently beat in the milk and cream. Stir in the bread crumbs, scallions, parsley sprigs, and thyme, then season to taste with salt and pepper.

Melt 2 Tbsp of the butter over medium-low heat in a large, heavy, ovenproof skillet, then pour in the egg mixture. Cook for 5 to 8 minutes or until the bottom of the pancake browns. Put the skillet in the oven and bake until the pancake puffs slightly and the top browns, 20 to 25 minutes.

Turn the pancake out onto a large plate and garnish with parsley leaves. To serve, divide the remaining 2 Tbsp of butter into 4 pats or knobs. Cut the pancake into 4 wedges, and put a bit of butter on each one.

Smoked Cod and Irish Cheddar Soufflé

Serves 4

Chef Kevin Dundon, proprietor of Dunbrody House in Arthurstown, County Wexford, likes cooking with smoked fish. This is one of his specialties.

2 TBSP BUTTER SOFTENED, PLUS MORE FOR GREASING

2 TBSP WHITE FLOUR

2/3 CUP/160 ML WARM MILK

2 EGGS, SEPARATED, PLUS 1 EGG WHITE

1/4 CUP/30 G GRATED IRISH CHEDDAR

1/2 CUP/100 G FINELY CHOPPED SMOKED COD, SMOKED HADDOCK, OR FINNAN HADDIE [SEE SOURCES, PAGE 369]

SALT AND PEPPER

Preheat the oven to 350°F/175°C (Gas Mark 4).

Generously grease four 4- to 6-oz/120- to 175-ml ramekins with butter, then put into the freezer for 5 minutes to let the butter harden.

Melt the 2 Tbsp butter in a medium saucepan over low heat, then sprinkle in the flour, stirring constantly with a wooden spoon. Continue cooking and stirring for 3 to 4 minutes to make a roux. Slowly pour in the milk, continuing to stir until sauce thickens. Remove from the heat and let stand for 5 minutes to cool slightly, then beat in the egg yolks one at a time. Mix in the cheese and smoked cod. Season to taste with salt and pepper and set aside to cool to room temperature.

In a medium bowl, whisk the egg whites until stiff peaks form, then gently fold the whites into the fish mixture.

Divide the soufflé batter evenly between the 4 ramekins and bake for 15 to 18 minutes, or until the soufflés have risen and turned golden on top.

IRELAND'S GOLDEN GLORY

In a country whose traditional diet is based on potatoes and bread, butter isn't just a nicety; it's a condiment as essential as salt. Fortunately, Ireland produces some of the world's best butter, and plenty of it. (No less a cooking authority than the distinctly non-Irish Marcella Hazan has written that she uses Irish butter exclusively in her kitchen.)

Butter has probably been churned in Ireland for at least two thousand years, and the early Irish considered it a symbol of abundance. It also helped give them strength: In the sixteenth century, Sir George Carew reported back to England that the Irish were too powerful to do battle with in the summertime, when they lived "upon the milk and butter of their kine." (He recommended that the would-be invaders wait until milk-less February to attack.) Sometimes, butter was salted or mixed with wild garlic or leeks; sometimes it was wrapped in cloth, enclosed in wicker, and buried in peat bogs to preserve and flavor it.

Ireland's commercial butter industry developed in the eighteenth century, and it is difficult to find a recipe of the period that does not contain it or call for it as an accompaniment. British food historian C. Anne Wilson reports that the Irish sometimes even salted a brick of butter and dredged it in oatmeal, then roasted it whole like meat and served it sliced at the table. Cork became the country's butter capital, and by the mid-nineteenth century, the city was shipping as much as thirty million pounds/fifteen million kilos of butter annually to markets as far away as India, Australia, and Brazil. (Today, Cork boasts the world's only butter museum, well worth a visit.)

In *The Farm by Lough Gur*, Mary Carberry evokes nineteenth-century butter making in rural County Limerick: "Here entered in a long file, the head dairywoman and her maids, carrying milk pails on their heads; lowering them carefully, they poured the milk through strainers into huge lead cisterns where the cream for butter-making was to rise. . . . A lovely, homely sight: rich, ivory milk, golden cream—all to be hand skimmed—firm one-pound pats of perfectly made butter ready to be sent off to special customers in Dublin and London."

In the late nineteenth century, Irish butter consumption dropped following the introduction of vegetable-oil margarine—that "rogueish compound," as the *Cork Examiner* once called it. The industry rebounded with the formation of the Irish Dairy Board in 1961, and today butter is Ireland's largest export by far, with some two billion dollars' worth shipped annually to ninety countries around the globe, much of it under the Kerrygold label. Closer to home, meanwhile, a smattering of small producers still make country butter by hand—people like Barbara Harding in Borrisokane, County Tipperary, or the Kingstons at Glenilen Farm in Drimoleague, County Cork. Kerrygold—which is widely available, happily, in American supermarkets—is about as good as commercial butter gets, but country butter, which you'll have to sample in Ireland itself, is a pure magic.

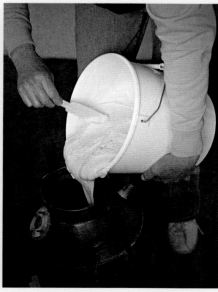

Molly Keane's Cheese Pudding

Serves 4

Irish author Molly Keane, née Mary Nesta Skrine, was born in County Kildare, but spent most of her life in what are sometimes called "the W's"—counties Wexford (where she grew up), Wicklow (where she went to boarding school), and Waterford (where she lived for years and died in 1996). Although she is best known for novels like *Good Behavior* and *Time After Time*, she also wrote a delightful, unpretentious cookbook called *Molly Keane's Nursery Cooking*, full of recipes for what a later generation would call "comfort food." This is a particularly tasty example.

2 TBSP COLD BUTTER, CUT INTO SMALL PIECES, PLUS SOFTENED BUTTER FOR GREASING

2 CUPS/120 G FRESH WHITE BREAD CRUMBS

2 1/2 CUPS/600 ML MILK

2 EGGS, SEPARATED

1 CUP/120 G GRATED WHITE IRISH CHEDDAR

SALT AND PEPPER

Preheat the oven to 350°F/175°C (Gas Mark 4). Generously grease a 1-qt/1-L baking dish.

Put bread crumbs into a medium bowl. Heat the milk in a small pan over medium heat until it starts to simmer. Pour the warm milk over the bread crumbs. Add the cold butter and stir until it melts, then set the mixture aside to cool for 10 minutes.

Whisk the egg yolks in a small bowl. Stir in the cheese, then fold the mixture into the bread crumbs. Season to taste with salt and pepper.

In a small bowl, beat the egg whites with an electric mixer until stiff peaks form, then fold the whites into pudding mixture.

Bake for about 1 hour, or until golden and set.

Fried Cooleeney Cheese with Beet Salad

Serves 6

This is a popular dish at Brocka on the Water in Ballinderry, County Tipperary. Cooleeney cheese, made by the Maher family in Moyne, near the Tipperary town of Thurles, is often available in the United States (see Sources, page 369). Camembert may be substituted.

2 EGGS, LIGHTLY BEATEN

1 1/2 CUPS/90 G DRY BREAD CRUMBS

THREE 7-OZ/200-G WHEELS COOLEENEY OR CAMEMBERT, QUARTERED

2 TO 3 CUPS/475 TO 720 ML CANOLA OR SUNFLOWER OIL

1 SMALL HEAD BUTTER LETTUCE, JULIENNED

1 RECIPE BEET SALAD [PAGE 260]

1 RECIPE CABBAGE WITH GINGER [PAGE 247]

CANNED FRUIT CHUTNEY [PAGE 330] OR ANOTHER CHUTNEY OF YOUR CHOICE FOR GARNISH [OPTIONAL]

Put the eggs and bread crumbs in separate shallow bowls. Coat the cheese wheels in the egg, dredge in the bread crumbs, then refrigerate for 1 hour.

Pour about 2 in/5 cm of oil into a deep medium skillet or heavy-bottomed pot and heat over high heat to a temperature of about 350°F/175°C on a candy/deep-fat thermometer. Working in batches, fry the cheese until golden brown, then drain on paper towels.

To serve, divide the lettuce evenly between 6 plates. Put the beet salad on top of the lettuce, dividing it equally, then arrange 2 cheese pieces on each serving of beets. Top the cheese and beets with cabbage, dividing it evenly. Garnish with Brocka on the Water's Canned Fruit Chutney or another chutney, if you like.

FRIED COOLEENEY CHEESE
WITH BEET SALAD

Baked Gubbeen with Garlic and Fresh Herbs

Serves 4

Gubbeen, from Schull in West Cork, is one of the most famous of Irish farmhouse cheeses, and one of the few that is widely available in the United States. This recipe, from Gubbeen cheese maker Giana Ferguson, appears in Clodagh McKenna's *Irish Farmers' Market Cookbook*.

TWO 14-OZ/400-G GUBBEEN CHEESES
[SEE SOURCES, PAGE 369]

1 TBSP CHOPPED FRESH THYME

1 TBSP CHOPPED FRESH ROSEMARY

4 CLOVES GARLIC, MINCED

PEPPER

Preheat the oven to 325°F/160°C (Gas Mark 3).

Cut each cheese in half to make 2 thinner rounds (4 all together). Sprinkle half the thyme, rosemary, and garlic on the cut side of each bottom half of cheese, then season both herbed rounds generously with pepper.

Replace the top halves of the cheeses, then wrap each cheese separately in foil, leaving a steam vent at the top of each package to let moisture escape.

Put the wrapped cheeses on a baking sheet and bake for 20 minutes. Serve hot with slices of country bread or toast or good crackers.

A FAMILY AFFAIR

"Why has West Cork become the food center of Ireland?" asks Giana Ferguson rhetorically. "It's the people." She should know: Born in England, brought up in Spain, and married to an Irish farmer, she's at the center of the region's artisanal food movement, *and* at the heart of a family that is helping to define the whole phenomenon. At Gubbeen, their farm in Schull, on the West Cork coast, Giana makes one of Ireland's oldest, most distinctive, and most celebrated artisanal cheeses, Gubbeen, a semisoft marvel made of raw cow's milk, with an attractive animal aroma and flavors that suggest wild mushrooms and hazelnuts. She and her husband, Tom, also raise grass-fed cattle (including native Kerry cows) and pigs, whose diet includes whey from the cheese-making process and herbs from the garden. In a facility of his own on the property, meanwhile, their son, Fingal, uses meat from those pigs to make a wide range of cured meats, including assorted sausages and salamis, back bacon, and ham. Fingal's sister Clovis tends the organic herb garden, whose yield goes into the sausages and is sold at shops and farmers' markets around West Cork. "What we're doing here," says Giana, "is breaking away from the great dream of industrial riches from the land. We are in effect creating a new peasantry."

A WORLD OF CHEESE

Ireland produces a wonderful range of first-rate farmhouse cheeses. Cheese, in fact, is not only one of the great success stories of modern Irish food, but the engine that has driven the island's whole artisanal food movement.

Almost every variety imaginable is made in Ireland—cheeses inspired by (though inevitably at least a little bit different from) Brie, Camembert, Reblochon, Montrachet, Feta, Tilsit, Port-Salut, Gouda, Wensleydale, Cheshire, Cheddar, Emmenthaler, Garrotxa, Gjetost, Parmigiano-Reggiano, Stilton, and more—and there are a number of unclassifiable originals. Cow's milk cheeses predominate, but a number of good ones are made from sheep's and goat's milk, too. Some cheese makers are farmers who wanted to get better value from their milk than a dairy cooperative could provide; some are retired or moonlighting professionals from other fields entirely—the philosophy department, the movie studio wardrobe shop. They're Irish, but also English, Australian, German, Italian, and Dutch, and their assistants come from all over. Fermoy Natural Cheeses in Fermoy, County Cork, for example, is owned by German-born Gudrun Shinnick and her husband, Frank, who calls himself "the token Irishman"; the workers hail from Poland, France, and Brazil.

Helen Finnegan at Knockdrinna, in Kilkenny, was a farmer's wife who wanted to get into food production. "Bread and jam were pretty well taken around here," she says, "but there was only one other cheese maker in the county—Lavistown." So she taught herself the cheese maker's art, found sources for cow's, sheep's, and goat's milk, and started making several types of cheeses. When the proprietor of Lavistown retired, she bought that operation, too. Jeffa Gill (facing page, top left), who makes Durrus (facing page, top right), near Bantry in West Cork, moved from Dublin to her Durrus farm because she wanted to "live off the land," and decided to make cheese, she says, for a simple reason: She had small children, and cheese making would let her work at home. Jane Murphy, whose Ardsallagh is arguably Ireland's best goat cheese, got into the business when a traveling salesman, noting her overgrown front yard and her childrens' eczema, told her, "What you need is a goat." (Goat's milk is an effective natural cure for the skin disease, and of course a goat would keep the yard mown.) Before long, she had a herd of goats and too much milk, and. . . .

Remarkably, good Irish cheeses can be hard to find in Ireland unless you visit their places of production. Even the best restaurants don't always offer good selections on their cheese boards, and what's found in shops isn't always in the best condition. A good source, though, is Trevor Irvine's Cheese, Etc. in Carrick-on-Shannon, County Leitrim (he also sells at the twice-weekly St. George's Market in Belfast, well worth a visit). Another is Sheridans, with branches in Galway, Dublin, and Waterford, and a thriving wholesale cheese business based in County Meath, which supplies Irish and other fine cheeses to purveyors both in Ireland and abroad. Importation of Irish cheeses into America is inconsistent, but at least one or two are usually available at good cheese shops. (See Sources, page 369, for mail-order purveyors.)

AN IRISH CHEESE PLATE

It is frustrating to have to report that very few Irish farm-house cheeses are currently available in the United States. The mother of them all, Milleens, for instance, isn't being imported right now, though it has been sold here in the past. First-rate goat cheeses like Ardsallagh and St. Tola haven't found their way to our cheese shop shelves recently, if indeed they ever did. You will look in vain for St. Gall, Knockdrinna, Lavistown, Glebe Brethan, Baylough or Hegarty's cheddar, or Wicklow Blue, not to mention Desmond or Gabriel (though, to be fair, those last two are hard to find even in Ireland). Just to make things even more difficult, no one merchant I've found sells all of the ones that *are* imported. (See page 369 for various sources.) Of course, one solution to the problem is simply to include one or two Irish cheeses, when you do find them, in a selection of artisanal cheese from the United States or other countries. If you want to stay Irish, though, and are willing do search around a little, here's what you can probably come up with:

- Ardrahan, a washed-rind cow's milk cheese from County Cork, with a full-flavored, sweetish interior contrasting with a salty rind
- Carrigaline Natural (the producers also make smoked and flavored cheeses), a mild and pale waxed cow's milk cheese from County Cork, reminiscent of Tilsit or Havarti
- Cashel Blue from County Tipperary, a comparatively mild cow's milk blue, less salty than many of its counterparts, with a creamy texture and a faint flowery aftertaste
- Coolea, a hard cow's milk cheese made in County Cork, with a pronounced caramel flavor and a rich aftertaste

- Cooleeney, a soft-ripe cow's milk cheese, also from County Tipperary, reminiscent of Camembert; very soft and delicate when young, growing more pungent with age
- Crozier Blue, Cashel Blue's sheep's milk sibling: creamy, toasty, and a little sweet
- Gubbeen, a semisoft cow's milk cheese, and one of the essentials (see page 61)

Because no Irish farmhouse cheddars or Cheddar-style cheeses are sold in the United States right now, you may wish to add a commercial cheddar or Cheddar-style cheese from Kerrygold, the brand of the Irish Dairy Board. These are widely available in U.S. supermarkets and include Irish cheddar, Blarney, Dubliner, and a very flavorful reserve Cheddar, more than two years old.

To serve 4 to 8:

Select at least four Irish cheeses, or as many as you can find.

If using Ardrahan, Carrigaline, Cashel Blue, Coolea, Crozier Blue, or Gubbeen, cut in 3- to 4-oz/85- to 125-g wedges. If using Cooleeney, serve a whole 4-in/10-cm wheel. Break Kerrygold cheddar or Cheddar-style cheese into irregular shards.

Arrange the cheeses on a cheese board or serving plate. Accompany with crisp apple slices, Rhubarb Chutney (page 331), and/or oatcakes, either homemade (page 351) or Robert Ditty's (see page 276).

FISH

The Generous Waters

The fish of both river and sea are so exquisite and abundant that the common Irish eat freely of pike, hake, salmon, trout, [and] indeed all sorts of fish are to be had for astonishing value.

—Archbishop Giovanni Battista Rinuccini, Papal Nuncio to Ireland [circa 1645]

[E]xplain to me why people have gone on for generations swallowing boiled-fish-and-white-sauce without even one cook having been assassinated.

—Maura Laverty, *Feasting Galore: Recipes and Food Lore from Ireland* [1961]

Albert Jouvin de Rochefort, a French visitor to Ireland in the late seventeenth century, wrote that "It is saying everything to relate that navigators who frequent these parts

complain that their vessels are sometimes obstructed by the quantities of fish they meet in their course." Indeed, the island's piscatorial abundance is remarkable.

The Irish coastline, deckled with inlets and bays, extends for more than 3,500 miles/5,600 kilometers, and the island is laced with an estimated 10,000 miles/16,000 kilometers of rivers and streams and dotted with about 50 fresh- and saltwater loughs (pronounced "locks"), or lakes. More than 150 species are caught in these waters: Cod, ling, hake, haddock, whiting, tuna, shark, turbot, plaice, sardines, herring, mackerel, and an array of shellfish are among the many sea creatures. Swimming in the island's fresh waters are perch, pike, bream, tench, trout, eel, pollen (a freshwater relative of the herring), and even arctic char, found wild in a few cold, nutrient-poor loughs and now being farmed in County Sligo. And, of course, journeying from salt to sweet, there is Ireland's emblematic fish, salmon (see Chapter No. 5).

There is no doubt that for many thousands of years, fish and shellfish have formed part of the Irish diet, on every socio-economic level. In 1750, the very well-to-do Mary Delany, wife of Jonathan Swift's friend Dean Patrick Delany, boasted that she was able to buy, at her Mount Panther estate in County Down, "fine salmon, lobster, trout, crabs, every day at the door." Two hundred years later, in Magherafelt, County Derry, baker Robert Ditty remembers the fishmonger who came by every Friday in a gray Morris Minor van selling pollen out of wooden crates. "The housewives would come out," he says "with fish plates already full of flour and put the fish right into them to be cooked later. They'd be eaten every Friday night, fried in bacon fat from the morning's breakfast."

Strangely, the Irish consume comparatively little seafood today. In earlier times, distribution was difficult; it was easier to transport salted mackerel to Holland than fresh cod to Tipperary. Thus, some parts of the country never developed a fish-eating tradition. Fish also had negative associations. I once overheard a gentleman in a pub in Skerries, County Dublin, declare that "Fish was what you ate if you didn't have any money, because anybody could go out and catch a few fish; if you were well off, you had meat." If you were Catholic, fish was also pretty much what you had to eat on Fridays and other days of abstinence; once dietary strictures were relaxed, many Irish no longer saw the point of it. (The fisherman–chef Enda Conneely reports that only about a quarter of the customers at his little restaurant on the island of Inishere, in Galway Bay, actually order fish—and the place is called Fisherman's Cottage!) Nonetheless, there are a lot of wonderful fish dishes cooked in Ireland today, some drawn from the traditional repertoire, others created by modern-day chefs and imaginative home cooks. Let us hope that boiled fish with white sauce is a thing of the past.

Trout Baked in Wine

Serves 4

Ireland's rivers, loughs, and streams teem with trout, in numerous varieties. Fish expert Ian Hill writes that in Lough Melvin (bordered by counties Leitrim and Fermanagh) alone there are five subspecies, including one called the "slob trout." Trout were frequent targets of poachers: Kathleen McClintock remembers the day, when she was a girl in Greenisland, County Antrim, a trout suddenly landed on the kitchen floor. A poacher had tossed it through the open door so the approaching police wouldn't find any evidence of his misdeeds. Today, rainbow trout, originally from California, are farmed in Ireland, but wild trout are greatly preferred for their flavor and richness. Theodora FitzGibbon credits this recipe to J. O'Brien of County Clare, circa 1880.

1/2 CUP/125 G BUTTER, SLIGHTLY SOFTENED, PLUS MORE FOR GREASING

2 TBSP MINCED FRESH PARSLEY

4 TROUT, CLEANED AND SCALED

SALT AND WHITE PEPPER

1/2 BOTTLE/375 ML DRY WHITE WINE, PREFERABLY UNOAKED

1/2 LEMON

Preheat the oven to 375°F/190°C (Gas Mark 5).

Combine 4 Tbsp of the butter with the parsley to form into 4 rectangular pats. Put one pat inside each fish, then arrange the fish side by side in a lightly greased baking dish with a cover. Rub salt and pepper into the top side of each fish, cover the dish, and bake for 20 minutes.

Divide the remaining 4 Tbsp of butter into 4 pats. Put 1 on top of each fish, then squeeze lemon juice over all 4. Cover again and return to the oven to bake for 10 minutes more.

Smoked Eel with Cucumbers and Brown Bread

Serves 4

Anthony Creswell produces some of Ireland's best smoked salmon at his Ummera Smokehouse in Timoleague, County Cork. But possibly even better are his remarkably delicate and seductively smoky silver eel fillets, boned and skinned (see Sources, page 369). Another of Ireland's best smokehouses, Frank Hederman's Belvelly, sells excellent smoked eel, too, with skin and bone still attached.

TWO 100-G PACKAGES IRISH SKINLESS SMOKED EEL FILLETS, OR 8 TO 10 OZ/225 TO 280 G DOMESTIC SKIN-ON SMOKED EEL

2 TBSP BUTTER

8 SLICES BALLYMALOE BROWN BREAD [PAGE 282] OR BROWN SODA BREAD [PAGE 272] OR ANOTHER DENSE BROWN BREAD

1/2 CUCUMBER, PEELED AND SLICED PAPER-THIN, PREFERABLY ON A MANDOLINE

1 LEMON, QUARTERED

If using skin-on eel, remove the skin, peeling it like a banana, then gently push the meat off the central bone with your thumb. Cut skinned eel or skinless eel fillets into lengths about 3 in/7.5 cm long, then cut each piece lengthwise into an even number of thin slices.

Generously butter the slices of bread, then top each with a layer of cucumber slices. Divide the eel slices evenly between the bread slices. Garnish with lemon quarters.

Smoked Eel Tempura

Serves 2 to 4

Stopping for lunch one day at Beech Hill Country House just outside the town of Derry, I ordered seared salmon fillet with a parsley and white bean purée, garnished with two or three little pieces of smoked eel, fried in a delicate batter. The whole dish was delicious, but I was particularly taken by the eel, which somehow seemed to get lighter rather than richer through the process of being battered and fried. By the time I got around to asking for the recipe, the chef who had prepared the dish, Sharon Harkin, had departed, but I managed to reproduce it fairly closely.

I EGG, BEATEN

I CUP/100 G WHITE FLOUR, SIFTED

2 TO 3 CUPS/475 TO 720 ML CANOLA OR
SAFFFLOWER OIL

TWO 100-G PACKAGES IRISH SKINLESS SMOKED EEL
FILLETS, OR 8 TO 10 OZ/225 TO 280 G DOMESTIC
SKIN-ON SMOKED EEL, SKINNED AND BONED
[SEE STEP I, PAGE 71], CUT INTO 2-IN/5-CM PIECES

Combine the egg and flour in a medium bowl and whisk in 1 cup/240 ml ice water to form a medium-thick batter. Do not overmix.

Pour about 2 in/5cm of oil into a deep medium skillet or heavy-bottomed pot and heat over high heat to a temperature of about 375°F/190°C on a candy/deep-fat thermometer.

Put the eel pieces into the bowl of batter and make sure they are well coated, then fry them in batches for 4 to 5 minutes, or until just golden brown. Drain on paper towels.

Toomebridge Eel Supper

Serves 6 to 8

Every Halloween, at hotels, restaurants, and private homes around Lough Neagh, the traditional evening meal is fried eel with onions. Toomebridge-born chef Noel McMeel remembers vividly his father preparing this feast every year. "As a child," he adds, "I always thought that eels were snakes, and I could never understand why St. Patrick had left some behind when he chased all the snakes from Ireland." This is McMeel's father's recipe. (Look for eels at Asian fish markets.)

2 CUPS/200 G WHITE FLOUR, SIFTED

SALT AND PEPPER

I TBSP BUTTER

I TBSP EXTRA-VIRGIN OLIVE OIL

5 FRESH SILVER EELS, SKINNED AND CUT INTO
2-IN/5-CM LENGTHS

1/2 LB/250 G IRISH BACON, PREFERABLY GALTEE'S
SLICED CURED PORK LOIN, TOMMY MOLONEY'S
MILD-CURED [NOT SMOKED OR BACK RASHERS],
OR DONNELLY'S [SEE SOURCES, PAGE 369],
I LARGE ONION, COARSELY CHOPPED

BOXTY [PAGE 217] FOR SERVING [OPTIONAL]

ROBERT DITTY'S WHEATEN BREAD [PAGE 275] OR
TREACLE BREAD [PAGE 282] FOR SERVING [OPTIONAL]

Put the flour into a medium bowl and season generously with salt and pepper, mixing them in well.

Melt the butter with the oil in a large skillet with a cover over medium-high heat. Roll the eel pieces in the seasoned flour and fry for 3 to 4 minutes on each side (including the edges) until golden brown all over.

Reduce the heat to low, add the bacon and onion, and cook for 3 to 4 minutes, stirring frequently. Cover the pan and cook for about 20 minutes more, or until the onion is soft.

Serve with Boxty and/or with Robert Ditty's Wheaten Bread or Treacle Bread, if you like.

FATHER EEL

According to legend, the hunter-warrior Fionn Mac Cumhaill—or Finn McCool—once scooped up a clod of earth from Ulster to hurl at a rival. He missed and the clod landed in the Irish Sea, where it became the Isle of Man; the divot left behind became Lough Neagh. Lough Neagh is the largest inland body of water in Ireland or Great Britain, covering almost 160 square miles/400 square kilometers and touching the shores of five Northern Ireland counties.

The lough is rich in fish, but its most valuable denizens are its eels. Salmon travel from salt water into freshwater rivers to spawn. Eels (*Anguilla anguilla*) do the opposite, leaving freshwater to swim all the way to the Sargasso Sea in the North Atlantic. Elvers spawned there turn around and, in the case of Lough Neagh's eels, swim some four thousand miles/ sixty-five hundred kilometers to Ireland, up the River Bann, and into the lough. Still tiny when they arrive, they fatten and mature there for anywhere from fourteen to eighteen years. Then they start heading back to the Sargasso Sea to spawn themselves, which is when some of them run right into the largest (and now possibly the only) wild eel fishery in Europe, at Toomebridge. As the poet Seamus Heaney describes it in "Up the Shore" from *A Lough Neagh Sequence*,

> "At Toomebridge where it sluices towards the sea
> They've set new gates and tanks against the flow.
> From time to time they break the eels' journey
> And lift five hundred stone in one go."

The man in charge of the fishery is a quiet, white-haired Catholic priest named Father Oliver Kennedy. "Fishing rights in the lough were owned by a company that didn't treat the fishermen particularly well," he explains, "and I wanted to help, so I founded a fishermen's cooperative in the 1960s. We now employ about three hundred people." The number of elvers coming into the lough has declined precipitously in the past thirty years, he says, but the fishery supplements the natural population with elvers bought from England. (Early in 2009, all eel fishing in Ireland—as opposed to Northern Ireland—was banned for an indeterminate period of time, to allow stocks to regenerate. The Toomebridge fishery was not affected by the ban and remains open.)

Very few of the eels—which are shipped live—stay in Ireland, and those that do mostly go to Chinese and Japanese purveyors, with only a few bought by Irish smokehouses and restaurants. The rest go to London, to be jellied, or to Holland and Germany, to be smoked. I mention to Father Kennedy that I've just had excellent eel tempura at a restaurant in Derry. "I prefer it simple," he replies. "Do you eat a lot of eel yourself, then?" I ask him. "Oh, no," he says with a smile.

Smoked Mackerel Pâté

Serves 6

Bad weather can shut down plane and ferry access to the Aran Islands, at the mouth of Galway Bay. At their café and cultural center, Fisherman's Cottage, on Inishere, the smallest of the Arans, Enda and Marie Conneely always keep long-lasting make-ahead dishes like this in the refrigerator, because they never know, from day to day, whether they'll be serving thirty dinners or none.

THREE 6- TO 8-OZ/175- TO 250-G SMOKED
MACKEREL FILLETS, SKINNED AND BONED

4 TBSP BUTTER, SOFTENED

1/2 TSP GROUND NUTMEG

PINCH OF PEPPER

3 TO 4 TBSP HEAVY CREAM

MELBA TOAST OR CRACKERS FOR SERVING

Put the mackerel, butter, nutmeg, and pepper into a food processor and pulse until well blended. With the processor turned to high, slowly add the cream, processing until the mixture is creamy but not liquid. Adjust the seasoning, adding more nutmeg and/or pepper if necessary.

Serve with melba toast or crackers.

Potted Herring

Serves 6 to 8

Potting fish and shellfish—packing the cooked, seasoned flesh into molds and sealing it with butter—is an ancient method of preservation, and herring, always cheap and plentiful in Ireland, lends itself particularly well to the process. Gerry Galvin (see page 79) serves this dish with salad and a Mediterranean-inspired spicy tomato dressing. I like it better with just good Irish-style bread.

1 1/2 LB/750 G HERRING FILLETS, BONED

2 BAY LEAVES

1 TBSP MINCED FRESH DILL OR FENNEL FRONDS

2 CLOVES GARLIC, CRUSHED

1/2 ONION, MINCED

1/2 TSP NUTMEG

8 BLACK PEPPERCORNS

SALT

1/2 CUP/120 ML WHITE WINE VINEGAR

1/2 CUP/120 ML DRY WHITE WINE

6 TBSP BUTTER, SOFTENED

Preheat the oven to 350°F/175°C (Gas Mark 4).

Roll up the herring fillets loosely and arrange them side by side in a single layer in a glass or ceramic baking dish with a cover. Add the bay leaves, dill or fennel, garlic, onion, nutmeg, peppercorns, and salt to taste. Gently pour in the vinegar and wine, then bake the herring, covered, for about 45 minutes.

Meanwhile, lightly grease 6 to 8 small molds or ramekins with some of the butter, then melt the rest.

Drain the herring, picking out and discarding the bay leaves and peppercorns. Pack the herring into the molds or ramekins, and pour a thin layer of melted butter over each one. Refrigerate for at least 4 hours and as long as 2 weeks before serving.

CURING FISH, DOWNINGS PIER, COUNTY DONEGAL.

Kedgeree

Serves 4

This is an Anglo-Indian dish that became popular throughout the United Kingdom and in Ireland in Victorian times. (The name derives from the Hindi *khichdi*, meaning a kind of rice and lentil dish.) It is thought of as a breakfast dish, but makes a good light lunch, too.

I LB/500 G SMOKED HADDOCK OR FINNAN HADDIE
[SEE SOURCES, PAGE 369], SMOKED SALMON,
WOK-SMOKED SALMON [PAGE III], OR COOKED
FRESH SALMON, OR A COMBINATION

2 CUPS/475 ML MILK [IF USING HADDOCK OR
FINNAN HADDIE]

3 CUPS/480 G COOKED RICE

I TSP CURRY POWDER

I TSP CAYENNE

SALT AND PEPPER

3 TBSP BUTTER

I ONION, MINCED

2 HARD-COOKED EGGS, CHOPPED

2 TBSP CHOPPED FRESH PARSLEY

I TBSP CHOPPED FRESH CHIVES

If using haddock, rinse the fish, then heat the milk in a small pan over medium heat (do not boil) and add the fish, breaking it up if necessary. Reduce the heat to low and poach the fish for about 10 minutes. Remove the fish from the milk and discard the milk. When the fish is cool enough to handle, remove and discard any skin and bones and break the fish into small pieces with your hands.

If using regular smoked salmon, cut it into small strips. If using wok-smoked salmon or fresh salmon, break the fish into small pieces with your hands. Set aside.

Put the rice into a large bowl, breaking it up with your hands if it has clumped together, and stir in the curry powder, cayenne, and salt and pepper to taste.

Melt 1 Tbsp of the butter in a large skillet over medium heat, then add the onion and cook for about 8 minutes.

Melt the remaining 2 Tbsp of the butter in a small pan, then drizzle it over over the rice. Add the onion and the butter it cooked in, then stir in the fish. Add the eggs and parsley and mix everything together well. Adjust the seasoning with salt and pepper, then scatter the chives over top. Serve warm or at room temperature.

Haddock Smokeys

Serves 4

Variations on this rich, satisfying dish are found in pubs and on restaurant lunch menus all over Ireland. This recipe comes from Kevin Dundon at Dunbrody House in Arthurstown, County Wexford—a talented contemporary chef who wisely, in this case, refrains from adding any contemporary-chef touches.

2 SMALL TOMATOES, SEEDED AND CHOPPED

I LB/500 G SMOKED HADDOCK OR FINNAN HADDIE
[SEE SOURCES, PAGE 369], SKINNED, BONED,
AND DICED

I CUP/120 G GRATED IRISH CHEDDAR

PEPPER

I $1/_3$ CUPS/320 ML HEAVY CREAM

BREAD AND BUTTER FOR SERVING

Preheat the oven to 350°F/175°C (Gas Mark 4).

Distribute half the tomatoes evenly between four 6- to 8-oz/ 175- to 250-ml ramekins or individual baking dishes. Scatter the smoked haddock over the tomatoes, dividing it equally between the ramekins, then sprinkle half the cheese over the haddock, again dividing it equally. Cover the cheese with the remaining tomatoes, and season generously with pepper. Pour the cream over the ingredients; and scatter the remaining cheese over the top of each.

Place the ramekins on a baking sheet and bake for 15 to 20 minutes or until the tops are golden brown. Serve with good bread and butter.

Fish Cakes

Serves 4

This recipe appears in Irish writer Molly Keane's wonderful *Nursery Cooking* book and is a signal example of the genre.

1 LB/500 G RUSSET POTATOES, COARSELY CHOPPED

3/4 LB/375 G COD, HAKE, OR HALIBUT FILLETS, SKINNED AND BONED

1 TBSP KETCHUP

1 TBSP MINCED FRESH PARSLEY

1 TBSP LEMON JUICE

3 EGGS, BEATEN

1/2 CUP/50 G WHITE FLOUR, PLUS MORE FOR DUSTING

SALT AND PEPPER

2 TO 3 TBSP CANOLA OIL

1/3 CUP/10 G CORN FLAKES, FINELY CRUSHED, OR 1/3 CUP/50 G IRISH ROLLED OATS

Put the potatoes into a medium pot and cover with cold water. Salt the water generously, then cover the pot and bring to a boil over high heat. Reduce the heat to medium and continue cooking the potatoes, still covered, for 15 to 20 minutes or until the potatoes are very soft.

Meanwhile, put the fish fillets into a medium skillet, add water to cover, bring to a boil over medium heat, and then reduce the heat to low and simmer for about 10 minutes or until just cooked through. Drain and set aside.

Drain the potatoes, then return them to the pot and mash them well. Flake the fish into the pot, then stir in the ketchup, parsley, lemon juice, and about two-thirds of the eggs, or just enough to bind the mixture. Stir the mixture vigorously until well combined.

Spoon the mixture into 4 mounds of equal size on a floured board, then, with floured hands, shape each mound into a round cake about ¾ in/2 cm thick.

Put the flour in a medium bowl and season generously with salt and pepper.

Heat the oil in a medium skillet over medium-high heat. Coat each fish cake in the seasoned flour, then in the remaining egg, and then dredge in the corn flakes or oats. Fry for 7 to 8 minutes per side, or until golden brown, turning once.

Skate in Brown Butter

Serves 4

Skate (or ray) is surprisingly popular in Ireland, and is sometimes even used for fish and chips. Sauced with brown (often called "black") butter, it was a staple of the affluent Anglo-Irish table for centuries.

1 1/2 LB/750 G SKATE WINGS, SKINNED [ASK YOUR FISHMONGER]

1 ONION, SLICED

1 BAY LEAF

3 OR 4 SPRIGS PARSLEY

JUICE OF 1/2 LEMON

SALT

4 TBSP BUTTER

2 TBSP WHITE WINE VINEGAR

2 TBSP CAPERS, DRAINED [OPTIONAL]

Lay the skate wings in a skillet large enough to hold them in one layer. Add the onion, bay leaf, and parsley, then pour in enough water to cover all the ingredients. Add the lemon juice and salt to taste and bring to a boil over medium-high heat. Reduce the heat to low, cover, and cook for 15 to 20 minutes, or until the flesh lifts easily from the cartilage.

Meanwhile, melt the butter in a small saucepan over medium heat and cook for 2 to 3 minutes, or until it begins to brown. Stir in the vinegar and capers (if using) and season the butter generously with salt.

Carefully remove the skate from the skillet and divide between 4 warm plates. Drizzle some brown butter over each portion.

KINSALE

Kinsale is a pretty little port town in County Cork, roughly twenty miles/thirty kilometers south of Cork City at the mouth of the River Bandon. It is famous in Irish history as the site of a battle in 1601 in which English forces defeated the Irish and their Spanish allies, precipitating the so-called "flight of the earls" to continental Europe, an event romantically considered to have signaled the end of the old Gaelic order. Kinsale is also famous in Irish gastronomy as Ireland's first modern culinary capital.

From the mid-1970s through the 1990s, the town had probably five or six of the best restaurants in the country. "There was a kind of pioneering spirit there," remembers Gerry Galvin (below), who had one of the most celebrated, The Vintage. "We had a Swedish couple, a German, an Italian, all kinds of interesting people, all cooking good food." Galvin himself, who comes from Drumcollogher in County Limerick, went to hotel school in Shannon and later worked in hotels, both in management and in the dining rooms, all over Ireland and in England, Switzerland, and South Africa. In 1974, after two seasons working as a manager at Kinsale's Trident Hotel, Galvin and his wife, Marie, rented The Vintage and opened it as a French restaurant. Galvin had an epiphany, though, when a visiting Belgian food writer, attracted by the French-language menu, came in for dinner and left very

disappointed. "I realized," he says, "that I was just pretending to be a French chef. That's when I began to see that what I really wanted to do was to make a personal statement of some kind—though I wouldn't have put it that way then—with all the lovely ingredients I saw all around me that were being covered up with heavy sauces." In so doing, he became one of the first "new Irish" chefs.

Galvin sold The Vintage in 1983, and the next year opened Drimcong House in Moycullen, County Galway. Today, he has retired from restaurant cooking but writes frequently about food. Most of the pioneers of good cooking in Kinsale gradually drifted away, and for a decade or so, the town lived mostly on its past reputation, gastronomically speaking. Today, there are again a number of good restaurants in town, most notably Martin and Marie Shanahan's Fishy Fishy Café, a stylish outgrowth of their original Fishy Fishy café and fish shop (still in business, too). Their seafood is impeccable and varied, and is cooked with skill and respect.

Kinsale is also noteworthy for its role as Ireland's first Transition Town—a community that has volunteered to seek out ways to reduce energy consumption and increase self-reliance through recycling, community gardens, and other programs. "Food feet, not food miles!" is one of the movement's mottos.

Arctic Char with Lemon Sauce

Serves 4

Arctic char or charr (*Salvelinus alpinus*), a mild-flavored relative of trout and salmon, is not traditional in the Irish diet, but it does exist in some loughs, and is now being farmed by the Carty-Johnson family at Cloonacool, in the foothills of the Ox Mountains in County Sligo. This is adapted from one of their recipes.

1 CUP/240 ML HEAVY CREAM

JUICE OF 1 LEMON

1/4 CUP/60 ML FISH STOCK [PAGE 356]

SALT AND PEPPER

FOUR 5- TO 7-OZ/150- TO 200-G ARCTIC CHAR FILLETS, SKIN ON

CANOLA OIL FOR FRYING

PARSLEY OR WATERCRESS LEAVES FOR GARNISH [OPTIONAL]

Combine the cream, lemon juice, and stock in a small saucepan. Bring to a boil over medium-high heat, then reduce the heat to low and simmer, covered, for about 10 minutes or until the sauce thickens slightly. Season to taste with salt and pepper.

Meanwhile, heat a large nonstick grill pan or cast-iron griddle or skillet over medium-high heat. Brush the fish on both sides with oil and season to taste with salt and pepper, then sear them for 2 to 3 minutes on each side or until they are golden brown and just cooked through (do not overcook).

To serve, arrange the fish on a serving platter and drizzle sauce over them. Garnish with parsley or watercress, if you like.

Monkfish in Beer Batter

Serves 4

Maurice Keller had a good French chef at his Arlington Lodge in Waterford. But when the man left to take another job, instead of hiring a replacement, Keller took over the kitchen and simplified the menu to include, as he puts it, "the kind of food I like to eat myself." One of his best dishes is that old Irish (and British) standby fish and chips, which he makes with small, sweet monkfish landed at nearby Dunmore East. Larger monkfish or any other firm-fleshed fish will work almost as well. "The secret of this dish," says Keller, "is fresh monkfish in freshly made batter, cooked and served immediately—that means now!" Noting that the recipe calls for only part of a bottle of beer, he adds, "I don't need to be told what to do with the rest, so I am not telling you!!"

1 CUP/100 G WHITE FLOUR

1 EGG, LIGHTLY BEATEN

1 CUP/240 ML BEER [LAGER, NOT STOUT], PLUS MORE AS NEEDED

SALT

1 1/2 LB/750 G BONELESS MONKFISH OR ANOTHER OCEAN FISH WITH FIRM WHITE FLESH, CUT INTO BITE-SIZE PIECES

OIL FOR FRYING

LEMON WEDGES FOR GARNISH

TARTAR SAUCE [PAGE 358] FOR SERVING

CHIPS [PAGE 229] FOR SERVING

MUSHY PEAS [PAGE 244] FOR SERVING [OPTIONAL]

Put the flour into a medium bowl, stir in the egg, then stir in the beer to make a light batter that will coat the fish almost translucently. Season the batter lightly with salt. (Add a bit more beer to thin the batter if necessary.)

Heat at least 6 in/15 cm of oil in a deep pot or deep fryer to 350°F/175°C on a candy/deep-fat thermometer, then fry the fish pieces in batches for about 3 minutes per batch, draining on paper towels as they're done.

Garnish with lemon wedges and serve with homemade tartar sauce, chips, and, if you like, mushy peas.

MONKFISH IN BEER BATTER

BLACK SOLE WITH GREEN GARLIC

Black Sole with Green Garlic

Serves 4

Black sole is what the Irish call Dover sole—for why would the Irish append an English name to this superlative fish, found amply in Irish waters? A few years back, in her cottage in Courtmacsherry, a fishing hamlet in County Cork, food writer Clodagh McKenna cooked some fresh local sole this way, flavoring them with the shoots and blossoms of wild flowering garlic from a nearby field. In springtime, farmers' markets in the United States often sell wild or cultivated green garlic shoots, perfect for this dish; garlic chives or even ordinary chives may be substituted. Don't be put off by the amount of butter in this preparation; the fish should luxuriate in it.

3/4 CUP/190 G BUTTER, SOFTENED

1 CUP/100 G CHOPPED WILD OR GREEN GARLIC
SHOOTS, GARLIC CHIVES, OR CHIVES

2 LARGE OR 4 SMALL SOLE
[ABOUT 2 LB/1 KG TOTAL], FILLETED

SALT AND PEPPER

In a medium bowl, mix the butter and garlic shoots or chives together well with a wooden spoon. Put about half the butter mixture into a small bowl and set aside.

Melt the remaining butter mixture in a large skillet over medium-high heat. Working in batches if necessary, fry the fillets, skin side up, for 1 to 2 minutes, or until just beginning to color. Turn the fillets over, quickly season with salt and pepper, then transfer to a warmed serving platter. Drizzle the melted butter and pan juices over the fish.

Serve with the remaining butter mixture on the side.

Baked Cod

Serves 4

Cod is the workhorse, if you will, of North Atlantic food fish, abundant (at least in earlier times) and adaptable to almost any method of cooking, including steaming, poaching, grilling, frying, and baking. It can also be preserved by salting and/or drying. It is a familiar fish in Ireland; some of the most famous is landed at Ballycotton, in County Cork, where its skin has been described as resembling Connemara marble in appearance, sandy but mottled with browns and greens.

2 TBSP BUTTER

4 COD FILLETS [ABOUT 1 1/2 LB/750 G TOTAL]

1 TSP CHOPPED FRESH THYME

SALT AND PEPPER

Preheat the oven to 375°F/190C° (Gas Mark 5).

Lightly grease a baking dish with a little of the butter. Put the cod fillets in the baking dish, side by side. Dot with the remaining butter, sprinkle the thyme over the fish, and season to taste with salt and pepper.

Bake for 20 to 30 minutes, depending on the thickness of the fillets, or until the cod is done.

Broiled Mackerel with Gooseberry Sauce

Serves 4

Gooseberries have been called "the lemons of the north" because they provide a fruity acidity in regions where citrus won't grow. They are a classic foil to rich, oily fish like mackerel and herring, in Ireland and in England alike.

2 TBSP EXTRA-VIRGIN OLIVE OIL

SALT AND PEPPER

4 SMALL WHOLE 8- TO 10-OZ/240- TO
300-G MACKEREL

2 CUPS/300 G FRESH GOOSEBERRIES

1/2 CUP/120 ML HARD CIDER

2 TBSP SUGAR

2 TBSP BUTTER

BOILED POTATOES [PAGE 229] FOR SERVING

Preheat the broiler.

Brush the mackerel on both sides with oil and season them generously with salt and pepper. Score both sides of each fish 2 or 3 times, cutting down to but not into the backbone. Broil the mackerel for 5 to 7 minutes per side, depending on size, or until done.

Meanwhile, put the gooseberries and cider into a medium saucepan and bring to a boil over high heat. Add the sugar and butter and stir well. Reduce the heat to low and cook, stirring occasionally, for 6 to 8 minutes, until the gooseberries start to break down but still maintain their shape.

Serve the mackerel with boiled potatoes, with the gooseberry sauce on the side.

Roast Pike with Lamb Sauce, Lovage, and Bacon

Serves 4

Pike was once abundant in Irish loughs and rivers and is still fished regularly. One old account claims that a 350-pound/ 160-kilo specimen was once caught in County Down (highly unlikely); a 90-pound/40-kilo pike caught in Lough Derg in 1862, on the other hand, has been documented. Today, 8 to 12 pounds/3.5 to 5.5 kilos is the usual weight. For some reason, while the Irish like to catch them, the idea of eating pike has rarely appealed to them. That may have something to do with its forbidding appearance: Ian Hill, in his book *The Fish of Ireland*, describes the creature as resembling "a mottled-olive carnivorous torpedo," and notes that a bone in the fish's

head takes the form of a cross and was once worn to ward off epilepsy and vex witches. The pioneering modern Irish chef Gerry Galvin created this unusual recipe. He suggests serving it with a mixed green salad enhanced with watercress, sorrel, and thinly sliced apple.

4 TBSP BUTTER

FOUR 6- TO 8-OZ/175- TO 250-G PIKE FILLETS

FLOUR FOR DUSTING

SALT AND PEPPER

CANOLA OR VEGETABLE OIL FOR GREASING THE
BAKING DISH

1 CLOVE GARLIC, CRUSHED

JUICE OF 1/2 LEMON

1 CUP/240 ML LAMB JUICES [SEE PAGE 166];
OR 2 1/2 CUPS /600 ML LAMB STOCK [PAGE 357],
REDUCED OVER MEDIUM HEAT TO ABOUT
1 CUP/240 ML

1 TBSP CHOPPED FRESH LOVAGE OR CELERY LEAVES

1 TBSP BALSAMIC VINEGAR

4 STRIPS BACON, COOKED UNTIL CRISP, DRAINED,
AND COARSELY CHOPPED

Preheat the oven to 400°F/200°C (Gas Mark 6).

Melt the butter in a large sauté pan over medium-high heat. Dust the pike fillets lightly on both sides with flour, season with salt and pepper, then sear them lightly for about 30 seconds on each side. Remove from the pan and transfer to a lightly oiled glass or ceramic baking dish.

Stir the garlic into the lemon juice in a small bowl, then drizzle it over the fish. Roast the fish in the oven for about 8 minutes.

Meanwhile, warm the lamb juices or reduced stock in a small saucepan, then stir in lovage leaves and balsamic vinegar. Keep warm.

To serve, divide the fish between 4 plates, scatter the servings equally with chopped bacon, and serve with the sauce on the side.

KING HERRING

The Atlantic herring (*Clupea harengus*), small, oily, and delicious, has always been plentiful off the coast of Ireland, and has been an important food fish on the island for hundreds of years, and an important item of trade. In the eighteenth century, salted herring packed in barrels was shipped regularly from Wexford to the West Indies. It was also common fare around Ireland on days of religious fast and abstinence. In fact it was so common that after forty days of Lent, during which devout Catholics would eat no meat, butchers in some towns held a "herring funeral," in which the fish was paraded down the main street and tossed into the sea or a nearby stream.

The hind section of a lamb, meanwhile, bedecked in ribbons, would be hung in the butcher-shop window to announce that meat was back.

Because herring was so plentiful and cheap, there was an old saying that "Stingy folks eat herrings and potatoes." On the other hand, in 1846, Alfred Perceval Graves, the bishop of Limerick (and grandfather of the writer and poet Robert Graves) paid this tribute to the humble fish: "Let all the fish that swim the sea, / Salmon and turbot, cod and ling, / Bow down the head and bend the knee / To herring, their King!— to herring, their King."

Fish sellers in Galway.

SALT FISH

I met Enda Conneely, a fisherman and chef from Inishere, one of the Aran Islands in Galway Bay, in 2006. We had both been invited to help cook a St. Patrick's Day dinner for the Tipperary Slow Food Convivium at Country Choice, a grocery shop and café in the North Tipperary town of Nenagh. Conneely brought mussels just picked off the rocks of the island and also packages of wrasse, a smallish rock fish, which he'd caught and then preserved in salt. He steamed the mussels in the usual way. The wrasse he steamed, too, over a bed of potatoes; then he mashed the two together to make a kind of Irish *brandade*. It was, well, unusual. (A little non-Irish aïoli would have helped.)

I'd become something of a student of salted fish in researching my books on the cooking of Catalonia and the Italian Riviera, but it had never occurred to me that there'd be such a thing in Ireland. I subsequently learned, though, that fish preserved in this manner—especially salted ling,

sometimes called "battleboard" for its stiffness—was eaten for hundreds of years around Ireland as Friday fare or a winter staple. The County Kilkenny diarist Amhlaoibh Ó Súilleabháin, who claimed not to like salted fish, nonetheless records that on St. Patrick's Day in 1829, "We had for dinner . . . salt ling softened by steeping, smoke dried salmon and fresh trout."

"It was hard to dry fish in this country," Conneely explained. "The climate wouldn't allow it. But people did used to leave salted ling on the rooftops to lose some moisture, and when I was young I did my time saving the fish from seagulls and any sneaky shower of rain. They used to go to a lot of trouble to wash and clean fish for salting in freshwater as opposed to salt water and I always wondered why— but then I read somewhere that in Norway they had some problems with a bacteria in seawater attacking fish for drying. I wonder if the old guys knew this? I'll bet they did!"

THE CLADDAGH

The Claddagh ring depicts hands clasping a heart, usually surmounted by a crown. The design dates from the seventeenth century, and is worn by men and women, boys and girls, all over the world today. Tradition has it that the way the ring is worn announces the wearer's romantic status: on the right hand with the heart pointing out betokens availability, on the left hand facing in says "I'm married," and so on. How many of its wearers know that the ring is intimately involved with the sea and with a unique group of men who harvested it?

The fishing grounds off Galway are perhaps the most famous in Ireland, and for centuries they were the effective preserve of the Claddagh colony, an insular, conservative community—supposedly descended from the ancient Celtic tribes—who lived in a cluster of brightly colored, thatch-roofed cottages across the River Corrib from Galway's Spanish Arch. (The name Claddagh comes from the Irish *cladach*, meaning "beach" or "shore.") The community, whose origins date back at least to the fifth century, was largely Irish-speaking, elected its own "mayor," and had its own laws and customs. The people were known to be superstitious, and discouraged marriage outside the confines of the settlement. The men of the Claddagh went out in small boats and took herring, mackerel, scad (a mackerel relative), turbot, haddock, sole,

hake, bream, gurnet, and some cod and ling. For its valuable oil, they also brought in sunfish—not the tropical flatfish also called opah, but *Mola mola*, the largest known bony fish in the world, with an average adult weight of over two thousand pounds/one thousand kilos. The Claddagh fishermen considered the waters in and around Galway Bay to be theirs alone, and were known to attack other fishing boats that strayed into the area.

According to tradition, the prototype for the famous ring was fashioned by a Claddagh fisherman named Richard Joyce in the late seventeenth century. Captured by Algerian pirates and sold into slavery, he became the property of a Moorish goldsmith, from whom he learned the art of jewelry making. Pining for his lover back in Galway, he created a ring with a heart for love, clasped hands for friendship, and a crown for fidelity. Joyce eventually won his freedom, returned home, and married the object of his affections.

The Claddagh community came to a bad end. During the famine years of the mid-nineteenth century, the catch was poor, and many of the fishermen sold their gear to buy grain or healthy seed potatoes. By the 1940s, they had pretty much disappeared, and the Claddagh is now considered part of Galway proper, with housing prices that are some of the city's highest.

SHELLFISH

The Pick of the Sea

Our shells clacked on the plates. / My tongue was a filling estuary, / My palate hung with starlight: / As I tasted the salty Pleiades / Orion dipped his foot into the water."

—Seamus Heaney, "Oysters" [circa 1975]

I find that lobster and peach champagne keeps one going.

—Molly Keane, anecdotal [circa 1990]

Ireland's shores and coastal waters teem with shellfish that is as good as any on Earth, from aristocrats like sweet-fleshed spiny spider crabs and meaty Atlantic lobsters to lowly limpets and winkles and Molly Malone's

renowned "cockles and mussels, alive alive-o." They thrive in the island's clean, cold waters, and end up on tables all over Europe and beyond. (Even back in the 1930s, pioneering English travel writer H. V. Morton described trying to buy lobsters from a fisherman on the coast of Connemara, only to be told that they were not for sale as they were destined for France.)

Zoologist and seafood expert Noël P. Wilkins believes that oysters and other molluscs were once widely eaten by the poor in coastal regions in Ireland, as a part of the *cnuasach mara*, or "sea pickings"—an "eclectic mixture of shellfish and seaweed that was traditionally gathered on Irish shores for human consumption." Wilkins also points out that Sligo, a town and county northeast of Galway, derives its name from the Irish word for shell, *sliogán*.

Mussels are, along with salmon, Ireland's most important seafood export today. (It is said that an Irishman named Walton, shipwrecked near La Rochelle in the thirteenth century, first showed the French how to raise mussels in vertical piles in shallow bays.) Dublin Bay prawns (*Nephrops norvegicus*), also called "Norwegian lobster," are another important commercial commodity. These are saltwater crayfish—actually little lobsters, not shrimp—that are exactly the same animal as the famous scampi of the Mediterranean. Mussels and Dublin Bay prawns are found frequently on Irish menus today, as are scallops, crab, and, of course, lobster. Although abalone are not associated with Ireland and has yet to find much of a place on the nation's tables, there are two kinds being farm-raised in the country. Ireland even has Europe's only sea urchin hatchery.

Potted Shrimp

Serves 4

In the days before refrigeration, this was an easy way to preserve fresh shrimp. At Ballymaloe House in County Cork, bits of leftover lobster are sometimes added to the shrimp, or even substituted for it.

I SMALL CLOVE GARLIC, PEELED

SALT

I/2 CUP/120 ML MELTED CLARIFIED BUTTER [PAGE 362]

I TSP MINCED FRESH THYME

I/2 LB/250 G SHELLED SMALL SHRIMP AND/OR CHOPPED LOBSTER MEAT

2 TSP LEMON JUICE

PEPPER

With a mortar and pestle, crush the garlic to a paste with a little salt.

Bring about three-quarters of the butter to a boil over medium heat and the add garlic paste and thyme. Reduce the heat to low, add the shrimp and simmer for about 5 minutes, then set aside and let cool to room temperature.

Stir the lemon juice into the shrimp and season to taste with salt and pepper.

Spoon the shrimp into 4 small ramekins, dividing it equally between them, then pour the remaining butter on top. Refrigerate immediately. Serve when the butter has solidified.

Hot Buttered Prawns on Toast

Serves 4

This very simple recipe for what might be called "scampi Irish-style" comes from food writer and television personality Clodagh McKenna of County Cork.

20 FRESH RAW DUBLIN BAY PRAWNS [LANGOUSTINES OR SCAMPI] OR MEDIUM SHRIMP, IN THEIR SHELLS [ABOUT I LB/500 G]

4 TBSP BUTTER

2 LEMONS, HALVED

SALT AND PEPPER

8 SLICES COUNTRY-STYLE BREAD, TOASTED

If using prawns, twist the heads and claws off, then pull the meat out of each shell in one piece. (Save the heads, claws, and shells to make stock for later use, or add to fish when making Fish Stock, page 356.) Or shell the medium shrimp.

With a small knife or shrimp deveiner, remove the vein from the back of each prawn or shrimp, then rinse and dry thoroughly with paper towels.

Melt 2 Tbsp of the butter in a large skillet over high heat, then add the prawns. Immediately squeeze the juice from both lemons into the skillet through a strainer and season generously with salt and pepper.

Stir prawns well and cook for about 2 minutes, or until they have just changed color. Do not overcook.

Butter the toast with the remaining 2 Tbsp of butter and divide the slices between 4 plates. With tongs put 5 prawns on top of each piece of toast, then drizzle pan juices over all the prawns.

Dublin Bay Prawns
with Mayonnaise

Serves 4

This simple preparation, sometimes found in seafood restaurants, especially along Ireland's southern and southeastern coasts, is a vast improvement on generic shrimp salad.

SALT

40 FRESH RAW DUBLIN BAY PRAWNS [LANGOUSTINES OR SCAMPI], IN THEIR SHELLS [ABOUT 2 LB/1 KG]

JUICE OF 1/2 LEMON

3 TBSP MAYONNAISE, PREFERABLY HOMEMADE [PAGE 357]

2 TBSP MINCED FRESH CHIVES

TOASTED WHITE BREAD OR SHREDDED LETTUCE FOR SERVING [OPTIONAL]

Bring a large pot of salted water to a boil over high heat. Put the prawns in the pot, return the water to a boil, then immediately drain the prawns in a colander and refresh with cold water.

Twist the heads and claws off the prawns, then pull the meat out of each shell in one piece. (Save the heads, claws, and shells to make stock for later use, or add to fish when making Fish Stock, page 356.) Set the meat aside to cool to room temperature.

With a small knife or shrimp deveiner, remove the vein from the back of each prawn, then rinse the prawns and dry thoroughly with paper towels.

Combine the prawns, lemon juice, mayonnaise, chives, and salt to taste in a medium bowl and toss to coat the prawns thoroughly with mayonnaise.

Serve atop toasted white bread or shredded lettuce, if you like.

Dublin Bay Prawns
with Garlic and Herbs

Serves 4

This is another simple, popular way of serving these Irish langoustines.

SALT

40 FRESH RAW DUBLIN BAY PRAWNS [LANGOUSTINES OR SCAMPI], IN THEIR SHELLS [ABOUT 2 LB/1 KG]

1 CUP/250 G BUTTER

1 TBSP EXTRA-VIRGIN OLIVE OIL

3 OR 4 CLOVES GARLIC, MINCED

1/4 CUP/10 G MIXED FRESH HERBS [SUCH AS PARSLEY, CHERVIL, THYME, OREGANO, MARJORAM, TARRAGON, BASIL, LEMON VERBENA, AND/OR SUMMER SAVORY]

JUICE OF 1/2 LEMON

Bring a large pot of salted water to a boil over high heat. Put the prawns in the pot, return the water to a boil, then immediately drain the prawns in a colander and refresh with cold water.

Twist the heads and claws off the prawns, then pull the meat out of each shell in one piece. (Save the heads, claws, and shells to make stock for later use, or add to fish when making Fish Stock, page 356.)

With a small knife or shrimp deveiner, remove the vein from the back of each prawn, then rinse the prawns and dry thoroughly with paper towels.

Melt the butter with the olive oil in a large skillet over high heat, then add the garlic, herbs, lemon juice, and plenty of salt. When the butter begins to foam, add the prawns and cook for 3 to 4 minutes, stirring constantly. Do not overcook.

NATIVE OYSTERS

The oysters most often found in Ireland today are *Crassostrea gigas*, the largish Pacific variety (below, left), introduced into Ireland in the 1970s. They're delicious; even major French oyster growers, for whom these are a major crop, mature some of their *huîtres* in Irish waters. But there's something better—native flat-shelled Irish oysters (*Ostrea edulis*; below, at far right). These can be comparatively difficult to find, since they're in season only from September through April, grow slowly and only in a few parts of Ireland (most notably Galway Bay), and have been afflicted off and on, since the 1980s, by a parasite called *Bonamia ostreae*. They are, however, well worth looking for. They're one of the great natural glories of Irish food, lean and sea-bright and faintly, pleasantly metallic.

Native oysters were once used in Anglo-Irish kitchens; several eighteenth- and nineteenth-century recipe manuscripts offer instructions for making oyster sausages by grinding oysters with beef or mutton and binding them with eggs. But modern chefs don't often cook with them. And they probably shouldn't, at least not very often, especially when the oysters are so glorious by themselves, fresh out of the water and served as they are at places like Moran's Oyster Cottage in Kilcolgan, County Galway (where Seamus Heaney penned his paean to them; see page 91): just opened and on the half shell, with at most a drop of lemon juice and maybe not even that as seasoning, and with brown bread and sweet Irish butter and a flagon of Guinness or Murphy's stout—an unlikely but superb accompaniment—on the side.

Oyster Rolls

Serves 4

The oyster sandwich, or oyster loaf, is usually thought of as a specialty of New Orleans (where it is more commonly called a po' boy), and possibly of the Chesapeake Bay region. I was surprised, then, to find recipes for oysters loaves (little more than French bread hollowed out and filled with the bivalves) in two early- to mid-nineteenth-century recipe manuscripts in the National Library in Dublin, one by Mrs. Creagh of Creagh Castle in Ballinrobe, County Cork, and the other by Mrs. A. W. Baker of Ballytobin, County Kilkenny. This modern version of the dish, which I'd recommend for its simplicity if you're going to cook oysters at all, is adapted from Máirín Uí Chomáin's *Irish Oyster Cuisine.*

4 SMALL FRENCH ROLLS, HALVED CROSSWISE

3 TBSP BUTTER, MELTED

$1/2$ CUP/120 ML HEAVY CREAM

$3/4$ CUP/175 ML CRÈME FRAÎCHE

16 TO 24 FRESH SEASONAL OYSTERS
[$1 1/2$ TO 2 LB/750 G TO 1 KG], SHUCKED,
WITH JUICES STRAINED AND RESERVED

PEPPER

Preheat the oven to 450°F/230°C (Gas Mark 8).

Scoop out and discard some of the soft interior from the roll halves (or save the interiors to make bread crumbs). Brush the cut surfaces generously with butter, then put the roll halves on a baking sheet and crisp them in the oven for 4 to 6 minutes or until golden brown.

Meanwhile, combine the cream, crème fraîche, and reserved oyster juices in a medium saucepan over medium-high heat and cook, whisking constantly, for 2 to 4 minutes or until the sauce thickens. Reduce the heat to low and add the oysters. Cook for 3 to 4 minutes or until the oysters are just cooked.

Put 2 roll halves on each of 4 plates and spoon oysters and sauce over them.

Mussels in Cream

Serves 2 to 4

Mussels have always been plentiful along the Irish coastline, so much so that, in addition to being used as bait and of course as food in themselves, they were spread in the fields as fertilizer, especially in Donegal and Cork. Though most mussels sold in Ireland today (and exported from it) are farmed, wild mussels still abound, and are preferred by connoisseurs. This is a simple Irish way of dressing up mussels without losing their precious flavor.

45 TO 50 MUSSELS [ABOUT $2 1/2$ LB/1.25 KG],
SCRUBBED AND DEBEARDED

$1/2$ CUP/125 G BUTTER

$1/4$ CUP/25 G WHITE FLOUR

2 CUPS/475 ML HEAVY CREAM

SALT AND PEPPER

Heat the mussels in a large, dry skillet over medium-high heat, shaking the pan constantly until the shells open. Remove the skillet from the heat and discard any unopened mussels.

Melt the butter over medium heat in a pot large enough to hold the mussels. Sprinkle in the flour and cook, whisking constantly, for about 1½ minutes to make a roux (don't let it brown). Slowly add 1 cup/240 ml of water and stir well, then slowly add the cream. Stir well, then continue cooking, stirring frequently, until the sauce thickens slightly. Season generously with salt and pepper, then put the mussels and the mussel juices into the pot and stir well to coat with the sauce.

Ivan Allen's Dressed Crab

Serves 4 to 6

"When I first came to Shanagarry," recalls Darina Allen in her *Ballymaloe Cooking School Cookbook,* "crabs were considered a nuisance by most fishermen because they found their way into the lobster pots and were much less lucrative to sell. The

MUSSELS IN CREAM

legendary Tommy Sliney, who sold his fish from a donkey and cart on Ballycotton pier, occasionally brought us a few, and it was always a cause for celebration." Darina's late father-in-law, Ivan Allen of Ballymaloe House (see page 242), prepared the crabs this way.

6 TBSP BUTTER, SOFTENED

4 CUPS/240 G FRESH WHITE BREAD CRUMBS

1 LB/500 G TOP-QUALITY RAW CRABMEAT,
AS FRESH AS POSSIBLE

2 TSP WHITE WINE VINEGAR

2 1/2 TBSP TOMATO CHUTNEY OR TOMATO RELISH

1 TSP DIJON MUSTARD

3/4 CUP/175 ML WHITE SAUCE [PAGE 360]

SALT AND PEPPER

Preheat the oven to 350°F/175°C (Gas Mark 4).

Melt 4 Tbsp of the butter in a medium saucepan over low heat, then stir in 2 cups/120 g of the bread crumbs. Remove the pan from the heat and set aside to cool.

Combine the remaining 2 Tbsp of butter and 2 cups/120 g of bread crumbs with the crabmeat, vinegar, tomato chutney or relish, mustard, and white sauce and season generously with salt and pepper. Put the mixture into a glass or ceramic baking dish (or into empty, washed and dried crab shells if you have them), and sprinkle with the reserved buttered bread crumbs.

Bake for 15 to 20 minutes. If the buttered bread crumbs don't turn golden brown, put the baking dish (or crab shells) under the broiler for a minute or two.

Lobster in Foaming Butter

Serves 4

This is one of the most popular seafood creations introduced at Ballymaloe House in County Cork by the legendary Myrtle Allen (see page 242). There are many theories, and much controversy, about the best way to kill live lobsters for cooking. Allen believes the method used below is the most humane.

2 LIVE LOBSTERS [ABOUT 2 LB/1 KG EACH]

ONE 750 ML BOTTLE DRY WHITE WINE

1 CARROT, SLICED

1 ONION, SLICED

3 SPRIGS PARSLEY

3 SPRIGS THYME

1 BAY LEAF

10 TBSP BUTTER

SALT

Put the lobsters into a large pot, cover them with lukewarm water, then bring the water to a simmer over medium heat. (This should take 20 to 30 minutes.)

Meanwhile, put 2 cups/475 ml of water, the wine, and the carrot, onion, parsley, thyme, and bay leaf into a large pot and bring to a boil over medium-high heat. When the water in the pot with the lobsters has begun to simmer and the lobsters have begun to turn red, transfer them to the pot with the wine and vegetables. Cover the pot, reduce the heat to medium, and steam for about 20 minutes, or until the lobsters turn bright red. Remove the lobsters from the pot, discarding the contents, and set the lobsters aside to cool.

Preheat the oven to 350°F/175°C (Gas Mark 4).

When the lobsters are cool enough to handle, remove the claws and carefully extract the meat, keeping it intact if possible. Halve the lobsters lengthwise and remove the meat.

Scrape out and discard the tomalley and other remaining materials in the shells and rinse and dry them. Put the shells, cut side up, on a baking sheet and put them in the oven to warm.

Cut the lobster body meat into pieces 1 to 1½ in/2.5 to 4 cm thick, keeping the claw pieces intact. Melt the butter in a large skillet over medium-high heat until it begins to foam, 1 to 2 minutes. Add the lobster meat and toss until it is just heated through. Remove the shells from the oven and fill them with lobster.

Serve the lobster with the melted butter and pan juices in a small bowl on the side.

ST. PATRICK

We honor St. Patrick each March 17—and when I say "we," I mean millions and millions of people, Irish and not, from Buenos Aires to Beijing, Sydney to Sitka—with all manner of Irish-themed folderol, including green beer, parades, and often corned beef and cabbage (see page 183). But in fact, St. Patrick wasn't Irish, and he was said to have been partial to lobster, not corned beef.

Patrick was probably born in Roman Britain, possibly in Cumbria or Wales, around A.D. 400. Some sources give his birth name as Maewyn Succat, and maintain that he was the issue of an Italian father and a Scots mother; others render his name as Patricius Maganus Sucatus and identify his father as a Briton called Calpernius. When he was about fifteen, Patrick was allegedly kidnapped by Irish slave traders and brought to the island, where he was put to work as a shepherd, possibly on Slemish Mountain in County Antrim. After six years, he escaped and returned to Britain. There he became a priest, and then a bishop. He may have spent time in France. After a vision in which the voice of the Irish begged him to return to the island, he did just that, apparently arriving around 432.

He proceeded to convert thousands of pantheistic Celts to Christianity, founded numerous churches, and established links with the Holy See in Rome. Most significant, Patrick set Ireland well on its way to becoming a Catholic nation, which it remained for well over a thousand years after his death, from natural causes, around 480. (Earlier he had supposedly survived an assassination attempt involving a poisoned cheese.) St. Patrick's Day has been observed since at least A.D. 900, but the first St. Patrick's Day parade wasn't held until 1737, the work of Irish immigrants in Boston.

Beyond his apparent fondness for lobster, we know little about what St. Patrick ate, but tradition has it that he was partial to garlic and that he carried a plentiful supply of it when he traveled around Ireland. There is also a reference in *The Annals of the Four Masters*, a chronicle of Irish medieval history compiled in the seventeenth century from earlier monastic sources, to St. Patrick's household staff, including "Aithchen his true cook." Aithchen, whoever he was, is now considered in some circles to be the patron saint of Irish chefs.

A POUND FOR A DOZEN

Tomás Ó Crohan (or Ó Criomhthain) lived in the late nineteenth and early twentieth centuries on Great Blasket Island, off the coast of County Kerry. He wrote two books about island life, and in one of them, *The Islandman*, first published in 1929, he tells a story about the early days of lobstering on the island:

Having gone "up the hill to fetch a load of turf" one day, he looks down and sees two men from Dingle in a small boat below him in the water, throwing "some objects" into the sea. That night he encounters the men in a pub and learns that "The things I had seen them throwing into the sea were pots to catch lobsters. The Blasket people were as strange to that sort of fishing tackle as any bank clerk at that time. Not much of the year had gone before there were four Dingle canoes fishing lobsters round the Blasket in this fashion. The Dingle fishermen took hundreds of pounds worth of lobsters from the waters around the Island before we had any notion how to make a shilling out of them. They fetched a pound the dozen, and, to make the story better, the dozen was easy got."

The islanders caught on soon enough, however, and before long ships from England and France were steaming into the harbor to buy lobsters from their boats, at ever-increasing prices. On one occasion, Ó Crohan and a friend are pulling up pots when a grand sailing ship comes by, "black with people, every one of them looking more of a gentleman than his fellows as far as dress and ribbons went." Ó Crohan had just hauled in a lobster and a crayfish and held them up, one in each hand. He continues the tale:

[N]o sooner had I done that than every soul in the ships [sic] *on deck, man and woman, was beckoning to us, and they stopped short on the surface of the sea till we came up to them. . . . We had a dozen lobsters and two dozen crabs and three dozen of other fish, and the gentry didn't worry about how we looked, or our little canoe; all they thought about was to get fresh fish from us. One of the crew lowered a bucket to take up the lobsters. . . . He lowered it again to take up the crabs, and a third time for the other fish. When he had collected all the contents of our little canoe . . . he lowered the bucket again without a moment's delay, and, upon my oath, I thought that it was a hunk of bread that we had in the stern of the canoe that he wanted this time. But it wasn't as I thought, for, when I caught it in my hand and looked at it, what was to be seen in it was money . . . a shilling for every fish I had sent up to him. . . . [B]efore long I saw [the bucket] coming down to me again, heaped up and running over. . . . The bucket was crammed with every kind of food . . . and I couldn't put a name to half of them.*

SALMON

The
Magical Fish

All my life I've heard of salmon lying in the river, four
and five deep, like sardines in a box.

—George Moore, *Hail and Farewell* [1912]

[A] taste of the wild will spoil your enjoyment of much of the farmed.

—Ian Hill, *The Fish of Ireland* [1992]

Salmon is Ireland's heraldic fish, or ought to be. It has been eaten on the island since prehistoric times, and figures prominently in ancient Celtic legend and mythology [see page 110].

It has even left its mark on topography, as in the town of Leixlip, County Kildare, a name derived from the Norse word for "salmon," *lax*—related of course to "lox." (The Irish name for Leixlip is Leim an Bhardain, meaning "salmon leap.") The old Gaelic chieftains gave salmon pride of place at their banquets, serving it roasted whole on a spit, basted with butter, honey, and herbs. And in County Kerry, until the mid-twentieth century, it would not have been uncommon to see a whole salmon as the centerpiece of a Christmas dinner, in place of goose or turkey. Of course salmon, being meaty and oily, with a distinctive flavor of its own, takes perfectly to smoking, and Irish smoked salmon (see page 115) is widely reckoned, by yours truly among others, to be the finest in the world.

The testimony by one S. Sweeney before the Northern Ireland Planning Appeals Commission in 2005, asking that some historic buildings associated with the salmon trade in Portballintrae, County Antrim, be preserved, gives a vivid picture of old salmon processing methods:

The Ice House was vital to the operation of the salmon fishery. The rear part of the building . . . was used for the storage of ice which, historically, was carted during winter months from the ponds at the Lissanduff earthworks. Every day after the caught salmon were brought ashore they were weighed and recorded by the Fishery Manager. The salmon were stored on the concrete floor of the Ice House until iced and packed in wooden boxes before being despatched to Portrush railway station. At the height of the season on St John's Day (24 June) the McNaughten Estate, employers of the fishermen, entertained the men to a Salmon Dinner in the upstairs loft of the Cottage. . . . These are the traditions which provide a community or a village with its heritage and the remnants of the past should be preserved to keep that memory alive.

The commercial fishing of wild salmon is pretty much a vanished tradition in Ireland today. In 2007, alarmed by a sharp decline in Ireland's salmon population, the Irish government banned offshore drift-netting (which employs immense free-floating nets buoyed at the top and weighted at the bottom). Salmon fishing is now limited to draft-netting (which uses smaller nets, with one end attached to the shore)—and angling—in rivers and estuaries. The measure has been controversial, to say the least. Sally Barnes, a onetime fisherman's wife who became an artisanal fish smoker (see page 108) in Castletownsend, near Skibbereen in West Cork, is one of the many interested parties who maintain that drift-netting was only a small part of the problem, and that salmon caught in freshwater, which may be polluted by agricultural runoff, are "not worth eating." Some smokehouses in Ireland now use "organic" farmed salmon, raised in low-population pens that allow them to swim (say some farmers) almost as much as wild salmon. That's admirable, but there's one problem: Farmed salmon, organic or not, is simply a pale shadow of the best of the wild in flavor. Famed West Cork salmon smoker Frank Hederman (see page 108), now forced to concentrate on farmed salmon, once showed a silvery twelve-pound/six-kilo wild salmon to the late R. W. Apple Jr. of the *New York Times*, and enthused, "These guys swim four thousand or five thousand miles to get here. By comparison, the farmed salmon, the ones who live in those cages off the coast, are essentially goldfish."

Frank Hederman's Smoked Salmon Pâté

Serves 12 to 16

At his Belvelly Smokehouse in Cobh, County Cork, master smoker Frank Hederman makes up batches of this simple pâté to sell at local farmers' markets. He notes that a more elegant version can be made by substituting an equal quantity of crème fraîche for the cream cheese and mayonnaise, but adds that "the cream cheese version lasts very well and is rich and delicious."

1 LB/500 G SMOKED SALMON, PREFERABLY IRISH [SEE PAGE 108], SKIN AND ANY BONES REMOVED, AND COARSELY CHOPPED [OR CUT INTO STRIPS IF ALREADY SLICED]

1 CUP/240 G CREAM CHEESE

1/4 CUP/60 ML MAYONNAISE, PREFERABLY HOMEMADE [PAGE 357]

JUICE OF 1/2 LEMON [OPTIONAL]

BUTTERED BREAD, TOASTED OR NOT, FOR SERVING

Put the salmon into the bowl of a food processor and pulse until it is coarsely puréed (do not process for too long or until too fine, or the pâté will separate).

Transfer the salmon from the processor bowl to a medium bowl and put the cream cheese and mayonnaise into the processor bowl. Process until well combined.

With a spatula, fold the cream cheese mixture into the salmon until very well combined (no white should be visible). Mix in lemon juice if you like. (Hederman notes that "you shouldn't need the lemon juice if the salmon is good enough.")

Serve on buttered toast or bread.

Salmon with Cabbage and Cider Vinegar

Serves 4

Denis Lenihan and Mike Crowe worked together for roughly twenty years as executive and head chef, respectively, at the vaguely Disneylandesque Ashford Castle in Cong, County Mayo. (Cong is famous to movie buffs as the backdrop for John Ford's classic 1952 film *The Quiet Man*, starring John Wayne and Maureen O'Hara.) This dish dates from Lenihan's Ashford Castle days, though he and Crowe now run, and cook at, Ryan's Hotel, a more modest property in the same town.

FOUR 6- TO 8-OZ/175- TO 250-G SALMON FILLETS, WILD-CAUGHT IF POSSIBLE, OF APPROXIMATELY THE SAME THICKNESS

1 TO 2 TBSP EXTRA-VIRGIN OLIVE OIL, PLUS MORE FOR BRUSHING FISH

SALT AND PEPPER

1/4 LB/125 G IRISH BACON, PREFERABLY GALTEE'S SLICED CURED PORK LOIN, TOMMY MOLONEY'S MILD-CURED [NOT SMOKED OR BACK RASHERS], OR DONNELLY'S [SEE SOURCES, PAGE 369], DICED

1 SMALL GREEN CABBAGE [ABOUT 1 LB/500 G], SHREDDED

1/4 CUP/60 ML DRY WHITE WINE

1/4 CUP/60 ML APPLE CIDER VINEGAR

1/2 CUP/120 ML FISH STOCK [PAGE 356]

1/2 CUP/120 ML HEAVY CREAM

1 TBSP CHOPPED FRESH DILL

1 TBSP CHOPPED FRESH CHIVES

Brush the salmon fillets lightly on both sides with olive oil and season with salt and pepper. Heat a large skillet or grill pan over high heat for about 2 minutes, then sear the salmon for about 2 minutes per side or until lightly browned. Transfer to a plate and set aside. Wipe out the pan with paper towels.

Add the olive oil to the same pan, then cook the bacon over medium heat until well browned. Drain the bacon on paper towels, leaving the oil and bacon fat in the pan. Put the cabbage in the pan and cook for about 5 minutes, stirring

frequently. Add the wine, vinegar, stock, and cream. Cover, reduce the heat to a simmer, and cook until the cabbage is wilted, 15 to 20 minutes. Put the salmon fillets on top of the cabbage, cover the pan, and cook for about 5 minutes more (do not overcook the salmon).

To serve, divide the cabbage equally between 4 plates and sprinkle with bacon. Put 1 salmon fillet on top of each serving of cabbage, moisten with a spoonful of pan juices, and sprinkle with dill and chives.

Pickled Salmon

Serves 6

According to *The Sportsman in Ireland* by "A Cosmopolite," originally published in 1840, the "Sportsman's breakfast" was "First, a large bowl of new milk which instantly disappeared; then a liberal allowance of cold salmon soaked in vinegar—a very common dish this . . . and a bottle of port wine." Because salmon was so plentiful in Ireland until recent times, it was often preserved, not only by smoking but also by salting and pickling. The salted and pickled fish was an important item of export, especially in the north of the country, for instance from the port of Ballyshannon in Donegal. I found this recipe (with no quantities specified) in "Mrs. A. W. Baker's Cookery Book, Vol. 1," a manuscript dating from the early nineteenth century, from Ballytobin, County Kilkinney. Mrs. Baker notes that her pickled salmon "will keep three months in cold weather."

I TBSP SALT

I TBSP WHOLE BLACK PEPPERCORNS

I TBSP GROUND MACE

I TBSP FRESHLY GRATED OR GROUND NUTMEG

I TBSP WHOLE ALLSPICE [JAMAICAN PEPPER] BERRIES

3 BAY LEAVES

2 LB/I KG SALMON FILLET, WILD-CAUGHT IF POSSIBLE, CUT CROSSWISE INTO 6 PIECES

6 BAY LEAVES

2 CUPS/475 ML WHITE WINE VINEGAR

BROWN SODA BREAD [PAGE 272] AND UNSALTED BUTTER FOR SERVING

Put 4 cups/1 L of water into a large pot, then add the salt, peppercorns, mace, nutmeg, and allspice. Bring to a boil over high heat, then turn off the heat and let rest for 10 minutes. Repeat the process twice more, then add the salmon to the pot and bring to a gentle boil over medium-high heat. Simmer for about 5 minutes, then carefully lift the fish from the pot with a slotted spatula, being careful not to let it break apart. Set aside and allow to cool.

Strain the poaching liquid through a fine strainer or cheesecloth into a medium bowl, stir in the vinegar, and set aside to cool.

Put the bay leaves in one layer on the bottom of a glass or earthenware crock or baking dish with a cover, then lay the salmon pieces side by side on top of them. Pour the cooled poaching liquid over the salmon, making sure that it covers the fish entirely (add more water and vinegar if it doesn't).

Cover and refrigerate for at least 3 days and as long as a week, turning the fish once a day. Bring to room temperature and serve with brown soda bread and unsalted butter.

SMOKING ENCOURAGED

In the 1960s, food writer Monica Sheridan described an old-fashioned version of smoked salmon as it was made in Ireland "before the invention of matches" (which were developed in the first half of the nineteenth century): Fishermen going out to sea would take along smoldering turf in an iron pot to ignite their pipes during the day. The turf wasn't hot enough to actually cook on, but they learned that they could skewer a boned, gutted, butterflied salmon on two sticks and lay it over the top of the pot to gently smoke for hours. Sheridan notes that "This particular smoked salmon later enjoyed quite a vogue with epicures," but is today "quite unknown, even among fishermen."

Irish smoked salmon today, though processed with slightly more sophisticated methods, is still an epicure's delight, and Ireland's artisanal fish smokers are among the best in the world. Three of the most celebrated work in County Cork. Frank Hederman (facing page, top left), at his Belvelly Smokehouse in Cobh, smokes salmon—wild when he can get it, but mostly now farmed—as well as mackerel, eel, and mussels, over beech chips. His salmon is elegant, with a deft balance of salt and smoke, and his mackerel, which is subtle and buttery, will make converts to that underappreciated fish. "For us," he says, "smoke is a condiment, not a preservative." Hederman also smokes oats for Robert Ditty's Oatcakes (page 276) and cheese for Gubbeen (see page 61). And, experimentally at this writing, County Cork cheddar producer Dan Hegarty with his wife, food writer Caroline Workman, runs a small food shop next to the smokehouse.

At his Ummera Smokehouse in Timoleague, in West Cork, Anthony Creswell has vowed to use organically farmed salmon exclusively unless and until wild stocks again become sustainable. He burns oak sawdust (which gives less "puff" than chips, he says) to smoke brined fish into a faintly sweet, slightly smoky marvel. (He also smokes eel and bacon and chicken; the latter two are unusual for fish smokers.) Sally Barnes (facing page, bottom left), at her Woodcock Smokery in Castletownsend, near Skibbereen, also in West Cork, goes for what she describes as "a proper smoke, not a cosmetic one—otherwise, you might as well just eat the fish fresh!" She uses oak, beech, ash, and elm shavings to both cold- and hot-smoke a variety of fish, including pollack, haddock, mackerel, sprats, and tuna. Her salmon is wild-caught and brought in from Scotland, and has a distinctive smoky flavor—not heavy, but rich and distinctive. (The perfect accompaniment might be a shot of good Irish whiskey.)

Creswell and Barnes are all willing to ship to the United States, under certain conditions (see Sources, page 369). Some other good Irish smokehouses, who may or may not ship at any given time, include Ballycotton Seafood in Ballycotton, East Cork; Kinvara Smoked Salmon Ltd. in Kinvara and Connemara Smokehouse in Ballyconneely, both in County Galway; Clarke's Master Fishmongers and Salmon Smokers in Ballina, County Mayo; and Burren Smokehouse in Lisdoonvarna, County Clare. I've also heard praise of Keem Bay Fish Products' salmon, made by Gerry Hassett on Achill Island, County Mayo, but haven't yet been able to track any down.

SALMON TALES

"In the centre of the pine wood called Coilla Doraca," wrote Dublin-born novelist and poet James Stephens in *The Crock of Gold*, "lived not long ago two Philosophers. They were wiser than anything else in the world except the Salmon who lies in the pool of Glyn Cagny into which the nuts of knowledge fall from the hazel bush on its bank. He, of course, is the most profound of living creatures."

Hazelnuts and a wise salmon figure in one of the most famous stories from the Fenian Cycle of Irish mythological tales. A young man named Demne, son of the slain warrior Cumhail Mac Art, fled his father's killers to become a poet, studying with an older bard named Finnéagas, who lived near the River Boyne. The Boyne was home to a magical salmon that fed on hazelnuts that dropped into the river, and drew so much intelligence from them that he became known as An Bradan Feasa, or "the Salmon of Knowledge." Finnéagas had tried for years to catch the fish, and finally succeeded. He gave it to his apprentice and asked him to roast it over an open fire on a spit, but warned him not to taste its flesh. As the fish cooked, a blister arose on its skin, and Demne unthinkingly reached out and pressed it down with his thumb. That burned, and to ease the pain, he stuck his thumb in his mouth—thereby tasting the fish and assimilating all its knowledge. Finnéagas was a good sport and told Demne that he had obviously been destined to consume the salmon. He dubbed the young man Fionn Mac Cumhail ("son of Cumhail"), Anglicized as Finn McCool, and sent him out in the world, where he became a great hero.

In a sense, though, salmon was to haunt McCool. He was betrothed to the princess Gráinne, but she ran off with one of his soldiers, Dermot Ó Duibhne. McCool followed them, each morning finding an unbroken crust of bread that Ó Duibhne had left behind to prove his continued loyalty. When the two reached Killarney in County Kerry, however, Ó Duibhne caught a salmon in the River Laune (to this day famous for its abundance of that fish) with a rowanberry as bait. Gráinne cooked it on a hazel-wood spit over an apple-wood fire and served it with fresh watercress and wine. The next morning, the two left behind a broken crust of bread, and when McCool arrived, he knew that he had lost his princess.

One more salmon tale: It is said that one day, back in the sixth century, the celebrated St. Columkille was sitting on the banks of Lough Finn in County Donegal, reading his breviary, when a salmon leapt out of the water, drenching him and ruining his holy book. Columkille promptly denounced the salmon and decreed that salmon would never again be found in that lough. Unfortunately for the saint's legacy, the River Finn, which flows into the lough, is one of the more famous salmon streams in Ireland, and the lough itself is full of salmon and its relative, the arctic char.

Broiled Salmon with Butter and Honey

Serves 4

This recipe is inspired by reports of ancient Irish methods of cooking salmon, which involved spit-roasting the fish and flavoring it with honey, among other things. Spit-roasting a tender-fleshed fish like salmon is tricky, unless you've got a spit that will hold a large fish on an acute angle. A light glaze of honey, though, works very nicely on simply broiled salmon fillets.

2 TSP COARSE SEA SALT

FOUR 6- TO 8-OZ/175- TO 250-G SALMON FILLETS, WILD-CAUGHT IF POSSIBLE, OF APPROXIMATELY THE SAME THICKNESS

1/2 CUP/120 ML DRY WHITE WINE

JUICE OF 1/2 LEMON

2 TBSP BUTTER

1 TBSP HONEY, PREFERABLY IRISH

Preheat the broiler.

Press the sea salt crystals into surface of the salmon fillets, dividing it evenly between them.

Combine the wine and lemon juice in a small saucepan and bring to a simmer over medium heat. Add the butter, stirring until it melts, then stir in the honey.

Brush the mixture over the salmon fillets and broil 4 to 6 in/ 10 to 15 cm from the heat for about 5 minutes, or until just done. (The salmon should be very pink inside.)

Wok-Smoked Salmon

Serves 4

This recipe won't yield "smoked salmon" in the usual sense, but it's an easy way to add a delicate but perceptible smoke flavor to fresh salmon fillets.

3 TO 4 GENEROUS HANDFULS OF OAK OR OTHER WOOD CHIPS, SOAKED IN WATER TO COVER FOR 30 MINUTES

FOUR 6- TO 8-OZ/175- TO 250-G SALMON FILLETS, WILD-CAUGHT IF POSSIBLE, OF APPROXIMATELY THE SAME THICKNESS

EXTRA-VIRGIN OLIVE OIL FOR BRUSHING

SALT AND PEPPER

Line a large wok with foil, add wood chips, then cover tightly with more foil. Turn on your exhaust fan, then put the wok over high heat for about 10 minutes or until the chips start to smoke.

Brush a round metal rack lightly with olive oil, remove the top layer of foil from the wok, and place the rack over the smoldering chips, making sure that none touch the bottom of the rack.

Brush the salmon with olive oil and season with salt and pepper. Place the salmon on the rack, and cover the wok tightly. Leave on high heat for about 10 minutes, then remove from the heat and let it sit, covered, for about 20 minutes.

Serve the salmon at room temperature, or sear quickly in a hot skillet and serve warm.

Poached Whole Salmon

Serves 8 to 10

A necessity for making this dish correctly is a fish poacher or deep elongated baking dish (with a cover) large enough to hold the salmon with a little room around the sides—typically at least 20 in/50 cm long and 5 in/12 cm deep.

12 CUPS/3 L FISH STOCK [PAGE 356]

2 CUPS/475 ML DRY WHITE WINE

SALT

1 WHOLE 6- TO 7-LB/2.5- TO 3-KG SALMON, WILD-CAUGHT IF POSSIBLE AND PREFERABLY WITH HEAD ON, CLEANED AND SCALED

LEMON SLICES FOR GARNISH [OPTIONAL]

GREEN MAYONNAISE [PAGE 357] FOR SERVING

Put 8 cups/2 L of the stock and the wine into a large fish poacher and season to taste with salt. Cover, then place over two burners on the stove. Bring just to a boil over high heat.

Meanwhile, wrap the salmon in several thicknesses of cheese-cloth, then tie the ends with kitchen twine. Put the remaining 4 cups/1 L of stock into a small pot and bring to a boil over high heat, for use as needed.

Carefully lower the salmon into the poacher. Add more hot stock, if needed, to cover the salmon entirely, then reduce the heat to medium-low and simmer until the salmon is just cooked through, about 30 minutes. Remove the poacher from the heat and set aside until the salmon and its liquid cool to room temperature.

Carefully remove the salmon from the poacher, holding the cheesecloth by the ends, and transfer to a cutting board, then gently cut off and discard cheesecloth. Keep the skin on, or carefully remove it from the top side of the fish, leaving it intact on the head and tail.

Garnish the salmon with lemon slices, if you like, and serve at room temperature with the mayonnaise.

Baked Salmon

Serves 6 to 8

The success of this very simple dish depends on the freshness and flavor of the salmon.

1/2 CUP/125 G BUTTER, SOFTENED

1 WHOLE 4- TO 6-LB/2- TO 3-KG SALMON, WILD-CAUGHT IF POSSIBLE, HEAD ON, CLEANED AND SCALED

1/2 BUNCH PARSLEY

JUICE OF 1 LEMON

SALT AND PEPPER

Preheat the oven to 375°F/190°C (Gas Mark 5).

With some of the butter, lightly grease a fish roaster or a roasting pan large enough to hold the whole fish.

Stuff the parsley into the cavity of the fish, then lay the fish in the roasting pan. Drizzle lemon juice over the whole fish, then dot with 2 to 3 Tbsp of the butter. Bake for 8 to 10 minutes per lb/15 to 20 minutes per kg, basting occasionally.

Melt the remaining butter in a small saucepan over low heat. Remove the parsley from the cavity of the fish and discard it, then gently lift the skin off the top side of the fish, drizzle the fish with melted butter, and season it generously with salt and pepper. Serve warm, either presenting the whole fish at the table or cutting it lengthwise into pieces about 3 in/7.5 cm wide.

BAKED SALMON

HOW TO SERVE IRISH SMOKED SALMON

If you're lucky enough to secure some Irish wild smoked salmon, or even the good-quality organic farmed variety (see page 104, and Sources, page 369), treat it with respect.

Vacuum-sealed smoked salmon generally will keep for at least a month in its original unopened package in the refrigerator (but honor the "sell by" or "best before" date on the label). Once the package is opened, rewrap the fish tightly in plastic wrap or seal it in a plastic bag so that it doesn't dry out. (You can freeze smoked salmon, but it always seems to lose at least a little something in flavor and texture when it's thawed out.)

Smoked salmon is best at room temperature, so remove it from the refrigerator a couple of hours before you plan to serve it (but leave it wrapped or covered as it warms up). If you've got a whole side of salmon, you will probably find tiny pin bones running down the center. Take the time to pull these out with tweezers.

The traditional way to slice smoked salmon is horizontally, at a very shallow angle, with a long, sharp knife (knives made especially for the purpose have very thin, scalloped blades). Start slicing 5 or 6 in/12 to 15 cm from the tail, cutting toward the tail and working your way backward toward the thick end, or shoulder, of the fish as you cut. (How thick you cut the slices depends on your skill and your personal taste.) Tradition notwithstanding, at least one prominent salmon smoker, Frank Hederman of East Cork's Belvelly Smokehouse, has another theory: Because the salt used in curing the salmon tends to soak into its flesh while the strongest layer of smoke flavor rests on its surface, he likes to slice the salmon vertically, cutting down from the top to the skin (this obviously yields smaller slices), so that salt and smoke are more perfectly balanced with every bite.

Serve Irish smoked salmon with slices of brown bread, soda or otherwise, and unsalted Irish butter (or some other butter equally rich and delicious). Add a few drops of lemon juice if you like, or even a few grindings of black pepper, but these are hardly necessary. Capers? Chopped eggs? Chopped onion? Save them for supermarket lox. Sally Barnes of Woodcock Smokery in West Cork, on the other hand, says, "We love our smoked salmon with scrambled egg (very softly scrambled, almost runny) and a scratch of black pepper, and no lemon in sight."

The Irish Touch

SAVORY PIES

I think it is time that people went back to the meat pie.

—Myrtle Allen, *Myrtle Allen's Cooking at Ballymaloe House* [1990]

We all ate [Dingle pie] as children and it can be glorious in the hands of a good cook or repulsive in the hands of a bad one.

—Séamus Hogan, chef at Glin Castle, County Limerick, in an e-mail to the author [2008]

In the Italian region of Liguria, which was one of the poorest in Italy before the advent of year-round tourism, flour was a luxury. Instead of eating huge bowls of pasta as many of their countrymen did then, locals made a little

precious flour go a long way by using it to make thin pastry crusts to enclose various combinations of vegetables, wild greens, and farmhouse cheeses in *tortas*—savory pies. No doubt inspired by similar economic restrictions, the Irish have created a number of variations on the savory pie themselves over the centuries, as ways to use up leftovers and to extend what meat became available. Sometimes they employed pastry dough, sometimes just leftover soda-bread dough, and sometimes no dough at all but something they usually had in abundance: potatoes, which they mashed and spread out as a crustlike topping.

Pizza, another sort of savory pie, isn't Irish, of course. As gratifying as it would be to be able to report that the ancient Celts topped their griddle breads with wild garlic, hunks of venison, and one of the early Irish cheeses, I can't find a shred of evidence that was true—but a handful of Irish chefs have found ways to give this much-loved Italian specialty a local accent.

Smoked Fish Pie

Serves 4

Potato-topped fish pies were a common Friday-night dinner back in the no-meat-on-Fridays days, and were obviously well liked enough that they have remained a staple of Irish home cooking, especially in coastal regions.

2 TBSP BUTTER

2 ONIONS, FINELY CHOPPED

I CUP/240 ML WHITE SAUCE [PAGE 360]

I TSP POWDERED MUSTARD

I 1/2 LB/750 G SMOKED HADDOCK OR
FINNAN HADDIE [SEE SOURCES, PAGE 369]
OR A COMBINATION OF SMOKED HADDOCK OR
FINNAN HADDIE AND UNSLICED SMOKED SALMON,
CUT INTO I-IN/2.5-CM CUBES

I CUP SHELLED FRESH PEAS
[ABOUT I LB/500 G PEAS IN PODS]

SALT AND WHITE PEPPER

2 CUPS/420 G FRESHLY MADE MASHED POTATOES
[PAGE 223]

Preheat the oven to 400°F/200°C (Gas Mark 6).

Melt the butter in a large saucepan over low heat, then add the onions and cook, stirring frequently, for 12 to 15 minutes or until soft, but not browned.

Remove the pan from the heat and stir in the white sauce, mustard, smoked fish, and peas, mixing together well. Season to taste with salt and pepper.

Put the smoked fish mixture into a casserole or glass or ceramic baking dish, then spread the mashed potatoes on top. Season the top of the potatoes lightly with salt and pepper.

Bake for 40 to 45 minutes, or until the top of potatoes has turned golden brown.

Colm Finnegan's Colcannon Pie with Spinach, Bacon, and Lavistown Cheese

Serves 6 to 8

When I visited Helen Finnegan's Knockdrinna cheese operation in Stonyford, County Kilkenny, she had just picked up her thirteen-year-old son Colm from a turn at the Savour Kilkenny cooking competition. The theme was potatoes, and he arrived bearing the leftovers of his entry, which I tasted and thought was pretty good. (He tied for second place.) His version was topped with Lavistown, a cheese his mother now makes; it's not currently available in America, but Wensleydale makes a good substitute.

4 CUPS/850 G FRESHLY MADE MASHED POTATOES
[PAGE 223]

20 LARGE LEAVES SPINACH, STALKS TRIMMED

1/2 LB/250 G IRISH BACON, PREFERABLY GALTEE'S
SLICED CURED PORK LOIN, TOMMY MOLONEY'S
MILD-CURED [NOT SMOKED OR BACK RASHERS], OR
DONNELLY'S [SEE SOURCES, PAGE 369], CHOPPED

SALT AND PEPPER

1/4 LB/125 G LAVISTOWN OR WENSLEYDALE CHEESE,
CRUMBLED

Wash but don't dry the spinach, then wilt it in a medium saucepan over low heat in the water that clings to the leaves. Do not overcook. Drain on paper towels.

Bring a small pot full of water to a boil, then add the bacon. Boil for 2 to 3 minutes, then drain. Fry in a small skillet in the bacon's own fat until lightly browned. Drain on paper towels.

Preheat the broiler.

Mix the spinach and bacon into the potatoes. Adjust the seasoning with salt and pepper if necessary.

Put the potato mixture into a 2-qt/2-L casserole or baking dish and sprinkle the cheese on top. Put the casserole under the broiler for 3 to 4 minutes or until the cheese is golden brown.

Hartichoake Pie

Serves 8 to 10

Globe artichokes—called "hartichoakes" or "harty choakes" in earlier times—have grown in the kitchen gardens of Ireland ever since the Norman conquest in the late twelfth century. Lady Rosse of Birr Castle, County Offaly, who still harvests them from land where they have grown for almost four hundred years, reconstructed and published this seventeenth-century recipe from a manuscript in the castle archives. There is one unusual feature: After the pie is baked, a caudel is added to it through a hole in the crust. A caudel is a warm drink of spiced or sweetened wine and egg, a relative of posset and an ancestor of eggnog. It was often added to savory pies, in old recipes, to replace the moisture that had been baked out of them. You will need thick beef bones with marrow for this recipe; request them from your butcher.

2 CUPS/200 G WHITE FLOUR,
PLUS MORE FOR DUSTING

1/2 TSP SALT

3/4 CUP/190 G COLD BUTTER, CUT INTO SMALL
PIECES, PLUS 4 TBSP BUTTER, SOFTENED

I EGG YOLK BEATEN WITH 2 TBSP COLD WATER,
PLUS 4 EGG YOLKS BEATEN WITH I TBSP WATER

2 BEEF MARROW BONES

10 COOKED SMALL ARTICHOKE BOTTOMS

MEAT FROM I SMALL COOKED CHICKEN
[I TO I 1/2 LB/500 TO 750 G], CUT INTO
I-IN/2.5-CM PIECES

I TBSP FINELY DICED CANDIED LEMON PEEL

I TBSP FINELY DICED CANDIED ORANGE PEEL

1/2 TSP GROUND NUTMEG

1/2 TSP GROUND MACE

1/4 TSP GROUND CLOVES

PEPPER

I CUP/240 ML DRY WHITE WINE

2 TBSP SUGAR

Combine the flour and salt in a large bowl and rub in the ¾ cup/190 g of cold butter with your fingertips until the mixture resembles coarse meal. Add the single beaten egg yolk and water, and stir with a fork, adding 1 to 3 Tbsp more cold water as needed to form a dough that can be gathered into a ball.

Turn the dough out onto a lightly floured board and shape it into a disk. Wrap the dough in plastic wrap and chill for at least 1 hour or as long as 24 hours before using.

Meanwhile, put the beef bones into a medium pot with salted water to cover. Bring to a boil over high heat, then reduce the heat to low and simmer until the marrow is set, 10 to 15 minutes, depending on the size of bones. Skim any foam that rises to the surface. Drain the bones and set aside to cool slightly. Cut the marrow out of each bone in one piece with a paring knife. Slice each piece of marrow crosswise into ½-in-/1.25-cm-thick rounds.

Generously grease a deep 6-cup/1.5-L baking dish or casserole with the remaining 4 Tbsp of the butter. Arrange the artichoke bottoms on the bottom of the baking dish in a single layer. Arrange the chicken pieces over the artichokes. Sprinkle the candied lemon peel, orange peel, nutmeg, mace, and cloves over the chicken. Arrange the pieces of marrow on top. Season to taste with salt and pepper.

Preheat the oven to 350°F/175°C (Gas Mark 4).

Roll the dough out onto a floured board to a thickness of about ¼ in/6 mm. Cut a 1-in/2.5-cm hole out of the center of the dough, discarding the cut-out piece. Drape the dough over the filling in baking dish, centering the hole. Trim off the excess dough, leaving 1 in/2.5 cm overhanging the edge. Crimp the edge of the dough, sealing the crust to the baking dish. Brush the crust with some of the beaten egg yolk–water mixture. Set the remainder aside.

Bake the pie until the crust is golden brown and the filling is bubbling hot, 45 to 60 minutes. Remove the pie from the oven and allow to stand for 10 minutes.

Meanwhile, put remaining beaten egg yolk mixture, the white wine, and the sugar into a small saucepan and cook over low heat, stirring constantly, until thickened, 3 to 4 minutes. (Do not allow it to boil or it will curdle.) Carefully pour the thickened sauce through the hole in the crust. Allow the pie to stand for about 10 minutes before serving.

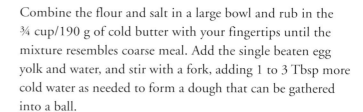

ADVICE TO EMIGRANTS

At the height of the famine in Ireland in the mid-nineteenth century, a would-be emigrant could buy passage to the United States or Canada, in steerage, for three-and-a-half English pounds. It was a grim voyage, lasting two months or more, with as many as four adults crammed into a 6-by-6-foot/ 2-by-2-m stall. Food was often rotten, and always scarce. On May 12, 1853, the *Anglo-Celt* in County Cavan published "Hints to Emigrants"—advice on how to make the journey slightly more bearable:

If emigrants would only use a little forethought we should not hear of so many complaints respecting their diet on board. . . . You should take with you some flour and suet cut up; mix both together dry—they will keep well, and be always ready. Onions, potatoes, and dried herbs, these three things are very useful in making a sea-pie of a stew out of your salt meat after it has been soaked. Wrap the potatoes and onions up separately, each one in paper, and stow them in a hamper; by doing this, if one gets bad it will not affect the rest. Pack your herbs and put them in papers; don't forget mint and a little celery-seed for your pea-soup. A few loaves of bread cut up and sent to the baker, with directions to put them in a slow oven and do them to a light brown. A few quarts of dried green and split peas. A couple of hams. A little pepper, mustard, salt, and pickles. A few raisins and currants, with the addition of a little tea, coffee, cocoa, and sugar. Now the major part of these things could be stowed in a flour-barrel, would be compact, and wouldn't cost much. . . . Among your other requirements, there are—a sponge, a scrubbing-brush, a frying-pan, a three-quart saucepan, a good stout fishing-line, and some large hooks, sufficient for a fish thirty or forty pounds weight. A two-gallon keg is much better for water than tin or earthenware, and would, in case of necessity, make a life-preserver.

SHEPHERD'S PIE

Séamus Hogan, chef at Glin Castle, County Limerick, has researched the origins of shepherd's pie (see page 126), and he generously shared these thoughts with me:

In one version of the story, the dish began life as a picnic food for the English aristocracy. Many picnic recipes were first devised for the Dukes of Bedford, who were exiled from court for several generations and had to find amusement on their own estate at Woburn Abbey. Their picnics were very elaborate affairs and the story goes that the idea of lamb and root vegetables in a pastry case was developed on their Devon estate at Tavistock. Of course they were probably influenced by the French court, which was famous for its "romantic" picnics, where everyone dressed as shepherds and so on. The dish was adapted as a large pie, with a raised pastry, for hunting lodges and winter house parties. For ordinary people who didn't have access to good ovens, it was changed to a casserole with potatoes and finally a deep dish with a potato topping. There is also the fact that that many farm recipes were either revised or reinvented by publishers or authors who felt that giving aristocratic cachet to peasant food would be a good sales technique, witness Mrs. Beeton. I mention this because shepherd's pie is supposed to be made from leftover roast lamb and that presupposes a roast to begin with, something which many peasants would not have had.

Donegal Pie

Serves 4

"This is the pie to make in an emergency, as most people usually have all these ingredients in the house," says Ruth Isabel Ross in *The Little Irish Baking Book*. In Ireland, pies like this are often served at room temperature as picnic fare.

2 TBSP MINCED FRESH PARSLEY

2 TBSP MINCED FRESH CHIVES

2 CUPS/420 G FRESHLY MADE MASHED POTATOES [PAGE 223]

SALT

2 HARD-COOKED EGGS, THINLY SLICED

4 SLICES IRISH BACON, PREFERABLY GALTEE'S SLICED CURED PORK LOIN, TOMMY MOLONEY'S MILD-CURED [NOT SMOKED OR BACK RASHERS], OR DONNELLY'S [SEE SOURCES, PAGE 369], FRIED [WITH FAT RESERVED], THEN FINELY CHOPPED

WHITE FLOUR FOR DUSTING

6 OZ/175 G SHORTCRUST PASTRY [PAGE 363]

Preheat the oven to 375°F/190°C (Gas Mark 6).

Mix the parsley and chives into the potatoes and season well with salt.

Line the bottom of a 9- to 10-in/22- to 25-cm pie dish with half the potatoes, smoothing them down with a dinner knife. Arrange the egg slices in a single layer on top of the potatoes, then sprinkle with the chopped bacon and drizzle with the reserved bacon fat. Spread the remaining potatoes over the top of the bacon, smoothing them down with a dinner knife.

Lightly dust a board with flour, then roll out the pastry to a circle large enough to fully cover top the layer of potatoes. Lay the pastry on top of the potatoes and bake for 25 to 30 minutes, covering the dish loosely with foil for the last 10 minutes.

Fermanagh Bacon and Potato Pie

Serves 8

This recipe comes from Enniskillen butcher Pat O'Doherty's *Fermanagh Black Bacon Cookbook*, and is meant specifically to utilize his trademark "black bacon." This is a nitrite-free product, with less fat than traditional Irish bacon (see page 154), cured for as long as three months, during which time its exterior gets very dark, if not quite really black. O'Doherty raises free-range pigs for the bacon on Inishcorkish Island in the middle of Lough Erne. Unfortunately, his bacon isn't available in America, so more prosaic Irish bacon will have to be substituted.

1/2 CUP/125 G BUTTER, PLUS MORE FOR GREASING

1/2 LB/250 G IRISH BACON, PREFERABLY GALTEE'S SLICED CURED PORK LOIN, TOMMY MOLONEY'S MILD-CURED [NOT SMOKED OR BACK RASHERS], OR DONNELLY'S [SEE SOURCES, PAGE 369], DICED

2 LB/I KG POTATOES, VERY THINLY SLICED, PREFERABLY ON A MANDOLINE

3 SHALLOTS, MINCED

SALT

2 TBSP FRESH TARRAGON LEAVES

2 TBSP MINCED FRESH CHIVES

PEPPER

1/2 LB/250 G PUFF PASTRY, HOMEMADE [PAGE 363] OR STORE-BOUGHT

WHITE FLOUR FOR DUSTING

2 EGG YOLKS, LIGHTLY BEATEN

I CUP/240 ML HEAVY CREAM

Preheat the oven to 350°F/175°C (Gas Mark 4).

Melt 4 Tbsp of the butter in a large skillet over low heat and cook the bacon for 8 to10 minutes or until slightly crisp. Remove the bacon with a slotted spoon and drain on paper towels, then put into a large bowl. Put the potatoes into the same pan and cook for 10 to15 minutes or until they are just cooked through but not browned. Put them into the bowl with the bacon and set aside.

Melt the remaining 4 Tbsp of butter in the pan over medium heat, then sweat the shallots for 2 to 3 minutes with a little

salt. Stir in the tarragon and chives and cook for about 2 minutes more. Allow the mixture to cool, then stir gently into the potatoes and bacon and season the mixture generously with salt and pepper.

Roll out half the pastry on a lightly floured board into a circle about 14 in/36 cm in diameter and transfer a lightly greased baking sheet. Brush the edges lightly with the beaten egg yolk, then mound the potato mixture in the center of the pastry. Flatten the potatoes out evenly with a dinner knife, spreading them to cover the whole pastry circle, but leaving about a 1-in/2.5-cm border with no potatoes.

Roll out the remaining pastry into a slightly larger circle to form a lid for the pie. Carefully place it over the filling and crimp the edges of the pastry inward. Cut a circle about 2 in/5 cm in diameter in the middle of the pie with a pastry cutter or sharp knife, but do not remove it. Brush the pie with beaten egg yolk.

Bake for 50 minutes, covering the top loosely with foil if it browns too quickly.

Warm the cream in a small pan over low heat. Remove the pie from the oven, gently lift off the pastry circle in the center of the pie, and slowly pour in the cream. Replace the circle and return to the oven for 10 minutes more.

Serve warm or at room temperature.

Dingle Pies

Serves 8

These savory little pies, a specialty of the Dingle Peninsula and the surrounding region in County Kerry, are featured at the centuries-old Puck Fair every August (see page 131). They were a popular food in general at public celebrations and on market days in the area, and were also taken up into the hills as lunch for local shepherds. Cathal Cowan and Regina Sexton, in their fascinating volume *Ireland's Traditional Foods: An Exploration of Irish Local and Typical Foods and Drinks*, note that the mutton for the filling was traditionally shredded very finely, on occasion even snipped with scissors, and that cold pies were sometimes reheated in broth and served in it. Dingle pies were originally made with mutton fat instead of lard, but butter is common today.

3 TBSP CANOLA OR SUNFLOWER OIL

I SMALL ONION, FINELY CHOPPED

I CARROT, FINELY CHOPPED

SALT AND PEPPER

I LB/500 G TRIMMED BONELESS MUTTON OR LAMB, PREFERABLY FROM THE SHOULDER OR LEG, FINELY CHOPPED

2 TBSP WHITE FLOUR, PLUS MORE FOR DUSTING

I 1/2 CUPS/360 ML BEEF OR LAMB STOCK [PAGE 357]

I TSP MINCED FRESH MINT

I TSP MINCED FRESH THYME

I RECIPE SHORTCRUST PASTRY WITHOUT SUGAR [PAGE 363]

2 TBSP MILK

Heat 1 Tbsp of the oil in a large skillet over medium heat. Add the onion, carrot, and salt and pepper to taste and cook, stirring occasionally, for 6 to 8 minutes, or until the vegetables begin to soften. Transfer the vegetables to a bowl and set aside.

Heat the remaining 2 Tbsp of oil in the same skillet over medium-high heat. Add the meat and cook, stirring often, until browned, 2 to 3 minutes. Sprinkle in the flour, reduce the heat to medium, and cook for 30 seconds, stirring constantly. Slowly add the stock, stirring to deglaze the pan. Return the vegetables to the skillet, add the mint and thyme, and season to taste with salt and pepper. Reduce the heat to medium-low, cover, and simmer until the meat is tender, about 45 minutes. Uncover the skillet and cook until thickened, about 5 minutes more. Set aside to let cool.

Preheat the oven to 400°F/200°C (Gas Mark 6).

Roll out half of the pastry on a lightly floured board into a disk about ¼ in/6.5 mm thick. Cut the disk into 8 rounds about 4 in/10 cm in diameter with a cookie cutter or the floured rim of a glass. Repeat the process with the remaining pastry to make 16 rounds in all.

Put about one-eighth of the meat mixture in the middle of a pastry round, then wet the edges with a bit of water. Top with a second pastry round, then press down the edges and crimp with the tines of a fork. Cut a slit in the top of the pie and transfer to a parchment paper–lined baking sheet. Repeat the process with the remaining meat filling and pastry, arranging the pies on the baking sheet about 1 in/2.5 cm apart. Brush the tops of the pies with milk and bake until golden brown, about 40 minutes. Serve hot or at room temperature.

Caherbeg Pork Pie with Caramelized Apples

Serves 4

Food writer and television personality Clodagh McKenna of County Cork developed this recipe, traditional in style, to use sausage meat and bacon made by Avril and Willie Allshire at Caherbeg Free Range Pork, Ltd. in Rosscarbery, in West Cork. They produce some of Ireland's best cured meats, but unfortunately, they can't ship to the United States. Use the best available substitutes, artisanal if possible.

1 TBSP BUTTER, PLUS MORE FOR GREASING

2 MEDIUM COOKING APPLES, PEELED, CORED, AND SLICED

2 TBSP HONEY

1 LB/500 G PORK SAUSAGE MEAT, CRUMBLED

1/2 LB/250 G IRISH BACON, PREFERABLY GALTEE'S SLICED CURED PORK LOIN, TOMMY MOLONEY'S MILD-CURED [NOT SMOKED OR BACK RASHERS], OR DONNELLY'S [SEE SOURCES, PAGE 369], DICED

SALT AND PEPPER

3 TBSP MINCED MIXED FRESH HERBS, SUCH AS THYME, ROSEMARY, SAGE, AND/OR WINTER OR SUMMER SAVORY, MINCED

1/2 LB/250 G PUFF PASTRY, HOMEMADE [PAGE 363] OR STORE-BOUGHT

1 EGG, BEATEN

Preheat the oven to 325°F/160°C (Gas Mark 3).

Melt the 1 Tbsp butter in a medium skillet over a medium heat. Add the apples and honey, stir well, then cook for about 10 minutes to caramelize, stirring frequently.

Grease a small casserole, then put about one-third of the sausage meat on the bottom, and top with about one-third of the bacon. Season with salt and pepper, sprinkle 1 Tbsp of the herbs on top, then cover with a layer of caramelized apples. Repeat the process twice to use up all the sausage meat, bacon, and herbs.

Roll out the pastry to a round big enough to cover the surface of pie. Cover the pie with pastry and press down lightly. Prick the pastry with a fork several times, then brush with the beaten egg.

Bake for about 1 hour, or until the pastry has puffed up and turned golden brown.

The Best Shepherd's Pie

Serves 6

Several years ago, two prominent West Cork food personalities—writer and TV host Clodagh McKenna and her friend the culinary historian Regina Sexton—got together and decided to come up with the ultimate shepherd's pie recipe. This was the result.

2 TBSP EXTRA-VIRGIN OLIVE OIL

1 ONION, MINCED

1 1/2 CARROTS, MINCED

1 1/2 POUNDS/750 G LAMB, MINCED OR GROUND

1 TBSP TOMATO PASTE

1 TSP DIJON MUSTARD

1 CUP/240 ML HOT BEEF OR LAMB STOCK [PAGE 357] OR CHICKEN STOCK [PAGE 356]

SALT AND PEPPER

4 CUPS/850 G FRESHLY MADE MASHED POTATOES [PAGE 223]

2 TBSP BUTTER, MELTED

Preheat the oven to 350°F/175°C (Gas Mark 4).

Heat the olive oil in a large skillet over medium heat. Add the onion and carrots and cook for 8 to 10 minutes or until they are soft but not browned.

Raise the heat to high, add the lamb, and cook until well browned. Stir in the tomato paste and mustard, then add the stock. Reduce the heat to low, season to taste with salt and pepper, and simmer for 15 to 20 minutes or until the stock is mostly but not completely evaporated.

Transfer the meat mixture to a round or rectangular ovenproof baking dish. Cover the meat with mashed potatoes, flattening the top with a knife. (Make a wave or crosshatch pattern in the top of the potatoes, if you like.) Brush the top with melted butter, then bake for 50 minutes.

Here Comes Everybody

[Steak and Kidney Pie]

Serves 4 to 6

Wexford-born cooking teacher Mary Kinsella gives this homey dish this appealing and evocative name in her book *An Irish Farmhouse Cookbook.*

1/2 LB/250 G LAMB'S KIDNEYS WITH MEMBRANES
REMOVED, CUT INTO 1-IN/2.5-CM CUBES

2 TBSP BUTTER

2 LB/1 KG BEEF ROUND, CUT INTO
1-IN/2.5-CM CUBES

1/2 LB/250 G CARROTS, TRIMMED AND SLICED

2 SMALL ONIONS, SLICED

1/4 CUP/25 G WHITE FLOUR, PLUS MORE FOR
DUSTING

1/4 CUP/60 ML BEEF OR LAMB STOCK [PAGE 357]

1 TBSP TOMATO PASTE

BOUQUET GARNI [2 SPRIGS PARSLEY,
2 SPRIGS THYME, AND 1 BAY LEAF, WRAPPED AND
TIED IN CHEESECLOTH]

SALT AND PEPPER

1/2 LB/250 G PUFF PASTRY, HOMEMADE [PAGE 363]
OR STORE-BOUGHT

1 EGG YOLK, BEATEN

3 OR 4 SPRIGS PARSLEY, TRIMMED AND MINCED

Bring a small pan of water to a simmer over medium-high heat (do not boil), then turn off the heat, add the kidneys, and cover, allowing the kidneys to steep for about 15 minutes. Drain and rinse in cold water.

Melt the butter in a medium saucepan over medium-high heat. Add the kidneys and beef and cook for about 8 minutes, stirring frequently and browning on all sides.

Remove the meat mixture from the pan with a slotted spoon and put the carrots and onions into the pan, adding a little more butter if necessary. Cook for 3 or 4 minutes, stirring frequently, then stir in the flour and cook for 1 or 2 minutes more.

Add the stock to the pan slowly, stirring as you do, then return the meat to the pan and stir in the tomato paste. Add the bouquet garni and season to taste with salt and pepper; then cover the pan and simmer for 1½ hours.

Transfer the mixture to a casserole, removing and discarding the bouquet garni.

Preheat oven to 400°F/200°C (Gas Mark 6).

On a board dusted with flour, roll out the pastry in the same shape as the casserole and about 1 in/2.5cm bigger than the dish. Cover the casserole with pastry, pressing the edges down gently on the edge of the casserole to seal. Brush the pastry with beaten egg, then bake for 30 minutes or until golden brown. Garnish with parsley before serving.

Leek and Black Pudding Pizza

Serves 1

Bernadette O'Shea introduced Mediterranean cooking—and good pizza—to Sligo with her Truffles restaurant, opened in 1989, and became a precocious supporter of the local organic food movement there. She closed the place in 1997, and now helps run Sligo's Model Arts and Niland Gallery, an art exhibition space and cultural center—but her pizza lore and recipes live on in her book *Pizza Defined*. Though she has real skill with traditional-style pizzas, she also freely improvises, sometimes with an Irish flavor. She says of this example, "This pizza was my response to the clutch of new recipes which were part of the nouvelle cuisine in Ireland, when age-old ingredients such as black pudding were 'outed.'"

1 LEEK, WHITE PART ONLY, SLICED INTO RINGS

SALT AND PEPPER

2 TO 3 TBSP EXTRA-VIRGIN OLIVE OIL

6 OZ/175G BASIC PIZZA DOUGH, HOMEMADE OR STORE-BOUGHT

FLOUR FOR DUSTING

2 TBSP MASCARPONE

6 OZ/175 G BLACK PUDDING [SEE PAGE 201], PREFERABLY GALTEE, SLICED

1/4 CUP/30 G PINE NUTS

LEAVES OF 2 TO 3 SPRIGS ROSEMARY, COARSELY CHOPPED

Put a large square of foil on the floor of your oven, then put a pizza stone on top of the foil, making sure a border of foil extends at least 1 in/2.5 cm around the stone (so that melting cheese won't drip onto the oven floor).

Preheat the oven to 550°F/290°C (at least Gas Mark 10).

Cook the leek in the olive oil in a small pan over medium heat until tender and slightly browned, 10 to 12 minutes. Season to taste with salt and pepper.

Stretch the pizza dough into a circle about 8 in/20 cm in diameter and put on a lightly floured surface.

Gently spread the mascarpone over the dough with your fingers, leaving about a ½-in/1.25-cm border around the rim without cheese.

Pile the leek in the center of the pizza, arrange black pudding slices around the leek, and scatter pine nuts in the middle.

Carefully transfer the pizza to the pizza stone and bake for about 10 minutes or until the crust is well browned. Scatter the rosemary over the top of the pizza.

FAIR TRADE

Since medieval times, country fairs have been an important feature of rural life in Ireland. One in Teltown (Tailten), County Meath, is celebrated in a poem dating from A.D. 885, In the thirteenth century, the locations and dates of fairs throughout the country were confirmed by legal charter. Fairs in Clogher, Muff, Limerick, Dublin, Kildare, and Cashel (the one in County Tipperary) became famous. The Tipperary agricultural town of Nenagh held one so important that its very name comes from *An tAonach*, Irish for "the fair."

Irish fairs were not necessarily the kind of thing we have in mind when we picture medieval carnivals. There may well have been jugglers and magicians at some of them, and displays of horsemanship or sword skills, but they were primarily commercial events—markets, if you will, and indeed the distinction between market and fair is a difficult one to pin down. From Norman times until well into the 1950s, most trading in horses and cattle in Ireland was effected at fairs. (The Ballinasloe fair in County Galway each October, once among the largest in Europe, is still the most important horse fair in Ireland, drawing up to 100,000 visitors annually.) Foodstuffs, both local and exotic, metal goods, cloth (Chinese silk, English wool), and more were on offer. In 1837, the catalog of goods for sale at the fair in Lisburn, a city split between counties Down and Antrim, included "oats, oatmeal, potatoes, fresh butter, beef, mutton, bacon, pork, fed veal, slink veal [the meat of newborn or aborted calves], cheese, saltherrings, duck eggs, hen eggs, turkeys, geese, ducks, hens, onions, salt, calf shins, woollen hats, mens

and womens shoes," and so on through sackcloth, kitchen stools, potato baskets, and pig troughs.

Jobs were sought out and dispensed at fairs, and marriages were arranged. And there was feasting galore. Historian and antiquarian P. W. Joyce describes one typical scene: "Just at the mouth of the tent it was common to have a great pot hung on hooks over a fire sunk in the ground underneath, and full of pigs cheeks, flitches [sides] of bacon, pigs' legs and croobeens [pig's feet] galore, kept perpetually boiling like the chiefs' caldrons of old, so that no one need be hungry or thirsty so long as he had a penny in his pocket. These pots were so large that they came to be spoken of as a symbol of plenty: 'Why you have as much bacon and cabbage there as would fill a tent-pot.'"

Fairs could also be rough-and-tumble; shopkeepers boarded up their windows when the fair was coming, and the annual fifteen-day fair at Donnybrook, in County Dublin, was so notorious that the town's name became a synonym for uproar or free-for-all.

One of the last of the old-style fairs is the annual Puck Fair held every August in Kilorglin, near Dingle Bay in County Kerry, which dates back to at least 1613. A wild goat is caught in the mountains each year and crowned King Puck, and for three days there is much merriment, and much alcohol consumed. A horse fair and a cattle fair figure in the proceedings, and the Puck Fair has its own "street food," the Dingle pie (see page 125), also called the Kerry pie, a sort of lamb-filled Irish empanada.

Chapter No. 6

POULTRY

*Fit for
a Feast*

[Irish] fowls, I think, are as delicate and highly flavored as those of Normandy.

—John Carr, *The Stranger in Ireland; or, a Tour of the Southern and Western Parts of That Country, in the Year* 1805

I find it hard to get good results from intensively-reared, frozen ducks. I was once overheard screaming down the telephone to an un-cooperative co-operative manager, "Do you freeze the ducks before you kill them, then?"

—Myrtle Allen, *The Ballymaloe Cookbook* [1977]

Chickens were most probably first brought to Ireland from Roman Britain, roughly two thousand years ago, and for many centuries at least a bird or two could be found scratching around farmyards all over the country. They

were typically fed on potato skins and other household scraps, and grew healthy, laying the eggs that became so important a part of the Irish diet. Of course, because chickens were more valuable over time for their eggs than for their meat, they were usually eaten only when they had grown old and barren— which is why they were typically stewed or braised. A younger bird, simply roasted, was a special treat, the centerpiece of a holiday feast or other celebratory meal. The best chickens in Ireland today are often those bought from small farmers, who raise them the old-fashioned way. As Myrtle Allen of Bally-maloe House in County Cork puts it, "Free range, grass fed chickens . . . grow slowly and are healthy. They have firm, slightly dry flesh, which smells wonderful when roasted."

Ducks were less common (their eggs were not as highly prized, for one thing), but they, too, would sometimes show up on the holiday table, simply roasted, or else braised with spring peas. Turkey was apparently introduced to Ireland by the English, and perhaps for that reason didn't find a large following for some time. In many ways, the quintessential Irish domestic fowl was the goose, traditional for Michaelmas (see page 140) and Christmas. Geese were a valuable commercial commodity because, unlike ducks or chickens, they could be driven to market on their own two feet. They also ate cheaper feed than chickens and their flesh had more calories, which would be seen as a disadvantage in many quarters today, but was important in a sustenance economy.

Irish geese were highly regarded across the Irish Sea, and the County Tipperary writer and retired farmer Marjorie Quarton remembers when the birds "used to be sold wholesale to dealers who shipped them to Liverpool, then marched them across Northern England in huge droves to Manchester, Leeds, York and even Newcastle. . . . No wonder Irish geese were renowned more for muscle than for fat." And the food writer Monica Sheridan tells the story of one of her cousins, a Kerryman, who sent a fat Irish goose every Christmas to his uncle in England. "Inside the goose," she writes, "he concealed a large bottle of poteen [Irish moonshine]. . . . There was one unfortunate occasion when the English landlady put the goose in the oven, not realizing that the illicit spirit was inside it. After some time there was an unmerciful explosion."

THE TRADITIONAL YEAR

The combination of pre-Christian and Catholic rituals has given Ireland an impressive procession of holidays and festivals. Here is a brief guide to some traditions:

- Imbolic, the first day of spring, celebrated on or around February 1 (Ireland, remember, has a temperate climate): This was an old Celtic festival associated with the "mother goddess" Brigit, or Brigid, who protected dairy production and grains grown for ale. The Catholic Church wisely adopted and canonized her, and today February 1 does double duty as her feast day. The fairies are thought to be particularly active on Imbolic, and in some homes in earlier times, a small ball of freshly churned butter was smeared on the top of the dresser as an offering to the little people. Colcannon (page 219), Barm Brack (page 293), apple desserts, and a kind of fermented oat gruel called "sowans" are associated with the day.

- Shrove Tuesday, the day before Ash Wednesday: Pancakes, made from all the sweet and milk-based products that would be given up for Lent, are the traditional meal.

- St. Patrick's Day, March 17 (see page 100): Once strictly a religious holiday, this occasion has become an excuse for green-hued revelry all over Ireland, and around the world. If this holiday falls during Lent, tradition permits the consumption of meat and alcohol, otherwise theoretically eschewed for the season.

- Easter Sunday: A grand repast of roast lamb or (less often these days) goat is traditional. Eggs, those ancient symbols of fertility, are eaten, both natural and chocolate.

- Bealtaine or May Eve, April 30 (*Bealtaine* is the modern Irish word for "May"): This was traditionally the day the cattle were sent out to pasture, and as such marked the beginning of summer. Because butter-stealing fairies were apt to be about, no milk was given away on this day, and no stranger was allowed near the cattle.

- Midsummer, June 24 (also St. John's Day): Just after the summer solstice, this occasion is celebrated with bonfires and much feasting.

- Lughnasadh, called Lammas in Northern Ireland. Celebrated on August 1 or on the Sunday nearest to that date. Dating back to the time of the Druids, this holiday is associated with fraughans, or wild bilberries, which are traditionally eaten on this day. So are the first potatoes of the summer crop, with fresh butter. In Ballycastle, County Antrim, at the Auld Lammas Fair, the confection of the moment is Yellowman (page 321).

- Michaelmas, September 29, the feast of St. Michael the Archangel (see page 141).

- Samhain, the harvest festival: The last traditional Celtic holiday of the year. This fête, celebrated on October 31, became known as All Hallows Eve—and eventually Halloween. Foods made with the fruits of the apple harvest and the last berries of summer are eaten, as is Boxty (page 217) in the northern counties, and, harking back to Imbolic, colcannon and barm brack.

- Martinmas, November 11: On this day the pig was traditionally killed and hams and sausages were made for winter. A pre-Christian tradition was to sprinkle the animal's blood on the doorstep and in the four corners of the house to ward off evil spirits.

- Christmas, December 25: Known for rich puddings and other sweets, and for extravagant banqueting by those who can afford it. Poet Thomas McCarthy, for instance, imagines his "gentleman–merchant" Nathaniel Murphy, sitting down for the occasion in Clonakilty, County Cork, in 1809, to "salted loins of beef, / Bacon and pullets, a roasted snipe, / And bread-stuffing bursting from the roasted goose."

- St. Stephen's Day, December 26: The day for Spiced Beef (page 179)—and the day when the "wren boys," dressed in flour sacks, with faces blackened with soot or shoe polish, carried a wren on top of a holly bush as they went from house to house playing tin whistles and singing, and collecting coins for their trouble.

- December 27 through January 6: Not an official holiday period, but Thomas McCarthy once described this span to me as "those ten best, best days in Irish life . . . days of horses, beagles, hunt teas, trad music sessions, family reunions, cousins from America, ghosts, goose, black pudding, and hot whiskey."

- January 6, celebrated in most of the Christian world as the Feast of the Epiphany: Called Nollaig Bheag, Little Christmas, or Nollaig na mBan ("Women's Christmas") in Ireland. Goose dinners are common, especially in rural areas, and in County Cork—and especially Cork City—it is the tradition to this day for men to take over women's chores and for women to go out and celebrate with parties and restaurant meals.

Braised Chicken with Bacon

Serves 4 to 6

In Ireland, chicken is traditionally cooked with ham or bacon, or served with ham or bacon on the side. The early-nineteenth-century Kilkenny diarist Amhlaoibh Ó Súilleabháin, for instance, notes on Easter Sunday of 1828, "I had chicken and smoked ham for my dinner."

2 TBSP CANOLA OIL

1/2 LB/250 G CURED PORK LOIN [SEE PAGE 154]
OR GOOD-QUALITY BAKED HAM, CUBED

ONE 3 1/2- TO 4-LB/1.75- TO 2-KG CHICKEN,
CUT INTO 8 TO 12 PIECES

1 TBSP WHITE FLOUR

2 CUPS/475 ML CHICKEN STOCK [PAGE 356]

12 SHALLOTS, MINCED

1/2 LB/250 G WHITE MUSHROOMS,
WHOLE IF SMALL, OTHERWISE HALVED

SALT AND PEPPER

1 CLOVE GARLIC, MINCED

Heat the oil in a large skillet over medium heat, then add the pork loin or ham and cook, stirring frequently, until it begins to brown, 4 to 6 minutes. With a slotted spoon, transfer the pork loin or ham to a Dutch oven or deep, heavy pot with a cover.

Brown the chicken pieces in the same skillet, turning them frequently and adding a little more oil if necessary, for 6 to 8 minutes in all. Sprinkle the flour evenly over them, stir the pieces, and cook for 1 minute more. Pour the stock into the pan gradually, stirring as you do. Add the shallots and mushrooms, stir well, and season to taste with salt and pepper.

Carefully pour the contents of the pan into the Dutch oven or pot, bring to a boil over high heat, then reduce the heat to low and simmer, covered, for 45 to 50 minutes, or until the chicken is cooked through.

Roast Chicken with Herb Stuffing

Serves 6 to 8

A properly cooked roasting chicken is one of the great monuments of honest home cooking, Irish or otherwise. Make sure you buy a roaster, not a broiling chicken. The latter is fine for frying or moist-baking in a Dutch oven, but if you try to roast it, as Myrtle Allen of Ballymaloe House, County Cork, puts it, "All your work will be wasted on the tasteless flesh." Allen serves her roast chicken with Bread Sauce (page 362), crisp-fried Irish bacon (see Sources, page 369), homemade sausages and black pudding, and Colcannon (page 219)—quite a serious repast.

2 CUPS/475 ML CHICKEN STOCK [PAGE 356]

ONE 4- TO 5-LB/2- TO 2.5-KG ROASTING CHICKEN
[WITH NECKS AND GIBLETS], FREE-RANGE IF
POSSIBLE, RINSED AND VERY THOROUGHLY DRIED

3 TBSP BUTTER OR 2 TBSP BUTTER
AND 1 TBSP CHICKEN FAT

1 ONION, CHOPPED

2 CUPS/120 G FRESH BREAD CRUMBS

1 TBSP CHOPPED FRESH PARSLEY

1 TBSP CHOPPED FRESH THYME OR WINTER SAVORY,
PLUS 5 TO 6 SPRIGS FRESH THYME

1 TBSP CHOPPED FRESH CHIVES

SALT AND PEPPER

1 TBSP WHITE FLOUR

Bring the stock to a boil over high heat in a medium pot, then reduce the heat to medium-low and add the chicken neck and giblets and any other trimmings. Simmer for 30 minutes, until the stock reduces by about one-third. Strain the stock, discarding solids.

Meanwhile, melt the butter in a medium saucepan over low heat. Add the onion and cook for 6 to 8 minutes or until just soft, then stir in the bread crumbs, parsley, thyme or savory, and chives, and season to taste with salt and pepper. Cook for about 3 minutes, then remove from the heat and set aside to cool to room temperature.

Preheat oven to 400°F/200°C (Gas Mark 6).

ROAST CHICKEN WITH
HERB STUFFING

Season the chicken all over, inside and out, with salt and pepper, then fill the cavity with stuffing, being careful not to pack it too tightly. Push thyme sprigs lightly into the stuffing so that they protrude. Secure the opening with a small skewer, then roast the chicken on a rack in a roasting pan for 20 minutes. (Put the leftover stuffing in a small baking dish and put it in the oven with the chicken, if you like.) Reduce the heat to 350°F/175°C (Gas Mark 4) and continue roasting for about 20 minutes per lb/40 minutes per kg (not counting the first 20 minutes). To test for doneness, stick a skewer into the thigh; if the juices run clear, the chicken is done.

When the chicken is cooked, remove the rack with the bird still on it and set aside to rest. Spoon the excess fat out of the roasting pan, then put the pan on the stove top over low heat. Sprinkle in the flour and stir until a roux forms. Add the reserved stock. Increase the heat to high and deglaze, scraping up the browned bits from the bottom of the pan. Continue to cook, stirring constantly, until the gravy is thick.

Carve the chicken and serve with the gravy on the side.

Duck with Sage and Onion Stuffing

Serves 4

This is the most traditional Irish preparation for domestically raised duck.

ONE 4- TO 5-LB/2- TO 2.5-KG DUCK
WITH NECK AND GIBLETS

2 ONIONS; 1 QUARTERED, 1 MINCED

1 CARROT, SLICED

BOUQUET GARNI [2 SPRIGS PARSLEY,
2 SPRIGS THYME, 1 BAY LEAF, WRAPPED AND
TIED IN CHEESECLOTH]

4 TBSP BUTTER

2 TBSP MINCED FRESH SAGE

2 CUPS/120 G FRESH BREAD CRUMBS

SALT AND PEPPER

Remove the giblets, neck, and any other trimmings from the duck and put into a small pot. Add the quartered onion, carrot, and bouquet garni and enough water to cover the duck parts and vegetables. Bring to a boil over high heat, then reduce the heat and simmer for 3 hours. Strain the stock, discarding the solids.

Meanwhile, melt the butter in a medium saucepan over low heat. Add the minced onion and cook for 6 to 8 minutes or until just soft, then stir in the sage and bread crumbs and season to taste with salt and pepper. Remove from the heat and set aside to cool to room temperature.

Preheat the oven to 350°F/175°C (Gas Mark 4).

Wash and thoroughly dry the duck inside and out, then season it generously, inside and out, with salt and pepper. Fill the cavity with stuffing. Truss the duck loosely with kitchen twine, then roast on a rack in a roasting pan for 1¼ to 1½ hours. To test for doneness, stick a skewer into the thigh; if the juices run clear, the duck is done.

When the duck is cooked, remove the rack with the duck still on it and set aside to rest. Degrease the roasting pan, reserving the fat to cook with. Put the pan on the stove top over high heat and deglaze with the stock, stirring constantly, until the liquid reduces by about one-half.

Carve the duck and serve with the gravy on the side.

Breakfast Duck

Serves 4

Mary Caherty, in her little booklet *Real Irish Cookery*, writes that this simple preparation was the traditional Christmas morning breakfast in "northern areas of the country." The skin won't crisp when cooked this way, but the meat will be moist and tender.

ONE 4- TO 5-LB/2- TO 2.5-KG DUCK

SALT AND PEPPER

1 SMALL ONION STUDDED WITH 6 CLOVES

4 SLICES BACON

BROWN SODA BREAD [PAGE 272] FOR SERVING

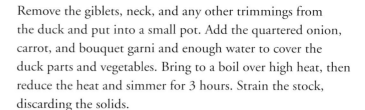

Preheat the oven to 400°F/200°C (Gas Mark 6).

Wash and thoroughly dry the duck inside and out, then season generously, inside and out, with salt and pepper.

Place the clove-studded onion in the duck cavity and truss the duck.

Put the duck on a rack in a covered roasting pan just large enough to comfortably hold it. Pour ½ cup/120 ml water around the sides. Drape the bacon slices over the duck.

Cover the pan and roast the duck for 45 minutes.

Uncover, baste well with pan juices, and roast for 30 to 45 minutes longer. To test for doneness, stick a skewer into the thigh; if the juices run clear, the duck is done.

Serve with unbuttered soda bread to sop up the juices.

Roast Turkey with Watercress Sauce

Serves 8 to 12

"Easter Sunday and Christmas Day are the two best days for eating," wrote the Kilkenny diarist Amhlaoibh Ó Súilleabháin. But that was almost two hundred years ago, and chances are that the Christmas feasting he had in mind didn't involve turkey. The bird has been known in Ireland at least since the mid-eighteenth century (Theodora FitzGibbon found a recipe in a manuscript from 1746, by one Sara Powers, for boneless whole turkey seasoned with nutmeg, mace, and cinnamon, then boiled in white wine and lemon-water), but didn't become associated with the holidays until the early twentieth century. Once it did take hold, it was usually cooked not at home but in the local baker's oven. Esther Barron of Barron's bakery in Cappoquin, County Waterford, recalls that when she was a young girl, "A stream of people would start coming in at 9 a.m. on Christmas morning with their turkeys, each with a name-tag on its leg." Everybody has his or her own favorite stuffed roast turkey recipe, but this one is a little different: It is Myrtle Allen's delicious way of treating a "summer turkey" or smaller bird.

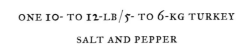

ONE 10- TO 12-LB/5- TO 6-KG TURKEY

SALT AND PEPPER

5 TBSP BUTTER

1 TBSP CANOLA OR SUNFLOWER OIL

6 MEDIUM ONIONS, CHOPPED

4 CLOVES GARLIC, CRUSHED

2 BUNCHES WATERCRESS, TRIMMED AND CHOPPED

2 TBSP CHOPPED FRESH PARSLEY

1 CUP/240 ML HEAVY CREAM

Preheat the oven to 375°F/190°C (Gas Mark 5).

Season the turkey all over, inside and out, with salt and pepper. Melt 4 Tbsp of the butter with the oil over medium-high heat in a heavy-bottomed roasting pan large enough to hold the turkey. Put the turkey into the pan, breast side down, and cook for 4 to 6 minutes to brown it.

Remove the turkey from the pan, and add the onions and garlic. Place the pan over 2 burners on the stove top and cook over medium heat for 5 minutes, stirring occasionally. Return the turkey to the roasting pan breast side up and bake for 2½ to 3 hours or until done. If the bottom of pan starts to dry out during cooking, add a little water to prevent the onions from burning. To test for doneness, insert a meat thermometer into the thickest part of the thigh; the temperature should be 175°F/80°C. Alternately, pierce the same place with a skewer; if the juices run clear, the turkey is cooked.

Remove the turkey from the pan and set aside to rest for about 15 minutes.

When ready to serve the turkey, pour the pan juices through a sieve into a small bowl, pressing through a little of the onion. Melt the remaining 1 Tbsp of butter in the roasting pan over medium heat, then add watercress and parsley, stir well, and cook for about 1 minute. Add the pan juices and cream, stir well, and cook for about 2 minutes more. Season to taste with salt and pepper.

Carve the turkey and serve with sauce on the side.

Michaelmas Goose

Serves 8

Goose is so firmly associated with Michaelmas, September 29, in Ireland that the old Irish name for the holiday was *Fómhar na nGéanna,* "the goose harvest." There are countless variations on the stuffing, but they usually involve apples and potatoes.

ONE 9- TO 11-LB/4.5- TO 5.5-KG GOOSE, WITH
GIBLETS, COMPLETELY THAWED IF FROZEN

3 ONIONS, CHOPPED

1 CARROT, CHOPPED

1 STALK CELERY, CHOPPED

BOUQUET GARNI [2 SPRIGS PARSLEY,
2 SPRIGS THYME, AND 1 BAY LEAF,
WRAPPED AND TIED IN CHEESECLOTH]

4 SLICES BACON, MINCED

2 TBSP BUTTER

3 COOKING APPLES, PEELED, CORED, AND CHOPPED

4 CUPS/850 G FRESHLY MADE MASHED POTATOES
[PAGE 223]

1 TBSP CHOPPED FRESH SAGE

1 TBSP CHOPPED FRESH THYME

1 TBSP CHOPPED FRESH PARSLEY

SALT AND PEPPER

APPLESAUCE [PAGE 333] FOR SERVING

Separate the liver from the giblets and set aside. Put the heart, neck, and gizzard in a medium pan. Add a third of the onion, the carrot, celery, and bouquet garni, then add enough water to cover all the ingredients. Bring to a boil over high heat, then reduce the heat, cover, and simmer for 2 hours.

Fry the bacon over medium heat in a large skillet with a lid (do not cover) until brown, then remove with a slotted spoon and set aside. Lower the heat, add the butter to the bacon fat, and when it has melted, add the remaining onions. Cook, stirring frequently, for 10 to 12 minutes, or until they soften.

Finely chop the reserved goose liver, then add to the onions. Cook for 3 to 4 minutes, then add the apples to the skillet. Cover the skillet and cook for 20 to 30 minutes, or until the apples have broken down and are very soft. Stir in the mashed potatoes, sage, thyme, and parsley, and season to taste with salt and pepper. Remove from the heat and set aside to cool.

Preheat the oven to 400°F/200°C (Gas Mark 6).

Wash and dry the goose thoroughly inside and out. Pull out any fat inside the cavity and reserve it to render later for cooking fat. Prick the skin of the goose all over with a fork, then rub salt all over the skin. Season the cavity with salt and pepper, then fill with the mashed potato–apple stuffing. Truss the goose with kitchen twine, binding the legs and wings close to its body.

Put the goose into a heavy roasting pan large enough to hold it, with a little room around the sides, and roast it for 30 minutes. Remove from the oven and draw off the rendered fat with a bulb baster or large spoon. (Reserve the fat for cooking.) Return the pan to the oven and decrease the temperature to 325°F/160°C (Gas Mark 3). Roast for about 2½ hours more, drawing off rendered fat at least once more as it cooks. Test for doneness by pricking the thigh at its thickest point with a skewer. If the juices run clear, the goose is done; if they're pink, roast for another 15 minutes, then check again

Meanwhile, strain the giblet stock, discarding the solids, and set aside.

When the goose is done, transfer it to a large serving platter to rest. Draw off any remaining fat, then set the roasting pan over 2 burners on the stove top. Deglaze with the stock, scraping up any browned bits on the bottom of the pan. Strain the gravy into a gravy boat or bowl.

Carve the goose at the table. Serve with applesauce and the gravy.

MICHAELMAS

Michaelmas, September 29, is the feast of St. Michael the Archangel—important not just because it honored the saint but because it was one of the traditional "quarter days" of the year. These were the days on which rents were due, accounts of all kinds were settled, and new servants were hired (the other quarter days were March 25, June 24, and Christmas). Michaelmas was celebrated with a special dinner in households that could afford it. Because the occasion also marked the end of the harvest, there was a custom of putting the season's last sheaf of wheat on the table as a centerpiece. (The girl who tied it was due the first dance of the evening with the farmer's son.)

The meal was always built around roast goose. Darina Allen remembers the preparations when she was a girl in Cullohill, County Laois: "The bird was smothered several days ahead and hung by the neck in the larder. It was then plucked in an open shed. The wings were kept (and much sought after for brushing out dusty corners), the large feathers were sometimes made into quills or fishing floats, and the smaller ones and the precious down were collected for stuffing pillows and feather beds." The final days of September also marked the beginning of the apple harvest, so applesauce was often served with the goose, and apple cake or tart was the typical dessert.

St. Stephen's Day Stew

Serves 6 to 8

In her delightful little book *The Festive Food of Ireland*, Darina Allen summons up the memory of the picnics her family would enjoy, when she was a girl, after the local fox hunt every St. Stephen's Day (Boxing Day), the day after Christmas: sandwiches of turkey and ham, smoked salmon, or spiced beef; Christmas cake, sponge cake, mince pie, and clementines; flasks of tea and of hot mulled wine. "But the real favourite," she writes, "was a bubbling stew transported in a haybox" (which held fodder for the horses on a journey, and was incidentally a naturally insulated container for hot food). The main ingredients of this stew, which must have seemed particularly appealing outdoors on a chilly winter day, were leftover ham and turkey from the Christmas table.

8 TBSP/125 G BUTTER

2 ONIONS, CHOPPED

6 TO 8 WHITE MUSHROOMS, THINLY SLICED

2 LB/1 KG LEFTOVER TURKEY MEAT, CUT INTO
1-IN/2.5-CM CUBES

1 LB/500 G LEFTOVER HAM,
CUT INTO 1-IN/2.5-CM CUBES

4 CUPS/1 L STRONG TURKEY OR CHICKEN
STOCK [PAGE 356] OR 3 CUPS/720 ML STOCK AND
1 CUP/240 ML LEFTOVER TURKEY GRAVY

3/4 CUP/175 ML HEAVY CREAM

1 TBSP MINCED FRESH PARSLEY

2 TBSP MINCED FRESH CHIVES

2 TBSP FLOUR

12 SMALL BOILED POTATOES
[SEE PAGE 229], PEELED

SALT AND PEPPER

Preheat the oven to 200°F/90°C.

Melt 6 Tbsp of the butter in a Dutch oven or heavy-bottomed pot over low heat, then add the onions and cook for 10 to 12 minutes, stirring frequently. Add the mushrooms and cook for about 10 minutes more, continuing to stir frequently.

Add the turkey and ham to the Dutch oven, stir well, and cook for about 10 minutes more, continuing to stir frequently.

Increase the heat to medium-high, add the stock, and deglaze the pot. Reduce the heat to low and stir in the cream, parsley, and half the chives. Season to taste with salt and pepper and continue cooking for 10 to 15 minutes.

Meanwhile, melt the remaining 2 Tbsp of butter in a small pan over low heat, then gradually whisk in the flour to make a roux. Continue whisking for 2 to 3 minutes or until the roux thickens. Stir the roux into the stew and cook for about 5 minutes more.

Take the stew off the heat, put the boiled potatoes on top of the stew, then cover the Dutch oven and let the stew rest in the preheated oven for 30 to 45 minutes before serving. Garnish with the remaining minced chives.

PORK

The Favored Meat

Like all intelligent creatures, pigs like to play, so you have to give them room. It's so satisfying, when you release them into the wood in the spring, to see them doing what pigs love to do most, which is rooting in the ground with their snouts.

—Giana Ferguson of Gubbeen, in an interview with the author [2005]

What a wonderful animal is the pig—dead, I mean.

—Monica Sheridan, *The Art of Irish Cooking* [1965]

Remains of roasted wild boar have been found at the Mesolithic site of Mount Sandel, County Derry, dating from around 7000 B.C., so it seems safe to say that the Irish have been eating pork for quite a while. Pigs were first

domesticated on the island in the Neolithic era, and ever since then, pork—fresh but especially in cured form—has been central to the Irish diet. (Just how highly pigs were valued, says A. T. Lucas in his paper "Irish Food Before the Potato," is suggested by the frequency with which swineherds are mentioned in early literature.) Pork has always been Ireland's favorite variety of animal flesh. Even today, the Irish consume more pork than any other meat, over eighty pounds/forty kilos of it per capita each year (most of it cured). Why? Its rich flavor (pigs traditionally fattened on mast, the wild fruits of the oak, beech, and chestnut) and suitability to various methods of preservation are probably the main reasons for its historical popularity. In addition, unlike sheep and cattle, pigs are worthless as dairy animals. They have no udders, making them difficult to milk, and they give low yields. Their milk also lacks the short-chain fatty acids that give the milk of cows, sheep, and goats the "dairy" flavor humans seem to like. And pig's milk doesn't coagulate, making it useless for the production of cheese. The only way to get food value out of a pig, then, is to eat it.

In the old days, farmers would typically fatten two pigs every year, one for family use and one to sell, which is why the animal became known as "the gentleman who pays the rent." The annual pig slaughter, writes Dublin chef and food historian Máirtín Mac Con Iomaire, was both a ritual and a social occasion. "Neighbours, who came to help," he explains, "brought a handful of salt for the curing, and when the work was done each would get a share of the puddings and the fresh pork."

The happy, rooting pigs Giana Ferguson describes at her Gubbeen farm (see page 61), unfortunately, are the exception rather than the rule in Ireland today. While small farmers around the island are beginning to raise organic, free-range sheep and cattle, often from heritage breeds, Irish pork is still largely the preserve of agribusiness—and though more than three million pigs are slaughtered in the country every year, some of the larger processors buy carcasses from Eastern Europe and elsewhere. The Fergusons and a handful of other pig farmers—among them Jill Dougan at Moyallen Foods in Craigavon, County Armagh; Trevor Barclay at Moss-Brook Farm in Desertmartin, County Derry; Marc O'Mahoney in Enniskeane, County Cork (he has a shop in Cork City's English Market; see page 212); and Joseph and Julie Delaney at Tully-wood Farm near Boyle, County Roscommon—are bucking the trend with Gloucestershire Old Spots, Tamworths, Saddle-backs, and other rare breeds. These animals are raised more humanely and sustainably than the factory pigs, often organically, and their meat almost invariably has more flavor. Most of the Irish pork products sold the United States are "Irish-style," but aren't made with Irish meat. One exception is Tommy Moloney's Mild-Cured Irish Bacon, produced under USDA supervision using pork "from local farms nestled in Ireland's southwest countryside." Other Irish-branded bacon sold in this country is, to the best of my knowledge, made with American or Danish meat. No sausages or black or white puddings based on Irish-grown pork are currently imported, though several producers make more than credible domestic substitutes, often using "Irish seasonings." If you want to taste the real thing . . . well, that's one more reason to visit Ireland itself.

Battered Sausages

Serves 4

A staple at gas-station food counters all over Ireland, battered sausages are usually grim and greasy. If made correctly, though, they can be a real treat—though admittedly dietarily excessive and nutritionally incorrect.

TWO $^1/_4$-OZ/7-G PACKETS ACTIVE DRY YEAST

1 $^1/_4$ CUPS/300 ML GUINNESS STOUT

2 3/4 CUPS/275 G WHITE FLOUR

1 TSP SALT

OIL FOR FRYING

12 SMALL IRISH-STYLE BREAKFAST SAUSAGES, PREFERABLY GALTEE OR WINSTON'S [SEE SOURCES, PAGE 369]

Put the yeast in a medium bowl and drizzle in the Guinness, stirring constantly with a small whisk until it is well incorporated.

Sift 2¼ cups/225 g of the flour and the salt into a large bowl. Make a well in the center and pour in beer and yeast mixture. Stir well, then cover the bowl and set aside for 1 hour.

Heat at least 6 in/15 cm of the oil in a deep pot or deep fryer to 350°F/175°C.

Dust the sausages with the remaining ½ cup/50 g flour, dip in the batter, and deep fry, a few at a time, for about 8 minutes each.

Drain the sausages as they're done and cover with foil to keep them warm.

Bacon and Cabbage

Serves 4 to 6

Máirtin Mac Con Iomaire, a lecturer in culinary arts at Dublin Institute of Technology, quotes the late Irish playwright and author John B. Keane on this basic Irish comfort food thusly: "When this kind of bacon is boiling with its old colleague, white cabbage, there is a gurgle from the pot that would tear the heart out of any hungry man." Every traditional Irish household has a recipe for bacon and cabbage (bacon in this case meaning cured pork); this one comes from Peter and Mary Ward of Nenagh, County Tipperary, who specify the use of local organic vegetables in its preparation.

ONE 3-LB/1.5-KG CURED PORK LOIN

1 CARROT, CHOPPED

2 STALKS CELERY, CHOPPED

2 LEEKS, WHITE PART ONLY, CHOPPED

1 TSP BLACK PEPPERCORNS

1 TBSP DIJON MUSTARD

1 TBSP FRESH BREAD CRUMBS, DRIED IN THE OVEN AT 250°F/120°C FOR 30 MINUTES

1 $^1/_2$ TSP BROWN SUGAR

2 TBSP BUTTER, SOFTENED

2 LB/1 KG WHITE CABBAGE, FINELY SHREDDED

SALT

MUSTARD SAUCE [PAGE 360] OR PARSLEY SAUCE [PAGE 360] FOR SERVING

BOILED POTATOES [PAGE 229] FOR SERVING

Put the pork loin into a large pot. Add the carrot, celery, leeks, and peppercorns and cover ingredients with cold water. Bring to a boil over high heat, then reduce the heat and simmer, uncovered, for about 1 hour.

Meanwhile, preheat the oven to 400°F/200°C (Gas Mark 6).

Remove the pork from the pot and set aside. Strain and reserve the cooking liquid.

Cut the rind off the pork and discard it, then score the fat all over with a small, sharp knife. Put the pork into a roasting pan just big enough to hold it.

In a small bowl, combine the mustard, bread crumbs, brown sugar, and 1 Tbsp of the butter and mix them together with a fork.

Spread the mixture over the top and sides of the pork loin, then roast in the oven for about 20 minutes.

Meanwhile, put the cabbage into a saucepan just big enough to hold it and add the reserved cooking liquid to cover, pouring in a little water if necessary. Bring the liquid to a boil, then reduce the heat to a simmer and cook until the cabbage is cooked through but still a little crisp, about 6 minutes. Drain well and toss in a bowl with the remaining Tbsp of butter. Season to taste with salt.

To serve, make a bed of the cabbage on a serving platter. Slice the pork loin about ½ in/1.25 cm thick and lay it on top of the cabbage. Serve with mustard sauce or parsley sauce, with boiled potatoes on the side.

Ulster Fry

Serves 2

The Ulster Fry is a slightly more elaborate Northern Irish version of the full Irish breakfast—or, as it is fondly known in some quarters, the "cardiac special"—offered all over the island, and probably eaten these days almost as often at midday as for the morning meal. The exact constituents of this extremely, well, hearty meal vary from county to county and even from house to house. Small quartered mushrooms, cooked in butter or bacon fat, are sometimes added; lamb kidneys occasionally join the other meats or substitute for one or more of them; scones may also be halved and fried. Baker Robert Ditty, of Castledawson, County Derry, says that in modest traditional homes, the Ulster Fry didn't include sausages or puddings, because people didn't have the equipment to make them, whereas they could always cure their own bacon. Ditty, who includes American-style streaky bacon as well as Irish bacon when he constructs an Ulster fry, has

strong ideas about the order and methods of cooking the ingredients, which I pass along below. (He adds, "People who throw soda bread and potato bread into a deep-fat fryer should be strangled.") In attempting to reproduce a real Ulster fry as accurately as possible in the United States, I sampled every example of Irish bacon, sausage, and black and white pudding that I could find in this country, both imported and American-made; my recommendations are below (see Sources, page 369). Serve with strong tea (see page 364) or freshly brewed coffee.

2 SLICES BACON

2 SLICES IRISH BACON, PREFERABLY GALTEE'S SLICED CURED PORK LOIN, TOMMY MOLONEY'S MILD-CURED [NOT SMOKED OR BACK RASHERS], OR DONNELLY'S

I TOMATO, HALVED [IN SEASON ONLY]

2 SMALL IRISH-STYLE BREAKFAST SAUSAGES, PREFERABLY GALTEE'S OR WINSTON'S

TWO ½-IN/1.25-CM SLICES BLACK PUDDING, PREFERABLY GALTEE'S

TWO ½-IN/1.25-CM SLICES WHITE PUDDING, PREFERABLY GALTEE'S OR DONNELLY'S

I SODA FARL [PAGE 279], HALVED CROSSWISE

2 WEDGES FADGE [POTATO CAKES, PAGE 225]

ABOUT I TBSP CANOLA OR SUNFLOWER OIL

2 EGGS

Fry the bacon over medium heat in a large skillet, preferably cast-iron. When done on one side, tip the pan slightly to distribute the bacon fat, then add the Irish bacon and tomato halves (if using), skin side down, to the skillet.

When the bacon is crisp on both sides, the Irish bacon is lightly cooked, and the tomatoes are soft, remove from the skillet. Set aside, covered with foil to keep warm.

Fry the sausages and black and white pudding in the same skillet until lightly browned on all sides, then add them to the other cooked ingredients.

While the sausages and puddings are frying, heat a small dry skillet, preferably cast-iron, over medium heat. When you've removed the sausages and puddings from the large skillet, dip both sides of the soda farl and fadge pieces in the fat in the pan.

Transfer them to the dry skillet and fry until crisp on both sides, turning once. Add them to the cooked meats and tomato.

Wipe out the large skillet, add a little oil, and fry the eggs over medium heat until done.

Put 1 egg in the middle of each of 2 large warmed plates, then arrange the bacon, Irish bacon, tomato halves (if using), sausages, black and white pudding, soda farl, and fadge around them.

Bacon Broth

Serves 6 to 8

Despite its name, this isn't a mere broth or even just a soup at all, but a hearty soup-plus-meat dish—a two-course meal in one, a bit like an Irish *pot-au-feu*. Theodora FitzGibbon suggests that other meats, including lamb, mutton, beef, or rabbit, can be substituted for the bacon (i.e., cured pork) or added to it, and opines that a combination of bacon and rabbit is particularly good.

ONE 3-LB/1.5-KG CURED PORK LOIN

1/2 CUP/90 G PEARL BARLEY

1/2 CUP/100 G BROWN LENTILS

2 ONIONS, SLICED

4 CARROTS, SLICED

2 PARSNIPS, SLICED

1 BAY LEAF

2 OR 3 SPRIGS PARSLEY

2 OR 3 SPRIGS THYME

1 LB/500 G POTATOES, SLICED

1 SMALL WHITE OR GREEN CABBAGE, QUARTERED

1 LEEK, WHITE PART ONLY, CHOPPED

SALT AND PEPPER

BOILED POTATOES [PAGE 229] FOR SERVING [OPTIONAL]

MUSTARD SAUCE [PAGE 360] FOR SERVING [OPTIONAL]

Put the pork loin into a large pot with water to cover. Bring the water to a boil over high heat, then add the barley and lentils. Return to a boil, then reduce the heat and simmer, uncovered, for 20 minutes.

Add the onions, carrots, parsnips, bay leaf, parsley, and thyme. Bring to a boil, then reduce the heat and simmer, uncovered, for 10 minutes.

Add the potatoes and cabbage. Bring to a boil, then reduce the heat and simmer, uncovered, for 20 minutes more.

Add the leek and continue simmering for about 10 minutes. Season to taste with salt and pepper (but be careful with the salt, as the pork loin will have added some to the soup).

To serve, carefully lift the pork loin from the soup with tongs. Let it cool slightly, then trim off any rind or excess fat. Wrap the pork loin in foil to keep warm.

Ladle the soup into bowls and serve first, then slice the pork loin into pieces about ½ in/1.25 cm thick. Serve with mustard sauce and boiled potatoes, if you like.

Alternatively, after removing the pork loin from the soup and trimming the skin and fat, cut it into small pieces, return it to the soup, and serve the soup in one course.

Dublin Coddle

Serves 4

A dish with "Dublin" in its name doesn't sound like it belongs in a book about country cooking, but this venerable classic, a favorite of Jonathan Swift's, has been around at least since the seventeenth century—and according to some reports, dates back to the time of the Vikings in the ninth century A.D. Though it may have been popular in Dublin, it is undeniably rural, if not positively rustic, in its heartiness and simplicity. As the chef and culinary historian Máirtín Mac Con Iomaire has pointed out, it is basically Irish stew made with bacon and sausage instead of mutton or lamb. He also notes that it was sometimes called "black coddle" because its surface could get dusted by soot falling from the chimney into the open cauldron where it simmered. (To coddle a dish is to cook it very slowly.) For Irish bacon and sausage, as well as Chef Sauce or YR Sauce, see Sources, on page 369.

8 SLICES IRISH BACON, PREFERABLY GALTEE'S
SLICED CURED PORK LOIN, TOMMY MOLONEY'S
MILD-CURED [NOT SMOKED OR BACK RASHERS],
OR DONNELLY'S, EACH PIECE QUARTERED

6 TO 8 LARGE IRISH-STYLE BREAKFAST SAUSAGES,
PREFERABLY GALTEE'S OR WINSTON'S,
CUT INTO LARGE PIECES

I LB/500 G POTATOES, SLICED I/4 IN/6.5 MM THICK

2 ONIONS, THINLY SLICED

PEPPER

2 TBSP CHOPPED FRESH PARSLEY

CHEF SAUCE, YR SAUCE, OR AI STEAK SAUCE
FOR SERVING

Preheat the oven to 325°F/160°C (Gas Mark 3).

Put the bacon and sausage into a medium saucepan with just enough water to cover them. Bring the water to a boil over high heat and cook for 8 to 10 minutes, or until the liquid is reduced by about one-third. Remove the bacon and sausage from the saucepan, reserving the liquid.

Mix the bacon, sausage, potatoes, and onions together in an ovenproof pot or baking dish with a lid. Season to taste with pepper. Pour the reserved cooking liquid into the pot, cover tightly, then bake for about 1 hour or until the liquid is reduced by about half.

Sprinkle the parsley on top of the coddle. Serve with Chef Sauce or YR Sauce or with A1.

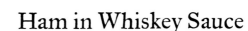

Ham in Whiskey Sauce

Serves 4

Use leftover Baked Christmas Ham (page 152) for this recipe.

2 TBSP BUTTER

4 HAM STEAKS, ABOUT I IN/2.5 CM THICK

I ONION, THINLY SLICED

I TBSP WHITE FLOUR

I TBSP BROWN SUGAR

I/4 CUP/60 ML IRISH WHISKEY

I/2 CUP/120 ML BEEF STOCK [PAGE 357]

I/4 CUP/60 ML HEAVY CREAM

SALT AND PEPPER

Melt 1 Tbsp of butter in a large skillet over medium-high heat, then brown the ham steaks, in batches if necessary, for 2 to 3 minutes per side. Remove the ham from the skillet when done and set aside, covering the steaks with foil to keep them warm.

Melt the remaining Tbsp of butter in the same pan, then add the onions. Cook for 10 to 12 minutes, or until golden brown. Remove the onions from the skillet with a slotted spoon and drain on paper towels.

Reduce the heat to low and sprinkle the flour into the pan, mixing it into the butter and pan juices. Repeat the process with the brown sugar, then add the whiskey and the beef stock and stir it in well. Whisk in the cream, then season to taste with salt and pepper.

To serve, put 1 ham steak on each of 4 plates, spoon a quarter of the onions over each steak, then gently pour sauce over the onions and ham.

Baked Christmas Ham

Serves 20 to 24

This recipe comes from Barbara Workman of Gray Abbey, County Down (grandmother of food writer Caroline Workman, now of East Cork). I first encountered the recipe in "Ditty's Digest," the newsletter of the northern Irish baker Robert Ditty (see page 276). He notes that this ham is "delicious hot with parsley sauce [page 360] and baked potatoes or in a 'doorstop sandwich' [made with a single long loaf of bread and then cut into individual sandwiches] with butter and honey mustard."

1 WHOLE 10- TO 15-LB/5- TO 7.5-KG HAM

20 TO 24 CLOVES

1 BOTTLE GUINNESS STOUT

2 CUPS/400 G DARK BROWN SUGAR,
PLUS MORE AS NEEDED

Put the ham into a pot large enough to hold it with some room left over, then fill with water to cover. Bring to a boil over high heat, then reduce the heat to medium-low and simmer, covered, for 3 hours, skimming off any foam that rises to the surface from time to time.

Preheat the oven to 475°F/250°C (Gas Mark 9).

Carefully remove the ham from the pot and pat dry, then peel off the skin, leaving a layer of fat. Stud the fat all over with cloves, spacing them as equally as possible.

Put the ham on a rack in a large roasting pan, drizzle with Guinness, then sprinkle brown sugar all over the ham, packing it down with your hands to form a crust. Add additional sugar if necessary to cover. Bake for 30 to 40 minutes or until the crust is dark golden brown.

Irish Schnitzel

Serves 4

In giving this recipe in her book *Feasting Galore: Recipes and Food Lore from Ireland*, Maura Laverty calls for griskins, which she describes as "odds and ends of lean pork that are cut off when the pig is trimmed." (Griskins were traditionally served to the parish priest when he came to lunch, while the rest of the family ate lesser cuts.) Unless you plan on trimming your own pig in the near future, I'd advise using slices of pork loin.

3 TBSP WHITE FLOUR

SALT AND PEPPER

1 EGG BEATEN WITH 1 TBSP WATER

1 CUP/60 G DRY BREAD CRUMBS

4 TBSP BUTTER

1 LB/500 G PORK LOIN, CUT INTO
1/2-IN/1.25-CM SLICES, POUNDED THIN
BETWEEN 2 PIECES OF WAX PAPER

MAURA LAVERTY'S ONION AND APPLE SAUCE
[PAGE 358] FOR SERVING [OPTIONAL]

Put the flour onto a plate and season well with salt and pepper, mixing the seasonings in. Put beaten egg into a wide, shallow bowl. Put the bread crumbs on a plate.

Melt the butter in a large skillet over medium heat. Working in batches, dredge each piece of pork in flour, then dip it in egg, then dredge it in bread crumbs. Fry for about 3 minutes per side, or until the breading is golden brown.

Serve with Maura Laverty's Onion and Apple Sauce, if you like.

THE ORIGINAL ARTISANS

Though the modern artisanal food movement in Ireland isn't much more than three decades old, many of the country's butchers, in both small towns and big cities, have maintained artisanal standards for centuries, making sausages, meat puddings, and bacon and other cured meats on a small scale, by hand, from local sources. When Ed Hick, a fourth-generation butcher from Dún Laoghaire, County Dublin, got started in the business, his family still bought pigs from their neighbors—the coal man, the bus driver, and other ordinary citizens who, as was common in those days, kept a few animals on the side and slaughtered them themselves. Today, laws forbid that kind of hands-on process. Butchers can't use wooden cutting blocks or scatter their floors with sawdust, either. Legislation and regulation, both Irish and from the European Union, have changed the old ways. Hick thinks that's a shame. "Our mothers learned food safety from their grandmothers," he says. "They'd never heard of bacteria, but somehow they lived to a ripe old age."

Legal restrictions aside, Hick continues to make some of Ireland's best old-style sausages and other specialty items, including a remarkable dry-cured smoked venison loin, which is served at Dublin's superb Chapter One, among other places. (Hick's operation is now wholesale only, but his wares—almost always identified by name—may be found in good restaurants and specialty food shops all over Dublin and beyond.) At his McGeough's Connemara Fine Foods, meanwhile, up in Oughterard, on the edge of Connemara in County Galway, second-generation, German-trained butcher James McGeough is exploring new territory with his prosciutto-like air-dried Connemara lamb (see page 172), heather-flavored salami, air-dried beef, sweet chili and pesto sausages, and other imaginative products, as well as traditional-style bacon and some of Ireland's best ham.

Elsewhere in Ireland, butchers like T. J. Crowe in Dundrum, County Tipperary; the Rudd family in Birr, County Offaly; Jack McCarthy in Kanturk, County Cork; Sean Kelly in Newport, County Mayo (a master of black and white puddings, see page 201); John Muldrew in Markethill, County Armagh; and Pat O'Doherty in Enniskillen, County Fermanagh (whose trademark is the long-cured Fermanagh black bacon) are producing wonderful pork products and other specialty meats in styles both ancient and modern. The American government restricts the importation of meat products from Ireland (and elsewhere), and though some producers will unofficially ship their products here (see Sources, page 369), they're best and most easily enjoyed in Ireland itself—a particularly salient, if you will, reason for a gastronomic visit.

Liam Morrissey's butchers, Waterford City.

IRISH BACON

The commercial bacon industry began to develop in Ireland in the 1800s, with Waterford as its capital. One factory alone—and there were at least four—slaughtered and processed more than a thousand pigs a day. Irish bacon makers became famous for their skills, helping to set up curing plants in Denmark and Russia and exporting their wares not just to London and Paris but to India and North and South America.

In Ireland, though, the term *bacon* is applied to virtually all cured pork except for ham (which is often called "gammon"). The bacon used in homey dishes like bacon and cabbage is usually, these days, what we'd call cured pork loin (it can also be shoulder or other cuts). The bacon eaten for breakfast and used for flavoring in cooking is usually lean back bacon, called "rashers" (facing page)—not dissimilar to what Americans know as Canadian bacon. American-style bacon, fatty and usually fried crisp, exists in Ireland, under the name "streaky bacon," but it is the exception rather than the rule.

Pork Rib Irish Stew

Serves 4

In *The Cookin' Woman*, Florence Irwin gives three recipes for Irish stew: the third one is made with leftover beef or lamb, the second one uses mutton, and the first one, presumably positioned to suggest its importance, is based on pork spare ribs, pork kidneys, and griskins (miscellaneous bits of pork). Irwin notes, in fact, that "any raw pork may be used" for this stew. Ask your butcher to cut the ribs for you.

3 LB/1.5 KG PORK RIBS [NOT BABY BACK RIBS], SEPARATED AND CUT INTO 2-IN/5-CM LENGTHS

2 ONIONS, SLICED

3 LB/1.5 KG POTATOES, ONE-THIRD SLICED, TWO-THIRDS CUT INTO LARGE CHUNKS

SALT AND PEPPER

Put the ribs in a large pot with salted water to cover. Bring to a boil, then reduce the heat to low and simmer for about 10 minutes, skimming off any foam that rises to the surface. Add the onions and sliced potatoes and cook for about 20 minutes more.

Adjust the seasoning with salt and pepper, then add the potato chunks, cover the pot, and simmer for about 2½ hours, stirring occasionally.

Roast Pork Belly

Serves 6 to 8

This recipe comes from J. J. Healy, a chef based in County Tipperary who has cooked at several country house hotels and is the South East Branch Chairman of the Panel of Chefs of Ireland.

1 ONION, SLICED

2 CLOVES GARLIC, MINCED

1 BUNCH SAGE, CHOPPED

4 CUPS/1 L BEEF OR CHICKEN STOCK [PAGE 357 OR 356]

ONE 3-LB/1.5-KG PORK BELLY

SALT AND PEPPER

1/2 CUP/120 ML HARD CIDER

8 CLOVES

PINCH OF ALLSPICE

PINCH OF CINNAMON

6 TBSP BROWN SUGAR

Preheat the oven to 300°F/150°C (Gas Mark 2).

Put the onion slices in a roasting pan large enough to hold them in a single layer, then scatter the garlic and half the sage over them. Pour in the stock. Season the pork generously with salt and pepper on all sides. Set it on top of the onions and spoon the cider over it. Scatter the remaining sage over the pork and then the cloves, allspice, and cinnamon.

Cover the pan tightly with foil and roast, basting occasionally with pan juices, for 2 to 3 hours, or until the pork is very tender.

Uncover the roasting pan and coat the top of the pork with the brown sugar. Increase the oven temperature to 400°F/200°C (Gas Mark 6) and continue roasting the pork, uncovered, for about 20 minutes or until sugar begins to brown. Spoon pan juices over sugar crust (sugar will dissolve). Continue roasting the pork for 10 minutes more or until the top is glazed and golden.

Transfer the pork to a warmed platter, reserving the pan juices, and let rest for 10 to 15 minutes. To serve, reheat the pan juices, deglazing pan with a little more stock or cider, if you like. Slice the pork, then strain the juices over it.

ROAST PORK BELLY

Pot-Roasted Pork with Root Vegetables and Apples

Serves 6

Chef-consultant Martin Dwyer, who used to run the acclaimed Dwyer's Restaurant in Waterford, developed this recipe for that city's best food shop, Ardkeen.

2 TBSP BUTTER

5 STRIPS BACON, FINELY CHOPPED

2 ONIONS, QUARTERED

3 CARROTS, COARSELY CHOPPED

3 PARSNIPS, COARSELY CHOPPED

6 CLOVES GARLIC, PEELED

ONE 2-LB/1-KG BONELESS PORK LEG OR SHOULDER ROAST, ROLLED AND TIED

SALT AND PEPPER

2 CUPS/475 ML APPLE JUICE OR CIDER

2 APPLES, PEELED, CORED, AND COARSELY CHOPPED

BOILED POTATOES [PAGE 229] FOR SERVING [OPTIONAL]

Melt the butter in a large skillet over medium heat. Add the bacon and cook for 10 to 12 minutes, stirring frequently, until well browned. Remove the bacon from the skillet with a slotted spoon and transfer it to a baking dish large enough to hold the pork roast, with room to spare.

Put the onions, carrots, parsnips, and garlic into the skillet and cook in the butter and bacon fat for 12 to 14 minutes, stirring frequently, or until well browned. Remove the vegetables from the skillet with a slotted spoon and transfer them to the baking dish, stirring to mix them with the bacon.

Preheat the oven to 400°F/200°C (Gas Mark 6).

Snip the twine off the pork and season it generously with salt and pepper. Put the pork into the same skillet, raise heat to high, and cook, adding more butter if necessary, for 4 to 6 minutes, turning frequently, until browned all over.

Transfer the pork to the baking dish. Deglaze the skillet with the apple juice or cider, letting it boil for 3 to 4 minutes to reduce slightly.

Put the apples in the baking dish, around the pork. Drizzle the reduced cider over all, then roast in the oven for about 20 minutes. Reduce the heat to 275°F/135°C (Gas Mark 1), cover the baking dish, and roast for about 1 hour more or until the meat is tender.

Remove the meat from the baking dish, let sit for 5 minutes, then carve. Serve with the vegetables and any cooking juices on the side, and with boiled potatoes, if you like.

THE WATER OF LIFE

There's an old saying that God invented whiskey so that the Irish wouldn't rule the world. In fact, divinely inspired though they may have been, it was the Irish themselves who created this famous liquor—even Scots distillers admit that. Missionary monks apparently brought the technique of distillation to Ireland sometime in the fourteenth (some say thirteenth) century, either from Spain or directly from the Middle East, where it was first developed. The earliest reference to whiskey in Irish literature is a report in 1405 that a chieftain named Richard Mac Rannal died of a surfeit of *uisge beatha*—literally (and ironically, under the circumstances) "water of life," and the Irish term from which the word *whiskey* is derived. (That word, by the way, is spelled with an *e* in Ireland and America, and without one in Scotland and Canada.)

The whiskey of earlier times didn't bear much resemblance to what we know today. English traveler Fynes Moryson, who roamed through Ireland in the late sixteenth and early seventeenth centuries, wrote that *usquebaugh*, as he called it, was preferable to English alcohol because "the mingling of raisins, fennel-seed, and other things, mitigating the heat and making the taste pleasant, makes it less inflame, and yet refresh the weak stomach with moderate heat and a good relish." It was, in other words, sweetened and herb flavored—perhaps more like Irish Mist liqueur than, say, Jameson or Bushmills. Irish whiskey today, on the other hand, is dry, clean, and accessible—"less boisterous" than Scotch, as spirits writer Stephen Beaumont put it—because it's distilled three times instead of two like its Scots sibling, and seldom has the latter's smoky peat character.

Speaking of Bushmills, that distillery was licensed in 1609, making it the oldest licensed distillery in the world. It sits in the small town of the same name in County Antrim, almost at the northeastern tip of the island and not far from the spectacular Giant's Causeway, a vast seaside formation of interlocking basalt columns that has been declared a World Heritage Site. Remarkably, while there are scores of whiskey varieties in Ireland, including an increasing number of single malts on the Scots model, Bushmills, now owned by the Diageo conglomerate, is one of only three distilleries on the entire island. The other two are Pernod-Ricard's New Midleton, outside Midleton in County Cork, which produces Jameson, Powers, and Paddy, among others; and the Irish-owned Cooley, on the Cooley Peninsula in County Louth, the source of boutique brands like Connemara, Kilbeggan, Locke's, and Tyrconnell. One other operation bottles whiskeys already distilled elsewhere under the Clontarf and Knappogue Castle labels; the latter includes old stocks from the long-defunct B. Daly Distillery in Tullamore, County Offaly.

THE CALIFORNIA OF IRELAND

"You could look at West Cork as the California of Ireland," says artisanal sausage maker Frank Krawczyk (below, left), Polish born but a resident of Eire since 1974. "Not in climate, of course," he continues, "but in its openness and creativity. It's very, very diverse, very cosmopolitan. It's one of the most forward-thinking counties in Ireland." It's also both the cradle and the hotbed of the modern Irish artisanal food movement. The pioneers here were cheese makers Norman and Veronica Steele at Milleens (see page 50), Jeffa Gill at Durrus, and Giana Ferguson at Gubbeen (see page 61), and there are many more cheese producers in the county today. (New Zealand author Sarah-Kate Lynch has even written a novel about the subject, the 2003 *Blessed at the Cheesemakers*, about a cheese-making West Cork country house run, in the words of one review, "by two old codgers and a handful of misfit pregnant milkmaids.") County Cork is also home to some of Ireland's best fish smokers, to Myrtle Allen's seminal Ballymaloe House and the world-renowned Ballymaloe Cookery School (see page 259), and to some of Ireland's best charcutiers. Chief among the latter are Fingal Ferguson of Gubbeen (see page 61) and Krawczyk—who handcrafts superb sausages, salamis, and specialties like Corcoppa (Cork coppa) and "Rebel County smoked beef" (Cork has a history of rebelling, or at least siding with unpopular political causes) at Dereenatra, Schull.

County Cork is also the home of one of Ireland's most unusual restaurants, Island Cottage (facing page), on a little piece of rock off Skibbereen alternately known as Hare and Heir Island. Here, chef John Desmond—Cork born and trained at the Ritz and Taillevent in Paris—cooks a single four-course fixed-price dinner for a maximum of twenty-four guests five nights a week from April through September, while his wife lays down the house rules and doles out the wine. Desmond's cooking is refined but not overly complicated. A dinner might include, for instance, risotto with fresh shrimp and bits of wild salmon, roasted duck legs with sauce béarnaise, and lemon soufflé crêpes. Diners travel to the island by ferry, then walk about half a mile/three-quarters of a kilometer to the restaurant; walking back in the dark is the tricky part.

Another individualistic County Cork chef was Otto Kunze, who ran the unfortunately named Otto's Creative Catering, a farm-cum-eatery in Dunworley. Kunze worked under Gerry Galvin at The Vintage in Kinsale (see page 79), but was always as interested in growing things as in cooking them. "He rode his Honda 50 motorcycle twenty-two miles to the restaurant every day," remembers Galvin, "laden down with fruit and vegetables and herbs for us to use." Kunze not only grew his own produce; he also raised pigs and made sausages, which he sent to Fingal Ferguson to smoke, and he canned his own jellies and relishes. Whatever he bought came from the immediate vicinity and was almost certainly organic. On the subject of genetically modified foods, he was unequivocal: "We should not let that rubbish into the country," he said. Kunze is now retired and Creative Catering closed, but his memory is still an inspiration in the region.

Chapter No. 8

BEEF

and

LAMB

From the Rich Pastures

[We] sit down Morning, Noon, and Night to the finest Beef in Christendom.

—A guest at the home of Rev. Nicholas Herbert in Knockgrafton, County Tipperary [1789]

As a young girl in the 1860s, my grandmother was warned never to let slip to the landlord's agent that her family ever ate meat.

—Malachi McCormick, *Irish Country Cooking* [1988]

The greatest glory of Irish agriculture is not the potato, or cabbage or kale, or those famous ancient apples. It's grass—the thick, nutrient-rich green that flourishes unstoppably in Ireland's damp, healthy earth, feeding the

island's celebrated farm animals, especially cattle and sheep, and flavoring their meat and their milk and the butter and cheese and other dairy products that are made from that milk. The quality of Irish grass has been remarked upon for centuries. Surveying Ireland in the late 1100s, Gerald of Wales correctly proposed that "this island is more productive in pasture than in corn, in grass than in grain." (Even today, 70 percent of Irish farmland is pasturage.) Visiting Killarney in 1775, English traveler Richard Twiss observed that the soil was "so rich as to fatten cattle almost into marrow in a very short time." Not quite two hundred years later, in County Tipperary, writer Marjorie Quarton heard an elderly farmer exclaim, as he gazed over a nearby plot of land, "Ah, that field would fatten a bicycle." Novelist J. P. Donleavy has evoked "chubby lambs and bullocks grazing . . . [and nurturing] themselves on grasses and herbs growing since Methuselah's time."

The Irish of an earlier era didn't eat a lot of those grazing animals, though; the beasts were more valuable for the *bánbhianna*, or "white meats"—dairy products—that they produced. When the Irish did slaughter them, it was almost always for a special occasion: a holiday or religious observance or a state banquet for a Celtic chieftain or an Anglo-Irish lord. Animals were generally roasted whole, often with honey and salt, and were commonly garnished with butter and watercress. What cut of meat you ate depended on your station in life. The ancient legal text the Senchus Mór (see page 304) specifies "A thigh for a king and a poet: a chine for a literary sage: a leg for a young lord: heads for charioteers:

a haunch for queens." A more prosaic version of this distribution, for the middle class, survives from the seventeenth century, giving "the head, tongue and feet to the smith . . . the neck to the butcher, two small ribs that go with the hindquarters to the tailor, the kidneys to the physician, the udder to the harper, the liver to the carpenter, and sweetbread to her that is with child."

Specialty beef and lamb producers around Ireland today are turning out meat of superb quality. Maurice Kettyle in Lisnaskea, County Fermanagh, raises sheep—a Suffolk-Cheviot and Dutch Texel cross—on islets in Lough Erne, and dry-ages their meat for ten days. He also butchers organically fed Angus and Hereford cattle, hand-selecting the meat for fat cover and internal marbling before selling it to some of Ireland's top restaurants. Joe and Eileen Condon raise "Omega beef" from Belted Galloway cattle, a heritage breed, in Clonmel, County Tipperary. Another Tipperary couple, Richard Auler and Stella Coffey, work with organic Angus at their Ladybird Organic Farm in Cahir. Paul Johnson specializes in heritage Dexter beef, from a native Irish breed, in Dunmanway, County Cork. The Burren Beef & Lamb Producers Group is a collective of producers in County Clare raising "conservation grade" beef and lamb with practices aimed at enhancing the Burren's incredible biodiversity. Their meat and that from other good sources is now in shops and on restaurant menus all over Ireland—proudly identified as Irish—and no meat-loving visitor to the island should go home without tasting a juicy Irish steak or piece of lamb.

NO "BROWN BEEF CONCOCTION"

Irish stew is the chili con carne, the paella, the tandoori chicken of Ireland—the emblematic dish, the one that seems (rightly or wrongly) to define an entire culture. Of course, as is the case with all definitive dishes, there is no definitive recipe. What kind of lamb does Irish stew contain, for starters? Mutton (see below), according to most sources. But what about neck chops (favored by Myrtle Allen)? breast? leg chops? shin or "scrag end"? Miscellaneous stew meat? Or is regular young lamb acceptable? I met a mother and daughter in County Antrim who have always made their Irish stew with mince, in this case ground lamb. There are even recipes that call for beef—and some food scholars believe that the dish was originally made with goat.

Next question: What, besides meat, goes into Irish stew? The basic recipe calls for little more than potatoes, onions, and water, plus maybe a little parsley. But I've seen versions that call for beef stock, Guinness stout, Worcestershire sauce, turnips, pumpkin, leeks, barley, thyme, and rosemary. Irish-American journalist Alexander Cockburn once went so far as to posit that without barley, "life—so far as Irish stew is concerned—lacks all meaning." But then, of course, he was born in Scotland. And there's the burning question of carrots. Some cooks think they're essential. Others would no sooner add them to their Irish stew than a right-thinking Texan would put beans in his chili or a Spaniard would make paella with instant rice. In his detective novel *The Price of Blood*, Dublin playwright, theatre director, and novelist Declan Hughes has his private detective, Ed Loy, note of an Irish stew he orders "[F]or once, it actually was Irish stew—mutton, potato, and onion in a white sauce—and not the brown beef concoction that often masqueraded in its place." And then there's this exchange in American thriller writer David Baldacci's *The Whole Truth*, which occurs as two of his main characters sit down to dinner in Dublin: "I still can't understand why Irish stew has no carrots," says one. "Even the British have carrots in their stew." The other replies. "And that's exactly why the Irish don't."

LAMB WITH SENIORITY

Mutton is old lamb—comparatively speaking, anyway. Though exact definitions vary from place to place, the meat of *Ovis aries* is usually considered spring lamb when it's younger than five months old (it is rarely sold at younger than three months, at least in the United States), and then becomes just plain lamb until its first birthday. Although the term is rarely used off the farm or outside the meat industry, hogget is the next stage, and refers to a sheep between the ages of one and two. Anything older than that is usually considered mutton. (Just to confuse things, in South Asia, *mutton* often means goat meat.)

Generally tougher than lamb and with a stronger flavor (from an increased concentration of fatty acids), mutton is generally not much appreciated in North America, and is difficult to find here. In Ireland, however, it is considered essential for real Irish stew and other stewed or braised lamb dishes—though it's also roasted like spring lamb. Theodora FitzGibbon, in her definitive book *Irish Traditional Food*, quotes a late-nineteenth-century French traveler to Ireland named Madame de Bovet, who, while mostly critical of the food she encountered, praised a baron of mutton with gravy that she was served one evening as "the only triumph of Irish cookery."

Ballyknocken Lamb Steaks Slow-Cooked in White Wine

Serves 8

The Byrne family has owned Ballyknocken Farm, in Ashford, County Wicklow, for three generations. Today, Catherine (Byrne) Fulvio runs the delightful Ballyknocken House (with five guest rooms) and Cookery School on the property, but it is still a working agricultural property. Wicklow lamb is famous all over Ireland, and Fulvio's, raised on the farm, is particularly flavorful. She serves it to guests frequently, and this is one of her favorite recipes.

3 TBSP BUTTER

1 TBSP EXTRA-VIRGIN OLIVE OIL

2 WHOLE HEADS GARLIC, UNPEELED, HALVED HORIZONTALLY, PLUS 8 CLOVES, UNPEELED, SLICED LENGTHWISE

1 BUNCH ROSEMARY

EIGHT 6- TO 8-OZ/175- TO 250-G LAMB STEAKS

SALT AND PEPPER

2 1/2 CUPS/600 ML DRY WHITE WINE

1 TBSP WHITE FLOUR

BALLYKNOCKEN GREEN MASHED POTATOES [PAGE 223] FOR SERVING [OPTIONAL]

MINT, ONION, AND APPLE CHUTNEY [PAGE 331] FOR SERVING [OPTIONAL]

Preheat the oven to 325°F/160°C (Gas Mark 3).

Melt 2 Tbsp of the butter with the oil in a large skillet over low heat. Add the sliced garlic cloves and rosemary and stir, crushing the garlic slightly into the butter and oil. Cook for about 5 minutes, then remove the garlic and rosemary from the skillet with a slotted spoon and set aside.

Season the lamb generously with salt and pepper. Increase the heat to medium-high and fry the lamb steaks for 3 to 4 minutes per side, or until well browned. Transfer the lamb to a baking dish large enough to hold them in a single layer with plenty of room at the sides. Put the garlic cloves and rosemary into the dish, then add the halved garlic heads, cut side up.

Bring the wine almost to a boil in a small pan over high heat, then pour over the lamb. Cover the lamb lightly with foil and roast for 45 minutes to an hour, or until the meat is very tender.

Remove the lamb from the dish and set aside on a plate, covering it loosely with foil. Remove the halved garlic heads from the dish and cut each one in half again Set aside. Strain the pan juices into a small bowl, pushing down on the sliced garlic cloves and rosemary with the back of a wooden spoon.

Melt the remaining 1 Tbsp of butter in a small saucepan over medium heat, then sprinkle in the flour, whisking constantly and cooking for about 1½ minutes to make a roux. Stir in the pan juices. Adjust the seasoning if necessary.

Serve the lamb garnished with pieces of garlic head. Serve with Ballyknocken Green Mashed Potatoes and Fulvio's Mint, Onion, and Apple Chutney, if you like.

Roast Leg of Lamb

Serves 6 to 8

It has been said that as roast beef is to England, roast lamb is to Ireland. If you have pan juices left over from this recipe, consider saving them to make Gerry Galvin's recipe for Roast Pike with Lamb Sauce, Lovage, and Bacon (page 84). Any leftover meat may be used for Jellied Lamb (page 168).

ONE 5- TO 6-LB/2.5- TO 3-KG LEG OF LAMB, TRIMMED OF EXCESS FAT

6 CLOVES GARLIC, PEELED AND QUARTERED LENGTHWISE

12 SMALL SPRIGS THYME

4 TBSP BUTTER, SOFTENED

SALT AND PEPPER

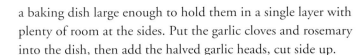

ROAST LEG OF LAMB

Preheat the oven to 500°F/260°C (Gas Mark 10).

With the tip of a small, sharp knife, make 24 small incisions all over the skin of the lamb. Push a quarter of a garlic clove into each of them. With the same knife, make 12 more incisions, evenly distributed around the leg, and push a sprig of thyme into each of them. Brush butter all over the lamb leg and season generously with salt and pepper.

Place the lamb on a low rack in a roasting pan and roast for 15 minutes.

Reduce the temperature to 350°F/175°C (Gas Mark 4) and continue to roast for about 1 hour for medium-rare lamb, basting occasionally. (For medium lamb, roast 20 minutes longer; for well-done lamb, roast another 20 minutes.)

Allow to rest for 15 to 20 minutes before carving.

Jellied Lamb

Serves 4 to 6

Florence Irwin, the "cookin' woman" who taught Northern Ireland's housewives the culinary arts in the early twentieth century and wrote a column on what were then called the "domestic sciences" for the *Northern Whig* for fifty years, identifies the recipe from which this one is adapted as her "second most popular recipe so far as my readers' letters showed" (she doesn't identify the most popular). This is a perfect way to use up the remains of a roasted leg of lamb (see page 166).

3 CUPS/720 ML LAMB OR BEEF STOCK [PAGE 357]

ONE 1/4-OZ/7-G PACKET POWDERED GELATIN

1/2 CUP/120 ML MINT SAUCE [PAGE 359]

1 CUP SHELLED FRESH PEAS
[ABOUT 1 LB/500 G PEAS IN PODS], COOKED

2 HARD-COOKED EGGS, 1 THINLY SLICED,
1 FINELY CHOPPED

1 TBSP CHOPPED FRESH PARSLEY

1/2 TO 3/4 LB/250 TO 375 G LEFTOVER COOKED
LAMB, FINELY CHOPPED

SALT AND PEPPER

Heat the stock in a medium saucepan over medium heat, then add the gelatin, stirring until it dissolves. Set aside to cool for about 10 minutes, then stir in the mint sauce.

Pour the stock into a glass or ceramic baking dish or terrine to a depth of about 1/2 in/1.25 cm and refrigerate until just set, 15 to 20 minutes. When set, scatter half the peas around the edge of the baking dish, arrange the egg slices in the center, and scatter the parsley between the two. Gently pour another 1/2-in/1.25-cm layer of stock over the peas, eggs, and parsley and allow to set in the refrigerator.

Meanwhile, add the lamb, the remaining peas, and the chopped egg to the remaining stock, season generously with salt and pepper, then gently pour over the gelled stock.

Chill until set, at least 1 hour, then unmold onto a serving plate.

Potted Meat

Serves 6 to 8

Though it's a technique usually applied to seafood, potting is also a way of preserving meat. Nineteenth-century Scottish novelist and poet Robert Louis Stevenson (of *Treasure Island* fame) wrote, "The traveller dines on potted meats; / On potted meats and princely wines, / Not wisely but too well he dines." There's also an exchange in Dublin-based novelist Tara French's mystery *The Likeness* in which one character asks, "What *is* potted meat?" and another replies, "Spam." Not so. You would do better to call this Irish pâté.

1 LB/500 G LEAN COOKED LAMB OR BEEF, SHREDDED
OR VERY FINELY CHOPPED

5 SLICES BACON; 4 FINELY CHOPPED, 1 LEFT WHOLE

2 TSP SALT

1/2 TSP PEPPER

1/4 TSP GROUND GINGER

1/4 TSP GROUND NUTMEG

1 1/4 CUPS/300 G BUTTER, MELTED,
PLUS MORE FOR GREASING

1 BAY LEAF

TOAST OR COUNTRY BREAD FOR SERVING

JELLIED LAMB

Preheat the oven to 300°F/150°C (Gas Mark 2).

Grease a 1-qt/1-L terrine or glass or ceramic baking dish with a lid and set aside.

Mix the lamb or beef, chopped bacon, salt, pepper, ginger, and nutmeg together in a large bowl, then transfer to the terrine. Pour the melted butter over the top, then gently stir the meat mixture to distribute the butter well and ensure there are no large gaps. Lay the remaining slice of bacon and bay leaf on top, then cover the terrine tightly with foil and put on the lid.

Put the terrine into a deep roasting pan, then pour in enough hot water to reach halfway up the sides of the dish. Bake, adding more water if necessary to maintain the same level, for 3 hours.

Remove the terrine from the water and set aside to cool to room temperature; then refrigerate, covered, until well chilled. Bring to room temperature before serving. Serve with toast or country bread, spreading the meat like pâté.

Irish Stew

Serves 6

I've eaten Irish stew in private homes and public eating places all over Ireland, north and south, probably twenty-five or thirty examples in all, and no two have been alike. (The most purely delicious example I remember came from Gleeson's Townhouse & Restaurant in Roscommon, though I suspect its appeal came not from any secret ingredient or magical cooking technique but from the flavor inherent in the raw materials that went into it. The very thick version offered at Belfast's historic Crown Liquor Saloon isn't bad, either.) Along the way, I've come to believe that the construction of this dish should

adhere to a few simple guidelines: (1) Given that you probably couldn't find mutton if you wanted it, at least not in America, use the best quality lamb you can find—locally raised farmers' market stuff, if possible—but use the less expensive, more flavorful cuts. (2) Keep it simple; improvisation is fine, and the world won't end if you add carrots or fresh thyme or whatever, but don't throw too many different things into the pot. (3) Cook it very slowly; an old adage has it that "a stew boiled is a stew spoiled." (4) Always make the stew 24 hours or so before you're going to serve it; a night in the refrigerator really will improve it. (5) As Theodora FitzGibbon notes, Irish stew is "frequently spoilt by too much liquid"; the finished product should be thick enough to stand a spoon in.

3 LB/1.5 KG MUTTON OR LAMB FROM THE NECK OR SHOULDER, TRIMMED AND CUT INTO CUBES

2 LB/1 KG RUSSET POTATOES, THICKLY SLICED

1/2 BUNCH PARSLEY, TRIMMED AND FINELY CHOPPED

1 LB/500 G ONIONS, THINLY SLICED

SALT AND PEPPER

Preheat the oven to 250°F/120°C (Gas Mark ½).

Put the lamb, potatoes, parsley, and onions into a heavy casserole with a lid and season generously with salt and pepper. (Or layer the ingredients, starting and ending with a layer of potatoes, and seasoning each layer to taste.)

Add 2 cups/475 ml of water or enough to barely cover the ingredients. Bring to a simmer over low heat (do not boil), then cover and put into the oven. Cook for 2½ to 3 hours or until the meat is very tender and the stew is thick, adding a little water if the stew dries out too much.

IRISH STEW

CONNEMARA LAMB

Almost anywhere you go in Ireland, if you go to the right homes or restaurants or butcher shops, you'll find locally raised lamb, proudly identified by its place of origin. County Wicklow is particularly famous for its lamb, and that from County Donegal has its partisans—as does the lamb of the Burren in County Clare, which feeds on wild herbs and wildflowers, some of them species unknown anywhere else in the world.

Arguably the best lamb in Ireland, though, and certainly the most unusual, is Connemara lamb from the mountains of northwestern County Galway. The Connemara lamb is a unique animal, descended from blackface sheep imported from Scotland in the nineteenth century, but bred, in these rocky fastnesses, into a smaller, leaner beast. Hardy and agile, these lambs feed on mountain herbs and grasses as they scramble up and down lush green slopes. The raw flesh of Connemara lamb is dark ruddy red in color, with little striation of fat. Cooked, the meat has extraordinary flavor, pronounced and intense without being gamy or muttony. Butcher James McGeough (facing page) from Oughterard turns Connemara lamb shoulder into a unique prosciutto-like cured meat, and restaurants around County Galway proudly feature Connemara lamb by name, especially in the fall. If you see it offered on a menu, don't even think about the pork chop or the monkfish.

Savory Mince

Serves 4

"This recipe came from my grandmother Elizabeth Hagan Millar, from Greenisland, County Antrim," says Irish quilt preservationist and collector Roselind Shaw. "She passed it on to my mother, Kathleen McClintock, who in turn passed it on to me. My mother used to make savory mince once a week, as I do to this day. Even though I have been to catering college in Belfast and the Cordon Bleu school in London, where I learned many interesting recipes, this simple one is my favorite of all." Bisto, beefy-flavored "gravy granules" (they actually contain no beef), is an essential of the British home kitchen.

3 TO 4 TBSP CORN OR CANOLA OIL

1 1/2 LB/750G GROUND BEEF

1 LARGE CARROT, THINLY SLICED

1 LARGE PARSNIP, THINLY SLICED

2 SMALL ONIONS, HALVED

2 TSP CORN FLOUR

2 TSP BISTO [SEE SOURCES, PAGE 369]

MASHED POTATOES [PAGE 223] FOR SERVING

Heat the oil over medium heat in a large skillet, and brown the ground beef, breaking it up into small pieces with a wooden spoon as it cooks.

Add the carrot, parsnip, and onion halves. Add water to cover and simmer for about 30 minutes, adding a bit more water if the mixture dries out.

Stir the corn flour and Bisto into ½ cup/120 ml of cold water until they dissolve. Add to the ground beef mixture, stir in well, and cook for about 5 minutes more. The finished mince should be like a thick stew in consistency.

Serve with mashed potatoes.

[Raw] Beef Sandwiches

Serves 4

This is one of the more unusual but appealing recipes from a household manuscript (the National Library in Dublin has a microfilm copy), apparently from the 1920s, by F. Eva Wisdom, "teacher of cooking, laundry, and other things." Wisdom lived in Rathmines, a suburb of Dublin, where she worked as a nurse, and at Wilmont House in Castlebridge, County Wexford. Prominent Irish philosopher J. O. Wisdom was her nephew, and her cousins, the Nunn family, owned a grand local house called Castlebridge Ho—at which, in 1954, the *Guinness Book of Records* was conceived: Two men hunting on the property, one of them Sir Hugh Beaver, then managing director of Guinness, had a friendly argument over whether the grouse or the golden plover was the world's fastest game bird (it turned out to be neither, but rather the Canadian long-tailed duck), and it occurred to Beaver that a compendium of similar statistics might find an audience.

1/4 LB/125G ROUND STEAK

SALT AND PEPPER

2 TBSP BUTTER, SOFTENED

16 SLICES THIN WHITE BREAD

1 TO 2 TBSP RED CURRANT JELLY

Grind the round steak finely in a meat grinder or pulse in a food processor until very fine but not quite a paste. Season the meat generously with salt and pepper, mixing them in well.

Butter all the bread slices on one side, then spread a very light film of red currant jelly over the butter on 8 of the slices.

Spread ground meat over the butter on the 8 slices of bread without the currant jelly, dividing it evenly between them and smoothing it down with a knife.

Assemble sandwiches, press them together, and cut off the crusts.

To serve, cut into fingers or (says Wisdom) "fancy shapes."

MAC CONGLINNE'S MENU

Aislinge Meic Con Glinne, or "The Vision of Mac Conglinne," is a rambling, colorful parody on inspirational texts, probably composed in the eleventh century. Satirical value aside, it happens to be a treasure trove of detail about the medieval Irish diet. The plot involves efforts by Aniér Mac Conglinne, a scholar from Armagh, to rid King Cathal Mac Finguine of a "demon of gluttony" that has taken up residence in his throat. Under the demon's power, Cathal consumes gargantuan meals, once putting away "a pig and a cow and a bull-calf of three hands, with three score cakes of pure wheat, and a vat of new ale, and thirty heathpoults' eggs"—and that was just as a snack before dinner. Clearly, thinks Mac Conglinne, this kind of thing has to stop.

In the course of his attempts to aid the monarch, our hero enjoys a vision in which, among other things, he visits a fortress "With works of custards thick . . . New butter was the bridge in front, the rubble dyke was wheaten white, bacon the palisade. . . . The door of it was dry meat, The threshold was bare bread, cheese-curds the sides." He also constructs a genealogy of food, which reads in part, "Son of honey-bag, son of juice, son of lard, son of stirabout, son of pottage, son of fair speckled fruitclusters, son of smooth clustering cream, son of buttermilk, son of curds, son of beer (glory of liquors!) . . . Son of twisted leek, son of bacon, son of butter, of full-fat sausage, son of pure new milk, of nut-fruit, son of tree-fruit, son of gravy, son of dripping, of fat, son of kidney, son of rib, son of shoulder, of well-filled gullet, son of leg, son of loin . . . son of cheese without decrease, of fish of Inver Indsén . . . son of fair oatmeal gruel, of sprouty meat-soup, with its purple berries, of the top of effeminate kale."

Finally, Mac Conglinne convinces Cathal to fast for two consecutive nights, then has the king tied up in his palace and, dressed like a chef, cooks a succulent meal to taunt the demon into abandoning his berth: "And he [Conglinne] called for juicy old bacon, and tender corned-beef, and full-fleshed wether, and honey in the comb, and English salt on a beautiful polished dish of white silver, along with four perfectly straight white hazel spits to support the joints. . . . Then putting a linen apron about him below, and placing a flat linen cap on the crown of his head, he lighted a fair four-ridged, four-apertured, four-cleft fire of ash-wood, without smoke, without fume, without sparks. He stuck a spit into each of the portions. . . . He rubbed the honey and the salt into one piece after another. And big as the pieces were that were before the fire, there dropped not to the ground out of these four pieces as much as would quench a spark of a candle; but what there was of relish in them went into their very center. And when this was ended . . . he stuck the spits into the bed before Cathal's eyes, and sat himself down in his seat, with his two legs crossed. Then taking his knife out of his girdle, he cut a bit off the piece that was nearest to him, and dipped it in the honey that was on the aforesaid dish of white silver." Between the aromas of the meat and the details of his vision, which he relates to Cathal, the demon is finally tempted forth, and, after muttering imprecations, flies away.

CORNED BEEF WITH PARSLEY SAUCE

Corned Beef with Parsley Sauce

Serves 4

This classic presentation of one of Ireland's most emblematic meats is served by Kay Harte at her indispensible Farmgate Café, overlooking the daily bustle at the English Market in Cork. Harte's parsley sauce is more subtle than Theodora FitzGibbon's version (page 360), but the latter may also be used for this dish. Use the recipe for Brine for Meats (page 361) with bottom round if you want to make your own corned beef. Serve with simply steamed cabbage, if you like, or with Champ (page 221), Colcannon (page 219), Carrot and Parsnip Mash (page 251), Glazed Carrots (page 251), Broccoli in Butter (page 251), and/or any other vegetable you favor.

2 LB/1 KG CORNED BEEF, PREFERABLY BOTTOM ROUND [SOMETIMES LABELED "SILVERSIDE" OR BRISKET]

2 CARROTS, CHOPPED

1 ONION, CHOPPED

2 TBSP BUTTER

2 TBSP WHITE FLOUR

3/4 CUP/175 ML MILK

2 TSP MINCED FRESH PARSLEY

1/2 TSP ENGLISH MUSTARD

PINCH OF NUTMEG

SALT AND PEPPER

Put the corned beef, carrots, and all but about 1 Tbsp of the onion into a large pot, cover with water, and bring to a boil over high heat. Reduce the heat to medium-low, and skim the foam from the surface of the water. Cover and simmer for about 2½ hours, or until the corned beef is tender. Remove from the liquid, wrap in foil, and set aside. Reserve about ¾ cup/175 ml of the cooking liquid.

Melt the butter in a small saucepan over medium heat. Mince the reserved onion and add to the butter. Cook for about 1 minute, then whisk in the flour and cook for about 1 minute more. Add the reserved cooking liquid, milk, parsley, mustard, nutmeg, and salt and pepper to taste, whisking the ingredients together until smooth. Cook 4 for 5 minutes more, whisking constantly, until the sauce thickens.

To serve, slice the corned beef and spoon the sauce over it.

Pink Lunch Pancake

Serves 2 to 4

In her 1947 book *Further Culinary Adventures*, Lady Pim—wife of Sir Richard Pim, inspector-general of the Royal Ulster Constabulary in the late 1940s—credits the recipe for this version of corned beef hash to Mrs. Frazer Mackie of Woodgarth, Newtownards, County Down.

1 MEDIUM ONION, MINCED

2 CUPS/450 G COOKED CORNED BEEF [AT LEFT] IN 1/4-IN/6.5-MM CUBES

2 CUPS/400 G BOILED POTATOES [PAGE 229] IN 1/4-IN/6.5-MM CUBES

2 CUPS/400 G COOKED BEETS IN 1/4-IN/6.5-MM CUBES

SALT AND PEPPER

1 EGG, LIGHTLY BEATEN

OIL FOR GREASING

Bring a small pot of salted water to a boil, then parboil the onion for about 3 minutes. When cool enough to handle, mince the onion.

In a large bowl, combine the onion, corned beef, potato, and beets, season to taste, and mix together well. Stir in the beaten egg.

Put a large, lightly greased nonstick skillet over medium-high heat, then add the corned beef mixture, forming it into a round cake about the size of a large dinner plate. Fry for 2 to 3 minutes or until nicely browned on the bottom. Place a large dinner plate on top of the mixture and turn the pan over to flip the pancake onto the plate. Carefully slide the pancake back into the pan, browned side up, and brown the underside for 2 to 3 minutes.

SPICED BEEF

Spiced Beef

Serves 10 to 12

This specialty of Cork, where it is particularly associated with the Christmas season, is just what its name suggests: beef (sometimes ox tongue) marinated or pickled in spices, almost always including peppercorns, allspice, and juniper. Salt and sugar, and sometimes vinegar or stout, are added as preservatives. Old recipes always called for saltpeter, later replaced by Prague powder, a sausage maker's concoction of salt and sodium nitrite. If you're going to eat your spiced beef within a week or so of making it, salt and sugar should be sufficient. Serve with a green salad or homemade chutney and soda bread, if you like.

2 TBSP WHOLE ALLSPICE BERRIES

2 TBSP WHOLE JUNIPER BERRIES

2 TBSP WHOLE BLACK PEPPERCORNS

2 TBSP CORIANDER SEEDS

2 TBSP BROWN SUGAR

2 TBSP TREACLE [SEE SOURCES, PAGE 369]
OR MOLASSES

1/2 CUP/125 G SALT

ONE 3- TO 4-LB/1.5- TO 2-KG BONELESS EYE OF
BEEF ROUND OR BRISKET, TIED INTO A COMPACT
SHAPE WITH KITCHEN TWINE

1 ONION, THICKLY SLICED

1 CARROT, COARSELY CHOPPED

Grind the allspice, juniper, peppercorns, and coriander seeds together in a spice mill or food processor until fine. Transfer to a medium bowl, add the brown sugar, treacle, and salt and mix well.

Rub the spice mixture all over over the surface of the beef and into any crevices. Put the beef into a nonreactive dish or bowl just wide enough to hold it, cover it tightly, and refrigerate for 1 week, turning it once a day.

Put the onion and carrot in the bottom of a pot wide enough to hold the beef, then put the beef on top of the vegetables. Add enough cold water to cover the beef, bring to a boil over high heat, then reduce the heat to low and simmer, covered,

until the beef is tender, occasionally skimming off any foam that rises to the surface. (The beef will take 3 to 5 hours to become tender, depending on the cut and quality of the meat.)

Remove the beef from the liquid, allow it to cool to room temperature, then put it into a nonreactive rectangular pan just big enough to hold it. Cut a piece of thick cardboard so it will just fit over the beef, wrap the cardboard in foil, and put it on top of the beef. Weigh the cardboard down with heavy cans or other weights and return the beef to the refrigerator for 12 to 24 hours.

To serve, remove the twine and cut the beef into thin slices.

Pot Roast of Brisket

Serves 4

Brisket is often corned in Ireland, but it is also appreciated in its native form; a tough but flavorful cut, it lends itself particularly well to long, slow pot-roasting. Serve with mashed or boiled potatoes, if you like.

1/2 TSP POWDERED MUSTARD

1 TSP CHOPPED FRESH THYME

SALT AND PEPPER

1/3 CUP/35 G WHITE FLOUR

ONE 2-LB/1-KG BEEF BRISKET

2 TBSP BUTTER

2 ONIONS, DICED

3 CARROTS, DICED

1/2 CUP/120 ML GUINNESS OR MURPHY'S STOUT

1/2 CUP/120 ML BEEF STOCK [PAGE 357]

MASHED [PAGE 223] OR BOILED POTATOES
[PAGE 229] FOR SERVING [OPTIONAL]

Mix the mustard, thyme, and flour together on a large plate, then season generously with salt and pepper. Roll the brisket in the flour mixture to coat it on all sides.

Melt the butter over medium-high heat in a heavy-bottomed pot large enough to hold the brisket. Cook the brisket on all

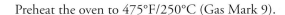

sides for 3 to 4 minutes per side or until it is well browned, then remove from the pot and set aside.

Put the onions and carrots in the pot and cook, stirring frequently, for 5 to 6 minutes, or until they begin to brown. Season to taste with salt and pepper.

Increase the heat to high and deglaze the pot with beer and stock, stirring well and scraping up the browned bits on the bottom. Set the brisket on top of the vegetables, reduce the heat to low, and cover the pot tightly. Simmer for about 2½ hours, or until the meat is very tender, turning about halfway through cooking. Check the meat occasionally, and pour a bit more stock or water into the pan if it gets too dry.

To serve, slice the brisket and arrange on a warmed platter, then drizzle the pan juices over it.

Roast Prime Rib of Beef

Serves 8 to 10

There is a tradition that one day, back in the sixth century, the celebrated St. Columcille of County Donegal roasted an ox for a couple of his companions. The first one fell on the beast and consumed it all, leaving the second one hungry. In a meaty variation on the parable of the loaves and fishes, Columcille blessed the animal's bones, upon which they reassembled themselves and filled again with roasted meat. Whole ox roasting has gone out of fashion today, but roast prime rib of beef on the bone became the traditional Sunday afternoon dinner in the Anglo-Irish manor houses in later centuries, and is still enjoyed today.

ONE 6- TO 8-LB/3- TO 4-KG PRIME RIB OF BEEF,
WITH UPPER CHINE BONE SAWED THROUGH
[ASK YOUR BUTCHER]

SALT AND PEPPER

3 CUPS/720 ML BEEF STOCK [PAGE 357]

HORSERADISH SAUCE [PAGE 358] FOR SERVING

Preheat the oven to 475°F/250°C (Gas Mark 9).

Score the fat with a sharp knife, then season the roast generously all over with salt and pepper. Place on a rack in a roasting pan with the fat side up and roast for 15 minutes, then lower the oven temperature to 350°F/175°C (Gas Mark 4) and continue roasting until the meat is cooked to your taste (about 10 minutes per pound for rare, 12 minutes per pound for medium-rare).

Remove roast from pan and set aside to rest for at least 20 minutes before carving, reserving pan juices in pan.

When pan juices have cooled slightly, skim off fat, then put pan on stovetop over high heat and deglaze with stock, stirring constantly, until liquid reduces by about one-half.

Carve the beef tableside and serve with the beef-stock gravy and horseradish sauce on the side.

Seared Filet Mignon with Jameson Sauce and Mushrooms

Serves 4

This dish is served, in one variation or another, at good restaurants all over Ireland.

3 TO 4 TBSP CANOLA OIL

1/2 LB/250 G MUSHROOMS, SLICED

1 CLOVE GARLIC, MINCED

SALT AND PEPPER

FOUR 6-OZ/175-G FILETS MIGNON

1/2 CUP/120 ML JAMESON
OR ANOTHER IRISH WHISKEY

1/2 CUP/120 ML HEAVY CREAM OR CRÈME FRAÎCHE

1/2 CUP/120 ML BEEF STOCK [SEE PAGE 357]

1 TBSP MINCED FRESH PARSLEY

Heat the oil in a heavy medium skillet over medium heat, then add the mushrooms and garlic. Season to taste with salt and pepper and cook, stirring frequently, for 8 to 10 minutes or until the mushrooms have given up their liquor.

Remove the mushrooms from the pan and set aside. Wipe out the pan and return to the heat, increasing it to high. Sear the filets on each side for about 1 minute, adding more oil to pan if necessary. Reduce the heat to medium and cook for about 4 minutes longer on each side for medium-rare.

Remove the steaks from the pan and set aside.

Pour the whiskey into the pan, warm it for about a minute, then carefully ignite it with a kitchen match. When the flames die down, scrape up any browned bits on the bottom of the pan. Add the cream or crème fraîche, stock, and parsley, stir well, and cook over high heat for 3 to 4 minutes. Add the mushrooms and continue cooking until the sauce thickens slightly. Adjust the seasoning if necessary.

Divide the steaks between 4 plates and spoon the sauce and mushrooms over them.

Veal Olives

Serves 4

"Olives" made of veal or beef are a French import, known in the better kitchens of England and Ireland at least since the mid-eighteenth century. The French call them *paupiettes* (originally from the Latin *pulpa*, "flesh"), or *alouettes sans têtes* ("headless larks," for their appearance). Since these little bundles of meat wrapped around a filling don't particularly resemble the fruit of the olive tree, it is thought that *olive* might be an English corruption of *alouettes*.

8 TO 12 VERY THIN VEAL SCALLOPS
[ABOUT 1 LB/500 G IN ALL]

1/4 CUP/15 G FRESH BREAD CRUMBS

1 ONION, MINCED

ZEST OF 1 LEMON

2 ANCHOVIES, MINCED

1 TBSP CHOPPED FRESH PARSLEY

1/2 TSP GROUND NUTMEG

2 EGG YOLKS, BEATEN

SALT AND PEPPER

2 TBSP BUTTER

1/4 CUP/25 G WHITE FLOUR

2 CUPS/475 ML BEEF STOCK [PAGE 357]

In a small bowl of cold water, soak as many wooden toothpicks as you have veal scallops.

Working in batches, put the veal scallops between 2 sheets of plastic wrap and pound with a kitchen mallet or the bottom of a heavy pan to flatten them until they are as thin as possible.

Mix together the bread crumbs, onion, lemon zest, anchovies, parsley, nutmeg, and about two-thirds of the egg yolks in a medium bowl. Season to taste with salt and pepper.

Lay the veal scallops out in a single layer on a board and brush one side of each one lightly with the remaining egg yolk.

Divide the filling evenly between the veal scallops, putting it in the center of each and flattening it slightly with the back of a spoon. Make "olives" by folding over 2 opposite sides of each scallop, then rolling it tightly from one unfolded side to the other. Secure each olive with a toothpick.

Melt the butter in a medium skillet over medium-high heat. Roll the olives lightly in the flour, then fry for 2 to 3 minutes per side until well browned on all sides. Remove the olives from the pan, then increase the heat to high and deglaze the pan with the stock, scraping up the browned bits on the bottom. Immediately reduce the heat to low, return the olives to the pan, cover, and simmer for 40 minutes, turning the olives in the liquid every 10 minutes.

To serve, remove the toothpicks from the olives and divide between 4 plates. Strain the pan juices and drizzle a little over the olives.

Boneless Oxtail Braised in Guinness

Serves 4

Oxtail is traditionally cooked in red wine, but Guinness stout makes a good substitute. Serve with buttered colcannon or champ.

4 TBSP BUTTER

I TBSP CANOLA OIL

5 TO 6 LB/2.5 TO 3 KG OXTAIL, CUT INTO 12 TO 16 PIECES TOTAL

2 ONIONS, CHOPPED

2 CARROTS, THINLY SLICED

2 TBSP WHITE FLOUR

I BOTTLE GUINNESS STOUT

I CUP GOOD-QUALITY CHOPPED OR PURÉED CANNED ITALIAN SAN MARZANO TOMATOES

2 BAY LEAVES

SALT AND PEPPER

BUTTERED COLCANNON [PAGE 219] OR CHAMP [PAGE 221] FOR SERVING

Preheat the oven to 350°F/175°C (Gas Mark 4).

Melt the butter with the oil over medium-high heat in a Dutch oven or flameproof casserole with a lid. Brown the oxtails on both sides, working in batches if necessary. As they brown, remove from the Dutch oven and set aside.

Reduce the heat to medium and put the onions and carrots into the Dutch oven, adding more oil if necessary. Cook, stirring frequently, for 10 to 12 minutes or until the onions and carrots soften and begin to brown. Sprinkle the flour over them and stir it in well. Return the browned oxtails to the pot, then add the Guinness and tomatoes and enough water to just cover all the ingredients, stirring everything together well.

Add the bay leaves to the oxtails and season to taste with salt and pepper. Cover the Dutch oven tightly and cook the oxtails for 4 hours, stirring the contents about every 45 minutes.

Remove the oxtails from the liquid and spread out on a baking sheet to cool. When cool enough to handle, pull the meat from the bones with your fingers or a knife and fork, saving the bones for stock. (If using your fingers, be very careful: the bones can be sharp.)

Return the meat to the Dutch oven or casserole dish and mix it in well. Cook over medium heat for 5 to 6 minutes to heat through. The liquid should be thick and dark. If it's still too thin, simmer, uncovered, over low heat, stirring frequently, for 20 to 30 minutes, or until it thickens.

CORNED BEEF AND CABBAGE

Asked to name one Irish dish, most Americans, if they didn't say "Irish stew," would say "corned beef and cabbage." This simple but hearty specialty became associated indelibly with the Irish-American community, and especially with American St. Patrick's Day celebrations, in the late nineteenth and early twentieth centuries. Helping its popularity was undoubtedly the George McManus comic strip "Bringing Up Father," which debuted in 1913. It featured a transplanted Irishman in New York named Jiggs, who preferred eating corned beef and cabbage at his friend Dinty Moore's tavern to stepping out with his social-climbing wife, Maggie.

A good many authorities these days take pleasure in announcing that corned beef and cabbage isn't a real Irish dish at all. Supposedly, it was developed by immigrants to the eastern United States in the nineteenth century as a substitute for their beloved bacon and cabbage because bacon in the Irish sense (which is to say cured pork loin) wasn't available here. I don't believe that for a minute. Let's leave aside the question of why the Irish couldn't have found an acceptable substitute for their bacon in East Coast cities that were full of German and Polish butchers (surely central European smoked pork was more like Irish bacon than beef pickled with spices and salt). The fact is that corned beef has been eaten, with and without cabbage, in Ireland since at least the 1600s. Under the name "salt beef" it was even exported in large quantities from Cork to continental Europe, the West Indies, and Newfoundland. I'll give the final word to eminent Irish historian and folklorist Bríd Mahon, who writes in her book *The Land of Milk and Honey*, "While Irish beef has always been noted for its flavour, corned beef was equally relished. Boiled and served with green cabbage and floury potatoes, it was considered an epicurean dish to be eaten at Halloween, at Christmas, on St. Patrick's Day, at weddings and at wakes, a tradition that was carried to the New World by the emigrants of the 18th and 19th centuries."

COW COUNTRY

The phrase "sacred cow" has come into our language from the observation that cattle are treated with great reverence in India. It might just as well have derived from Ireland. St. Patrick once declared that the three most heinous crimes imaginable were the killing of trained oxen, the rustling of cattle, and the burning of byres (cow barns) and cattle enclosures. In the early seventeenth century, English traveler Fynes Moryson noted of the Irish that "they watchfully keep their cows, and fight for them as for religion and life; and when they are almost starved, yet they will not kill a cow except it be old and yield no milk. Yet will they upon hunger, in time of war, open a vein of the cow and drink the blood, but in no case kill or much weaken it." (In drinking blood from a live cow, which they often mixed with its milk, the ancient Irish showed an unlikely kinship with the Masai people of Kenya and Tanzania, who do the same thing in tribal villages to this day.)

Cattle raising was a central part of Irish life in ancient times, but so was cattle raiding, which became practically the national pastime. Cattle were a measure of wealth and prestige—it wouldn't have been unusual for a prominent chieftain to run five or six thousand head—so to harm your enemy or express your disrespect to him, you stole his cows. One of the most famous of Irish epics is "Táin Bó Cúailnge," literally "The Driving-Off of Cooley's Cows," but popularly known as "The Cattle Raid of Cooley." It tells the tale of attempts by Queen Medb (who was later slain with a hard cheese hurled from a sling) and her husband, Ailill, to steal a prized stud bull from her enemies in Ulster. The tale has continued to inspire storytellers: Irish rock group Horslips released a concept album called *The Táin* in 1973, composer Terry Riley interpreted the epic in his 1987 saxophone piece "Chanting the Light of Foresight," and alternative band the Decembrists devoted a 2003 EP to a five-part retelling of the story.

Farmers at a cattle auction, Nenagh, County Tipperary.

GAME

Wild Ireland

[O]n the sides of these hills I wonder'd to see some hundreds of stately red deer,
the stags bigger than a large English calfe.

—John Dunton, *Teague Land, Or a Merry Ramble to the Wild Irish* [1698]

The game larder, too, was full all the winter with pheasant, snipe and other game,
hung the exact number of days to make them just right for the table.

—Alison, Lady Rosse, on Birr Castle in the 1940s, in *Traditional Country House Cooking* [1993]

Since prehistoric times, inhabitants of Ireland—an island once overrun with wild creatures, both furred and feathered—have been expert hunters, bringing down wild boar and red deer with spears and later with bows

and arrows and the help of trained hunting dogs, and taking wild birds in traps and (in medieval times) by falconry. One early game recipe appears in the humorous, food-filled utopian fantasy "Land of Cokaygne," written by Brother Hugh Fitz-Bernard, the so-called Grey Friar of Kildare, around 1315: "The larks, which are renowned, come down to man's mouth fully dressed in a great stewpan, sprinkled with clove and cinnamon."

Game birds of a kind figured in a minor but significant episode in Irish history: At Christmastime in 1171 or 1172 (accounts differ), when the English king, Henry II, received the submission of the Irish chieftains at Dublin Castle, he entertained them in a temporary palace built of painted wicker-work in the Irish style outside the castle walls. This may have seemed like a conciliatory gesture—but at the banquet he served them, the pièce de résistance was roasted crane, a bird hunted and enjoyed at table by the English but (as Henry must have known) not eaten by the Irish, who thought that cranes sometimes carried the reincarnated souls of their ancestors. Gerald of Wales, a contemporary of Henry's, maintained that the chieftains at that moment "learnt to eat cranes, a species of food which they had previously loathed," and in general were impressed with the greatness and glory of their conqueror. The Irish, on the other hand, are more likely to believe that the chieftains refused the bird's flesh and left the banquet with reinforced disdain for the English.

Rabbit isn't really game, of course, at least not today when virtually all of it is factory- or farmyard-raised (just like chicken), but it would have been trapped or shot in Ireland in earlier times, and often ended up in the soup pot or braised as "frigasse." Hare, on the other hand, has never been very popular in Ireland, though it was reckoned to make a good soup ("You can eat the soup but not the meat," it was said).

Wild porcines were once so numerous in Ireland that Gerald of Wales declared that "In no part of the world are such vast herds of boars and wild pigs to be found." Deer were also plentiful, and venison was regarded highly enough that it was one of the foods specified as a tribute due annually to the Irish king—specifically the venison of Naas—along with the fish of the Boyne and the cresses of the Brosna. Good restaurants in Ireland today still serve wild-shot deer meat in season, but it is also common to find farm-raised Finnebrogue Oisín venison from Northern Ireland, whose flesh is very flavorful as well.

STONE HOT COOKING

The *fulacht fiadh*—which means either "cooking pit of the Fian warriors [followers of Finn McCool]" or, more likely, "cooking pit of the deer"—is the most common type of archeological site in Ireland. The remains of *fulachtaí* (the plural form) survive as arrangements of stones, usually around an indentation in the earth. They are found all over the island, but particularly in counties Waterford, Tipperary, Kilkenny, Clare, and Cork (the last of which can claim more than 2,000 of the 4,500 or so known to exist). There are many references to spit-roasting deer and other animals in old Irish texts, but the pits were sometimes also used as massive outdoor ovens, with meat wrapped in hay or straw cooked between layers of hot stones. And the Irish developed another technique, as well: Some of the pits were filled with water (these were usually dug near bodies of water or in marshy lands so the water may simply have seeped in). Stones heated on an open fire were tossed in, bringing the water to a boil, and then the meat was added and simmered until it was done.

Caiman O'Brien, an archeologist with the National Monuments Service based in Nenagh, County Tipperary, warns against misinterpreting the *fulachtaí*. To begin with, he says, they're not exclusively Irish, but exist all over Northern Europe. And he notes that the proper term for the remains isn't "cooking pits" but "burnt mounds." "They were an example of hot-stone technology," he says, "which could be used for several things besides cooking: tanning leather, working metal, brewing beer, even producing steam for sweat lodges."

Nonetheless, you *can* cook in them. In 1952, Limerick-born archeologist M. J. O'Kelly and his colleagues restored one of the pits, at Ballyvourney, County Cork, and experimented with the technique, successfully poaching, to perfect doneness, a 10-lb/5-kg leg of mutton, wrapped in straw, in 3 hours and 40 minutes—exactly the 20 minutes per pound plus 20 recommended in many modern recipes for cooking the same cut of meat.

BRAISED RABBIT

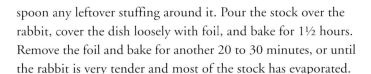

Stuffed Rabbit Armagh Style

Serves 4

I don't know the origins of this recipe, in which the rabbit is stuffed and pot-roasted, or even whether it is really typical of Armagh, but it appears in Mary Caherty's little book *Real Irish Cookery*, and has been widely appropriated in other recipe collections.

4 TBSP BUTTER

1 ONION, CHOPPED

2 COOKING APPLES, PEELED, CORED, AND CHOPPED

1 CUP/60 G FRESH BREAD CRUMBS

1 TBSP CHOPPED FRESH PARSLEY

1 TSP CHOPPED FRESH THYME

1 TSP SUGAR

1 EGG, BEATEN

ONE 3- TO 4-LB/1.5 KG- TO 2-KG WHOLE RABBIT [COMPLETELY THAWED IF FROZEN], WASHED AND DRIED INSIDE AND OUT

1^1/$_2$ CUPS/360 ML CHICKEN OR RABBIT STOCK [PAGE 356]

SALT AND PEPPER

Preheat the oven to 350°F/175°C (Gas Mark 4).

Melt 2 Tbsp of the butter in a medium skillet over medium-low heat, add the onion, and cook, stirring occasionally, for about 10 minutes. Add the apples and continue cooking for 10 to 15 minutes more, or until the apples are very soft.

Put the onion-apple mixture into a large bowl, then stir in the bread crumbs, parsley thyme, sugar, and egg. Season the mixture generously with salt and pepper.

Melt the remaining 2 Tbsp of butter in the same skillet over medium-high heat, then add the stuffing and cook for 3 to 4 minutes, stirring constantly. Set aside to cool.

When the stuffing is cool enough to handle, pack it loosely into the cavity of the rabbit. Put the rabbit into a baking dish and spoon any leftover stuffing around it. Pour the stock over the rabbit, cover the dish loosely with foil, and bake for 1½ hours. Remove the foil and bake for another 20 to 30 minutes, or until the rabbit is very tender and most of the stock has evaporated.

To serve, cut the rabbit into serving pieces with poultry shears. Put the stuffing in the middle of a serving dish and arrange the rabbit over it.

Braised Rabbit

Serves 4

Rabbit was a staple of Irish country kitchens in earlier times. A dish like this would have been cooked over the fire in a cast-iron bastable, or pot-oven (see page 287).

1 ONION, FINELY CHOPPED

3 CARROTS, FINELY CHOPPED

ONE 2^1/$_2$- TO 3-LB/1- TO 1.5-KG RABBIT, CUT INTO 6 SERVING PIECES

1 CUP/240 ML HARD CIDER

1 SPRIG FRESH THYME

3 TBSP CANOLA OR SUNFLOWER OIL

1 TBSP WHITE FLOUR

2 CUPS/475 ML CHICKEN OR RABBIT STOCK [PAGE 356]

SALT AND PEPPER

Put half the onion and half the carrots on the bottom of a nonreactive bowl or baking dish just large enough to hold the rabbit pieces in one layer. Lay the rabbit on top, then press the remaining onions and carrots lightly into the meat. Pour the cider over the rabbit and press the thyme sprig down lightly into the meat. Cover the bowl and marinate the rabbit for about 24 hours in the refrigerator, turning 2 or 3 times.

Preheat the oven to 350°F/175°C (Gas Mark 4).

Remove the rabbit from the marinade. Strain the marinade, reserving the cider and vegetables separately. Pat the rabbit dry.

Heat the oil in a Dutch oven or another heavy-bottomed oven-proof pot over high heat. Fry the rabbit, turning frequently, for 6 to 8 minutes, or until browned on all sides. Remove the rabbit from the Dutch oven and set aside. Reduce the heat to low, add the reserved vegetables, and cook, stirring frequently, for 10 to 12 minutes, or until the vegetables are soft and starting to brown. Sprinkle flour over the vegetables and stir well.

Slowly pour in the reserved cider and then the stock, stirring well. Season to taste with salt and pepper, then return the rabbit to the Dutch oven, turning it over in the liquid so that it is well coated. Cover the pot and braise the rabbit in the oven for 30 minutes. Lower the temperature to 300°F/150°C (Gas Mark 2), turn the rabbit pieces over in liquid and cook for another 1½ hours, turning the rabbit every 30 minutes.

Roast Loin of Venison

Serves 4 to 6

Legend has it that when St. Patrick died, sometime in the latter fifth century, two oxen from Finnebrogue, near Down-patrick, County Down, were harnassed to pull his funeral cart, and that he was buried where they stopped, unbidden by a drover. Today, Finnebrogue Estate is famous for animals of a different kind: red deer, raised for Finnebrogue Ois'in venison, an excellent meat found on some of the best restaurant tables of Ireland and the United Kingdom. The Finnebrogue deer, slaughtered between the ages of nine and twenty-one months (*ois'in* is Irish for "fawn"), aren't exactly wild, but they range free over a 600-acre/243-hectares property feeding on a natural diet. Their meat is tender and delicious, if not as gamy as some connoisseurs would like. Finnebrogue is worth ordering if you encounter it on an Irish menu. Unfortunately, it is not available in the United States, though good-quality farmed venison is (see page 369). This is a classic recipe.

TWO 12- TO 16-OZ/375- TO 500-G
VENISON TENDERLOINS

SALT AND COARSELY GROUND BLACK PEPPER

4 SLICES BACON, COARSELY CHOPPED

1 TBSP EXTRA-VIRGIN OLIVE OIL

1 TBSP CRUSHED JUNIPER BERRIES

1 SPRIG FRESH ROSEMARY

1 SPRIG FRESH THYME

1 ½ CUPS/360 ML RED WINE

4 TBSP BUTTER

1 TBSP ARROWROOT

Preheat oven to 350°F/175°C (Gas Mark 4).

Rub venison loins all over with salt and pepper. Tie the loins together with kitchen twine to make one loin and set aside.

Cook bacon in a heavy ovenproof skillet over medium-high heat until crisp, then remove the bacon and drain on paper towels. Add the olive oil to the skillet, then add the juniper, rosemary, and thyme. Cook for 1 minute over medium-high heat. Add the venison loin and brown well on all sides, about 5 minutes.

Roast the venison in the skillet for 25 to 30 minutes, or until the internal temperature is 125°F/50°C.

Meanwhile, bring the red wine to a boil in a heavy-bottom saucepan over medium-high heat and continue boiling until reduced by half. Season with salt and pepper to taste. Reduce the heat to low and whisk in the butter 1 Tbsp at a time. Dissolve the arrowroot in ⅓ cup/80 ml cool water. Stir the mixture into the red wine sauce and cook for 2 or 3 minutes, stirring frequently, until the sauce begins to thicken (don't allow to boil).

Remove the venison from the oven and let rest for 10 minutes. Strain any accumulated juices from the meat into the sauce, discarding the juniper, rosemary, and thyme. Slice the venison into thick medallions. Serve garnished with bacon, with the sauce on the side.

Marinated Venison Loin

Serves 4

This recipe comes from Darina Allen's *Ballymaloe Cooking School Cookbook*. She credits it to Canice Sharkey, chef at the lamented Arbutus Lodge in Cork, Ireland's first Michelin-starred restaurant. Sharkey—who is now a partner in Isaac's restaurant in Cork City—served it with puréed celeriac, but Carrot and Parsnip Mash (page 251) is a good accompaniment, too.

1/2 CUP/120 ML PLUS 1 TBSP EXTRA-VIRGIN OLIVE OIL

3/4 CUP/175 ML DRY WHITE WINE

DASH OF SHERRY VINEGAR

1 CLOVE GARLIC, PEELED AND SMASHED

4 JUNIPER BERRIES

1 SMALL ONION, SLICED

1 SMALL CARROT, SLICED

1 BAY LEAF

2 SPRIGS THYME

ONE 1- TO 1 1/2-LB/500- TO 750-G BONELESS VENISON LOIN

3 TBSP BUTTER

2 SHALLOTS, MINCED

2 CUPS/475 ML BEEF STOCK [PAGE 357]

Preheat the oven to 200°F/90°C (Gas Mark ¼).

Combine the ½ cup/120 ml oil, ½ cup/120 ml of the wine, the vinegar, garlic, juniper berries, onion, carrot, bay leaf, and thyme in a terrine or baking dish just large enough to hold the venison.

Put the venison into the marinade for 15 minutes, turning it once. Remove it, reserving the marinade, and slice into about 12 pieces (noisettes) about ¼ in/6.5mm thick.

Melt 2 Tbsp of the butter with the remaining Tbsp of olive oil in a heavy skillet over high heat and, working in batches, sear the venison for 1 to 2 minutes per side. As the venison is done, remove from the skillet, put it on a tray, and put into the oven to keep warm.

Deglaze the skillet with the remaining ¼ cup/60 ml of white wine over high heat, scraping up the browned bits on the bottom of the pan. Reduce the heat to medium, add the shallots, and cook for about 2 minutes. Add the stock and 2 Tbsp of the marinade (liquid only) and increase the heat to medium-high. Reduce by about half, then swirl in the remaining 1 Tbsp of butter.

Divide venison slices equally between 4 plates and spoon the sauce over the meat.

Game Pie

Serves 8

This is not only a delicious, extravagant dinner-party dish but also a conversation piece: The original version of the recipe (which included a rather leaden pastry casing, better left aside), published in Rosie Tinne's *Irish Countryhouse Cooking* in 1974, comes from Mrs. Derek Le Poer Trench of Wood-lawn House, County Galway, who in turn ascribes it to May A. Carroll (a friend? the estate's cook?). The Trenches are an old Irish family of French descent (the name was originally de la Tranche). In 1978, four years after Tinne's book was published, Derek Le Poer Trench, forced to sell Woodlawn House, shot himself in the head on the estate grounds. Today, the house is derelict and is widely rumored to be haunted. One visitor called it "one of the most terrifying places I have ever been." This wonderful old-fashioned recipe may be a bit daunting, but it's nothing to be scared of. Needless to say, if you have access to wild pheasant and/or hare, their flavor will improve this pie.

YES TO SEAL, NO TO HORSE

When people are hungry—and the Irish have certainly been hungry frequently, sometimes to the point of starvation—they tend to eat anything. In less dire times, some uncommon meats are more appreciated than others. Tomás O'Crohan notes that in the 1800s on the Blasket Islands, off the coast of County Kerry, seal meat was highly thought of, to the point that "anywhere you liked to take a lump of seal's flesh you could get the same weight of pork for it." (He adds, "[T]he men that ate that kind of food were twice as good as the men of to-day.") As late as 1947, Lady Pim, writing in Belfast, was able to give a recipe for whale meat, braised in stock with parsnip, carrot, onion, bacon rinds, vinegar, and a "little Marmite." (She also gave one for "Cabbage—as an Entrée," a reminder that Northern Ireland, unlike the rest of the island, suffered from postwar rationing.)

In the early seventeenth century, Fynes Moryson wrote of the eating habits of the Irish, a people of whom he had a low opinion in general, that "they will feed on horses dying on themselves, not only upon small want of flesh, but even for pleasure." Still, though it was doubtless eaten in times of siege or famine, horsemeat has generally been disdained in Ireland, probably for its association with paganism. (Served horse meat at a banquet, St. Moling, the seventh-century bishop of Ferns in County Wexford, reportedly blessed it and turned it into mutton as a sign of Christian disapproval.)

Another food the Irish apparently never considered eating was frogs' legs. There is a very funny account from the early nineteenth century by Stephen Moore, the second earl of Mount Cashel, of the time he "assailed boldly a dish of Frogs, and made my dinner on them" while in Paris. His opinion? "They are not like chickens as I was taught to think, but have an amphibious taste between Fish and Flesh and are exactly that Jesuitical sort of food, that might be safely eat while the midnight clock was striking twelve, announcing the black commencement of Lent."

6 TBSP BUTTER

1 SHALLOT, MINCED

1 CLOVE GARLIC, MINCED

2 TBSP MINCED FRESH PARSLEY

1 TSP THYME LEAVES

SALT AND PEPPER

1 LB/500 G IRISH BACON,
CUT INTO 1-IN/2.5-CM CUBES

1 PHEASANT, BONED AND CUT INTO
1-IN/2.5-CM CUBES

1 SMALL RABBIT OR 1/2 HARE, BONED AND
CUT INTO 1-IN/2.5-CM SQUARES

2 LB/1 KG CALF'S LIVER,
CUT INTO 1-IN/2.5-CM CUBES

1 TSP GROUND ALLSPICE

1 BLACK TRUFFLE, CHOPPED
[OPTIONAL]

1/2 CUP/120 ML COGNAC

1/2 CUP/120 ML CLARIFIED BUTTER
[PAGE 362]

Melt 1 Tbsp of the butter in a small pan over low heat, then cook the shallot and garlic for 2 to 3 minutes. Put the shallot and garlic into a mortar, add the parsley, thyme, and a little salt and pepper, and pound into a paste with the pestle. Set aside.

Melt 3 Tbsp of the butter in a large skillet over medium heat and cook the bacon for 3 to 4 minutes, stirring often, until it is just cooked through but not browned. Remove from the pan and repeat the process with the pheasant, rabbit, and liver, seasoning each batch with salt and pepper and a little allspice as they are done. Set each meat aside separately.

Grease a deep, round 12-cup/2.5-L lidded earthenware or ceramic casserole or terrine with the remaining 2 Tbsp of butter. Lay half the liver on the bottom of the dish, then add layers of half the pheasant, half the bacon, and half the rabbit. Dot the rabbit with the reserved shallot-garlic paste. Add layers of the remaining pheasant, bacon, rabbit, and liver. Scatter the truffle over the liver, if using. Drizzle cognac over the liver.

Cover the casserole or terrine, then set it into a large, deep pot, big enough to hold it with at least 2 in/5 cm around the side. Fill the pot with water to about 2 in/5 cm below the top of the casserole or terrine, cover the pot, and bring the water to a boil over medium-high heat. Reduce the heat to low and steam the pie for 3 hours, adding more hot water as necessary to keep the level approximately constant.

Allow the pie to cool slightly in the water bath, then remove the casserole from the pot and lift off the lid. Carefully pour the clarified butter over the top of the pie, put the lid back on, and put the casserole into the refrigerator.

Let the pie sit for at least 3 days or as long as a week before eating to let flavors marry. Serve cold or at room temperature.

The Irish Touch

OFFAL

Mr. Leopold Bloom ate with relish the inner organs of beasts and fowls.

—James Joyce, *Ulysses* [1922]

Sweetbreads . . . are easily eaten and very digestible, but they must
be nicely prepared and cooked.

—Florence Irwin, *The Cookin' Woman: Irish Country Recipes* [1949]

Americans don't eat a lot of offal, which might be loosely defined as, well, "the inner organs of beasts and fowls," and certain of their appendages. Despite the fact that many of our ancestors came from countries where

offal is an important part of the diet, we've never *had* to eat it. We can afford the chicken breast, the pork loin, the filet mignon (at least in times of economic health), so we tend to give the liver and the jowls and the tongue to our animals, or at least grind them up for sausages so that we're not reminded of their true identity.

In Ireland, as in so many places, people ate offal originally because they had to, because they couldn't afford to waste precious meat, no matter what its original function. (In Rome, offal is known as the *quinto quarto*, or "fifth quarter"—meaning that after the animal carcass has been quartered, its organs still add up to quite a bit of food.) In more recent times, the Irish, or some of them at any rate, have taken to eating offal simply because they like it. An American swell named Bruce Reynolds, visiting Dublin around the time Joyce published *Ulysses*, went out for a typical local meal one night and found, among other things on the menu at a "plain little Irish eatery," steak and kidney pie, mutton and kidney pudding, and calf's heart—the makings of a good Bloomsian repast. Because the pig was the animal most often slaughtered in Ireland, pork offal—like black and white pudding (see facing page) and pig's feet and heads—is particularly popular, but lamb's liver is highly regarded, too, and is often considered superior to, and specifically more flavorful than, calf's liver (I concur). Both veal and lamb kidneys and sweetbreads can also be found, and again the lamb seems to yield tastier cuts.

STUDY IN BLACK AND WHITE

Black and white puddings are the Irish equivalent of France's *boudin noir* and *boudin blanc*, respectively: The former is blood sausage, which is basically congealed blood, seasoned and bulked up with filler (typically including onions in France, oatmeal in Ireland). The latter is a mousselike filling of miscellaneous pork parts in a sausage casing.

The idea of black puddings is ancient: There is mention of blood cooked in a sheep's stomach in *The Odyssey*, and there is a detailed Roman recipe for blood sausage dating from the fourth or fifth century A.D. The Irish have been eating black pudding at least since medieval times. It has evolved over the years, though. It used to be made primarily with pig's blood mixed with oatmeal, flavored with tansy, and packed in pig's intestines. (Theodora FitzGibbon reports that when she was growing up, it was often made with turkey or goose blood, too.) Today, cow's blood is usually used, the most common flavoring is thyme, and the casings are artificial; the oatmeal, though, has remained a constant. Artisanal producers of blood sausage, of whom there are happily still quite a number in Ireland, like to work with fresh blood; mass-market black pudding is usually made with dried blood, which gives the sausage less flavor. White pudding has a similar consistency to black, but contains no blood—just pork fat and usually a bit of meat, again seasoned and bound with oatmeal.

The best-known black pudding in Ireland today—you'll find it identified by name on restaurant menus all over the country—is Edward Twomey's Clonakilty, from the town of the same name in West Cork. Among the other good producers of both black and white pudding—and no two butchers make either in exactly the same way—are O'Flynn's in Cork City; Staunton's in Timoleague, County Cork; Thomas Ashe in Annascaul, County Kerry; P. J. Burns in Sneem, County Kerry; Tournafulla in Wexford; Whelan Brothers in Carrick-on-Suir, County Waterford; T. J. Crowe in Dundrum, County Tipperary; Wysner Meats in Ballycastle, County Antrim; and my own favorite, Seán Kelly in Westport, County Mayo. Kelly not only makes subtly flavored conventional black and white puddings but also a "white in black" specialty (a core of white pudding surrounded by black) and what he calls putóg, which is the old Irish name for pudding and is in this case a massive old-style black pudding in a thick, almost hamlike shape (it was originally stuffed into a sheep's stomach).

ARLINGTON CHICKEN
LIVER PÂTÉ

Arlington Chicken Liver Pâté

Serves 12 to 16

This country-style pâté is one of the most popular appetizers and bar snacks at Maurice Keller's Arlington Lodge in Waterford. He says to serve "with a crisp salad, melba toast, and any sweet chutney or relish."

1 LB/500 G SLAB BACON, CHOPPED

1 LARGE ONION, COARSELY CHOPPED

4 CLOVES GARLIC, MINCED

2 LB/1 KG LARGE CHICKEN LIVERS,
MEMBRANES REMOVED

3/4 CUP/190 G BUTTER

SALT AND COARSELY CRACKED BLACK PEPPER

LEAVES OF 1/2 BUNCH PARSLEY, MINCED,
PLUS 15 TO 20 WHOLE LEAVES FOR GARNISH

LEAVES OF 1/2 BUNCH CILANTRO, MINCED
[OPTIONAL]

Fry the bacon over medium heat in a large skillet until lightly browned. Add the onion and garlic, reduce the heat to low, and cook until the vegetables are soft and lightly browned, about 10 minutes.

Add the chicken livers and cook for another 8 to 10 minutes, until they are cooked through but still slightly pink inside. As the livers cook, add butter, a few Tbsp at a time, stirring in well.

When the liver are cooked, season them with salt and plenty of pepper, then stir in the parsley and (if using) cilantro. Put the mixture into a food processor and pulse 3 or 4 times to get a coarse paste.

Line a 1½-qt/1.5-L terrine or glass loaf pan with plastic wrap and pour in the chicken liver mixture. Cover the terrine with plastic wrap and refrigerate until the butter solidifies, or as long as 5 days.

Turn the terrine out onto a serving plate, distribute the parsley leaves evenly over the top, and serve.

Crubeens [Pig's Feet]

Serves 4

Until the middle of the twentieth century, crubeens (from the Irish word *crúb*, "hoof") were common fare in pork-loving Ireland, sold at streetside stands and in pubs all over the island. (They were usually salted, and the hind feet were particularly favored, as they have more meat on them than the front ones.) As prosperity brought the Irish access to more refined foods, this particular variety meat fell out of favor. In recent years, though, along with such other gutsy fare as black pudding and lamb's liver, it has made something of a comeback, often showing up in contemporary guise on the menus at some of Ireland's better restaurants, for example the thin-sliced crubeens with salad of Maris Piper potatoes, crispy pork, poached quail egg, and Meaux mustard served at Patrick Guilbaud in Dublin (for about sixty dollars a portion!). This is a considerably simpler, more traditional preparation. Soda bread and Guinness stout are the classic accompaniments.

8 BRINED [PICKLED] PIG'S FEET

2 ONIONS, HALVED

2 CARROTS, CUT INTO LARGE CHUNKS

2 BAY LEAVES

6 TO 8 SPRIGS PARSLEY

2 TO 3 TBSP BACON FAT

1 EGG, BEATEN

1 CUP/60 G DRY BREAD CRUMBS

SALT AND PEPPER

Put the pig's feet into a large pot with the onions, carrots, bay leaves, and parsley. Add enough water to just cover all the ingredients, then bring to a boil over high heat. Reduce the heat to low, cover the pot, and simmer for 2 to 3 hours or until the meat is almost falling off the bone.

Preheat the oven to 450°F/230°C (Gas Mark 8).

Remove the pig's feet carefully, pat dry with paper towels, and set aside to dry further.

Melt the bacon fat over low heat in a roasting pan large enough to hold the pig's feet in a single layer. When the pig's feet are cool enough to handle, brush with the beaten egg, roll in bread crumbs, and season generously with salt and pepper.

Put the pig's feet into the roasting pan, spoon the bacon fat over them, and roast for 20 to 30 minutes, turning once, or until golden brown.

Crubeen Tortellini with Almond Butter

Serves 4

Pasta first became truly popular in Ireland in the mid-twentieth century; one theory is that a taste for it was brought home by Irish Catholics who had gone on the Irish National Pilgrimage to Rome for the Holy Year Jubilee in 1950. But, says archeologist and food historian Caiman O'Brien of Nenagh, County Tipperary, pasta may have been eaten on the island as early as the fourteenth century—specifically, an Anglo-Norman specialty called "cressee." This was a dish of thick, wide noodles flavored with sugar and ginger, some of them colored with saffron, which were interleaved in a crosshatch pattern, boiled, then served with butter and cheese. Today, of course, there are Italian restaurants all over Ireland and pasta is found in many guises on "new Irish" menus. With this dish, the talented Paul Flynn, at his Tannery in Dungarven, an attractive little port town in County Waterford, successfully marries pasta with traditional Irish cooking.

4 BRINED [PICKLED] PIG'S FEET

1 TBSP DIJON MUSTARD

DASH OF SHERRY VINEGAR

PEPPER

1 TBSP ALMOND SLIVERS

3 CUPS/300 G WHITE FLOUR,
PLUS MORE FOR DUSTING

1/2 TSP SALT

2 EGGS, PLUS 1 EGG BEATEN WITH 1 TBSP WATER

1 TBSP EXTRA-VIRGIN OLIVE OIL

1/2 CUP/120 ML CLARIFIED BUTTER [PAGE 362]

TURNIP PURÉE [PAGE 253] FOR SERVING [OPTIONAL]

BUTTERED KALE [PAGE 245] FOR SERVING [OPTIONAL]

Rinse the pig's feet thoroughly, then put them into a large pot with water to cover. Bring to a boil over high heat; then reduce the heat to low and simmer, covered, for 2 to 3 hours or until meat is almost falling off the bone. Skim any foam off the surface of the water as the pig's feet cook, and replenish the water as needed to keep the level constant. Set aside to cool.

Remove the meat and some of the fat from the pig's feet and put into the bowl of a food processor; add the mustard, sherry vinegar, and pepper to taste. Pulse the ingredients 3 or 4 times (do not process to a paste), then transfer to a medium bowl, cover, and refrigerate for 3 to 4 hours.

Heat a small nonstick pan over medium-high heat, then add the almond slivers and toast them, shaking the pan frequently, for 4 to 6 minutes or until dark brown but not burned. Set aside.

When the pig's feet mixture is almost ready to come out of the refrigerator, combine the flour and salt in the clean bowl of a food processor and pulse 2 or 3 times. Whisk the 2 eggs, oil, and 3 Tbsp of water together in a small bowl, then pour the mixture into the food processor in a slow, steady stream while processing, until the dough begins to pull away from the sides of the bowl.

Roll out the dough as thinly as possible on a floured board, then cut into rounds 3 to 4 in/7 to 10 cm in diameter with a cookie cutter or the floured rim of a glass.

Assemble the tortellini by putting ¼ tsp of the pig's feet mixture in the center of each dough round. Brush beaten egg on the bottom half of each round and fold over, pressing down gently to seal. Fold each sealed dough round over your finger, then turn down one edge of it to form each of the tortellini. Set the tortellini aside on a lightly floured baking sheet as they're done. Cover lightly with waxed paper and set aside.

Bring a large pot of salted water to a boil over high heat.

Heat the clarified butter in a small, heavy-bottomed pot over medium-low heat for 10 minutes or until it begins to turn amber. Remove from the heat and stir in the almond slivers.

Cook the tortellini for 4 to 5 minutes or until they bob to the surface of the pot. Carefully drain.

To serve, divide between 4 warmed plates and spoon the almond butter over the tortellini. Serve with turnip purée and buttered kale, if you like.

CORK CITY

Cork City was founded around a monastery dating back to at least the seventh century, and subsequently invaded and then built up by the Vikings and the Anglo-Normans. By the thirteenth century, it had become an important commercial center. Its harbor is the second-largest natural harbor in the world (after Sydney, Australia's), and through it Cork merchants exported wool, hides, live animals, meat, fish, and grain, and brought in wine, oil, utensils, and finished cloth. In the seventeenth century, Cork became the principal port in Ireland for the importation of sugar and tobacco from America. In the same era, after the British passed protectionist laws prohibiting the exportation of fresh Irish beef to England, Cork entrepreneurs became masters at producing provisions like butter, salted fish, and salted and spiced beef—which *could* be sent across the Irish Sea (and beyond). The by-products of the slaughterhouses, being perishable, mostly stayed in Cork, and the city became famous throughout Ireland for its offal. That term even took on a specific meaning in Cork: pig's backbone (now forbidden in Europe because of the association of spinal marrow with BSE or mad cow disease). Other organ meat specialties of Cork are drisheen (a type of blood sausage, see below), crubeens (pig's feet, page 203), tripe (which here is usually the first stomach or rumen of the animal, known locally as "plain," "blanket," or "vein," and not the second stomach or teticulum, which is the honeycomb tripe sold in America), and skirts-and-kidneys (cow diaphragm—the same cut used in Tex-Mex fajitas, but with the kidneys still attached).

DRISHEEN

People make the same kinds of jokes about drisheen in Ireland as they do about haggis in Scotland: It's sometimes foisted upon unsuspecting visitors, and in general considered to be a daunting food, eaten only by those with, well, special tastes. In fact, it's pretty inoffensive stuff, so much so that it was traditionally recommended as fit food for the infirm and elderly and for pregnant women. What is it? Contrary to some sources, drisheen is not just the local name for black pudding in Cork. It a very particular thing: a kind of blood sausage made from boiled blood serum, the yellowish liquid component of blood, separated overnight from the thicker part. The scholar Eugene O'Curry called it "probably . . . an example of one of the most ancient of Irish puddings," and food historian Regina Sexton reports that it has been eaten at least since the eleventh century. It's mentioned (as *dressan*) around that time in the satirical work "The Vision of Mac Conglinne." What does it taste like? Frankly, not very much. It's liver hued, slippery, and bland. Irish writer and bookbinder Malachi McCormick describes it as having "a most unusual texture, a bit like a savory caramel pudding." English traveler H. V. Morton thought it looked "like a large and poisonous snake . . . a chocolate-covered python." He sampled it cooked the traditional way, with tripe in a white sauce with lots of black pepper, and reported that "It is a peculiar, subtle dish, pleasant and ladylike," adding, "I believe that I would have liked it better fried."

COLLARED HEAD

Collared Head

Serves 10 *to* 12

Collared head, also known as brawn, is a kind of terrine of pressed pork—not fancy cuts, but the sweet, flavorful bits picked from brined, long-cooked pig's head, often with the meat of pig's feet or slices of salted ox tongue added. (It may be called "collared" because it's traditionally pressed in a metal ring.) When butcher T. J. Crowe of Dundrum, County Tipperary, makes his collared heads, they're immense, with bits of pig's ear included and two whole tongues positioned tip to tip in the middle. This less daunting recipe is adapted from one used by Peter Ward of Country Choice in the Tipperary town of Nenagh.

I PIG'S HEAD, HALVED FROM TOP TO BOTTOM,
BRINED [SEE PAGE 361]

I BEEF TONGUE, BRINED [SEE PAGE 361]

I ONION, HALVED

2 CARROTS, CHOPPED

2 BAY LEAVES

12 BLACK PEPPERCONS

3 CLOVES

2 WHOLE ALLSPICE

I WHOLE STAR ANISE

I TBSP KOSHER SALT

I/8 TSP GROUND NUTMEG

I/8 TSP GROUND ALLSPICE

6 TO 8 GARLIC CHIVES [OPTIONAL]

CRABAPPLE JELLY [PAGE 329] FOR SERVING
[OPTIONAL]

Put the pig's head, beef tongue, onion, carrots, bay leaves, black peppercorns, cloves, whole allspice, star anise, and salt into a large pot. Cover with cold water and bring to a boil over high heat; then reduce the heat and simmer, partially covered, for 3 to 4 hours, or until the head and tongue are tender.

Allow the ingredients to cool in the cooking liquid, then remove from the pot and set aside. Strain the cooking liquid, reserving 2 cups/475 ml. Discard the vegetables and the remaining cooking liquid (or save the liquid for soup or stock).

Pull and cut as much skin and fat as possible from the pigs' heads, then remove and finely chop the remaining meat. (Discard the fat, bones, and cartilage.) Peel the tongue, discarding the skin, and dice the meat.

Combine the meat from the pig's head and beef tongue, the reserved stock, and the ground nutmeg and allspice in a large bowl and mix together well. If using garlic chives, lay them flat in a single layer in the bottom of a 2-qt/2-L bowl or pudding basin, so that their ends curve up the sides of the bowl a little. Spoon the pig's head mixture into the bowl and tamp down lightly. Cut a piece of wax paper to exactly cover the top and lay it over the mixture. Weigh down with a plate or pie pan that fits the space exactly, and set 1 or 2 cans of canned food on top.

Refrigerate for at least 24 hours and for as long as 3 days. Remove the weights and plate and invert the collared head onto a large plate (wrap a very hot, damp kitchen towel around the bowl to help loosen the collared head if necessary).

Serve sliced, with crabapple jelly on the side, if you like.

Black Pudding with Cabbage and Apples

Serves 4

Despite the changes in modern Irish eating habits, black pudding remains popular, not only as part of an old-fashioned Irish breakfast (or Ulster Fry, page 149) but also in a number of more elaborate cooked dishes both homey and sophisticated. Along with pork belly, it is found in some form on almost every "new Irish" restaurant menu. To find Irish bacon and black pudding, see Sources on page 369.

2 TBSP BUTTER

2 SLICES IRISH BACON, PREFERABLY GALTEE'S
SLICED CURED PORK LOIN, TOMMY MOLONEY'S
MILD-CURED [NOT SMOKED OR BACK RASHERS],
OR DONNELLY'S, CUT INTO STRIPS ABOUT
2 BY I/4 IN/5 CM BY 6.5 MM

I LB/500 G BLACK PUDDING, PREFERABLY GALTEE,
CASING REMOVED, CUT ON THE DIAGONAL
INTO I/2-IN/1.25-CM SLICES

I ONION, DICED

1 SMALL HEAD GREEN OR WHITE CABBAGE,
THINLY SLICED

2 GREEN COOKING APPLES, PEELED, CORED, THINLY
SLICED, AND CUT INTO 1/4-IN/6.5-MM STRIPS

1/2 CUP/120 ML BEEF OR CHICKEN STOCK
[PAGE 357 OR 356]

SALT AND PEPPER

Melt the butter in a large skillet over medium heat, then fry the bacon for 2 to 3 minutes or until it begins to brown. Remove with a slotted spoon and drain on paper towels.

Working in batches if necessary, add the black pudding slices to the pan and cook for 2 to 3 minutes per side. Remove and set aside in a bowl covered with foil to keep warm.

Add the onion to the pan and cook for 2 to 3 minutes, stirring frequently; then add the cabbage, apples, reserved bacon, and stock. Increase the heat to high and bring to a boil, then reduce the heat to low, cover, and cook for about 15 minutes, or until the cabbage is cooked but still slightly crunchy. Season to taste with salt and pepper.

To serve, divide the cabbage mixture evenly among 4 plates and top with the black pudding.

Sweetbreads Wrapped in Bacon

Serves 4

Cookbook author Theodora FitzGibbon describes this as a family recipe from County Tipperary.

1 LB/500 G VEAL SWEETBREADS, WELL RINSED

SALT

1/2 TO 3/4 LB/250 TO 375 G BACON

BUTTER OR BACON FAT FOR GREASING

SALT AND PEPPER

1 SMALL ONION, MINCED

1 LARGE TOMATO, CHOPPED

1 TBSP CHOPPED FRESH PARSLEY

Put the sweetbrads into a medium pot of salted water. Bring to a boil over high heat, then reduce the heat to low and simmer, uncovered, for 10 to 15 minutes, or until the sweetbreads are firm.

Preheat the oven to 350°F/175°C (Gas Mark 4).

Drain the sweetbreads and refresh in a bowl of ice water. Peel off the membranes and cut out the fibers, then cut the sweetbreads into pieces slightly smaller than a Ping-Pong ball. Wrap each piece in a slice of bacon, securing it with a wooden toothpick.

Put the sweetbreads into a lightly greased baking dish large enough to hold them in a single layer. Season to taste with salt and pepper, then scatter the onion and tomato over the sweetbreads. Moisten with about 1/2 cup/120 ml of water, and bake until the bacon gets crispy, 20 to 30 minutes. Garnish with chopped parsley.

Creamed Sweetbreads

Serves 4

My wife and I got talking one afternoon with David Costelloe, the young Irish-born real estate agent who found us our new Manhattan apartment, and he mentioned that his mother, back in Galway, was a terrific cook. Of course, many young Irishmen (and -women) will say that about dear old mum—but after I tried a few of Anne Costelloe's recipes, which she generously forwarded, I was willing to believe David. This is one of her favorite dishes.

1 LB/500 G VEAL OR LAMB SWEETBREADS

1 SMALL ONION, SLICED

4 CUPS/1 L BEEF STOCK [PAGE 357]

SALT AND PEPPER

2 TBSP BUTTER

1/4 CUP/25 G WHITE FLOUR

1 EGG YOLK, BEATEN

2 TBSP HEAVY CREAM

1 LEMON, SLICED

THE POLISH CONNECTION

That non-English chatter you hear from the desk staff at the hotel or the bartenders and servers at the restaurant or the assistants in the market or boutique probably isn't Irish. It might be Czech, Russian, or Lithuanian—but it's probably Polish. J. M. Synge recorded the presence of German and Polish peddlers in Ireland, even in the isolated Aran Islands, in the early 1900s, but the real influx came much later. Following the demise of communism in Eastern Europe in the late 1980s and early 1990s and the almost concurrent unleashing of the so-called Celtic Tiger—the buoyant new Irish economy—thousands of young Poles (among others) began flooding into Ireland, where they found ready employment in the service sector.

Today, as the tiger sulks in the back of his cage while Poland's own economy is at least relatively healthy, some of these visitors are going home. But they're leaving behind Polish grocery shops, in small towns as well as cities around the island, and they have had at least a minor influence on Irish food: Northern Irish baker Robert Ditty says that Poles started coming into his shop in Castledawson, County Derry, complaining that the regular loaf he sold wasn't "real bread"; now he makes one labeled "Polish bread," from dough fermented for forty-eight hours. ("I don't know why we call it 'Polish,'" he says. "It's just good bread.") And Kay Harte of the Farmgate Café in Cork's English Market reports that market butchers specializing in offal have seen increased demand for their products from Eastern European customers, and that as a result, at least a few Irish shoppers are getting more interested in them as well. Now the question is whether a visitor to Warsaw in a few years time will find interpretations of boxty and Irish stew on Polish menus.

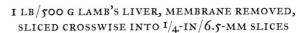

Bring a medium pot of salted water to a boil, then reduce the heat to low, add the sweetbreads, and simmer, uncovered, for about 1 hour.

Drain the sweetbreads and refresh in a bowl of ice water. If using veal sweetbreads, peel and discard all membranes and fibers. (The membranes are usually thin enough on lamb sweetbreads so that this is not necessary.)

Put the sweetbreads in a saucepan, add the onion and stock, and season to taste with salt and pepper. Bring to a boil over high heat, then reduce heat and simmer for 1 hour, uncovered. Remove the sweetbreads and onion from the pan with a slotted spoon and set them aside. Strain and reserve the stock, then wipe out the saucepan with paper towels.

Melt the butter in the same saucepan. Stir in the flour and cook over low heat, stirring constantly, for 3 minutes to form a roux. Stir in the reserved stock and simmer for about 5 minutes. Stir in the egg yolk and cream, return the sweetbreads to the sauce, and heat through.

Serve garnished with lemon slices.

Lamb's Liver with Whiskey Cream Sauce

Serves 4

I first tasted this dish at Peter and Mary Ward's house in Nenagh, County Tipperary. I've had several restaurant versions since, but prefer the simplicity of this one. Ask your butcher to order lamb's liver for you. (If it comes frozen, be sure to thaw it thoroughly before cooking.)

1 LB/500 G LAMB'S LIVER, MEMBRANE REMOVED, SLICED CROSSWISE INTO 1/4-IN/6.5-MM SLICES

2 CUPS/475 ML MILK

SALT

1/2 CUP/125 G BUTTER

1 ONION, MINCED

2 TBSP IRISH WHISKEY

1/2 CUP/120 ML HEAVY CREAM

1 TBSP WHOLE-GRAIN MUSTARD

1 TBSP CHOPPED FRESH CHIVES

PEPPER

Put the liver into a shallow dish large enough to hold it in a single layer; then cover with the milk and sprinkle lightly with salt. Cover and refrigerate overnight.

Rinse the lamb's liver, discarding the milk, and pat dry with paper towels. Melt half the butter in a large skillet over medium heat. Cook the onions, stirring frequently, until soft and beginning to brown, 10 to 12 minutes. Remove the onions from the skillet with a slotted spoon and set aside. Melt the remaining butter in the same skillet and, working in batches, sear the liver over high heat for about 1½ minutes on each side. As the liver is done, transfer to a plate and set aside.

Pour the whiskey into the pan, warm it for about a minute, then carefully ignite it with a kitchen match. When the flames die down, stir in the cream and mustard, scraping up any browned bits on the bottom of the pan. Cook for about 1 minute, then return the onions and liver to the skillet, along with any juices that may have accumulated.

Stir well, season to taste with salt and pepper, and cook for 1 to 2 minutes or until the liver is heated through. Garnish with the chives.

ENGLISH MARKET

There has been a market on what is now Grand Parade in the heart of Cork City since around 1610, and a covered market was first built there in 1788. It was originally a meat market. When a clock was installed on the façade, a wag suggested that on the city seal above it, Cork's motto should be changed from *Statio bene fida carinis,* "a safe harbor for keels" (i.e., ships) to *Statio bene fida carnis,* "a safe harbor for meat." A list of purveyors from 1845 identifies eighty-five butcher's stalls and no other kind at all.

In addition to the nature of their trade, those merchants had one thing in common: They were all Protestant; Catholics were barred from the market. When St. Peter's Market opened in 1843 in another part of the city specifically for the Irish, the Grand Parade market became known as the English Market, and it kept that name long after Catholics were allowed in. While the Irish market declined in the early twentieth century, closing in 1955, the English Market lasted, expanding to take up much of the block bordered by Grand Parade and Patrick, Oliver Plunkett, and Princes streets. It was modernized in the 1960s, escaped being torn down for the sake of an office building and garage in the 1970s, and suffered devastating fires in 1980 and again in 1986. Since the 1990s, however, it has been thriving again.

There are about forty-five purveyors in the market today, and they're a diverse lot. Old-style butchers, poultry stands, greengrocers, and fishmongers alternate with boutique bakeries and specialty shops. The Kay O'Connell stand offers an array of fish like you might find in Brittany, or even Marseilles—monkfish, John Dory, slabs of tuna, whole salmon, turbot, sole, Dublin Bay prawns, rock oysters, brill, loup, smoked salmon, cured fish, anchovies, salt cod stacked in a mound of salt. . . . Nearby, On the Pig's Back sells homemade pâtés, terrines, and rillettes as well as the best West Cork charcuterie from Frank Krawczyk and Gubbeen and Willie and Avril Allshire's Rosscarbery sausages and Caherbeg free-range pork.

Upstairs, around the central atrium, at Kay Harte's Farmgate restaurant, the freshest market fare is prepared simply but well—the fish pie, corned beef with parsley sauce, and tripe with drisheen are essentials—in both an open café setting and a small glass-enclosed dining room. Over lunch at the Farmgate one day, the poet Thomas McCarthy remarked, "When you go downstairs, you can buy olive oil from Trás-os-Montes in Portugal. Oil from Trás-os-Montes has been sold on this site for four hundred years." The English Market is that kind of place.

 POTATOES

The Definitive Food

[A]bout thirty five years ago . . . every capable farmer had peas and beans; but the potato put them out of date.

—Amhlaoibh Ó Súilleabháin, *The Diary of an Irish Countryman* 1827—1835

Upon an average, a man, his wife, and four children [in Ireland], will eat thirty-seven pounds of potatoes a day.

—John Carr, esq., *The Stranger in Ireland; or, a Tour of the Southern and Western Parts of That Country, in the Year* 1805

The potato—or pratie, as it is commonly known—is practically synonymous with Ireland. How it got there in the first place is a bit of a mystery [see page 231], but it didn't

take long: It is mentioned in a farm lease in County Down in 1606, not quite seventy years after conquistador Juan de Castellanos first discovered the thing (for Europeans) in a village on the western coast of South America. It was soon being grown all over the island. As the chef and food scholar Máirtín Mac Con Iomaire puts it, "The Irish were the first Europeans to seriously consider the potato as a staple food."

What accounted for its popularity? According to Larry Zuckerman in his definitive book *The Potato: How the Humble Spud Rescued the Western World,* "It was genuinely liked." The Irish climate, moist but temperate, was perfect for growing potatoes, and they took up less land and required less work than oats, the staple crop they quickly replaced. It was said that one acre of potatoes could feed a family of six for a year, and that one industrious farmer with a larger plot could grow enough potatoes to feed forty. By 1845, there were about 65,000 farms in Ireland of an acre or less that grew potatoes as their only crop, which may be why the term "garden" became a synonym for "potato field." An estimated 40 percent of the population ate only potatoes. This wasn't necessarily a bad thing: Potatoes are in fact very nutritious, a good source of protein, starch, vitamins, and such minerals as zinc and iron; they're one of the few vegetables that people *can* live on exclusively. (Interestingly, in October 2008 the *New York Times* reported that "scientists, nutritionists, and aid specialists are increasingly convinced that the potato should be playing a much larger role to ensure a steady supply of food in the developing world.") In fact, the more potatoes they ate, the healthier the Irish people became, and the population of the island soared as a result. In the late sixteenth century, there were about a million people in Ireland; by the mid-nineteenth, there were more than eight million, making it the most densely populated country in Europe. This turned out not to be a good thing, of course, when famine struck (see page 227).

The most popular potato in Ireland in the nineteenth century was the so-called lumper, imported from Scotland in 1808 as animal fodder. It was nutritionally almost worthless, didn't have much flavor, and went bad quickly. But it required little fertilizer, and was said to yield 70 or 80 barrels of spuds per acre, compared to the 50 or 60 that other kinds produced. In the late 1800s, its place was largely taken by the superior Champion. Today, the most widely grown potato is the Rooster (don't be dismayed if you see "mashed Roosters" offered on an Irish menu), followed by the Kerr's Pink. English Queens (which the Irish often label simply as Queens), Pentland Dells, Caras, Maris Piper, and Golden Wonders are other potatoes you'll see identified by name in Ireland. Seed Savers and other champions of heirloom vegetable varieties are attempting to revive potatoes with evocative names like the Sharpe's Express, the Arran Banner, the Bally Doan, and the Red Duke of York—and John Clarke of Broughgammon near Ballycastle, County Antrim, and other specialists are continually developing new varieties.

Considering their history with potatoes, it's not surprising that the Irish have as many recipes for them as the Bedouins have for dates. A number of the best ones appear in the pages that follow.

Boxty

Serves 4 to 6

An old verse says "Boxty on the griddle, / Boxty in the pan, / If you can't make boxty, / You'll never get a man." Boxty, occasionally spelled *boxdy*, is basically a potato cake, eaten mostly in the north of Ireland, especially in counties Cavan, Fermanagh, Derry, and Tyrone. (Its name perhaps derives from the Irish *bocht*, meaning "poor.") Tokens predicting the future state of those who find them are sometimes secreted inside boxty, as they are in Barm Brack (page 293) and Colcannon (page 219). Not all recipes call for the extra step of separating out the potato starch and then adding it to the cake, as required here, but that process seems to help hold the boxty together. (Potato starch extracted in this manner was also used to stiffen men's collars and various undergarments.)

I MEDIUM RUSSET POTATO [ABOUT 1/2 LB/250 G], GRATED ON THE LARGE HOLES OF A BOX GRATER

I CUP/210 G FRESHLY MADE MASHED POTATOES [PAGE 223]

I CUP/100 G WHITE FLOUR, PREFERABLY IRISH [SEE SOURCES, PAGE 369], PLUS MORE FOR DUSTING

I TSP BAKING SODA

SALT

2 TO 3 TBSP BACON FAT OR BUTTER

Wrap the grated potatoes in a clean tea towel or several thicknesses of cheesecloth. Working over a medium bowl, tightly twist the ends of the towel in opposite directions, to squeeze out as much liquid as possible. Set the bowl of potato water aside for 10 minutes.

Put the grated potato into a large bowl, add the mashed potatoes, and mix well to combine thoroughly.

Carefully pour off and discard the liquid from the bowl with the potato water, leaving a layer of thick white potato starch at the bottom. Add the starch to the potato mixture, then add the flour and baking soda and season to taste with salt. Transfer the mixture to a lightly floured surface and knead for 1 or 2 minutes or until a thick dough forms.

On a lightly floured surface, press the dough with your hands into a disk, then roll it out into a circle about ¾ in/2 cm thick. Using a cookie cutter or the floured rim of a drinking glass, cut the dough into 3-in/7.5-cm rounds.

Melt the bacon fat or butter in a large skillet over medium heat. Add the boxty in a single layer and fry for 3 to 4 minutes per side or until golden brown.

There are two other common ways of cooking boxty:

1. Cut the dough into cakes as described and then drop them into a large pot of gently boiling salted water and cook for about 40 minutes. (Be sure to use very starchy potatoes if you're going to make boiled boxty, or they'll fall apart in the water.) Carefully drain and cool to room temperature, then halve crosswise and fry as above. (Boiled boxty cakes are sometimes called "hurleys.")

2. Shape the dough into a circle about ¾ in/2 cm thick and cut into wedge-shaped farls (quarters). Put onto a lightly greased baking sheet and bake in a preheated 300°F/150°C (Gas Mark 2) oven for 45 to 50 minutes, or until done, turning them halfway through.

Boxty Pancakes

Serves 6 to 8

This variation on boxty can be eaten with butter and sugar, or used—nontraditionally—as a wrap for savory ingredients, for instance, Savory Mince (page 174) or Kedgeree (page 76).

2 LB/1 K RUSSET OR OTHER FLOURY POTATOES, PEELED AND FINELY CHOPPED

I CUP/100 G WHITE FLOUR

I TO I 1/2 CUPS/240 TO 360 ML MILK

3/4 TSP SALT

BUTTER FOR GREASING

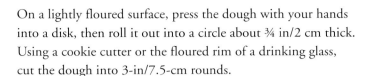

Purée the raw potatoes in a blender or food processor until smooth, then put into a large bowl. Stir in the flour, then slowly add the milk, stirring constantly until the mixture takes on the consistency of pancake batter. Season with the salt.

Lightly grease a small nonstick skillet with a bit of butter, then heat it over medium heat. Pour about ⅔ cup/160 ml of the batter into the pan, swirling it so that it covers the bottom evenly. Neaten the edges with a rubber spatula.

Cook the pancake for 4 to 5 minutes on one side, shaking the skillet gently every minute or so, so that the pancake doesn't stick. Carefully flip the pancake and continue to cook for 4 to 5 minutes more. Transfer pancake to a warm plate and tent it with foil. Stir the batter well, then repeat the process to use all the batter, adding the cooked pancakes to the foil-covered plate as you work to keep them warm.

Colcannon

Serves 4 to 8

In speaking of this most celebrated of Irish potato dishes, musician Mick Bolger—whose Denver-based contemporary Celtic band is *called* Colcannon—notes that it has a "wonderful affinity" for corned beef and cabbage. And he confesses that he has also eaten it "with filet mignon and port sauce; with rashers [bacon], tomatoes, and kidneys-in-their-jackets at 4 A.M.; and—God forgive me—wrapped in a tortilla, microwaved, and eaten, over the sink, with salsa." It is, in other words, a versatile creation. It is also one that exists in numerous variations, depending on the season, the region of the country, and of course personal taste. It is often made with just butter, milk, and kale, but scholar P. W. Joyce defines "caulcannon" as "potatoes mashed with butter and milk, with chopped up cabbage and pot-herbs." Mary Ward, when she makes colcannon at her house in Nenagh, County Tipperary, starts with a trip to the kitchen garden, armed with a basket and a pair of shears. This is her recipe.

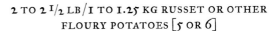

2 TO 2 ½ LB/1 TO 1.25 KG RUSSET OR OTHER FLOURY POTATOES [5 OR 6]

6 TO 8 TBSP BUTTER

2 TO 3 LIGHTLY PACKED CUPS/400 TO 800 G CHOPPED KALE OR ASSORTED CHOPPED GREENS [SUCH AS KALE, PARSLEY, SORREL, SPINACH, AND/OR BROCCOLI OR CAULIFLOWER LEAVES]

1 ⅓ CUPS/320 ML MILK

4 SCALLIONS, GREEN PART ONLY, MINCED

SALT AND PEPPER

Put the potatoes into a large pot, with the larger ones on the bottom, and add water to come halfway up the potatoes. Cover the pot and bring to a boil over high heat. When the water begins to boil, carefully drain off about half of it, then return the pot to the heat, cover it again, reduce the heat to low, and let the potatoes steam for about 40 minutes. Turn off the heat; cover the potatoes with a clean, damp tea towel; and let sit for 5 minutes more.

Melt 4 Tbsp of the butter in a large skillet over medium-high heat. Add the kale or assorted greens and cook until just wilted, about 5 minutes.

Combine the milk, scallions, and remaining butter in a medium pot and bring to a simmer over medium heat. Cook for about 2 minutes, then add the greens and stir in well. Remove the pot from the heat, cover, and set aside.

Drain and carefully peel the potatoes, then return them to the pot. Add the greens and their liquid and mash until smooth, leaving a few small lumps in the potatoes. Season to taste with salt and pepper.

To serve in the traditional Irish manner, push the back of a large soup spoon down in the middle of each portion to make a crater, then put a large pat of room-temperature butter into each one to make a "lake." Diners dip each forkful of colcannon into the butter until its walls are breached.

COLCANNON CAKES

Colcannon Cakes

Serves 6

There isn't usually any colcannon left over when Mary Ward (see page 246) makes up a batch, but if there is, her husband, Peter, likes to fry up these cakes to serve along good Irish bacon and black pudding for breakfast.

2 CUPS LEFTOVER COLCANNON [PAGE 219]

2/3 CUP/65 G WHITE FLOUR

4 TBSP BUTTER

SALT AND PEPPER

Combine the colcannon and the flour in a medium bowl, mixing together well. Form the mixture into 6 cakes of equal size, about ¾ in/2 cm thick. Season to taste with salt and pepper.

Melt butter in a large, heavy skillet over medium heat, then fry cakes on both sides, turning once and pressing down lightly on them with a spatula, until golden brown, about 4 minutes per side.

Champ

Serves 4 to 8

Like colcannon, champ is a perfect partner for almost any kind of meat or poultry. See following for a recipe for pea champ.

2 TO 2 1/2 LB/1 TO 1.25 KG RUSSET
OR OTHER FLOURY POTATOES [5 OR 6]

1 1/3 CUPS/320 ML MILK

2 SMALL BUNCHES SCALLIONS,
TRIMMED AND MINCED

1/2 CUP/125 G BUTTER, SOFTENED

SALT AND PEPPER

Put the potatoes into a large pot, with the larger ones on the bottom, and add water to come halfway up the potatoes. Cover the pot and bring to a boil over high heat. When the water begins to boil, carefully drain off about half of it, then return the pot to the heat, cover it again, reduce the heat to low, and let the potatoes steam for about 40 minutes. Turn off the heat; cover the potatoes with a clean, damp tea towel; and let sit for 5 minutes more.

Meanwhile, bring the milk to a simmer in a small saucepan, then add the scallions and simmer for 10 to 15 minutes or until soft. Strain the milk, reserving the scallions and milk separately.

Drain and carefully peel the potatoes, then return them to the pot and mash them well. Stir in the scallions and butter, then drizzle in the milk, continuing to mash, until the potatoes are fluffy. Season to taste with salt and pepper.

Pea Champ

Pea champ is a specialty of Ireland's northern counties: Prepare Champ as directed, substituting 1½ cups shelled fresh peas (about 1½ lb/750 g peas in pods) for the scallions, and mashing them into the potatoes.

COLCANNON AND CHAMP

Among the many things the Irish do, and have traditionally done, with potatoes are two versions of potatoes mashed with, well, some other vegetable. The common names for these two preparations are colcannon and champ, and the simple definitions are that colcannon is muddled up with kale or cabbage, while champ involves some variety of the onion family—usually spring onions (scallions) or leeks. Both preparations also typically include plenty of butter and salt and often milk or cream. The simple definitions only begin to tell the story, though.

Both colcannon and champ have probably been around for centuries, at least since the 1700s. Colcannon, in fact, seems to have been introduced to England from Ireland in the first half of the eighteenth century—doubtless by one of the frequent English travelers to the island—and is considered responsible for the growth in popularity of potatoes in general there. Colcannon takes its name from the Irish term *cál ceann fhionn* (the *f* and *h* are silent), meaning "white-headed kale" or "cabbage." Kale is the preferred ingredient, though cabbage and other greens are sometimes utilized; just to confuse things, it's not unknown for leeks or onions to find their way in, too.

Champ (the word may come from an old Scots term meaning "mash" or "crush") and its relatives—which go by names like cally, poundies, pandy, stelk, thump, bruisy, and cobbledy—are more popular in the north of Ireland than the south. Though spring onions and leeks are the most common constituents (white onions for cobbledy), early-twentieth-century cooking teacher Florence Irwin wrote, "I have known of carrot, cabbage, and even lettuce being made into champ." And there are references to versions made with chives, nettles, and even dulse. A very nice version is also made in Ulster with peas.

Ballyknocken Green Mashed Potatoes

Serves 6 to 8

At her Ballyknocken House in Ashford, County Wicklow, Catherine Fulvio serves this side dish with various preparations of lamb raised on Ballyknocken Farm.

2 LB/1 KG RUSSET OR OTHER FLOURY POTATOES [4 OR 5], PEELED AND QUARTERED

6 SPRIGS THYME, TIED IN A BUNDLE

1 BUNCH CHIVES, SNIPPED

1 CUP/35 TO 40 G LOOSELY PACKED CHOPPED FRESH PARSLEY

1/4 CUP/60 ML EXTRA-VIRGIN OLIVE OIL

3/4 TSP SALT

1/2 CUP/120 ML MILK

1/4 CUP/60 ML HEAVY CREAM

PEPPER

Put the potatoes and thyme bundle into a large pot with cold salted water to cover. Bring to a boil over medium-high heat, then reduce the heat to low and simmer for 20 to 30 minutes or until they are easily pierced with a fork.

Meanwhile, put the chives, parsley, olive oil, and salt into a blender or the bowl of a food processor and process until a smooth paste is formed.

When potatoes are done, drain and set aside, discarding the thyme bundle. Pour the milk and cream into the same pot and bring to a simmer over medium heat; then press the potatoes through a ricer directly into the pot or mash them in a large bowl, then add them to the pot. Stir the riced potatoes into the milk mixture, then stir in herb paste, mixing well until it is completely incorporated. Season to taste with salt and pepper.

Mashed Potatoes

Serves 4 to 6 [makes about 6 cups/1.25 kg]

For speed and convenience, many cooks like to peel and quarter their potatoes and boil them in salted water when making mashed potatoes (often called just "mash" in Ireland, and known as "pandy" in Cork). But steaming them in their skins leaves them drier and thus better able to soak up the cream and butter. See the following variation for Cheddar Mash.

2 1/2 LB/1.25 KG RUSSET OR OTHER FLOURY POTATOES [5 OR 6]

1 CUP/240 ML HEAVY CREAM

6 TO 8 TBSP BUTTER, SOFTENED

SALT AND PEPPER

Put the potatoes into a large pot, with the larger ones on the bottom, and add water to come halfway up the potatoes. Cover the pot and bring to a boil over high heat. When the water begins to boil, carefully drain off about half of it, reserving 2 Tbsp of the water you pour off. Return the pot to the heat, cover it again, reduce the heat to low, and let the potatoes steam for about 40 minutes. Turn off the heat; cover the potatoes with a clean, damp tea towel; and let sit for 5 minutes more.

Meanwhile, put the cream, butter, and reserved cooking water into a small pot and bring to a simmer over medium-high heat.

Remove the potatoes from the pot with a slotted spoon and carefully peel them while they are still hot. Return them to the pot and mash them well while slowly pouring in the cream mixture. Season generously with salt and pepper and finish by whisking the potatoes vigorously.

Cheddar Mash

For cheddar mash, stir 1/2 cup/60 g of grated Irish white cheddar into the potatoes after adding the cream mixture.

FADGE

Fadge [Potato Cakes]

Serves 4

In England, fadge is a small, flat bread loaf, but in Northern Ireland, the term refers to a variety of fried or baked potato cake. (*Fadge* is an Elizabethan word meaning "to fit, agree, or turn out well.") Similar cakes are also sometimes called "tatties" or "parleys." Some recipes add an egg to help bind the cakes, but if you use very floury (starchy) potatoes, an egg shouldn't be necessary. Fadge is an essential constituent of the traditional Ulster Fry (page 149).

I TBSP BUTTER, SOFTENED, PLUS 4 TBSP BUTTER
OR BACON FAT IF YOU'RE FRYING THE FADGE

I TSP SALT

4 CUPS/850 G FRESHLY MADE MASHED POTATOES
[PAGE 223]

I/2 TO 3/4 CUP/50 TO 75 G WHITE FLOUR,
PLUS MORE FOR DUSTING

In a medium bowl, mix 1 Tbsp of the butter and the salt into the potatoes. With your hands, work in enough flour to form a pliable dough.

Turn the dough out onto a lightly floured board and shape into a round about ¾ in/2 cm thick. Cut into 8 wedges.

To fry: Melt the butter or bacon fat in a large skillet and fry wedges, in batches if necessary, for about 5 minutes per side, turning once, or until cakes are golden brown on both sides.

To bake: Preheat the oven to 400°F/200°C (Gas Mark 6). Bake on a lightly greased baking sheet for 12 to 15 minutes or until the cakes are golden brown, turning once.

Miss Jane Bury's Potato Pancakes

Serves 6 to 8

In the recipe collections I've encountered from eighteenth- and early-nineteenth-century Anglo-Irish country house kitchens (many of them in the archives of the National Library in Dublin), potatoes are rarely mentioned. This may be because potatoes were considered "poor food" and thus not much eaten at fancy tables—or, more likely I think, because recipes were written down for the use of hired cooks, who may not have known how to make lobster fricassée or turkey en gelée without instruction, but would certainly have known what to do with potatoes. This exception to the rule, however, does appear in "Miss Jane Bury's Receipt Booke," part of the Townley Hall papers, from Drogheda, County Louth, now residing at the National Library. It apparently dates from the early 1700s. These pancakes are simultaneously richer but lighter in texture than Boxty Pancakes (page 217).

4 CUPS/850 G FRESHLY MADE MASHED POTATOES
[PAGE 223]

3 EGGS, LIGHTLY BEATEN

I TSP SALT

I CUP/240 ML HEAVY CREAM

3/4 CUP/175 ML MILK OR WATER, OR AS NEEDED

4 TO 6 TBSP CLARIFIED BUTTER [PAGE 362]

Put the potatoes, eggs, salt, and cream into a large bowl and stir well to form a thick batter. If the batter is too thick to flow from a spoon, dilute with a little milk or water.

Heat 2 Tbsp of the clarified butter in a large nonstick skillet over medium heat. Working in batches, pour about ¼ cup/60 ml of the batter to form each pancake (they should be 4 to 5 in/10 cm to 12.5 cm in diameter); then cook for 6 to 8 minutes, flipping once. Transfer the pancakes to a warm plate tented with foil to keep warm as they're done.

Serve topped with smoked salmon or as a side dish with meat or fish. Or serve with butter and sugar as a breakfast dish or dessert.

A FARMER'S LIFE

In his book *A Boy in the Country: An Antrim Peat Bog*, Belfast author John Stevenson paints this picture of farm life in County Antrim in the early twentieth century:

At dawn the farmer is up and out. He ploughs, harrows, carts, spreads lime or manure, cuts hay, does everything, indeed, that his men do, and in all weathers. Inside, his wife bakes griddle bread for household and servants, makes butter, helps a woman servant to milk, and prepare food for, fowls and pigs. . . . All through the day the kitchen is cumbered by great potfuls of food for beast or for the servants, whose last meal in the evening is, in summer, of potatoes and buttermilk. A huge potful of potatoes is emptied directly on the table, little heaps of salt are placed, also on the wood, beside tins of buttermilk; the men all sit round and peel and eat their potatoes without knife or fork.

Poet Patrick Kavanaugh harvesting potatoes.

IN PRAISE OF THE MURPHY

Many varieties of potatoes—also known as "praties" or "murphys"—were (and still are) grown in Ireland, each with its own characteristics and making its own demands on the farmer. In the early years of the twentieth century, writer John Stevenson offered a short course in potato diversity in his "Ode to a Pratie," written in the voice of an imagined Antrim farmer–poet named Pat M'Carty. An excerpt:

*Thy name is Murphy. On the Antrim hills
There's cruffles and white-rocks; there's skerries, too, and dukes,
And kidneys—which is early; and champions and flukes—
Which doesn't help the farmer much to pay his bills:*

*The sort's not recommended. Then there's early rose,
And forty-folds, and flounders—which is bad;
And magnum bonums:—if good seed's to be had
It is the biggest pratie that the country grows,
And tastes not bad. Some grows best in rigs
And some in drills. There's sorts ye cudn't ate;
There's others dry and floury that's a trate;
And weeshy kinds, that's only fit for pigs.
Some likes a sandy sile and some a turfy,
Others do their best in good stiff clay:
There's new varieties appearin' iv're day;
But, as I said, thy fam'ly name is Murphy.*

FAMINE

Unfortunately, it's impossible to talk about food in Ireland without talking about "the potato famine." It's important to understand, though, that the island didn't suffer from just one famine, and that the one everybody talks about, in the mid-nineteenth century—the one that changed the history not only of Ireland but also of England and America—wasn't really a famine at all.

Legend has it that when his enemies sent the High King Tuathal into exile in the first or second century A.D., God was angry and visited famine upon Ireland. What is not legend is that in the early fourteenth century, as much as a quarter of the Irish population may have perished during the great famine that swept through Europe, and that another 250,000 died from famine in 1741. Between 1816 (the so-called "year of no summer," when volcanic ash from the eruption of Mount Tambora in Indonesia covered skies worldwide for months, blocking out the sun) and 1842, some fourteen famines were recorded in Ireland. As Fionnuala Carragher, curator of domestic life at the Ulster Transport and Folk Museum in Cultra, County Down, puts it, "The nineteenth century was just *miserable* in Ireland."

The low point came with the appearance in Ireland of the potato blight, *Phytophthora infestans*. The Irish called the blight *mí-ádh*, literally "bad luck." It was worse than that. Between 1846 and 1851, more than a million poor Irish died of starvation, malnutrition, and opportunistic infections. More than a million more left Ireland. (Another five million emigrated between 1852 and 1916, three-quarters of them to the United States.) It's an oversimplification to say that

the blight hit Ireland so hard because of its overdependence on the potato. A decade before the blight arrived, a government official named Thomas Kelly told the celebrated Alexis de Toqueville, who was visiting the country, that "The Irishman raises beautiful crops, carries his harvest to the nearest port, puts it on board an English vessel, and returns home to subsist on potatoes. He rears cattle, sends them to London, and never eats meat." In fact, Ireland grew a number of crops besides potatoes in the mid-nineteenth century, and in the midst of the so-called potato famine the island remained a net exporter of foodstuffs. As George Bernard Shaw's character Malone says in *Man and Superman*, "When a country is full of food and exporting it, there can be no famine."

There are monuments all over the world memorializing the tragedy of the era; there is also a famine museum at Strokestown Park, County Roscommon, and a famine exhibition at the Skibbereen Heritage Center in County Cork. Giana Ferguson, who makes the renowned cheese Gubbeen in West Cork, has suggested another kind of commemoration. Speaking to the writer Betsy Klein about Ireland's burgeoning artisanal food movement, she said, "In terms of Irish country families there is still a traditional memory of famine. Finding something that you can make on an Irish farm . . . that gets accolades abroad and is seen as coming from the Irish land culture, that was a wonderful thing. Perhaps as well it was part of a healing process to do with recovering from the experience of famine. . . . To get back faith in the land is a sort of rebirth of our agriculture, of real food. It is hugely satisfying."

BOILED POTATOES

Chips

Serves 4

As in England, "chips" in Ireland are of course French fries (while what Americans call potato chips are known as "crisps"). Proper chips are thicker than typical French fries, though not as thick as what we call "steak fries"; unlike French fries, chips are traditionally fried only once, not twice.

2¹/₂ TO 3 POUNDS / 1.25 TO 1.5 KG MEDIUM RUSSET
POTATOES [ABOUT 6 OR 7]

SUNFLOWER OR PEANUT OIL FOR FRYING

SALT

Cut the potatoes into strips about 1 in/2.5 cm thick and 3 in/7.5 cm long, then soak them in a large bowl of cold water for 30 minutes. Rinse, then dry very thoroughly with paper towels.

Pour oil into a large, deep, heavy-bottomed pot to a depth of 3 in/7.5 cm, then heat over medium-high heat until the oil reaches 325°F/160°C on a candy/deep-fat thermometer. Fry the potatoes in small batches, stirring occasionally with a slotted spoon, for 5 to 8 minutes per batch or until golden brown.

Drain the chips on paper towels as they are cooked. Salt generously.

Boiled Potatoes

Serves 4 to 8

For the Irish poor, for generations, boiled potatoes weren't a side dish—they were dinner. One old tradition was to place two crossed metal spoons on the bottom of the pot to keep the potatoes from sticking. Irish cooks usually add new potatoes to salted water that is already boiling, but start older, larger potatoes in cold water, then bring it to a boil.

2 LB / 1 KG SMALL NEW POTATOES OF
APPROXIMATELY EQUAL SIZE, LIGHTLY SCRAPED
BUT NOT PEELED

SALT

BUTTER FOR SERVING [OPTIONAL]

CHOPPED FRESH PARSLEY OR MINT FOR GARNISH
[OPTIONAL]

Bring a large pot of water to a boil over high heat. Reduce the heat to medium-high and add the potatoes. Cook for 15 to 25 minutes or until soft but not disintegrating. (The cooking time will vary according to the variety, age, and size of potatoes.) Test for doneness with a skewer or sharp-tined fork.

Drain the potatoes, then pat dry lightly with a clean towel.

Serve traditional style, in a bowl at the table with a dish of salt on the side; or return the potatoes to the pot and toss with plenty of butter and salt, and with finely chopped parsley or mint, if you like.

Panhaggerty

Serves 2 to 4

Although the name Haggerty (or Hegarty) is known in Northern Ireland and in County Cork, this gratin is English in origin—probably from the vicinity of Newcastle. One theory is that the Haggerty in question is not a family name at all, but a Northumberland corruption of the French word *hachis*, meaning a dish of chopped or minced ingredients. It is nonetheless eaten in Ireland, sometimes under the name "farmhouse bake."

4 TBSP BUTTER OR BACON FAT

4 TO 5 SLICES BACON, CHOPPED

1 ONION, THINLY SLICED

¹/₂ LB / 250 G WAXY POTATOES, THINLY SLICED

SALT AND PEPPER

6 OZ / 175 G IRISH CHEDDAR, GRATED

Preheat the oven to 350°F/175°C (Gas Mark 4).

Melt half the butter or bacon fat in a large ovenproof skillet, preferably cast-iron, over low heat. Fry the bacon, stirring frequently, for 10 to 15 minutes, or until crisp.

Remove the bacon from the skillet with a slotted spoon and set aside to drain on paper towels.

Cook the onions in the same skillet for 6 to 8 minutes, or until they soften but don't brown, then remove them from the skillet and add to bacon, mixing the onions and bacon together.

Remove the pan from the heat, then carefully lay a thin layer of potatoes, about a third of them, on bottom of the pan so that they completely cover it. Season it lightly with salt and pepper. Cover with a layer of onions and bacon, about half of them, then a layer of cheese, about a third of it.

Add a layer of half the remaining potatoes and season lightly with salt and pepper. Cover with a layer of all the remaining onions and bacon, then a layer of about half of the remaining cheese. Finish with a layer of the remaining potatoes and season lightly with salt and pepper.

Dot or drizzle the remaining butter or bacon fat over the final layer of potatoes; then bake for 45 minutes.

When dish is done, top with the reserved cheese and put under the broiler for 3 to 4 minutes until the cheese has melted and begun to brown.

Potato Apple Cakes

Serves 4

These cakes were served in Northern Ireland at afternoon teas during apple harvest season and on Halloween.

I RECIPE FADGE [POTATO CAKES, PAGE 225] DOUGH, CUT INTO 8 WEDGES BUT NOT COOKED

I SMALL COOKING APPLE, PEELED, CORED, AND VERY THINLY SLICED

1/4 CUP/25 G FLOUR, PLUS MORE FOR DUSTING

4 TBSP BUTTER

2 TBSP SUGAR

Preheat the oven to 375°F/190°C (Gas Mark 5).

Put 4 wedges of fadge on a well-floured surface. Layer the apple slices evenly on top of the wedges, leaving a ½-in/1.25-cm border around the edges. Top each wedge with another wedge, then gently pinch the edges together to seal. Dredge each assembled wedge in flour, neatening its shape and shaking off any excess flour as you go.

Melt 3 Tbsp of the butter in a large skillet or nonstick pan over medium heat. Fry the cakes for about 5 minutes on each side or until they are nicely browned and cooked through, turning them once, very carefully. Transfer the cakes to a large baking sheet and set them aside until they're cool enough to handle.

Using a sharp knife, carefully halve each cake lengthwise along the seams, dot the interiors with the remaining tablespoon of butter, and sprinkle them with sugar.

Pinch the cake halves back togther and bake them, without turning, for about 15 minutes.

SIR WALTER RALEIGH AND THE SPUD

The usual story is that English courtier, poet, soldier, and explorer Sir Walter Raleigh (circa 1552–1618) brought the potato to Ireland. He came there to help the English Crown suppress the so-called Desmond Rebellions between 1579 and 1583, and stayed on to become the not particularly successful landlord of several seized estates. Raleigh supposedly discovered the spud through his ill-fated expeditions to Virginia. One version of the tale has him planting seed potatoes on his property at Killua Castle, County Westmeath (an obelisk on the site commemorates the occasion today). Another claims that he cultivated them at Myrtle Grove, his estate in Youghal, County Cork. Still another variation involves English poet Edmund Spenser (author of *The Faerie Queene*), who spent some years in Ireland and, for his own services in the Desmond Rebellions, was given property in County Cork near Raleigh's. Spenser and Raleigh are said to have met in 1580 at Castle Matrix in Rathkeale, County Limerick, where Raleigh gave potatoes to both the poet and the castle's owner, Lord Southwell, whereupon one or both promptly propagated them.

The trouble with these stories is that they're all speculation; no surviving estate records or contemporaneous accounts betray an early association of potatoes with any of the properties usually named. As for still another theory about how potatoes got to Ireland, that they came ashore with shipwrecked sailors from the Spanish Armada, there *is* documentary evidence that there were no potatoes on Armada ships. Anyway, most of the Spanish sailors who came ashore in Ireland were promptly executed, and it seems highly unlikely that the locals would have pulled soggy tubers out of the dead men's garments and rushed them off to their gardens. There is, however, almost certainly a connection with Spain, because an early name for potatoes in Ireland was an *spáinneach*. or Spanish, and it is likely that potatoes in fact first reached the island through something so prosaic as commercial trade with the Iberian Peninsula.

ODE TO COLCANNON

Who but the Irish would write a ballad praising potatoes mashed with kale? This traditional song, called "Colcannon or The Skillet Pot," probably dates from the late nineteenth century. It is offered here in one of its countless variations. The line about the ring, incidentally, is a reference to the fact that tokens supposedly predicting one's future state in life were sometimes hidden in the colcannon, as they were in boxty, a potato cake, and barm brack, a tea bread. A "sprissman" is presumably a *sprissaun*, from the word for twig or the spray of a bush and by extension someone of little significance.

Did you ever eat colcannon when 'twas made with yellow cream
And the kale and praties blended like the picture in a dream?
Did you ever eat colcannon when 'twas made with thickened cream
And the greens and scallions blended like the picture in a dream?
Did you ever take a forkful and dip it in the lake
Of the clover-flavored butter that your mother used to make?
Did you ever scoop a hole on top to hold the melting cake
Of the heather-flavored butter that your mother used to make?
Oh, you did, yes you did! So did he and so did I
And the more I think about it, sure, the more I want to cry.
Did you ever eat and eat, afraid you'd let the ring go past,
And some old married sprissman would get it at the last?
God be with the happy times, when trouble we had not
And our mothers made colcannon in the little skillet pot.

LADY MOUNT CASHEL'S POTATOES

Stephen Moore, the second earl of Mount Cashel, and his wife, Margaret, Lady Mount Cashel, who maintained residences in counties Antrim, Cork, and Kildare, traveled to the Continent in the early years of the nineteenth century. While in Paris, they passed time with the Polish Countess Myscelska, their son's godmother. Stephen tells the following story:

This Godmother of his is a very amiable Being. She has just arriv'd at that unbounded extent of Aristocracy which always produces the utmost republicanism of manners, and with more than regal revenues, she is the most simple and unpretending of any one in Society; the other day she call'd in here, and saw Lady Mount Cashell eating plain boil'd Potatoes for her luncheon in the middle of the day. She then heard for the first time that that was the principal Food of the Irish, and immediately resolv'd on giving Lady Mount Cashell a breakfast in compliment to her country. We went there and literally found nothing but Potatoes dress'd in fifty different fashions. I thought the repast would never have been at an end, such was the torture she had put her fancy to in devising methods to diversify the cookery.

THE NATURAL HEALTH FO

HIGH FIBRE • HIGH QUALITY

IRISH GARDEN
POTATOES

LOW FAT

MARIS PIPER	RECORD
KERRS PINK	HOME
GOLDEN WONDER	QUEENS
PENTLAND DELL	ROGSTER

NET W

THE NATURAL HEAL

HIGH FIBRE • HIGH

IRISH GA
POTA

LOW FAT

| MARIS PIPER |
| KERRS PINK |
| GOLDEN WONDER |
| PENTLAND DELL |

NET W

IRISH GARDEN
POTATOES

LOW FAT

MARIS PIPER	RECORD
KERRS PINK	HOME
GOLDEN WONDER	QUEENS
PENTLAND DELL	ROGSTER

NET WE
-80

IRISH GARDEN
POTATOES

LOW FAT

MARIS PIPER	RECORD
KERRS PINK	HOME
GOLDEN WONDER	QUEENS
PENTLAND DELL	ROGSTER

HIGH

IRIS

Treasures from the Garden

Garlic with May butter / Cureth all disease.

—Old Irish poem

A forest tall of real leeks, of onions and of carrots, stood behind the house.

—"The Vision of Mac Conglinne" [circa eleventh century A.D.]

Because potatoes are so overwhelmingly identified with Ireland, with cabbage probably a close second, people are sometimes surprised to learn that vegetables of almost every type

thrive on the island—some of them indigenous and wild or descended from wild, some of them imported by various invaders over the centuries, some of them relative newcomers planted to satisfy increasingly sophisticated eaters and an ever more diverse citizenry.

Wild mushrooms and herbs were used in earlier times for purposes both culinary and medicinal. Watercress (see page 262) was a staple, but the Celts also ate nettles, charlock (*Sinapis arvensis* L.), sorrel, the unrelated wood sorrel (sometimes confused with the shamrock; see page 264), sea kale or strand cabbage (*Crambe maritima* L.), and spinachlike *Chenopodia,* popularly known as "fat hen" and "good King Henry." They also pulled wild celery, carrots, and parsnips from the ground, and consumed large quantities of wild onions, leeks, and garlic—the last of these memorialized today in place names like Cloncraff (County Offaly), from *cluain creamha,* meaning "garlic meadow," and Glencrew (County Tyrone), from *gleann creamha,* meaning "garlic glen." Jonathan Swift once penned a little verse paean to onions that went "They make the blood warmer, / You'll feed like a farmer, / For this is every cook's opinion / No savoury dish without an onion." It is an expression of Irish affection for these plants that onions and leeks, along with parsnips, are believed to have been the first vegetables cultivated in Ireland.

Peas and beans arrived in the country with the Normans in the twelfth century, and were probably first grown in monastery gardens. Potatoes and cabbage are sixteenth-century imports. By the eighteenth century, an astonishing variety of vegetables and herbs was available, at least to the wealthy. A bill of sale from Dublin nurseryman Daniel Bullen, dated February 1755, reveals that William Balfour of Townley Hall in Drogheda,

County Louth, purchased seeds for his kitchen garden for the following items: leeks, two kinds of onions, carrots, parsnips, four kinds of turnips, two kinds of salsify, shallots, garlic, three kinds of radish, four kinds of lettuce, spinach, beets, sorrel, cardoons, parsley, cress, endive, purslane, asparagus, cauliflower, four kinds of cabbage, two kinds of cucumber, celery, thyme, hyssop, two kinds of marjoram, winter savory, marigold, four kinds of beans, and ten kinds of peas and field peas.

About the only thing not grown much in Ireland until the twentieth century were what we think of as Mediterranean vegetables (though they mostly come from the Americas): Squash was rare, as were tomatoes—though I did find a recipe for tomato sauce in an undated, but probably nineteenth-century, recipe manuscript. Peppers and chiles, though much appreciated in modern Ireland, were similarly absent, and it was clear that even the titled classes had no experience of the exotic eggplant, which the English (and French) call *aubergine*. Traveling in the Drôme in southeastern France in the early nineteenth century, Stephen Moore, the second earl of Mount Cashel, reports that his hosts "gave us for supper, instead of soup, the Food of the Country call'd . . . Oberginne which is a sort of purple Fruit fried in little slices."

Today, Ireland is notably hospitable to vegetarians. Almost every restaurant and café, even the ones with Michelin stars, offers meatless options, conceived with some imagination. And the best restaurant in Cork City is arguably Denis Cotter's all-vegetarian Café Paradiso, whose food is so imaginative that Darina Allen of Ballymaloe once told me that she'd eaten there three times before she "tumbled to the fact that there was no meat or fish on the menu."

Buttered Leeks

Serves 4 to 8

I had this dish, made from beautiful dark green leeks just out of the garden, alongside perfect roast lamb at Ballyvolane House in Castlelyons, County Cork.

8 MEDIUM LEEKS, THOROUGHLY WASHED,
TRIMMED TO LEAVE APPROXIMATELY AS MUCH
GREEN AS THERE IS WHITE, AND CUT ON THE
DIAGONAL INTO PIECES ABOUT 1 IN/2.5 CM LONG

1/2 CUP/125 G BUTTER, PLUS MORE
[OPTIONAL] FOR SERVING

SALT AND PEPPER

Put the leeks and butter into a large saucepan with a lid. Add ½ cup/120 ml water, cover, and bring to a boil over high heat. Reduce the heat to medium and cook for 5 to 8 minutes, or until the leeks are tender but not mushy.

Drain and season to taste with salt and pepper. Let a pat or two of additional butter melt over the hot leeks if you wish.

Leeks Cooked in Milk

Serves 4 to 8

This simple preparation would have been a popular side dish in the dining rooms of the old Anglo-Irish estates.

8 MEDIUM LEEKS, THOROUGHLY WASHED AND
TRIMMED TO LEAVE APPROXIMATELY AS MUCH
GREEN AS THERE IS WHITE

ABOUT 3 CUPS/720 ML MILK

4 TBSP BUTTER

SALT

Put the leeks into a large skillet, in two layers if necessary, and pour in the milk, adding more if needed to completely cover the leeks.

Bring just to a boil, then immediately reduce heat, cover the skillet, and simmer for 15 to 20 minutes or until the leeks are tender.

Transfer the leeks (without the milk) to a serving dish, slather with butter, and season to taste with salt.

Leek Pie

Serves 6

This recipe was developed by Kevin Driver, a chef at Kelly's Resort Hotel and Spa on the sea in Rosslare, County Wexford.

3 TBSP WHITE FLOUR, PLUS MORE FOR DUSTING

3/4 CUP BUTTER/180 G, SOFTENED,
PLUS MORE FOR GREASING

4 CUPS/500 G FINELY CHOPPED LEEKS
[WHITE PART ONLY]

1 CUP/240 ML HEAVY CREAM

1/2 LB/250 G GRUYÈRE CHEESE, GRATED

1 1/2 LB/750 G PUFF PASTRY, HOMEMADE [PAGE 363]
OR STORE-BOUGHT

1 EGG, BEATEN

Work the flour into about one-third of the butter to form a beurre manié.

Melt the remaining butter in a large skillet over low heat, then add the leeks. Cook for 15 to 20 minutes or until the leeks are very soft, stirring frequently.

Stir in the beurre manié and cream, increase the heat to high, and bring to a boil. Remove from the heat immediately and set aside to cool. When the mixture has reached room temperature, stir in the cheese.

Meanwhile, preheat the oven to 400°F/200°C (Gas Mark 6).

Divide the pastry in half and roll out each piece on a floured board into a disk 10 in/25 cm in diameter. Put one disk on a lightly greased baking sheet and brush some of the egg over its surface. Put the leek mixture in the middle of the disk and smooth out so that it comes to within about 1 in/2.5 cm of the edges. Cover with the remaining disk and crimp the edges. Brush the remaining egg over the top and cut a few X's in the dough with a knife.

Bake the pie for 10 minutes, then lower the oven temperature to 325°F/160°C (Gas Mark 3) and bake for 20 to 25 minutes more or until the crust is golden brown.

Baked Onions

Serves 4 to 6

"[L]est your kissing should be spoiled," Jonathan Swift once proposed, "The onion must be thoroughly boiled." Nonetheless, those onions were often roasted in the embers of the hearth in modest Irish homes, or in the all-purpose cauldron called the "bastable" (see page 287).

12 SMALL ONIONS [ABOUT 2 IN/5 CM IN DIAMETER], UNPEELED

BUTTER FOR SERVING

COARSE SEA SALT FOR SERVING

Preheat the oven to 400°F/200°C (Gas Mark 6).

Spread the onions out on a baking sheet and roast for 20 to 30 minutes or until soft.

Let the onions cool slightly and, when they are cool enough to handle, cut off the root ends. Serve with the skins still on, to be squeezed out by each diner, who should add butter and salt to taste.

Peas with Mint

Serves 6

Peas are mentioned in documents in Ireland as early as the mid-fourteenth century. The famous preparation of "mushy peas" (the name is self-explanatory; see page 244) is traditionally made with a variety of dried field peas. Fresh Irish peas right out of the garden, which should never be cooked until they're mushy, are often served with mint, with which peas have a natural affinity.

1 TSP SUGAR

2 SPRIGS FRESH MINT,
PLUS 1 TBSP MINCED FRESH MINT

3 CUPS SHELLED FRESH PEAS
[ABOUT 3 LB/1.5 KG PEAS IN PODS]

SALT

2 TBSP BUTTER

Combine the sugar, mint sprigs, peas, and salt to taste in a medium saucepan and add cold water to just cover. Bring to a boil over high heat, then reduce the heat to low and simmer for 4 to 5 minutes, or until the peas are just cooked.

Drain the peas, return them to the pan, and stir in butter and minced mint leaves. Adjust the seasoning if necessary.

PEAS WITH MINT

WHERE IT ALL BEGAN

"I was away at school when my mother told me that she was opening a restaurant at our house," Tim Allen, one of Myrtle Allen's six children, told me one night. "I was very excited. I thought I'd come home and have chips and mixed grills and all. I was so disappointed when I got back and discovered that she was serving the same food I'd eaten all my life."

As it turned out, the idea of serving that "same food" in a restaurant instead of just at the kitchen table was revolutionary. Ireland had never before seen a nice dining room in which fresh, honest products, many of them grown or raised either on the property or within a few miles of the place, were served simply but perfectly cooked—and the idea ended up galvanizing the Irish food scene.

The site was Ballymaloe House, a seventeenth-century country complex built around a fifteenth-century Norman castle in the East Cork village of Shanagarry. (*Ballymaloe* means "the place of sweet honey." Shanagarry takes its name from the Irish for "old garden.") A local fruit grower named Ivan Allen and his wife, the former Myrtle Hill, moved there in 1948. Myrtle taught herself to cook, using the riches of the farm. In 1964, she opened what was originally called the Yeats Room in one section of the house. As the restaurant gained popularity, Allen became an enthusiastic and vocal advocate for Irish food. At the time, the idea that there might

be something seriously worth eating in the country seemed like heresy, if not sheer madness, to many people, even (especially?) in Ireland itself.

Convinced that Irish raw materials were as good as any in the world, and that the traditions of real Irish farmhouse cooking were worth preserving and refining, Allen began encouraging other farmers and food producers, as well as chefs and restaurateurs, to look in their own backyards, literally and metaphorically, for quality. (Many of the most prominent "food people" in Ireland today have worked at Ballymaloe.) For three years in the early 1980s, she even ran a well-received Irish restaurant in Paris, La Ferme Irlandaise. It would be facile but not at all inaccurate to call Allen the Alice Waters of Ireland—except that she opened her restaurant and began her own crusades not in cosmopolitan Berkeley in the early '70s, but in isolated, unsophisticated southern Ireland almost a decade earlier.

Today, in her late eighties, Myrtle Allen is still going strong, and the food at Ballymaloe—the garden-fresh soups, fresh fish from nearby Ballycotton, summer turkey (see page 139), East Cork lamb, vegetables and salads from the soil outside, and all the rest—is better than ever. Still no chips or mixed grills, though.

Mushy Peas

Serves 4

A popular accompaniment, in Ireland as in England, to fish and chips or any kind of simply fried fish, mushy peas—which are pretty much just what they sound like—also go nicely with grilled or roasted salmon or roast chicken. In some of Ireland's better restaurants, fresh peas are used in this dish, but traditionalists insist on a variety of dried field peas called "marrowfat peas."

1/2 LB/250 G MARROWFAT PEAS
[SEE SOURCES, PAGE 369], SOAKED OVERNIGHT

2 TBSP BUTTER

SALT AND PEPPER

Drain the peas and put them into a large saucepan with enough water to cover them by about 2 in/5 cm. Bring the water to a boil over high heat, then reduce the heat to low, cover the pan loosely, and simmer, stirring occasionally, for 1½ to 2 hours or until the peas are very soft. If the peas dry out, add enough water to just cover them and continue cooking.

Drain the peas, then return them to the same saucepan and stir them for 1 to 2 minutes to dry them out. Add the butter and plenty of salt and pepper to the peas and stir well until the butter is melted. Beat the peas with a heavy whisk or wooden spoon until smooth but with some lumps remaining.

Artichokes in Butter

Serves 6

The artichoke has been grown in Ireland at least since the time of the Norman invasion of the island in the latter part of the twelfth century. Recipe collections from the seventeenth and eighteenth centuries include them, usually under the name

"harty choakes" (or "choaks"). They were sometimes baked into pies (see page 120); in one recipe dating from 1683, the pie includes grapes, dates, and hard-cooked eggs. Darina Allen teaches this simple preparation of the vegetable at her Ballymaloe Cookery School in Shanagarry, County Cork.

2 TSP SALT

2 TSP WHITE WINE VINEGAR

6 ARTICHOKES, BASES TRIMMED SO THAT THEY
WILL SIT FLAT ON A PLATE

3/4 CUP/190 G BUTTER

JUICE OF 1/2 LEMON

MELTED BUTTER FOR SERVING

Bring 5 cups/1.2 L water to a boil in a large pot over high heat. Add the salt and vinegar, then add the artichokes and return to a boil. Reduce the heat to low and simmer for 25 to 30 minutes, or until one of the larger leaves pulls away easily from one of the artichokes.

Meanwhile, melt the butter in a small saucepan and stir in the lemon juice.

Serve the artichokes on heated plates with melted butter for dipping in small bowls on the side.

Stewed Lettuce

Serves 4

This is an adaptation of a recipe that I found in "Mrs. A. W. Baker's Cookery Book, Vol. 1" a handwritten manuscript of "receipts" compiled in Ballytobin, County Kilkenny, circa 1810, now in the National Library in Dublin. Whoever originated the recipe—it was possibly a Mrs. Ellis, presumably either one of Mrs. Baker's cooks or one of her friends—recommends serving the lettuce with lamb.

4 LARGE HEADS BUTTER LETTUCE, TRIMMED

8 CUPS/2 L STRONG BEEF OR LAMB STOCK [PAGE 357]

3 OR 4 SORREL LEAVES

1 WHOLE ONION, PEELED

1 LEMON, QUARTERED

SALT

Bring a large pot of salted water to a boil, plunge in the lettuce heads, and boil for about 1 minute. Remove the lettuce heads from the pot and drain in a colander.

When the lettuce is cool enough to handle, halve the heads down to but not through the stem, leaving the stems intact to hold the heads together.

Combine the stock, sorrel leaves, and onion in the same large pot, bring to a boil, then reduce heat to low. Add the lettuce heads to the pot and simmer, uncovered, for 10 to 15 minutes, or until tender.

Remove the lettuce heads from the pot and drain in a colander. (Reserve the stock for another use.) Squeeze 1 lemon quarter over each head before serving, then season with salt.

Buttered Kale

Serves 4

This is a quick and useful—and very Irish—side dish for almost any meat, poultry, or offal dish.

2 TBSP BUTTER

1 LB/500 G KALE, STALKS TRIMMED, COARSELY CHOPPED

SALT

Melt the butter in a large skillet over medium heat. Dunk the kale into a large bowl of cold water, then shake off the excess moisture (do not dry) and add to the skillet. Season to taste with salt, then stir the kale until wilted, 3 to 5 minutes.

Kale with Cream

Serves 4

This recipe is adapted from one offered by Theodora Fitz-Gibbon in her invaluable book *Irish Traditional Food*. It was, she says, her father's favorite method of cooking kale. She recommends serving it as a side dish with pork or red meat.

1 LB/500 G KALE, STALKS TRIMMED, COARSELY CHOPPED

2 TBSP BUTTER

2 TBSP HEAVY CREAM

PINCH OF NUTMEG

SALT AND WHITE PEPPER

Bring a large pot of salted water to a boil, add the kale, and cook for about 20 minutes, or until the leaves are very tender.

Drain the kale, reserving about 2 Tbsp of the cooking water, then chop kale more finely.

In a large saucepan, melt the butter over medium heat. Add the cream, nutmeg, and salt and pepper to taste. Add the kale and reserved cooking water. Stir well and cook, continuing to stir, until the sauce is slightly reduced, 3 to 5 minutes.

RAGGEDY JACK AND FRIENDS

Kale, one of the essential vegetables of Irish cuisine, is a variety of wild mustard, closely related to collard greens and cousin to cabbage, broccoli, Brussels sprouts, cauliflower, and kohlrabi. Known in some northern counties as Raggedy Jack for its serrated leaves, it is, like its relations, high in vitamins C and K and many other beneficial compounds (including sulforaphane, believed to be an anticarcinogenic), and keeps its nutritional value well into the winter. It is more or less impervious to frost and, like cabbage, actually tastes better—and sweeter—after it has frozen. There is a variety of perennial kale, in fact, that is never taken from the ground. Known in Ireland as "cut-and-come" or "cottier's kale" (a *cottier* is someone who lives in a cottage), it doesn't flower or seed and is harvested by simply cutting off its leaves, leaving the plant behind to regenerate. Peter Ward (below, right, with his wife Mary) of the grocery shop and café Country Choice in Nenagh, County Tipperary, maintains (with a bit of a grin)

that colcannon, that definitively Irish mélange of potatoes and kale, should always have a bit of wool in it: "After the grass is gone in the winter and all that's coming up is the kale in the kitchen garden," he explains, "the sheep would slip under the fence and come nibble on it, leaving a bit of wool behind."

While it's likely that kale has been cultivated in Ireland since medieval times, cabbage seems to be a more recent arrival. The earliest reference to its cultivation on the island dates from 1690. There are a number of different varieties grown there today, some with loose leaves, some tight heads; white cabbage is particularly prevalent. There is an old Irish folk custom that involves sending a young woman of marriageable age blindfolded into the fields at night to pull up a cabbage. When it is cut open, if its heart is sweet, then so too will be the heart of her future husband; if it's hard and bitter, well . . .

Cabbage with Ginger

Serves 6

There has been a thriving spice trade in Ireland since at least the early sixteenth century, and probably earlier. (Recipes for curry powder and for fish and meat pickled with spices appear in seventeenth-century Irish recipe manuscripts.) Ginger somehow came to be particularly associated with Michaelmas, September 29, perhaps because it was a popular remedy for many illnesses, and St. Michael the Archangel, whom the feast honors, is the patron saint of healers. This recipe comes from Brocka on the Water in Ballinderry, County Tipperary.

I CUP RED WINE VINEGAR

I CUP SUGAR

I SMALL HEAD RED CABBAGE CORED AND
THINLY SLICED

ONE I- TO I $^1/_2$-IN/2.5- TO 4-CM PIECE
FRESH GINGER, PEELED AND MINCED

2 CLOVES GARLIC, MINCED

SALT AND PEPPER

Combine the vinegar, sugar, cabbage, ginger, and garlic in a medium nonreactive pot. Season to taste with salt and pepper. Bring to a boil over high heat, then reduce the heat to medium-low and simmer, uncovered, for about 40 to 45 minutes, or until the liquid is reduced to a syrup and the cabbage is soft.

Serve warm or cold.

Souffléed Cauliflower

Serves 4 to 6

"How many gardeners grow the same vegetables year after year, more cauliflower than can possibly be used before they burst with glorious yellow bloom and eventually reach the compost heap?" wrote Florence Irwin in introducing the "Vegetables and Salads" chapter of her famous book *The Cookin' Woman*. "The same with all the other cabbage tribe." She then went on to give recipes for such less common vegetables as salsify, sugar peas, celeriac, and kohlrabi—and also this one for, well, cauliflower.

I LARGE CAULIFLOWER, TRIMMED AND DIVIDED
INTO FLORETS

I $^1/_2$ CUPS/360 ML WHITE SAUCE [PAGE 360]

$^1/_2$ TSP POWDERED MUSTARD

SALT AND PEPPER

2 EGGS, SEPARATED

$^1/_2$ CUP/60 G GRATED IRISH CHEDDAR CHEESE

Put the cauliflower into a large bowl and cover with cold salted water. Set aside for 30 minutes.

Bring a large pot of salted water to a boil over high heat and add the cauliflower. Boil for 10 minutes, then drain and refresh in a large bowl of cold water.

Preheat the oven to 400°F/200°C (Gas Mark 6).

In a medium saucepan, heat the white sauce over medium heat, stirring constantly. Do not boil. Remove from the heat and stir in the mustard and salt and pepper to taste. Add the egg yolks one at a time, whisking them in until well combined, then stir in all but about 1 Tbsp of the cheese.

Whip the egg whites until stiff and fold them into the soufflé mixture.

Drain the cauliflower and put into a baking dish just large enough to hold it in a single layer. Spoon the soufflé mixture over the cauliflower. Bake for 20 to 30 minutes, or until the soufflé has risen and just started to brown. Sprinkle the remaining Tbsp of cheese over the soufflé just before serving.

LEAVES

Though we know from historical evidence that wild greens and other vegetables were eaten raw by the ancient Irish, in forms that would probably qualify as "salad," it's safe to say that salads as we know them were never a staple of the traditional Irish farmhouse table. Well into the twentieth century, even in fancy restaurants, salad—if it was served at all—was apt to be a sorry affair, not much more than soggy lettuce laden with bottled dressing. County Galway–based chef Gerry Galvin, for instance, notes, "I was in my late teens before I realised that a salad should not automatically include cooked ham and salad cream." In his book *The Drimcong Food Affair,* a collection of recipes from his now-closed Drimcong House in Moycullen, he passes along approvingly his interpretation of his friend Joachim Beug's recipe for salad. (It might be noted that one important step—call it 3.a.—is missing: dry the salad very well.)

1. Find the garden.
2. Pick as much salad as you need to fill a large bowl.
3. Wash it under the tap.
4. Toss it in oil, lemon juice, salt, pepper, and a pinch of sugar.
5. Assemble the guests.
6. Eat!

GLAZED CARROTS

Broccoli in Butter

Serves 4

Main dishes in Irish restaurants, even in the most sophisticated ones, are almost always served with additional vegetables (including potatoes) on the side. Simply cooked broccoli is a common offering.

I HEAD BROCCOLI, TRIMMED AND
CUT LENGTHWISE INTO FLORETS WITH
STEMS 3 TO 4 IN/7.5 TO 10 CM LONG

3 TBSP BUTTER

SALT AND PEPPER

Fill a large bowl with cold water and ice from 1 ice cube tray.

Bring a large pot of salted water to a boil over high heat. Blanch the broccoli until just cooked, 4 to 5 minutes, then drain and immediately plunge it into the ice water bath. Let sit for 3 to 4 minutes, then drain and pat dry with paper towels.

Melt the butter in a large skillet over medium heat, then add the broccoli and toss to coat well with butter. Cook for 2 to 3 minutes or until heated through. Season generously with salt and pepper.

Glazed Carrots

Serves 4

Wild carrots were part of the Irish diet in prehistoric times, and their cultivated cousins figure in many traditional Irish dishes.

I LB/500 G CARROTS, TRIMMED, PEELED,
AND CUT INTO BATONS ABOUT 3 IN/7.5 CM LONG
AND I/2 IN/1.25 CM WIDE

2 TBSP BUTTER

PINCH OF SUGAR

SALT

I TBSP MINCED FRESH MINT [OPTIONAL]

Put the carrots in a medium saucepan with the butter, sugar, salt to taste, and about ½ cup/120 ml water. Cover the pan, bring the water to a boil over high heat, then reduce the heat to low, and cook for 6 to 8 minutes or until the water has nearly evaporated.

Shake the saucepan so that the glaze covers all the carrots. Garnish with mint, if you like.

Carrot and Parsnip Mash

Serves 4 to 6

Darina Allen notes that this dish is sometimes called "Green, White, and Gold" or "Sunshine."

I TSP SUGAR

3 TO 4 CARROTS, CUT INTO I/4-IN/6-MM SLICES

5 TO 6 PARSNIPS, CUT INTO I/4-IN/6-MM SLICES

3 TBSP BUTTER

SALT AND PEPPER

LEAVES OF 5 OR 6 SPRIGS PARSLEY, MINCED

Bring a large pot of water to a boil over high heat. Add the sugar, then the carrots and parsnips. Continue boiling for 10 to 12 minutes or until the vegetables are very soft.

Drain the vegetables and mash them together in a large bowl, adding butter and plenty of salt and pepper.

Serve sprinkled with minced parsley.

Parsnip Cakes

Serves 4

Parsnips have been part of the Irish diet for many centuries. Cookbook author and culinary historian Theodora FitzGibbon, for example, cites an account from 1673 in which a traveler notes that "The Irish feed much also on parsnips." Northern Irish author and journalist Clare Connery writes that her recipe for parsnip cakes was one of her grandmother's favorites, "made from fresh parsnips grown in her cottage garden."

1 LB/500 G PARSNIPS, PEELED AND SLICED

2 TBSP WHITE FLOUR

PINCH OF GROUND MACE

2 TBSP BUTTER, MELTED

SALT AND PEPPER

1 LARGE EGG, BEATEN

1/2 CUP/30 G DRY BREAD CRUMBS

OIL FOR FRYING

Boil the parsnips in a large pot of salted water until tender, then drain and mash them well in a medium bowl. Stir in the flour, mace, butter, and salt and pepper to taste, then form the parsnips into small, flat, round cakes.

Dip the cakes, one at a time, into the beaten egg, and then into the bread crumbs. Put about 1 in/2.5 cm of oil into a large skillet and heat over medium-high heat. Fry the cakes for 5 to 6 minutes, turning once, until brown on both sides.

Rutabagas with Caramelized Onions

Serves 6

In Ireland, "turnip" usually means rutabaga, the yellow-orange version of the vegetable, called "swedes" (short for "Swedish turnips") in the United Kingdom. Turnips, of whatever color, were apparently a bit of a hard sell to the Irish in earlier years (farmers didn't like them because they required manure they thought better saved for the potatoes), but during the famine years of the nineteenth century, they were planted in some areas where potato crops failed. Darina Allen cites a report from Barnesmore, County Donegal, that in some places peoples' "skin turned yellow from the eating of swedes." For more modest consumption, she notes, in her *Irish Traditional Cooking*, that "If you are going to serve [rutabagas] mashed in the usual way, you should perk it up with caramelized onions."

3 TBSP CANOLA OR EXTRA-VIRGIN OLIVE OIL

3 ONIONS, SLICED

SALT

6 TO 8 RUTABAGAS [ABOUT 2 LB/1 KG IN ALL], CUT INTO 3/4-IN/2-CM CUBES

6 TBSP BUTTER

PEPPER

Heat the oil over low heat in a large skillet. Add the onions and stir to coat them all, then season generously with salt. Cook very slowly for 45 to 60 minutes, stirring occasionally, until the onions are golden brown and almost marmalade-like in consistency.

Meanwhile, put the rutabagas into a large pot of salted water and bring to a boil over high heat. Reduce the heat to medium and boil slowly for 20 to 30 minutes or until the rutabagas are soft. Drain, transfer to a medium bowl, and mash thoroughly, beating in the butter. Season generously with salt and pepper, then stir in the onions.

Turnip Purée

Serves 4

At the Tannery in Dungarvan, County Waterford, chef Paul Flynn serves this purée with his Crubeen Tortellini (page 204). It's also a good side dish for pork or duck.

1 LARGE RUTABAGA OR 2 TO 3 TURNIPS [1 TO 1 1/4 LB/ 500 TO 625 G TOTAL], CHOPPED

3 TBSP BUTTER, SOFTENED

1/2 TSP GROUND NUTMEG

SALT AND PEPPER

Bring a medium pot of salted water to boil over high heat, add the rutabaga or turnips, return to a boil, and cook for 15 to 20 minutes or until very soft.

Drain; then put into a medium bowl. Mash in the butter and season with nutmeg and salt and pepper to taste. Purée in a blender or food processor.

Candied Turnips with Crozier Blue

Serves 4

Paul Flynn developed this recipe for the Bord Bía, the Irish Food Board.

2 TBSP SUNFLOWER OIL

1 SMALL RUTABAGA OR WHITE TURNIP, CUT INTO 1/2-IN/1.25-CM CUBES

1 1/4 CUPS/300 ML HARD CIDER

1 TBSP BROWN SUGAR

PINCH OF ALLSPICE

SALT

1/2 LB/250 G CROZIER BLUE CHEESE [SEE PAGE 64] OR ANOTHER FIRM SHEEP'S MILK BLUE, CUT INTO 4 THIN SLABS OF EQUAL SIZE

1 CUP/50 G MIXED SPROUTS, SUCH AS RADISH, ALFALFA, LENTIL, AND MUNG BEAN, OR CHOPPED WATERCRESS

Put a shallow roasting pan into a cold oven, then preheat the oven to 400°F/200°C (Gas Mark 6).

When oven is preheated, put the oil and rutabaga into the roasting pan and stir to coat well. Bake for 5 minutes, then stir in the cider, sugar, and allspice, stirring to coat the rutabaga thoroughly.

Bake for 20 minutes or until the liquid has evaporated and the turnips are beginning to caramelize. Remove from the oven and season to taste with salt.

To serve, divide the rutabaga evenly among 4 plates. Top each serving with a slab of cheese, then scatter a few sprouts on top of the cheese.

Tomato Pie

Serves 4

Though Ireland is capable of producing excellent tomatoes, Irish recipes employing them are rare—at least until the "Mediterranean period" of the late twentieth century. (This is hardly surprising when you consider that even in Provence and the northern half of Italy, tomatoes were very seldom used until a hundred years ago or so.) This recipe comes from an unnamed member of the Portstewart (County Derry) Women's Institute and dates from the mid-1940s.

2 TBSP BUTTER, PLUS MORE FOR GREASING

1 CUP/60 G FRESH BREAD CRUMBS

3 LARGE TOMATOES, SLICED ABOUT 1/2 IN/1.25 CM THICK

1 ONION, MINCED

SALT

Preheat the oven to 400°F/200°C (Gas Mark 6).

Lightly grease a baking dish large enough to hold 4 tomato slices in a single layer.

Sprinkle a thin layer of bread crumbs on the bottom of the baking dish, then put one layer (4 slices) of tomato on top of them. Scatter some onion over the tomatoes, then season lightly with salt. Repeat the process to use up all of the tomatoes, onion, and bread crumbs, ending with a layer of bread crumbs on top.

Dot the top of the bread crumbs with butter and bake for 20 to 25 minutes or until the tomatoes are soft and the bread-crumb topping is golden brown.

"Serve with fried sausage and bacon for high tea or supper," counsels the Portstewart Women's Institute, "or for lunch with hot roast beef as an extra vegetable dish."

Creamed Mushrooms on Toast

Serves 6

Though the Irish are not great mushroom eaters, a wide variety grows around the island, as might be expected given its damp climate. Among those found are field or meadow mushrooms (*Agaricus campestris*), which are a wild relative of the common white or brown supermarket mushroom; hedgehogs (*Hydnum repandum*); giant puffballs (*Calvatia gigantea*); and chanterelles (various species of *Cantharellus*). Any of these or any other wild or cultivated mushroom may be used in this preparation. The recipe, written as "To Stue Museroons," comes from Ellinor, Lady Bellew's collection of eighteenth- and nineteenth-century recipes from Barmeath Castle in Dunleer, County Louth. She recommends serving it over a "frin rool [French roll] well tosted and buttered and crisp it before the fire."

4 TBSP BUTTER, PLUS MORE FOR BUTTERING ROLLS

2 LB/1 KG ASSORTED WILD AND/OR CULTIVATED MUSHROOMS, BRUSHED CLEAN AND CUT INTO PIECES OF APPROXIMATELY EQUAL SIZE [OR LEFT WHOLE IF THEY ARE SMALL]

6 SMALL OR 3 LARGE FRENCH ROLLS

1 CUP/240 ML HEAVY CREAM

SALT

CHOPPED FRESH PARSLEY FOR GARNISH [OPTIONAL]

Preheat the broiler.

Melt the butter in a large skillet over medium-low heat. Add the mushrooms and cook, stirring frequently, for about 20 minutes, or until they have released their liquor and reabsorbed some of it.

Meanwhile, split the French rolls, butter them lightly, and toast them lightly under the broiler. Divide the toasted rolls equally between 6 plates (2 small halves or 1 large half on each plate).

Add the cream to the mushrooms, stirring it in well, and continue to cook for another 8 to 10 minutes, or until the sauce thickens. Season to taste with salt, then spoon the mushrooms and sauce over the rolls. Garnish with some chopped parsley, if you like.

CREAMED MUSHROOMS ON TOAST

BAKED BEANS

Baked Beans

Serves 8

Baked beans are sometimes served as part of an Ulster Fry (page 149) or full Irish breakfast, or as an accompaniment to Irish sausages. They are nearly always canned (Heinz is the predominant brand, with Batchelors a close second), but it's easy to make them from scratch.

> 1 LB/500 G NAVY BEANS, WASHED, WITH ANY STONES OR SHRIVELED BEANS DISCARDED
>
> 1/2 CUP/100 G DARK BROWN SUGAR
>
> 1 SMALL ONION, MINCED
>
> 1/3 CUP/80 ML BLACK TREACLE OR MOLASSES
>
> 1 TSP WORCESTERSHIRE SAUCE
>
> 1/2 TSP POWDERED MUSTARD
>
> SALT

Put the beans in a large pot with water to cover, then bring to a boil over high heat. Reduce the heat to low and simmer, adding more water if necessary to keep the beans just covered, for 1 to 1½ hours, or until the beans are very tender but not split.

Drain, reserving the cooking water, and set the beans aside.

Preheat the oven to 275°F/135°C (Gas Mark 1).

Put the beans, sugar, onion, treacle, Worcestershire sauce, mustard, and salt to taste into a bean pot or deep baking dish. Add the reserved cooking water and a little more water, if necessary, to just cover the beans. Bake, uncovered, for 5 to 6 hours. The top of the beans should brown, but if they start to get too dark, cover the pot.

Coleslaw of Cabbage, Dulse, and Scallions

Serves 4 *to* 6

One mid-September day, the Slow Food Convivium in Cork gave a picnic with a particularly appealing menu—international in inspiration but resolutely local in its use of raw materials. Among the offerings were bruschetta with rocket (arugula), Bill Hogan's superlative Desmond cheese from Dereenatra in West Cork, and bresaola made by his neighbor, Frank Krawczyk; lightly pickled oysters from Sherkin Island, southwest of Cork in Roaringwater Bay; gumbo based on duck from Skeaghnore, at the top of the bay, and chorizo from Fingal Ferguson of Gubbeen; and an unusual slaw made with locally gathered dulse. I wasn't at the picnic, alas, and couldn't track down the recipe for the slaw, but this is a pretty good approximation, I think, of what it must have been like.

> 1 OZ/30 G DULSE [SEE PAGE 264], SOAKED FOR 5 MINUTES IN WARM WATER, DRAINED, AND FINELY CHOPPED
>
> 1/2 LB/250 G WHITE CABBAGE, FINELY SHREDDED
>
> 4 SCALLIONS, FINELY CHOPPED
>
> 1 CARROT, GRATED
>
> 1/4 CUP/60 ML MAYONNAISE, PREFERABLY HOMEMADE [PAGE 357]
>
> 2 TBSP APPLE JUICE
>
> SALT AND PEPPER

Combine the dulse, cabbage, scallions, and carrots in a large bowl.

Whisk the mayonnaise and apple juice together in a small bowl, then add to the slaw and toss well. Season generously with salt and pepper.

CONTINUING THE TRADITION

Shortly after Myrtle Allen opened her restaurant at Ballymaloe House, an aspiring chef from County Laoise, Darina O'Connell (facing page), sent her a letter asking for a job. "You could just about count the good restaurants in Ireland on one hand in those days," Darina says, "and even the good ones tended to write the menu the day they opened and it would be exactly the same ten years later. Myrtle wrote her menu every day, which was seen as an amateurish thing to do. I was brought up in the country, though, and my mother was a wonderful cook, and this sounded right to me." Darina got the job and ended up marrying Allen's son Tim. In 1983, the two started the Ballymaloe Cookery School a couple of miles down the road. It is now one of Europe's best and most famous institutions of culinary learning, offering a wide range of classes and programs in not just Irish cooking but the cuisines of the world—and Allen has gone on to become a celebrated cooking teacher, TV personality, and prolific author. She also started Ireland's farmers' market movement (see page 262), and is the Slow Food councillor for Ireland, among many other things. She is as much a champion of Irish food as her mother-in-law has been—and now her daughter-in-law Rachel Allen is herself a prominent television chef and cookbook author. The Ballymaloe spirit flourishes.

Sorrel, Beet,
and Watercress Salad

Serves 4 to 6

Caiman O'Brien, an archeologist with Ireland's National Monuments Service and a great lover of food and of culinary history, called my attention to a passage in a seventeenth-century chronicle that describes an early Irish salad. The author, a French cartographer named Albert Jouvin de Rochefort (circa 1640–1710), is describing a visit to Dundalk, County Louth: "I remember I eat of a salad made according to the mode of the country, of I know not what herbs; I think there were sorrel and beets chopt together; it represented the form of a fish, the whole without oil or salt, and only a little vinegar made of beer, and a quantity of sugar strewed over it, that it resembled Mount Etna covered with snow, so that it is impossible to be eaten by any one not accustomed to it. I made my host laugh heartily. . . on asking for oil to season this salad, according to the French fashion." This recipe is based very loosely on de Rochefort's description.

1/2 LB/250 G BEETS [1 OR 2], UNPEELED

1 TSP SUGAR

1 TBSP MALT VINEGAR

2 TBSP EXTRA-VIRGIN OLIVE OIL

SALT AND PEPPER

1 SMALL BUNCH SORREL, TRIMMED AND
FINELY CHOPPED

1 SMALL BUNCH WATERCRESS, TRIMMED AND
FINELY CHOPPED

Put the beets into a small pot, cover with salted water, and bring to a boil over high heat. Reduce the heat to medium-low and simmer, partially covered, for 1½ to 2 hours or until the beets are soft.

Drain the beets and set aside to cool slightly; then peel, slice, julienne, and chop into very small pieces.

While the beets cool, dissolve the sugar in vinegar in a small bowl, then whisk in the olive oil and season to taste with salt and pepper.

Combine the beets, sorrel, and watercress in a salad bowl, add the dressing, and toss well.

Beet Salad

Serves 6

This simple preparation is served with fried Cooleeney cheese (see page 64) at Brocka on the Water in Ballinderry, on the shores of Lough Derg in County Tipperary.

1 LB/500 G BEETS [3 OR 4], UNPEELED

1/4 CUP/60 ML EXTRA-VIRGIN OLIVE OIL

2 TBSP BALSAMIC VINEGAR

SALT AND PEPPER

Put the beets into a medium pot, cover with salted water, and bring to a boil over high heat. Reduce the heat to medium-low and simmer, partially covered, for 1½ to 2 hours or until the beets are soft.

Drain the beets and set aside to cool slightly; then peel them and cut them into 1-in/2.5-cm cubes.

In a medium bowl, toss the beets with olive oil, vinegar, and salt and pepper to taste. Let cool to room temperature or refrigerate before serving.

Celeriac Slaw

Serves 4 to 6

One Saturday I stopped at the Midleton farmers' market in East Cork just before it closed down for the afternoon. Fish smoker Frank Hederman and his wife, food writer Caroline Workman, were packing away their wares and invited me to come back to their house, next to their Belvelly Smokehouse in Cobh, for an impromptu lunch. There, while Frank went to get a plump smoked mackerel next door, Caroline put loaves of home-made bread and country butter on the table and then quickly and deftly peeled a knobby celeriac root and made this simple, delicious salad—which went perfectly with the mackerel and would be a good match for smoked salmon or eel as well.

I CELERIAC, PEELED AND CUT INTO BATONS
ABOUT 3 IN/7.5 CM LONG AND 1/4 IN/6.5 MM THICK
ON A MANDOLINE OR WITH A SHARP KNIFE

I CUP/240 ML CRÈME FRAÎCHE

SALT AND PEPPER

Bring a medium pot of salted water to a boil over high heat. Blanch the celeriac in boiling water for 2 minutes, then drain well and rinse in cold water.

In a medium bowl, mix the crème fraîche into the celeriac and season generously with salt and pepper.

Variation

Workman sometimes roasts whole hazelnuts in a 400°F/200°C (Gas Mark 6) oven for 10 minutes, chops them, and stirs them into the celeriac.

FARM TO SHOPPER

Ireland's Green Party has called for the establishment of farmers' markets in every city and town in Ireland. That may seem like asking a lot, but there are already at least 150 of them in Ireland and Northern Ireland as I write this, most operating once a week and year-round, including twenty-one in the greater Dublin area, nineteen in County Cork, and twelve each in counties Mayo and Kerry.

Darina Allen of Ballymaloe Cookery School (see page 259) set up Ireland's first modern-day farmers' market in 1999, on Saturday mornings in the East Cork town of Midleton, and it remains the most famous in Ireland. It's not a huge market, but a number of the most important figures in County Cork's artisanal food movement have regular stands there, including charcutier Frank Krawczyk (see page 160), fish smoker Frank Hederman (see page 108), goat cheese maker Jane Murphy of Ardsallagh (see page 62), Declan Ryan of Arbutus Bakery, and, of course, the Allens of Ballymaloe, who sell both organic vegetables and prepared foods. (Writer and TV personality Clodagh McKenna used to have a stand here as well, starring her very good chicken liver pâté, but she now lives in Turin, where she is active in the Slow Food movement. She has written a very good cookbook based on farmers' market foods; see page 367.)

"The problem with farmers' markets in Ireland can be summed up in one word—inconsistency," wrote County Waterford–based writer and broadcaster Michael Kelly in his blog "Tales from the Home Farm" in 2008. He also points out that you sometimes go to a so-called farmers' market and find generic bakers, T-shirt vendors, and stands selling such distinctly non-Irish produce as oranges and bananas—everything but farmers. The market held Saturdays and Sundays near St. Nicholas Church in Galway (facing page) is a case in point. There are real farmers there, a few of them, including organic activist Cait Curran, as well as a seller of locally caught oysters, cockles, and mussels and a fish smoker. But there are also stands selling South African sausages, crêpes, bagels, and Indian vegetarian food, as well as purveyors of jewelry, candles, incense, and, yes, T-shirts. On the other hand, it's a lively scene, full of good food smells (even if they do come from curried lentils)—and it beats a neon-lit, everything-in-plastic-wrap supermarket any day.

WATERCRESS

The most popular green vegetable in Ireland, at least before the arrival of cabbage, may well have been watercress, which goes by the healthy-sounding name of *biolar* in Irish. (The word is related to the Spanish term for the same thing, *berro*, and may also have some connection with the name of Birr in County Offaly.) Watercress was among the foods once specified as tributes owed to the Irish king, along with venison and fish. Some monks were known to subsist on almost nothing but watercress. It is said that the illustrious St. Brendan (who according to legend discovered America in a little cowhide boat a thousand years before Columbus) made it the main portion of his diet, and lived to be 180. The most famous references to watercress in Irish literature, though, come from the medieval tale of *Buile Shuibhne*, usually translated as "The madness of Sweeney" or "Sweeney's frenzy," Sweeney having been a legendary king of Ulster. In the saga, which alternates between poetry and prose, the deranged monarch at one point calls watercress "our desire," and later says, "Green watercress / and a draft of pure water, / I fare on them, I smile not." And in Glen Bolcain, the tale reports, "The madmen . . . used to smite each other for the pick of watercress." Eating wild watercress in Ireland today, unfortunately, would probably not be a good idea; the inland waters are too polluted with agricultural runoff.

SEAWEED

About the most succinct expression I can imagine of the cyclical nature of sustenance agriculture is this offhanded sentence by Tomás Ó Crohan in his 1929 book *The Island-man*, about life on Great Blasket Island, County Kerry: "Away I went to the strand to get seaweed for manure so that we could have more potatoes to rear pigs on."

Seaweed of many kinds washes up on or grows in the shallows of the Irish shoreline, and it has long been used as fertilizer, and also burned to produce ash used in the traditional manufacture of linen, soap, and glass. But seaweed—some prefer the term "sea vegetables"—has also long formed an important part of the Irish coastal diet. During times of famine, it was a source of vitamins and minerals, and in happier times it has been used in desserts, stews, salads, and other dishes just because people like its flavor and texture.

The two varieties of seaweed most often eaten in Ireland are dulse and carrageen. Dulse, also called "dillisk" and "seagrass," is a leathery-looking red or reddish-brown plant, harvested in spring and summer, then typically sun-dried on nets and salted before sale. Carrageen, also called "Irish moss," takes its name from Carrageen Head in County Donegal. A bushy little plant that can be anything from greenish purple to dark red when growing (becoming lighter when sun-dried), it is widely used in commercial food products as a thickening agent and emulsifier. A third type of seaweed sometimes eaten in Ireland is sloke or laver, which is what the Japanese call *nori*.

Cheese maker Maya Binder at her Dingle Peninsula Cheese Company in Castlegregory, County Kerry, flavors some of her cheeses with dulse, which is one of the seven varieties of sea vegetable harvested by her partner, Olivier Beaujouan.

THE SHAMROCK

The shamrock (*Trifolium repens*), a kind of three-leaved clover, is perhaps the single most evocative symbol of Ireland; the Irish government has even registered it as a trademark. It isn't exactly something you'd think of throwing into the salad, though, so it's a little startling to read the English traveler Fynes Moryson's report, from around the turn of the sixteenth century, that "[The Irish] . . . willingly eat the herb Shamrock, being of a sharp taste, which, as they run and are chased to and fro, they snatch like beasts out of the ditches." In fact, what he's talking about is almost certainly the botanically unrelated plant called wood sorrel (*Oxalis acetosella*), which is similarly three-leafed, and in fact so closely resembles the true shamrock that it is often given as a token on St. Patrick's Day. Wood sorrel is only distantly related to common sorrel (*Rumex acetosa*), though that plant, too, has long been eaten in Ireland.

Chapter No. 12

The Basic Pleasures

Next comes the well-bred men, who know the way / To please the ladies
in their bread at tea, / And with their white, their wheaten, and their brown /
Can please the palate of the lord or clown

——From the papers of the Bakers Guild of Ireland [founded in 1478]

Rye bread will do you good; / Barley bread will do you no
harm. / Wheaten bread will sweeten your blood; / Oaten bread will
strengthen your arm

——Nineteenth-century Irish rhyme

The earliest breads were probably pastes of crushed grain and water cooked on hot stones into little more than oversize wafers. Wild

airborne yeasts settling on the dough may have accidentally resulted in the first risen breads, but in any case these apparently existed by at least the seventh century A.D., when Ireland's ancient Brehon Laws (see page 304) included provisions regulating the size of loaves appropriate, respectively, for men and women to consume.

Despite the association of soda breads (leavened with bicarbonate of soda instead of yeast) with Ireland, these were unknown before the nineteenth century. The rising agent used was barm, the foam on top of fermenting ale or cider, which contains a yeast strain that is the ancestor of brewer's yeast.

"The Vision of Mac Conglinne," from around the eleventh century, enumerates eight kinds of grain that would have been available in Ireland at the time: rye, wild oats, *beare* (possibly either spelt or millet), buckwheat, wheat, barley, *fidbach* (literally "wood-gland," possibly meaning either acorn or hazelnut flour); and oats. They were all used for bread; oats and barley were initially more common than wheat (ground dried peas and beans and later potatoes were baked into bread, too). The first bakers to make bread in wood-burning ovens instead of the cast-iron pots called "bastables" (see page 287) were probably monks in their monasteries. The tradition of monastery baking has mostly died out in Ireland. One of the few exceptions—possibly the only one—is the bakery at the Cistercian Abbey of Mount St. Joseph in Roscrea, County Tipperary, where several monks—in their seventies and eighties, and with no apparent successors—produce hearty brown yeast loaves from turf-fired ovens.

White bread, and store-bought bread in general, is a phenomenon of the nineteenth century in Ireland. Local bakeries—often opened by farm wives who had followed their job-seeking husbands to the cities—began to proliferate in the latter years of that epoch, and were soon part of the fabric of urban life. Every city dweller had his or her favorite, and established close relationships with them. Esther Barron of Barron's Bakery in Cappoquin, County Waterford, has customers to this day who know her ovens well enough to ask specifically for loaves baked around the perimeter if they like crusty bread, or near the door, where it's cooler, if they prefer a softer exterior.

Once white loaves, sometimes known as "baker's bread" or "priest's bread" (because it was bought only when the priest came to say Mass) became popular, brown bread began to be seen as a sign of poverty. The Nenagh writer Marjorie Quarton recalls that during World War II, white flour was so scarce that, she says, "A friend of my mother's was the only person who still had white soda-bread on her table and she explained that her cook sieved the flour [to remove the coarser brown flour and bran]. Sieving it at our house only resulted in beige flour instead of brown. My mother asked the cook in question what she sieved it through. 'One of my stockings,' she said." In some parts of Ireland, brown bread was so associated with poverty that schoolchildren who had it in their lunch used to eat it on the way to school to avoid the noontime taunting of their peers. Today, of course, brown bread—called "wheaten bread" in Northern Ireland—is very much in favor again, for its nutritional value and its flavor, and also for its authenticity.

Northern Ireland is particularly known for its old-style griddle breads, like Soda Farls (page 279), but local bakers were often innovative. The Ormeau Bakery in Belfast, which delivered loaves around the city in electric vans in the early twentieth century, was the first bakery on the island to make soda bread commercially, the first to bake on a "traveling hot plate" conveyor belt, and the first to sell bread in wrappers. There are also a number of regional specialties in Northern Ireland, including the dense, bready currant cakes called Paris buns (immortalized by Van Morrison in his song "Cleaning Windows"); and Veda bread, a soft, sweetish, caramel-brown loaf made with malted wheat. Invented in Scotland by one Robert Graham in 1904, it was once baked all over the United Kingdom, but is now found only in Northern Ireland. The exact recipe remains a closely guarded secret.

SODA BREAD SECRETS

I baked scores of loaves of soda bread in testing recipes for this book, and in the process figured out a few important things about it. Most if not all of what follows will be old news to accomplished bakers, but to those who seldom bake, or who never have but want to try, these tips might come in handy.

1. First of all, do try. Soda bread is quick and quite forgiving, though it will admittedly probably take the novice baker at least a few tries to perfect it. Even the estimable Myrtle Allen once revealed, "I was many years married before I first triumphantly put a really good brown soda loaf on the tea table."

2. Use Irish flour if possible—the Odlums brand is available in the United States in specialty shops and by mail order. Or try King Arthur's American-made Irish-style flour. (See Sources, page 369.) These really do produce better results. Because Irish wheat is softer than American wheat, the closest substitute for Irish white flour would be pastry flour. Whatever flour you buy should be unbleached and, if possible, stone-ground and organic. "You can't underestimate the impact your flour choice will have on the outcome of your baking," says Tod Bramble of King Arthur. "Try different ones, and once you've found the one you like best, stick to it. Getting to know your flour is a great step toward becoming a better baker."

3. Use fresh flour—don't bake with something that's been sitting around the house for months or buy a dusty-looking bag from the back of the grocer's shelf. And if you store your flour in the refrigerator, which is a good way to keep mites and other little creatures out, bring it to room temperature before using it. Some bakers even recommend warming it very slightly in a low oven.

4. Sift your flour, or at least break up any lumps with your fingers.

5. While yeast breads should be made with warm milk or buttermilk (to help raise the temperature of the dough to the point at which the yeast works best), soda breads are best made with cold buttermilk. This, explains master baker Robert Ditty, is because warm milk will activate the baking soda prematurely and prevent the bread from rising in the oven. He notes that about 40°F/4°C is the ideal temperature for the buttermilk.

6. If your soda bread is too crumbly, try reducing or eliminating the butter—if you used any to begin with. Increasing the percentage of white flour slightly in recipes using white and brown might help, too.

7. Some recipes call for light kneading of the dough, others don't, but in any case don't knead very much. None is better than too much.

8. Until you get the ideal baking time figured out (this will vary according to the recipe, the nature of your ingredients, and your oven), err on the side of overbaking. It's pretty hard to bake a loaf too long (as long as it isn't starting to look burnt), but once you cut into an underbaked loaf, you might as well toss it.

9. Soda bread tastes best within 24 hours or so of baking. If you need to revive bread that's a day or two older than that, Ann De Piero of Annie's Irish Kitchen (in the little Irish village of Naples, Florida) taught me this trick: Put the loaf into a damp brown paper bag (like a lunchbag) and heat it in a 225°F/100°C oven for about 15 minutes.

10. Unbaked soda bread dough, rolled or patted out fairly thin, makes a good, quick crust for savory pies.

Brown Soda Bread

Makes 1 loaf

This straightforward recipe is Myrtle Allen's, from Ballymaloe House in Shanagarry, County Cork—except that she calls for sour milk, instead of the more readily available buttermilk. She allows considerable variation in the amount of milk used, which I find to be liberating: I just keep adding it until the dough reaches the perfect consistency. Allen calls for this loaf to be baked in the traditional round, scored form. I've found that it also works well in a loaf pan, producing a dense bread, which can be sliced fairly thinly–just right to accompany smoked salmon, mackerel, or eel.

BUTTER FOR GREASING

4 CUPS/400 G WHEAT FLOUR, PREFERABLY IRISH
OR IRISH STYLE [SEE SOURCES, PAGE 369]

1 CUP/100 G WHITE FLOUR, PREFERABLY IRISH,
OR UNBLEACHED PASTRY FLOUR,
PLUS MORE FOR DUSTING

1/2 CUP/80 G IRISH STEEL-CUT OATMEAL OR OAT BRAN

1 TSP BAKING SODA

1 TSP SALT

2 TO 4 CUPS/475 ML TO 1 L BUTTERMILK

Preheat the oven to 375°F/190°C (Gas Mark 5).

Grease a baking sheet and set aside.

Mix the wheat flour, white flour, oatmeal, baking soda, and salt together in a large bowl.

Make a well in the middle of the flour mixture and gradually pour in the buttermilk, stirring with a wooden spoon in a spiral motion from the center to the edge of the bowl. The dough should be soft but not too wet, with no raw flour left. (This will probably take about 2½ cups/600 ml of buttermilk, but use more or less if necessary.)

Turn the dough out onto a floured board. Flour your hands lightly, then shape the dough into a flat round about 3 in/7.5 cm thick. Cut a deep cross in the top of the loaf with a wet or floured knife.

Transfer the loaf to a baking sheet and bake for 45 to 60 minutes, or until nicely browned and the bottom of the loaf sounds hollow when tapped. (Alternatively, gently push the dough into a nonstick loaf pan and bake until done. The bread should slide out of the pan easily if done.)

Pint-Glass Bread

Makes 1 loaf

Peter and Mary Ward bake several varieties of bread every day, both at their home in Nenagh, County Tipperary, and at Country Choice, their store and café on Nenagh's Kenyon Street. It's hardly surprising, then, that when their son, Jeff, went off to college in Dublin, he found it hard to stomach the commercial breads and rolls served in the student cafeteria. Peter suggested that he try baking his own, but Jeff had never learned the baker's craft, and had few utensils in his student-housing kitchen. "I figured," says Peter, "that every university student has at least one pint glass that he's brought home from the pub, so I invented this very easy soda bread, using only a pint glass as a measure. I told him he could even mix it up in the washbasin if he had to."

1 PINT GLASS [2 1/2 CUPS/250 G] WHITE FLOUR,
PREFERABLY IRISH [SEE SOURCES, PAGE 369],
OR PASTRY FLOUR, PLUS MORE FOR DUSTING

1 PINT GLASS [2 1/2 CUPS/250 G] STONE-GROUND
WHOLE WHEAT FLOUR, PREFERABLY IRISH OR
IRISH-STYLE

ENOUGH BAKING SODA TO COAT THE BOTTOM
OF A PINT GLASS [3/4 TSP]

ENOUGH SALT TO COAT THE BOTTOM OF A
PINT GLASS [3/4 TSP]

ENOUGH BUTTER TO COAT THE BOTTOM
OF A PINT GLASS [1 TBSP]

3/4 PINT GLASS [1 3/4 CUPS/420 ML] ROOM-
TEMPERATURE BUTTERMILK, PLUS MORE AS NEEDED

Preheat the oven to 375°F/190°C (Gas Mark 5).

Sift the white flour, whole wheat flour, baking soda, and salt together in a medium bowl and stir with a fork until they're

PINT-GLASS BREAD [UNBAKED]

well combined. Rub the butter in with your fingers until the mixture resembles coarse bread crumbs.

Form a well in the middle of the flour mixture and pour the buttermilk into the well. Form your hand into a rigid claw and stir the buttermilk into the flour slowly but steadily in a spiral motion, starting in the middle and working outward. The dough should be soft but not too wet or sticky. (Add more buttermilk if necessary.)

Turn the dough out onto a floured board. Flour your hands lightly, then shape the dough into a flat round about 2 in/5 cm high. Cut a deep cross in the top of the loaf with a wet or floured knife, then bake for 45 to 60 minutes, or until nicely browned and the bottom of the loaf sounds hollow when tapped.

Kitty's White Soda Bread with Thyme

Makes 1 loaf

Though soda bread made entirely of white flour has been baked in Irish homes since the early twentieth century (which was, not coincidentally, about the time that white bread became common in bakeries), it is frequently made today, with currants or other fruit included, as a sweet tea bread. Most savory soda bread recipes (that is, those without fruit) call for white and whole wheat (which the Irish call "wholemeal") flours, combined in various proportions—sometimes with as little as 2 oz/60 g of white to 14 oz/400 g of whole wheat, and sometimes more like half and half. The late Kitty Timmons, of Ballyknocken House in Ashford, County Wicklow, liked to put raisins in her white soda bread—turning it into what the Irish call "spotted dog." Her granddaughter, Catherine Fulvio, who runs the country house hotel and cooking school at Ballyknocken, makes this savory version with thyme (sometimes substituting parsley or chives), but it is also good with no herbs at all.

3 1/2 CUPS/350 G WHITE FLOUR, PREFERABLY IRISH [SEE SOURCES, PAGE 369], OR UNBLEACHED PASTRY FLOUR, PLUS MORE FOR DUSTING

1 TSP SUGAR

1 TSP BAKING SODA

1 TSP SALT

3 TBSP CHOPPED FRESH THYME

1 1/2 TO 2 CUPS/360 TO 475 ML BUTTERMILK

Preheat the oven to 450°F/230°C (Gas Mark 8).

Sift the flour, sugar, baking soda, and salt together into a large bowl. Mix in the thyme.

Form a well in middle of flour mixture and pour at least 13 oz/385 ml of buttermilk into the well. Form your hand into a rigid claw and stir the buttermilk into the flour slowly but steadily in a spiral motion, starting in the middle and working outwards. Add more of the buttermilk if necessary. The dough should be soft but not too wet or sticky.

Turn the dough out onto a floured board and knead lightly; then flour your hands and shape the dough into a flat round about 1½ in/4 cm thick. Cut a deep cross in the top of the loaf with a wet or floured knife, then put on a lightly floured baking sheet and bake for 15 minutes. Lower the oven temperature to 400°F/200°C (Gas Mark 6) and bake for 20 minutes more, or until nicely browned and the bottom of the loaf sounds hollow when tapped.

Kelly's High-Fiber Brown Loaf

Makes 1 loaf

Kelly's Resort Hotel and Spa on the sea in Rosslare, County Wexford, started life as a modest tearoom, opened by William J. Kelly in 1895. Today, still under Kelly family ownership, it is a luxury property with a well-regarded restaurant and bistro (and a family connection with the French wine business: the modern-day Bill Kelly is married to Isabelle Avril, whose father, Paul, is one of the leading producers of Châteauneuf-du-Pape). This rich but traditional-style bread is a house specialty, particularly good alongside homemade soup.

3 CUPS/300 G STONE-GROUND WHOLE WHEAT FLOUR, PREFERABLY IRISH OR IRISH-STYLE [SEE SOURCES, PAGE 369]

1 TSP BAKING SODA

1/2 TSP SALT

2 TBSP WHEAT GERM

1/4 CUP/15 G WHEAT BRAN

4 TBSP BUTTER

1 MEDIUM EGG

1 1/2 CUPS/360 ML BUTTERMILK

Preheat the oven to 350°F/175°C (Gas Mark 4).

Sift the whole wheat flour, baking soda, and salt together in a large bowl, then add the wheat germ and wheat bran and stir with a fork until the ingredients are well combined. Rub the butter in with your fingers until the mixture resembles coarse bread crumbs.

In another bowl, beat the egg with the buttermilk until well combined. Add to the dry mixture, stirring it in with a fork to form a thick batter.

Pour the batter into a lightly greased loaf pan and bake for about 1 hour or until nicely browned and the bottom of the loaf sounds hollow when tapped.

Robert Ditty's Wheaten Bread

Makes 2 loaves

This is one of the celebrated baker's recipes for brown bread. He adds oatmeal flour and wheat bran so that the flour more closely resembles the less refined variety of earlier times, he says. "This is a very moist bread, hence needs to be baked in a tin and needs no hand molding," he notes. See page 369 to find sources for Irish and Irish-style flour as well as brans.

4 1/2 CUPS/450 G COARSE STONE-GROUND WHOLE-WHEAT FLOUR, PREFERABLY IRISH OR IRISH-STYLE

6 TBSP WHITE FLOUR, PREFERABLY IRISH, OR UNBLEACHED PASTRY FLOUR

3 TBSP OATMEAL FLOUR

3 TBSP WHEAT OR OAT BRAN, PLUS MORE FOR DUSTING

2 TSP BAKING SODA

2 TSP SALT

2 1/4 CUPS/530 ML BUTTERMILK

2 TBSP BUTTER, MELTED

4 TSP HONEY

Preheat the oven to 475°/250°C (Gas Mark 9).

Combine the whole wheat, white, and oatmeal flours and the wheat bran, baking soda, and salt in a large bowl and mix together well.

Pour the buttermilk into a medium bowl, then stir in the butter and honey, mixing well.

Pour the buttermilk mixture into the flour mixture and mix well with a wooden spoon. The dough should have the consistency of porridge.

Transfer the dough to 2 loaf pans. Score the top of each loaf once and dust with additional bran.

Lower the oven temperature to 425°F/220°C (Gas Mark 7) and bake the loaves for about 35 minutes or until nicely browned and the bottom of the loaves sound hollow when tapped.

THE BAKER'S ART

The best-known baker in Ireland today is Northern Ireland's Robert Ditty, who has shops in Castledawson and nearby Magherafelt, both in County Derry. You sometimes hear a craft baker described as an artist, but in Ditty's case that's literally true. Though his father was a baker, Ditty went off to study sculpture in England, doing postgraduate work at London's Slade Institute of Fine Art. Back home, in 1976, he mounted a show of his work and of paintings by the now prominent Donegal-born artist Felim Egan in Castledawson. Before it was to open, though, an IRA bomb destroyed the gallery building and, as Ditty puts it, "I watched my art go out in the rubbish bin." Discouraged, he turned to the family business—and soon earned a reputation far beyond the Northern Irish border for his wheaten loaves, soda farls, oatcakes, and other traditional items. A sign over Ditty's bakery counter reads "All our soda breads and wheaten breads were still flour at 3 A.M. this morning."

Ditty is more than just a baker, though: He's an innovator and a creative engine for the revival of traditional foodways. He experiments with new products, like oatcakes flavored with Gubbeen cheese and made with oats smoked by Frank Hederman at his Belvelly Smokehouse in Cobh. He also encourages locals who make traditional products or have traditional skills. He asked some of his customers, local women with garden plots, to grow rhubarb for him, and then put signs in his windows reading "Pies from Mrs. So-and-So's Rhubarb." The next thing he knew, he says, "People started ringing up saying 'I've got some black currants, you wouldn't want those, would you?' and the same with apples and pears and so on." He went on to discover that there was more going on in his part of the country than he'd thought: he found a woman making very small batches of jams and preserves, a man who makes his own bacon and ham, even a coffee roaster, and now he features their wares in his shops. Ditty also inspired the bakery school at the Dublin Institute of Technology to shift their focus from commercial production to artisanal baking, helped turn a private mansion across the street from his Castledawson shop into an inn with raised organic vegetable beds and a restaurant showcasing local foods, set up a traditional butcher shop down the street, and has been promoting "family breakfast" every Saturday morning (a boon to local commuters who get home too late for family dinner). Among his future projects: beehives with Italian bees producing honey that he's thinking of trying as a bread starter, and the construction of a theaterlike environment where visitors can watch and participate in the bread-making process. He may even, he says, go back to sculpture.

Soda Farls

Serves 4

Soda farls are the simplest of Irish pan breads. Their name derives from the old Lowland Scots word *fardell*, meaning "a fourth"; each farl is one quarter of a round piece of dough. Traditionally, farls were cooked on round iron griddles hung over the fire, and such griddles, or large cast-iron skillets, are still best for the purpose. Baker Robert Ditty, from Castledawson, County Down, still makes farls on the vintage 14-in/36-cm American-made Eagleware model that his aunt used during World War II when she cooked breakfast for GIs stationed nearby.

2 CUPS/200 G WHITE FLOUR, IRISH IF POSSIBLE [SEE SOURCES, PAGE 369], OR UNBLEACHED PASTRY FLOUR, PLUS MORE FOR DUSTING

2 TSP BAKING SODA

1 TSP SALT

1 CUP/240 ML BUTTERMILK, PLUS MORE AS NEEDED

3 TO 4 TBSP BUTTER OR BACON FAT FOR FRYING

Sift the flour, baking soda, and salt together into a medium bowl.

Make a well in the middle of the flour mixture, then slowly pour in the buttermilk, stirring the buttermilk into the flour with a wooden spoon in a spiral motion, working from the center to the sides of the bowl. The dough should be soft but not too wet, with no raw flour left. (Use a bit more buttermilk if necessary.)

Turn the dough out onto a floured board. Flour your hands lightly and knead for about 1 minute, then shape the dough into a flat round about ¾ in/2 cm thick.

Melt the butter or bacon fat in a large skillet over medium-low heat. Cut the dough round into wedge-shaped quarters with a wet or floured knife, then fry the quarters for 5 to 8 minutes on each side, or until they are nicely browned and cooked through.

Yogurt Soda Farls

Serves 4

The recipe for this modern version of soda-leavened griddle bread, from Pat Dennis of Coolnagoppah, near Ballycastle, County Antrim, appears in a book called *Fadge Farls and Oven Pots: Glens of Antrim Traditional Breads*, assembled by Helen McAlister and Fionnuala Carragher.

3 CUPS/300 G IRISH WHITE FLOUR [SEE SOURCES, PAGE 369] OR UNBLEACHED PASTRY FLOUR, PLUS MORE FOR DUSTING

1 TSP BAKING SODA

1/2 TSP SALT

3/4 CUP/175 ML PLAIN FULL-FAT YOGURT MIXED WITH 3/4 CUP/175 ML COLD WATER

4 TBSP BUTTER

Sift the flour, baking soda, and salt together into a medium bowl.

Make a well in the center of the ingredients, then slowly pour in about half the yogurt mixture, stirring the yogurt into the flour with a wooden spoon in a spiral motion, working from the center to the sides of the bowl. Continue pouring in the yogurt until the dough becomes slightly sticky and elastic.

Turn the dough out onto a lightly floured board and knead gently, forming a round about ¾ in/2 cm thick. Cut the dough into wedge-shaped quarters with a wet or floured knife.

Melt 2 Tbsp of the butter in a large skillet over medium heat. Fry the quarters for 7 to 8 minutes or until deep golden brown on the bottom. Transfer them to a plate, cooked side down. Reduce the heat to medium-low, melt the remaining 2 Tbsp butter in the skillet, then return the quarters to the skillet, raw side down. Cook for about 10 minutes more, or until the bottoms are deep golden brown.

Oaten Bread

Makes 1 loaf or sheaf

Oatcakes and oaten bread are foods commonly associated with St. Brigid (or Brigit) of Kildare (circa 451–525). In traditional Irish households of an earlier time, this bread would have been eaten on her feast day, February 1. The bread is sometimes baked in the shape of a sheaf of wheat.

3 CUPS/300 G WHITE FLOUR, PREFERABLY IRISH [SEE SOURCES, PAGE 369], OR UNBLEACHED PASTRY FLOUR, PLUS MORE FOR DUSTING

1 3/4 CUPS/275 G IRISH STEEL-CUT OATMEAL

2 1/2 TSP BAKING SODA

1 1/2 TSP SALT

2 TBSP BUTTER, CUT INTO SMALL PIECES, PLUS MORE FOR GREASING

1 EGG

1 3/4 CUPS/420 ML BUTTERMILK

Preheat the oven to 375°F/190°C. Mix the flour, oatmeal, sugar, baking soda, and salt together in a large bowl. Rub the butter into the mixture until it resembles coarse meal.

Lightly whisk the egg into the buttermilk. Make a well in the middle of the flour. Flour your hand and form it into a rigid claw, then stir slowly but steadily in a spiral motion, starting in the middle and working outwards. The dough should be firm.

Turn the dough out onto a floured board. Flour both hands lightly, then knead the dough two or three times. Shape the dough into a flat round about 2½ in/6.5 cm thick and cut a deep cross in the top of the loaf with a wet or floured knife.

Alternatively, to shape the dough into a sheaf of wheat, divide it into 4 pieces, 3 of equal size and 1 about one-third the size of the others. Shape each of the 3 large pieces into a long strip about 2 in/5 cm wide, then gently press them together side by side. Curve the tops and bottoms of the two outer pieces slightly (away from the middle one). With a wet or floured knife, cut shallow vertical lines from top to bottom on all three pieces, to suggest stalks of wheat. Gently shape the remaining piece of dough into a thin strip just long enough to stretch cross-wise across the 3 assembled pieces and drape down the sides by ½ in/1.25 cm or so. Lay it across the center of the assembled

pieces and press it down slightly. With a wet or floured knife, mark a shallow crosshatch pattern over its surface.

Put the loaf or sheaf on a lightly greased baking sheet and bake for 50 to 60 minutes, or until nicely browned and the bottom of the loaf sounds hollow when tapped.

Yalla Male Bread

Makes 1 loaf

I found the recipe for this variation on soda bread in *Maura Laverty's Cookbook*, by the eponymous Irish author and playwright. "Yalla male" is of course "yellow meal"—that is, cornmeal. Also known as "golden drop," it was first introduced to Ireland in the 1840s to help relieve famine.

3 1/2 CUPS/350 G WHITE FLOUR, PREFERABLY IRISH [SEE PAGE 369], OR UNBLEACHED PASTRY FLOUR, PLUS MORE FOR DUSTING

3/4/130 G CUP CORNMEAL

1 TSP SUGAR

1 TSP SALT

1 TSP BAKING SODA

2 1/4 CUPS/530 ML BUTTERMILK

BUTTER FOR GREASING

Preheat the oven to 450°F/230°C (Gas Mark 8).

Mix the flour, cornmeal, sugar, salt, and baking soda together in a large bowl with your hands. Don't overmix.

Form a well in the middle of the flour mixture and pour all but 2 Tbsp of the buttermilk into the well. Form your hand into a rigid claw and stir the buttermilk into the flour slowly but steadily in a spiral motion, starting in the middle and working outwards to the rim of the bowl. The dough should be soft but not too wet or sticky.

Turn the dough out onto a floured board. Flour your hands lightly, then knead the dough lightly for 2 to 3 minutes. Pat the dough out into a disk about 1½ in/4 cm high. Cut a deep cross in the top of the loaf with a wet or floured knife and brush the loaf with the remaining buttermilk. Bake on a lightly greased baking sheet for 40 to 45 minutes, or until done.

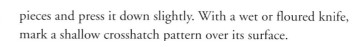

Treacle Bread

Makes 1 loaf

"When I was a boy and we worked all day bringing in the hay," recalls Noel McMeel, now chef for the restaurants at the Lough Erne Golf Resort in Enniskillen, County Fermanagh, "you felt a real sense of accomplishment when evening came, like you'd gone out and played football and won. We always had a celebration, the full works, a three-course dinner that night. And there was always treacle bread." Though they are produced by slightly different processes, treacle and molasses are essentially the same thing. At least one brand of British black treacle, Lyle's, is available in America (from merchants specializing in British products), but American blackstrap molasses may be substituted. Either will mix better with other ingredients if it has been slightly warmed by standing the open container in a bowl of hot water for 10 minutes or so. Rinsing the cup out with hot water before measuring will make it flow more smoothly when poured. This is author/playwright Maura Laverty's recipe.

3 1/2 CUPS/350 G WHITE FLOUR, PREFERABLY IRISH [SEE SOURCES, PAGE 369], OR UNBLEACHED PASTRY FLOUR, PLUS MORE FOR DUSTING

1 TBSP SUGAR

1 TSP SALT

1 TSP BAKING SODA

1/2 CUP/120 ML BLACK TREACLE OR MOLASSES

1 3/4 CUPS/420 ML BUTTERMILK

BUTTER FOR GREASING

Preheat the oven to 450°F/230°C (Gas Mark 8).

Mix the flour, sugar, salt, and baking soda together in a large bowl with your hands. Don't overmix.

Form a well in the middle of the flour mixture and pour the treacle and all but 2 Tbsp of the buttermilk into the well. Flour your hand generously, then form it into a rigid claw and stir the liquid into the flour slowly but steadily in a spiral motion, starting in the middle and working outward to the rim of the bowl. The dough should be soft but not too wet.

Turn the dough out onto a floured board. Flour your hands generously—the dough will be sticky—then knead the dough

lightly for 2 to 3 minutes. Pat the dough out into a disk about 1½ in/4 cm high. Cut a deep cross in the top of the loaf with a wet or floured knife and brush the loaf with the remaining 2 Tbsp of buttermilk. Bake on a lightly greased baking sheet for 40 to 45 minutes, or until done.

Ballymaloe Brown Bread

Makes 1 loaf

I watched Tim Allen, Myrtle Allen's son (and Darina Allen's husband) make this famous loaf one day at the Ballymaloe Cookery School. Doris Grant (see page 285), who created the original recipe and was a great foe of white flour, presumably would have been horrified when he added a couple of ounces of same to the mix, but Allen believes that it improves the texture. This recipe is based on his demonstration, rather than on Grant's (or Myrtle Allen's) written version—though I did honor Grant by specifying sea salt over ordinary table salt (she liked it for its trace minerals).

1 TSP BLACK TREACLE OR MOLASSES

1 OZ/28 G FRESH ACTIVE YEAST, CRUMBLED, OR ONE 1/4-OZ/7-G PACKET ACTIVE DRY YEAST

5 CUPS/500 G STONE-GROUND WHOLE WHEAT FLOUR, PREFERABLY IRISH OR IRISH-STYLE OR 4 1/2 CUPS/450 G STONE-GROUND WHOLE WHEAT FLOUR MIXED WITH 1/2 CUP/50 G WHITE FLOUR, PREFERABLY IRISH [SEE SOURCES, PAGE 369], OR UNBLEACHED PASTRY FLOUR

1 TSP FINE-GROUND SEA SALT

SUNFLOWER OR CANOLA OIL FOR GREASING

Dissolve the treacle in ⅔ cup/160 ml warm water in a small bowl. (Around 100°F/40°C is ideal; Grant calls it "blood heat," and notes that the easiest way to obtain this temperature without a thermometer is to bring 1 cup/240 ml of water to a boil, then add it to 3 cups/720 ml of cold water.) Stir in the yeast and set aside for 8 to 10 minutes or until the yeast begins to froth.

Put the flour into a large bowl and mix in the salt.

Lightly grease a nonstick loaf pan with oil.

BALLYMALOE BROWN BREAD

Make a well in the flour, pour in the yeast mixture, and let it sit for a minute. Pour in about 1¼ cups/300 ml warm water (see above), then form your hand into a rigid claw and stir the liquid into the flour slowly but steadily in a spiral motion, starting in the middle and working outwards to the rim of the bowl. The dough should be soft and too wet to knead (add more water if necessary).

Let the dough rest in bowl in a warm place for about 15 minutes.

Transfer the dough to the greased loaf pan, cover loosely with a damp towel, and set in a warm place to rise for about 20 minutes. ("The bread should be what we call 'proud,'" says Tim Allen, "just beginning to peer over the top of the pan.")

Meanwhile, preheat the oven to 450°F/230°C (Gas Mark 8).

Bake the bread for 20 minutes, then lower the oven temperature to 400°F/200°C (Gas Mark 6) and bake for 35 to 45 minutes more. If you like a crisp crust, remove the bread from the pan about 10 minutes before it's done, then return it to the oven, placing it upside down directly on the oven rack to finish cooking.

Maura Laverty's Wholemeal Yeast Bread

Makes 1 loaf

"Unpatriotic though it may seem," writes novelist and playwright Maura Laverty in her book *Feasting Galore* (originally published in 1952), "pride of place in any modern cookbook must be given to yeast bread—for the very good reason that yeast bread is better for us. When we add bicarbonate of soda to foods, we reduce their content of Vitamin B_1. . . . Yeast is especially rich in Vitamin B_1." This is her recipe for a no-knead, yeast-risen whole wheat bread, not much more difficult to make than soda bread. She notes, incidentally, that most cooks add a small portion of white flour to the wheat flour "to ensure better cutting consistency." Her recipe doesn't—but I have taken the hint and added some. Laverty believes that "Wholemeal bread is best kept for twenty-four hours before cutting," but that would take impressive will power.

2 CUPS/200 G WHOLE WHEAT FLOUR, PREFERABLY IRISH OR IRISH-STYLE [SEE SOURCES, PAGE 369]

1/2 CUP/50 G WHITE FLOUR, PREFERABLY IRISH, OR UNBLEACHED PASTRY FLOUR

1 TBSP SALT

ONE 1/4-OZ/7-G PACKET ACTIVE DRY YEAST

3 TBSP SUGAR

3/4 CUP/175 ML WARM MILK [NOT BUTTERMILK] MIXED WITH 3/4 CUP/175 ML WARM WATER [AROUND 100°F/40°C IS IDEAL; SEE THE FIRST STEP OF BALLYMALOE BROWN BREAD, PAGE 282]

BUTTER FOR GREASING

Preheat the oven to 200°F/100°C. Mix the whole wheat flour, white flour, and salt together in a large bowl, then set in the preheated oven for 10 to 15 minutes to warm slightly.

Mix the yeast and sugar together in a small bowl and add one-quarter of the milk mixture.

Make a well in the middle of the flour and pour in the yeast mixture. Sprinkle a little of the flour on top. Set the bowl aside in a warm place for 10 to 15 minutes or until the yeast begins to froth. Slowly pour the remaining milk mixture into the well, stirring the liquid into the flour with a wooden spoon in a spiral motion, starting in the middle and working outward to form a wet dough.

Warm a loaf pan in the oven, then grease it lightly and spoon the dough into it. Cover the pan with a clean dish towel and set aside in a warm place for about 20 minutes or until the dough approximately doubles in size.

Meanwhile, increase the oven temperature to 450°F/230°C (Gas Mark 8).

Bake for 50 to 60 minutes or until nicely browned and the bottom of the loaf sounds hollow when tapped. Turn the loaf out of the pan and let it rest upside down on a wire rack until cooled to room temperature.

THE GRANT LOAF

In restaurants and country house hotels all over Ireland (and in at least some private homes), you'll be served a kind of moist, slightly crumbly, dark brown yeast bread that is the perfect foil for rich Irish butter. This bread didn't come from Ireland originally, though: It is the creation of a remarkable Scots-born Englishwoman named Doris Grant, who died in 2003 at the age of 98. Grant was an early and vocal supporter of pesticide-free vegetables and what we would now call "whole foods." She thought factory-baked white bread was poison, literally. "If you love your husbands," she once wrote to her housewife readers, "keep them away from white bread. . . . If you don't love them, cyanide is quicker but bleached bread is just as certain, and no questions asked." In 1944, Grant published a little volume called *Your Daily Bread*, which became famous above all for one recipe: a foolproof, no-knead, one-rise whole wheat yeast bread that became known as "the Grant Loaf." When Myrtle Allen (below) started cooking for the public at her Ballymaloe farm in 1964, this was one of the breads she served. Distinctly different from brown soda bread but attractive to diners raised on the latter, it became very popular—and was soon being baked and served from one end of the island to the other.

THE REAL THING

Novelist and playwright Maura Laverty of Rathangan, County Kildare, once wrote, "Every time Ireland is put in the dock, I feel our diplomats are sadly lacking as a counsel for the defense that they don't bring forward in mitigation of our crimes the fact that we have given a four-leaved shamrock to the world. One leaf is W. B. Yeats, another is boiled potatoes in their jackets, another Barry Fitzgerald. The fourth is soda-bread. And the greatest of these is soda-bread."

Chances are that soda bread isn't what you think it is. All over America, and probably elsewhere in the world, a sweetened cakelike loaf, speckled with raisins or currants and sometimes softened with eggs, is sold as "soda bread"—or even "traditional Irish soda bread." It isn't, any more than flatbread covered with Thai barbecued chicken and goat cheese is "traditional Neapolitan pizza." True soda bread is the simplest of things: bread made with nothing more than flour, salt, sour milk or buttermilk, and—in place of yeast—baking soda, which reacts with the milk to have a leavening effect. Soda bread that's full of fruit is called "spotted dog" or "railway cake" in Ireland, and can be very nice in itself—but it's not soda bread as the Irish understand it.

There are countless recipes for making soda bread, and countless theories about how to do it right. The Northern Irish baker Robert Ditty told me that when he was growing up, his grandmother always let her buttermilk come to room temperature in the parlor overnight before baking her version, while her immediate neighbor, a woman of about the same age, took hers down the road and put it down a well overnight to chill. "Both claimed to make the best soda bread," he adds, "and both were very good, but we know today that chilled buttermilk is better."

Soda bread is indeed traditional to Ireland, but it hasn't been traditional for all that long: Its essential leavening agent, baking soda or bicarbonate of soda, was invented only in 1846—by two New York bakers whose companies eventually became Arm & Hammer—and reached Ireland a few years after that.

THE BASTABLE

In Irish farmhouse kitchens, well into the early twentieth century, the most often used cooking vessel was the bastable (or bastible). This was a cast-iron pot, similar to what we'd call a Dutch oven, with three or four legs and a concave lid. (The name comes from the town of Barnstable in Devon, England, where the pots were originally made.) The bastable had a handle so that it could be suspended above the fire in the hearth, but it could also be rested directly on top of smoldering coals or turf, with more of them banked around the sides and spread out in the shallow indentation on the lid.

This created an ovenlike environment in which the contents of the pot would cook more or less evenly from all sides. Irish stew was always made in a bastable, sometimes with the top sealed with a flour and water paste to keep in moisture. It was also the perfect vessel for roasting a chicken or baking bread. As part of a program called the West Cork Country Life Show, the Michael Collins Centre in Clonakilty, County Cork, offers a demonstration of how to bake a loaf of brown soda bread in a bastable over a peat fire. Tasting samples are available.

Bread sellers in the market.

THE WATERFORD BLAAS

"To us in Waterford," says Maurice Keller, proprietor of the city's Arlington Lodge, "the blaa is like the croissant is to a Frenchman." The Waterford blaa, occasionally spelled "bla" or "blah," is a soft, square white bun coated in flour. (Californians who remember the remarkable flour-dusted square hamburger buns used by the Blum's restaurant chain—the last of which closed in the 1970s—will have a rough idea of what they're like.) This style of bread is thought to have been introduced to the city by Huguenot immigrants in the seventeenth century, and the name may derive from the French *blanc*, "white," or *blé*, a term for wheat flour. (Author and linguistics scholar Diarmaid O'Muirithe suggests that the name might also come from the old Irish word *bleathach*, which described a small, flat flour cake.) Whatever its origins, the blaa is today a fact of daily life in Waterford, sold all over the city every morning, even at gas stations and newsstands— and at least half the city's population seems to have one for breakfast every day. While they're eaten plain, with morning tea or coffee, they're also used for sandwiches (ham is a popular filling). Maurice Keller toasts them and tops them with poached eggs and Kilmeaden cheddar. Nobody bakes them at home, incidentally; they're always produced by specialist bakeries, none of whom will part with the recipe.

BUTTERMILK

Buttermilk used to literally be that, the milk left over from churning the cream into butter. The Irish have consumed it since they first got cows, around the second century A.D. Peter Ward of Country Choice in Nenagh, County Tipperary, has particularly fond memories of the buttermilk he drank decades ago. "When I was a boy," he says, "we'd cut peat in the bog, and we'd carry a gallon can of buttermilk with us. We'd dig a hole in the cold peat with our hands, and it would fill with black water, and we'd set the can down into it to chill. Cutting peat is hard, back-breaking work, and when we'd take a rest, we'd pass the buttermilk around, drinking it so fast we practically poured it on our heads. It was the best thing in the world!"

When the Irish started leavening bread with baking soda in the mid-nineteenth century, they figured out that buttermilk could provide the acidity necessary to help soda bread rise—though soured regular milk was the preferred medium at first. (Alternatives were so-called buttermilk plant and winter buttermilk; the first was ordinary milk partially fermented with sugar and yeast; the second was, in author Maura Laverty's words, "an excellent substitute for buttermilk when the cows go dry," made by soaking oatmeal and cooked and raw potatoes in water in a warm place.) Unless you've got a friend or relative who churns butter, you won't find true buttermilk anymore. The substitute is so-called cultured buttermilk, milk to which *Streptococcus lactis* bacteria have been added, and even this is nearly always sold in reduced-fat form. This works perfectly well in baking, though it would probably be less of a treat after a hot morning in the peat bog.

CAKES

and

SWEET BREADS

Sheer Indulgence

Mrs. Vermont . . . went on to the chocolate cake, then to orange layer cake, to which she returned again and again. An idea she had had, that one should not eat very much when invited out, languished.

—Elizabeth Bowen, *The Last September* [1929]

Children always love helping with cake-making. I think it particularly appeals to them because of the almost magical way in which the raw, runny ingredients puff up in the oven.

—Darina Allen, *Irish Traditional Cooking* [1995]

The distinction between cake and sweet bread in Ireland is sometimes a very fine one. Many Irish cakes are little more than bread dough enhanced with dried fruit and sugar. Something as simple as an unsweetened griddle cake,

or at most the fruit bread called Barm Brack (see facing page), was the centerpiece of the festive cake dance traditional on Easter Sunday. A prize cake was displayed atop a butter churn or even high on a pole, and young couples danced around it; the pair judged best or most energetic were allowed to "take the cake."

That's not to say that there isn't more refined cake baking going on in Ireland, too, though. The grand Anglo-Irish kitchens often turned out elaborate confections in the French style. Bakeries, from the nineteenth century onwards, offered customers all manner of frosted and frilled "biscuits" (cookies) and cakes, as well as creations like the Chester or gur cake, invented to use up day-old bread. And home bakers took pride in the special sweets they made for holidays and other noteworthy occasions. Indeed, Darina Allen writes that "Having 'a light hand with a sponge' used to be the highest compliment a woman could be paid. Indeed, her status in her village or community would virtually depend on how high her sponge cakes rise!"

Sweet tea breads became popular in Ireland in the late nineteenth century, after the custom of afternoon tea—said to have been created by Anna Stanhope, the Duchess of Bedford in the 1880s—reached Ireland from England. The Irish love tea (the beverage), so over the years they have developed an impressive repertoire of accompaniments. The most famous of these, barm brack, has a less genteel association, too: "It was customary for the woman of the house in many parts of the country to bake a large barm brack on New Year's Eve," according to historian Bríd Mahon. "As night approached, the man of the house took three bites out of the cake and dashed it against the front door in the name of the Holy Trinity, expressing the pious hope that starvations might be banished from Ireland to the land of the Turks."

Barm Brack

Makes 1 *loaf*

There's some confusion about the correct name for this fruit-filled tea bread. The undisputed part of the name, "brack," comes from the Irish *breac*, meaning "speckled" (the speckles being the sultanas and currants). Barm is the yeasty foam that rises to the top of beer and other alcoholic beverages as they ferment, and it was once used to leaven bread, becoming a latter-day Irish synonym for baker's yeast. Because this tea bread is typically leavened with yeast instead of baking soda, "barm brack" would seem to be a reasonable description of it. But it's also possible that a better name for it is barn brack, "barn" perhaps deriving from the Irish *bairín* (or *bairgín*), an obscure word for "loaf." Whatever it's called, this bread is traditionally eaten at Halloween, when a token is baked into it: The eater may find a ring (predicting impending marriage), a button or thimble (portents of bachelor- or spinsterhood, respectively), or a coin (presaging wealth). In earlier, less sensitive times, items might also have included a rag or a dried pea (for poverty) or a matchstick (for an abusive spouse). Today, the tokens are usually wrapped in waxed paper or cloth, to lessen the possibility that they will be accidentally ingested, thereby provoking a different prognosis altogether.

TWO ¼-OZ/7-G PACKETS ACTIVE DRY YEAST

6 TBSP SUGAR

2 TBSP COLD UNSALTED BUTTER,
CUT INTO SMALL PIECES

4 ½ CUPS/450 G FLOUR, PLUS MORE FOR DUSTING

1 TSP GROUND GINGER

1 TSP GROUND NUTMEG

¼ TSP SALT

1 CUP/150 G SULTANAS [GOLDEN RAISINS]

1 CUP/150 G DRIED CURRANTS

½ CUP/40 G CANDIED ORANGE OR LEMON PEEL
[OR A COMBINATION], FINELY CHOPPED

Put the yeast and 1 Tbsp of the sugar into a medium bowl and gradually stir in 2 cups of warm water (about 100°F/40°C). Set aside for about 10 minutes, or until the mixture becomes frothy.

Meanwhile, rub the butter into the flour in a large bowl until the mixture resembles coarse bread crumbs. Stir in 4 Tbsp of the sugar, the ginger, nutmeg, salt, sultanas, currants, and candied peel. Make a well in the center, pour in the yeast mixture, and stir the liquid into the flour in a spiral motion, from the middle outward, until the dough pulls away from the sides of the bowl.

Turn the dough out onto a floured surface and knead, dusting with more flour as needed, until elastic and just slightly sticky, about 5 minutes. Put the dough into a large greased bowl, cover with a clean kitchen towel, and set aside in a warm place for about 1 hour, until dough has doubled in size.

Turn the dough out onto a lightly floured surface again and knead lightly for a minute or two, then shape it into a large round or oval and put it on a lightly greased baking sheet. Cover with a clean kitchen towel and set aside in a warm place for 30 minutes.

Meanwhile, preheat the oven to 450°F/230°C (Gas Mark 8).

Bake the bread for 15 minutes. Tent with foil, then reduce the oven temperature to 350°F/175°C (Gas Mark 4) and bake about 40 minutes more, or until a toothpick inserted in the center comes out clean. Dissolve the remaining 1 Tbsp of sugar in 1 Tbsp of hot water and brush over the loaf. Return the loaf to oven for 5 to 7 minutes, then transfer to a wire rack to cool.

Farmer's Sunday Cake

Makes 2 loaves

This tea bread, from County Tyrone, is essentially Barm Brack (page 293) risen with soda instead of yeast. The recipe comes from Florence Irwin's *The Cookin' Woman*.

6 1/4 CUPS/625 G WHITE FLOUR

I TSP BAKING SODA

I TSP CREAM OF TARTAR

I CUP/200 G SUGAR

3/4 CUP/170 G BUTTER, SOFTENED,
PLUS MORE FOR GREASING

I CUP/150 G SULTANAS [GOLDEN RAISINS]

I CUP/150 G DRIED CURRANTS

2 TBSP CANDIED ORANGE OR LEMON PEEL
[OR A COMBINATION], FINELY CHOPPED

GRATED ZEST OF 1/2 LEMON

2 EGGS, BEATEN

2 1/2 TO 3 CUPS/600 TO 720 ML BUTTERMILK

Preheat the oven to 450°F/230°C/(Gas Mark 8).

Lightly grease 2 loaf pans.

Sift the flour, baking soda, cream of tartar, and sugar together into a large bowl and mix well.

Rub the butter into the flour mixture with your hands until the mixture resembles coarse bread crumbs. Add the sultanas, currants, orange or lemon peel, and lemon zest and mix well.

Make a well in center of the flour mixture, and pour in the eggs and 2½ cups/600 ml of buttermilk. Stir the liquid into the flour mixture, working in a spiral motion from the middle toward the sides of the bowl, and adding a bit more buttermilk if necessary to make a moist but cohesive batter. Do not overmix.

Spoon the batter into the loaf pans and bake for 15 minutes. Reduce the oven temperature to 400°F/200°C (Gas Mark 6) and bake for 20 to 30 minutes longer.

Sultana Scones

Makes 20

Mary Carberry, in her *West Cork Journal 1898–1901*, describes at one point how "the scent of hot scones bores thro' the mist." Peter and Mary Ward (see page 301) serve their own scones—this is their recipe—with plenty of farmhouse butter and homemade orange marmalade for breakfast. I liked them so much, I put them on the cover of *Saveur*.

6 1/4 CUPS/625 G WHITE FLOUR,
PLUS ADDITIONAL FOR DUSTING

1/2 CUP/100 G SUGAR

2 TSP BAKING SODA

I CUP/220 G COLD BUTTER, CUT INTO PIECES

3/4 CUP/115 G SULTANAS [GOLDEN RAISINS]

I 3/4 CUPS/420 ML MILK

I EGG

Preheat the oven to 400°F/200°C (Gas Mark 6).

Line 2 baking sheets with waxed or parchment paper and set aside.

Mix the flour, sugar, and baking soda together in a large bowl. Using a pastry cutter or 2 table knives, cut the butter into the flour mixture until it resembles coarse meal flecked with pea-size pieces of butter. Stir in the sultanas, then add the milk and stir until the dough just comes together.

Turn the dough out onto a lightly floured surface. Dust your hands with flour and gently knead the dough with the heels of your hands several times, until the dough forms a rough ball. (Do not overknead.)

Divide the dough into 20 equal pieces, gently shape each into a round, and arrange the rounds on the prepared baking sheets at least 1 in apart. Beat the egg with 1 tsp of water in a small bowl, then brush the tops of the dough rounds with the egg wash.

Bake until the scones are golden brown, 30 to 35 minutes. Set aside to cool slightly on wire racks; then serve warm with butter and marmalade or preserves.

SULTANA SCONES

GOOD FOOD IRELAND

The strawberries of County Wexford are famous all over Ireland, but the county is also Ireland's black currant capital—and Des Jeffares (below, on left), who farms in the local community of Drinagh, is something of a black currant celebrity: He stars in commercials, shown all over Europe, for the Ribena brand of black currant juice, for which he supplies a portion of the fruit. Des's wife, Margaret (below, on right), is involved in a different kind of growing: She has formed an organization, called Good Food Ireland, that aims to do nothing less than establish a worldwide reputation for the island's food products, artisanal producers, shops and markets, cooking schools, restaurants, and gastronomically inclined hotels.

Margaret's background is in marketing and tourism, and Good Food Ireland, which she established in 2006, is above all a marketing network, composed of individuals and institutions from every part of Ireland's food world (and nearly every part of Ireland, Northern Ireland included) who pay a modest fee—and undergo a vetting process—to join. In return they receive marketing support and advice, with the opportunity to take part in trade and consumer shows, food showcases, direct marketing, e-marketing, media visits, and more. GFI asks that members sell only Irish beef and give priority to other Irish products, including pork, lamb, seafood, produce,

and dairy products, and that they support craft baking and other artisanal enterprises. Members include a number of the key food figures mentioned elsewhere in this book, among them Darina Allen, Peter Ward, Enda Conneely, Robert Ditty, Maurice Keller, and Kay Harte; others range from Redmond O'Donoghue, former group chief executive of Waterford Crystal and former chairman of Fáilte Ireland, the Irish tourism board, to Michelin-starred chef Derry Clarke of L'Écrivain in Dublin, Roscommon innkeeper Eammon Gleeson, and artisanal fish smoker Birgitta Curtin of Burren Smokehouse.

Good Food Ireland's website, www.goodfoodireland.ie, offers detailed profiles of the organization's two hundred–plus members, along with photos, recipes, videos, an online shop, an events calendar, and suggested food-related itineraries around the island—as well as a direct booking service for member establishments. Members are also listed in a terrific full-scale map of the island, available through the website (and handed out with all Hertz car rentals in Ireland). Even the most enthusiastic champions of Ireland's gastronomy will admit that great meals can be elusive in some parts of the country; the Good Food Ireland makes it easy to find, well, good food in Ireland.

Gingerbread

Serves 10 to 12

Gingerbread—not the dense confection often shaped into "men" or frosting-trimmed little houses, but rather a moist, sweet cake—has been popular in Ireland since the seventeenth century. There were even specialty gingerbread shops in Armagh in the late 1800s.

1/2 CUP/110 G BUTTER, PLUS MORE FOR GREASING

1/2 CUP/100 G BROWN SUGAR

1/2 CUP/120 ML LYLE'S GOLDEN SYRUP
[SEE SOURCES, PAGE 369] OR DARK CORN SYRUP

1/2 CUP/120 ML BLACK TREACLE OR MOLASSES

1/4 CUP/60 G PRESERVED [CANDIED]
GINGER, MINCED

1/2 CUP/75 G SULTANAS [GOLDEN RAISINS]

I EGG, BEATEN

1/2 CUP/120 ML WARM MILK

2 1/2 CUPS/250 G CUPS WHITE FLOUR

I TBSP GROUND GINGER

I TSP BAKING SODA

I TSP BAKING POWDER

1/2 TSP SALT

WHIPPED CREAM OR POWDERED SUGAR
FOR SERVING

Preheat the oven to 350°F/175°C (Gas Mark 4). Grease an 8- or 9-in/20- or 23-cm square baking pan with butter, then line the bottom with waxed or parchment paper. Set the pan aside.

Put the butter, sugar, syrup, and treacle into a medium saucepan over medium heat. Whisk constantly until the butter melts and the sugar is dissolved. (Do not boil.) Stir in the preserved ginger and sultanas. Let cool to room temperature, then stir in the egg and the milk until they are well combined.

Sift the flour, ginger, baking soda, baking powder, and salt together into a large bowl. Make a well in the middle of the flour mixture and pour in the butter mixture. Stir with a wooden spoon, working from the middle to the sides of the bowl, until the ingredients are well combined. Add a little more warm milk if necessary to absorb all the flour.

Spoon into the baking pan and smooth out the top with the back of a large spoon. Bake for 40 to 50 minutes or until cooked through and slightly risen. Allow to cool slightly, or cool to room temperature, before cutting.

To serve, cut into squares and serve with whipped cream or powdered sugar.

Theodora FitzGibbon's Apple Bread

Makes 1 loaf

This tea bread, says Theodora FitzGibbon, is "pleasant served warm, sliced with butter."

I 3/4 CUPS/175 G WHITE FLOUR

I CUP/200 G SUGAR

1/2 CUP/110 G COLD BUTTER, CUT INTO PIECES,
PLUS MORE FOR GREASING

4 COOKING APPLES, PEELED, CORED,
AND FINELY CHOPPED

I EGG, BEATEN

Preheat the oven to 350°F/175°C (Gas Mark 4).

Grease a shallow 2-qt/2-L rectangular baking dish.

Mix the flour and sugar together in a large bowl. Using a pastry cutter or 2 table knives, cut the butter into flour mixture until it resembles coarse meal flecked with pea-size pieces of butter.

Add the apples and egg to the flour mixture and mix well, then spoon the batter into the baking dish. Bake for 40 to 45 minutes or until the bread is brown and cooked through.

Apple Cake

Serves 6

Darina Allen remembers that when she was a farm girl growing up in County Laois, children who helped with the annual hay making were rewarded with a treat of fruit bread with butter, followed by apple cake washed down with sweet tea. This is her apple cake recipe. A cake like this would, she says, "originally have been baked in an iron bastible or pot oven beside an open fire."

2 CUPS/200 G WHITE FLOUR, IRISH IF POSSIBLE [SEE SOURCES, PAGE 369], OR UNBLEACHED PASTRY FLOUR, PLUS MORE FOR DUSTING

1/4 TSP BAKING POWDER

1/2 CUP/110 G COLD BUTTER, CUT INTO PIECES, PLUS MORE FOR GREASING

1/2 CUP/100 G SUGAR, PLUS MORE FOR DUSTING

2 EGGS, BEATEN, 1 WITH A PINCH OF SALT, IN SEPARATE BOWLS

1/4 TO 1/2 CUP/60 TO 120 ML MILK

2 OR 3 COOKING APPLES, PEELED, CORED, AND FINELY CHOPPED

Preheat the oven to 350°F/175°C (Gas Mark 4).

Sift the flour and baking powder into a large bowl, then rub in the butter until the mixture resembles coarse meal. Add about two-thirds of the sugar, the egg beaten without salt, and enough milk to form a soft dough.

Lightly grease a 10-in/24- to 26-cm pie pan. Divide the dough into 2 equal parts. Put one part into the pan and pat it out until it covers the surface. Spread apples across the top of the dough and sprinkle with the remaining sugar.

On a lightly floured board roll out the remaining dough into a circle large enough to cover the apples. Carefully lift the dough onto the apples, then press down around the edges, sealing it to the bottom round of dough. Cut a slit in the middle of the top crust, then brush all over with the egg beaten with salt.

Bake for about 40 minutes or until top crust is golden-brown. Dust with a little more sugar. Serve warm or at room temperature.

Cashel Blue Cheesecake with Apricots

Serves 8

Food writer and television personality Clodagh McKenna, who trained at Ballymaloe Cookery School and later cooked for three years at Ballymaloe House, graces this baked cheesecake with various fruits, according to the season.

7 OZ/200 G CASHEL BLUE CHEESE [SEE SOURCES, PAGE 369]

14 OZ/400 G MASCARPONE

5 CUPS/1 KG SUPERFINE SUGAR

6 EGGS, SEPARATED

1/2 CUP/75 G CORNSTARCH, SIFTED

PINCH OF SALT

8 APRICOTS, HALVED AND PITTED

Preheat the oven to 325°F/160°C (Gas Mark 3). Line the bottom of a 9-in/23-cm springform baking pan with waxed or parchment paper.

Mix the Cashel Blue and mascarpone together with a fork in a large bowl.

Put 2½ cups/500 g of the sugar and ¼ cup/60 ml water into a small saucepan, bring to a boil over high heat, and stir until the sugar is dissolved. Remove from the heat and set aside.

Beat the egg yolks in a large bowl until light and fluffy, then stir in the sugar water and cornstarch. Continue stirring until the mixture has cooled to room temperature; then fold in the cheese mixture. Set aside.

In another large bowl, whisk the egg whites with salt until they form stiff peaks. Carefully fold the egg whites into the cheese mixture with a spatula until well mixed. Pour into the baking pan and bake for 25 to 30 minutes.

Meanwhile, put the remaining 2½ cups/500 g of sugar and 2 cups/475 ml of water into a medium saucepan, bring to a boil over high heat, and stir until the sugar is dissolved. Add the apricots, reduce the heat to medium, and cook for about 15 minutes or until the apricots are very tender.

When the cheesecake is done, set aside to cool to room temperature. To serve, remove the side of the pan, transfer the cake to a serving plate, and cut into 8 wedges. Top each wedge with 2 apricot halves and a spoonful or two of the syrup.

Chester Cake

Serves 6 to 8

This cake is essentially bread pudding encased in pastry. It goes by many monikers, including donkey's wedding cake, Paddy's wedding cake, wacker's wedding cake, gudge, or donkey's gudge. In Ireland, where it has been a specialty of Dublin bakeries since the early twentieth century, it is most often called "gur cake." The name may derive from the Urdu word for jaggery (raw brown sugar loaves), or from the Irish slang word for street urchins, "gurrier." The cake also goes by the name "Chester cake," which would seem to suggest a relation with the town of that name, the county seat of Cheshire in England. That, in any case, is how it's sold at the historic Barron's Bakery (whose motto is "You can butter but you cannot better Barron's bread") in Cappoquin, County Waterford. This is the recipe of third-generation baker Esther Barron.

1 1/2 LB/750 G [ABOUT 1 STANDARD SIZE LOAF] STALE GOOD-QUALITY SLICED WHITE BREAD, SOAKED OVERNIGHT IN WATER TO COVER

2 TBSP SUGAR

1 TBSP BLACK TREACLE OR MOLASSES

2 TSP APPLE PIE SPICE

3/4 CUP/115 G SULTANAS [GOLDEN RAISINS]

1 RECIPE SHORTCRUST PASTRY [PAGE 363]

WHITE FLOUR FOR DUSTING

1 EGG YOLK, LIGHTLY BEATEN WITH 1 TSP COLD WATER

Preheat the oven to 450°F/230°C (Gas Mark 8).

Squeeze the water from the bread until it's dryish, then put the bread into a medium bowl. Add the sugar, treacle or molasses, apple pie spice, and sultanas, and mix together well.

Divide pastry dough into 2 uneven pieces: three-quarters for the bottom crust and one-quarter for the top crust. Roll out the larger piece of dough on a lightly floured board to a thickness of about 1/4 in/6.5 mm to fit into bottom and up the sides of a loaf pan. Lightly press the dough into the pan, prick all over with a fork, and spoon in the bread filling.

Roll out the remaining piece of dough on a lightly floured board into a 5-x-10-in/12-x-25-cm rectangle about 1/4 in/6.5 mm thick and carefully lay it on top of the filling. Crimp the edges and brush the pastry top with the egg wash. Prick the top crust all over with a fork. Bake for 20 minutes; then reduce the oven temperature to 400°F/200°C (Gas Mark 6) and bake for 20 minutes more. Allow to cool in the pan before serving.

To serve, turn the cake out of the pan and cut into slices 1 1/2 to 2 in/4 to 5 cm thick.

Mrs. Lamb's Sponge Cake

Makes one 8-in/20-cm cake

In her original *Ballymaloe Cookbook*, Myrtle Allen recalls that when she was learning to cook, in the 1940s, she "destroyed so many precious ingredients in war time." But fortunately, she adds, the ingredients were from her own farm. On one occasion, she reveals, "I beat 16 eggs with their weight in sugar by hand for a whole day, in an effort to achieve the smooth mousse-like texture that I had been taught was the correct basis for a sponge cake. It never happened and the result was finally fed to the chickens. Good came out of this episode in the end, however, when a friend came to my rescue with a much more foolproof recipe." Here it is.

BUTTER FOR GREASING

3 EGGS, SEPARATED

1 CUP/200 G SUGAR

1 CUP/100 G WHITE FLOUR, PLUS MORE FOR DUSTING

1 TSP BAKING POWDER

1/2 CUP/120 ML HEAVY CREAM

FRESH FRUIT OR POWDERED SUGAR FOR GARNISH

Preheat the oven to 375°F/190°C (Gas Mark 5). Grease two shallow 8-in/20-cm round baking pans, then dust them with flour.

Beat the egg yolks with the sugar in a large bowl for 2 minutes, then slowly blend in ⅓ cup/80 ml water. Whisk the mixture for about 10 minutes, or until it is firm and creamy. Sift the flour and baking powder together, then fold them into the egg yolk mixture.

Beat the egg whites until they form stiff peaks, and then very gently fold them into the egg yolk mixture.

Divide the batter evenly between the baking pans and bake for about 20 minutes.

Meanwhile, whip the cream until it forms stiff peaks.

Turn the cakes out onto a wire rack to cool. Transfer one cake to a serving plate and spread the whipped cream over the top. Set the second cake on top of the filling. Serve at room temperature or chilled, with fresh fruit and/or powdered sugar on top.

Guinness Cake

Makes one 9-in/23-cm cake

This is one of the many Irish variations on fruitcake, moistened not with the usual whiskey, rum, or brandy, but with rich brown stout. The recipe is Darina Allen's.

1 CUP/220 G BUTTER, PLUS MORE FOR GREASING

1 ½ CUPS/300 G BROWN SUGAR

8 OZ/120 ML GUINNESS STOUT

GRATED ZEST OF 1 ORANGE

1 CUP/150 G SULTANAS [GOLDEN RAISINS]

1 CUP/150 G RAISINS

½ CUP/40 G CANDIED LEMON OR ORANGE PEEL,
OR A COMBINATION OF THE TWO

4 CUPS/400 G WHITE FLOUR

½ TSP BAKING SODA

2 TSP PUMPKIN PIE SPICE

½ CUP/40 G CANDIED CHERRIES

3 EGGS, LIGHTLY BEATEN

Preheat the oven to 350°F/175°C (Gas Mark 4). Lightly grease a deep 9-in/23-cm cake pan with butter.

Combine the butter and sugar together in a small saucepan and melt the butter over low heat, stirring to dissolve the sugar, then stir in the stout. Add the orange zest, sultanas, raisins, and candied lemon and/or orange peel. Raise the heat to high, bring to a boil, and boil, stirring frequently, for 3 to 4 minutes. Remove from the heat and set aside to cool.

Sift the flour, baking soda, and pumpkin pie spice together into a large bowl. When the Guinness mixture has cooled to lukewarm, stir it into the flour mixture. Stir in the cherries, then slowly add the eggs, mixing well. Spoon the batter into the pan, and bake for 1 ½ hours or until done.

A COUNTRY GROCER

Peter and Mary Ward run a small specialty grocery shop and café in Nenagh, a prosperous agricultural town in County Tipperary not very well known outside Ireland. If you happened into Country Choice on, say, a Wednesday morning or a Saturday afternoon, you might find Ward (below), in his striped grocer's apron, behind the counter weighing out a slab of local Baylough cheddar, or in the back of the shop, making pots of tea for a couple of locals sitting at a little table over copies of the *Nenagh Guardian*—and you might think, yep, a provincial country grocer. If you got talking to him, though—and like so many of his countrymen and women he is a fluent and engaging conversationalist—you might find out that he has just come back from Alicante or even Capetown, where he was cooking Irish food for local journalists and dignitaries; that he was in Dublin the other day addressing a government panel on food regulation policies; that he has a warehouse nearby many times the size of the shop, stocked with the finest Irish and imported foodstuffs, which he not only sells but distributes to others; and that he sells not only Baylough cheddar but fine cheeses from France and Italy, including a splendid Parmigiano-Reggiano that he and Mary helped make when they were in Emilia-Romagna last year.

A onetime grocery-chain troubleshooter from Dunderry, near Trim in County Meath, Ward moved to Nenagh because it was Mary D'Arcy's hometown, and he was going to marry her. He soon became part of the community, opening Country Choice in 1982. Today, Ward seems to know everybody of import in the food world in Ireland, from the country's minister for Agriculture, Fisheries and Food to the best chefs in Dublin. He also knows everybody in his own community, from the woman who makes country butter by hand for him a few miles away to the retired Nenagh homeowners who bring him onions and asparagus and strawberries from their little garden plots. ("And when they bring their food in," he says, "they use the *front* door. We're proud of them.") He also travels around the country—the world—talking to large groups about the glories of real Irish food and cooking and serving it to back up his words.

Ward isn't afraid to speak his mind: At the Irish Food Board's specialty food symposium in Kinsale, County Cork, in 2002, he told the audience "When people come here from another country and want to taste Irish food and we serve them something from a German-owned supermarket, that ought to be considered an act of treason!" And he'll interrupt a conversation on the high quality of Irish cattle or sheep to say, "A lot of farmers in Ireland have surrendered their skill for subsidies." Ward is, above all, a knowledgeable, passionate advocate of Irish raw materials and culinary traditions. Ireland needs more people like him—but for now, he's doing a pretty good job himself.

Ballymaloe Chocolate Almond Cake

Makes one 7- or 8-in/18- or 20-cm cake

There's nothing particularly Irish about this moist, extremely rich cake, except for the fact that it's served at the legendary Ballymaloe House in Shanagarry, County Cork—which is good enough for me.

For the cake:

4 OZ/125 G LESMÉ BELGIAN DARK CHOCOLATE OR ANOTHER TOP-QUALITY BITTERSWEET CHOCOLATE

2 TBSP DARK JAMAICAN RUM

1/2 CUP/110 G BUTTER, SOFTENED, PLUS MORE FOR GREASING

1 CUP/85 G GROUND ALMONDS

1/2 CUP/100 G PLUS 1 TBSP SUPERFINE SUGAR

3 EGGS, SEPARATED

PINCH OF SALT

1/2 CUP/50 G WHITE FLOUR, SIFTED, PLUS MORE FOR DUSTING

For the frosting:

1/4 LB/125 G LESMÉ BELGIAN DARK CHOCOLATE OR ANOTHER TOP-QUALITY BITTERSWEET CHOCOLATE

1 TBSP DARK JAMAICAN RUM

1/2 CUP/110 G BUTTER, SOFTENED

SLIVERED ALMONDS FOR DECORATION [OPTIONAL]

CANDIED VIOLETS FOR DECORATION [OPTIONAL]

Preheat the oven to 350°F/175°C (Gas Mark 4). Grease two 7- or 8-in/18- or 20-cm round cake pans. Line the bottom of each pan with a circle of waxed or parchment paper cut to fit exactly. Grease the paper and the sides of the pans and dust the pans with flour.

To make the cake: melt the chocolate and rum together in a double boiler or a heatproof bowl set over a pot of gently simmering water over medium-low heat, stirring frequently until smooth. Remove the top of the double boiler or the bowl from the pan with simmering water and set the chocolate aside to let cool.

In a medium bowl, beat the butter with an electric mixer on medium speed until smooth. Mix in the ground almonds. Add 1/2 cup/100 g of the sugar and beat on medium speed until fluffy. Beat in the egg yolks one at a time, beating well after each addition.

In another medium bowl, beat the egg whites with the pinch of salt with an electric mixer on medium-high speed until soft peaks form. Add the remaining 1 Tbsp of sugar and beat until stiff, but not dry, peaks form.

Pour the melted chocolate mixture into the bowl with the butter and almond mixture and stir in well. Fold in one-quarter of the egg white mixture, then one-quarter of the flour. Repeat the process 3 times to use up the egg white mixture and flour.

Divide the batter equally between the prepared cake pans. Bake the cakes for 20 to 25 minutes, or until the sides of the cakes are firm and the centers are slightly underdone.

Remove the cakes from the oven and allow to cool slightly in the pans. Turn out onto wire racks, peel off and discard the paper, and let the cakes cool to room temperature.

To make the frosting: Melt the chocolate and the rum together in a double boiler or a heat-proof bowl set over a pot of gently simmering water over medium-low heat, stirring frequently until smooth. Set the chocolate aside to let cool.

Beat the butter into the cooled chocolate mixture with an electric mixer on medium speed, a little at a time, until the frosting is light and smooth. If it's too soft, refrigerate until it starts to stiffen, then beat again until smooth.

Place one cake layer on a cake plate and spread frosting evenly over the top. Set the second layer on top; then spread the remaining frosting over top and sides. Decorate the cake with slivered almonds and/or candied violets, if you like.

BREHON LAWS

The statutes and rules that governed Gaelic Ireland—the country's Napoleonic Code, if you will—are known collectively as the Brehon Laws, after the Irish word for "judge" (*breitheamh* in modern Irish). The laws date back to pre-Christian times, but St. Patrick was smart enough to have them edited and adapted to the Christian ethic instead of rejecting them outright. The laws exist in the form of a number of tracts, amply glossed and annotated over the centuries. The oldest extant tract, the so-called Senchus Mór, meaning "old knowledge," was concerned with civil law. Another tract, the Book of Achill, consisted of the legal opinions of two great scholars on criminal matters. The brehons, who interpreted these tracts, were considered particularly wise and intelligent, and they would have had to have been. The tracts were written in an ancient dialect of Irish so obscure that many later commentators had trouble deciphering parts of them.

The Brehon Laws—which remained in use well into the sixteenth century, and even longer in areas outside the English realm—deal with virtually every aspect of daily life, and are full of regulations pertaining to food and drink. The kinds of crops that could be planted and the uses to which they could be put are specified (barley, for instance, was to be grown only for brewing). There are catalogues of the appropriate food and drink to be offered as tribute to various rulers under various circumstances. A section of the criminal code computed fines to be paid to a wounded man by his attacker according to how many cereal grains or dried beans could be placed into the wound. Another prescribed periods of enforced fasting as punishment for certain crimes. Some of the most important provisions had to do with hospitality. The hearth was to be open to all, and hosts were expected to provide food, drink, and if possible a warm bed to anyone who visited, even strangers. Guests in turn were expected to make an offering of bread, cakes, wine, or other nourishment, or at the very least be expected to sing a song or spin a tale.

Closer to our own time, historian A. T. Lucas wrote that for the Irish, hospitality was "not merely a virtue, it was an over-riding duty." The traveler in Ireland today, at least outside the big cities (and often even there) will likely find that this is still the case—even though the Brehon Laws have long since been shelved.

PUDDINGS

and

CONFECTIONS

Sweet Rewards

A proper appreciation of the sweet course is of great importance in
courtship and marriage.

—Maura Laverty, *Maura Laverty's Cookbook* [1947]

Did you treat your Mary Anne to dulse and yallaman
At the auld Lammas Fair of Ballycastle, oh?

—"The Auld Lammas Fair," an old Irish ballad

The sausagelike specialties known as black and white pudding [see page 201] are basic to Irish cuisine, but sweet puddings have also been very popular for centuries, in farm cottages and grand houses alike. They were especially well

suited to frugal kitchens, since they were made mostly with eggs, milk, and butter—products of the farm—and used little or no flour (which had to be purchased). Sugar was a luxury, of course, but a little could be made to go a long way by introducing the natural sweetness of fruit or even carrots to the recipe, and honey was often available as a substitute. Historian Bríd Mahon writes that in the late seventeenth century, an Englishman traveling through County Westmeath reported the appearance on Irish tables on Mayday of "a type of thick milk pudding, rather like a blancmange, [made] as a celebration and proof that the good housewife through careful management had sufficient flour to keep bread on the table during the winter months."

Anglo-Irish recipe manuscripts from the seventeenth and eighteenth centuries are full of recipes for pudding-style desserts. Florence Irwin, in *The Cookin' Woman*, includes at least thirty sweet puddings, many of them made with fruit, some of them eggless. The most famous pudding of all, of course, is Christmas pudding. One theory is that this developed out of the practice of eating oatmeal porridge, or stirabout, on Christmas Eve, as sustenance after a day of fasting. Gradually, honey or sugar and bits of dried fruit were added, along with a shot or two of whiskey or poitín (see page 341), and eventually the Christmas pudding as we now know it came to be.

Ice cream probably first arrived in Ireland from France, by way of the Anglo-Irish estate kitchens. It became a popular treat in the 1920s, after the Hughes Brothers started making it commercially at their Hazelbrook Dairy in Bunratty, County Clare (HB is still Ireland's best-known ice cream brand). Today the Irish can enjoy the products of Baskin-Robbins and Ben & Jerry's, but also of a number of small artisanal producers, some of them organic.

The most famous nonchilled confection in the country is almost certainly yellowman, or yallaman, a hard, caramel-based sweet particularly associated with the Auld Lammas Fair in Ballycastle, County Antrim, and prominent in the famous ballad quoted on the previous page. Another, more sensual, version of the song has a verse that goes "[T]he scene that haunts my memory is kissing Mary Anne / Her parting lips all sticky from eating 'yellowman.'"

Bread and Butter Pudding

Serves 6

A homey dessert, bread and butter pudding has been showing up in recent years, with various refinements, on menus at good restaurants all over Ireland. This is a traditional version.

2 TBSP BUTTER

8 THICK SLICES FROM A PULLMAN LOAF OR ANOTHER GOOD QUALITY WHITE BREAD, CRUSTS TRIMMED

1/2 CUP/75 G SULTANAS [GOLDEN RAISINS]

2 TBSP CANDIED ORANGE OR LEMON PEEL, MINCED

3/4 CUP/150 G SUGAR

1/2 TSP GROUND NUTMEG

1/2 TSP GROUND CINNAMON

2 EGGS

1 CUP/240 ML CREAM

3 CUPS/720 ML MILK

1 TSP VANILLA EXTRACT

2 TBSP BROWN SUGAR

Preheat the oven to 350°F/175°C (Gas Mark 4).

Butter the bread on one side, then break each slice into large pieces. Put into a 2-qt/2-L rectangular baking dish, then mix in the sultanas and orange or lemon peel.

In a small bowl, mix one-quarter of the white sugar, the nutmeg, and cinnamon, and then sprinkle the mixture over the bread.

In a small bowl, lightly beat the eggs with the remaining sugar; then whisk in the cream, milk, and vanilla extract. Pour the mixture over the bread, and then dust the top with brown sugar.

Bake for 50 to 60 minutes, or until all the liquid is absorbed and top is golden brown.

Milky Rice Pudding

Serves 4

Florence Irwin, the Northern Irish "Cookin' Woman," tells of an encounter she had with an elderly housewife in one of the villages she visited: The woman thanked her for publishing a rice pudding recipe in her column in the Belfast newspaper the *Northern Whig.* "For many years," explained the woman, "I had a cup and pie-dish. The cup held just enough rice to make the pudding as [my husband] liked it, but the pie-dish got broken. The new pie-dish was a different size. After that the pudding was different every day, which led to much 'conversation.'" Irwin's recipe, giving exact quantities, brought domestic tranquility to the woman's home. This is more or less that formula, though using butter instead of the margarine she called for, and employing short-grain rice—in place of the long-grain Carolina rice she recommended—which yields a creamier pudding.

2 TBSP BUTTER

2 CUPS/475 ML MILK

1/3 CUP/70 G ABORIO OR ANOTHER SHORT-GRAIN RICE

2 TBSP BROWN SUGAR

PINCH OF SALT

1 TSP GROUND CINNAMON [OPTIONAL]

Preheat the oven to 325°F/160°C (Gas Mark 3). Generously butter an 8- to 9-in/20-cm pie pan.

Put the milk, rice, sugar, and salt into the pie pan and stir to combine well.

Bake for 1 hour or until the rice is thoroughly cooked, stirring every 10 minutes or so.

Spoon the hot pudding into bowls. Sprinkle the cinnamon over the top, if using.

TIPSY PUDDING WITH MULLED WINE

Tipsy Pudding
with Mulled Wine

Serves 8

Gerry Galvin used to prepare this dessert at his Drimcong House in Moycullen, County Galway.

2 TBSP BUTTER, SOFTENED

1 1/2 CUPS/90 G DRY BREAD CRUMBS

4 EGGS, SEPARATED

3/4 CUP/150 G PLUS 2/3 CUP/125 G SUPERFINE SUGAR

1 TSP FINELY GRATED LEMON ZEST

2 1/2 CUPS/600 ML DRY RED WINE

JUICE AND WIDE STRIPS OF ZEST FROM 1 LEMON

JUICE AND WIDE STRIPS OF ZEST FROM 1 ORANGE

4 WHOLE CLOVES

1 STICK CINNAMON

1 CUP/240 ML HEAVY CREAM, WHIPPED

Preheat the oven to 350°F/175°C (Gas Mark 4). Grease 8 ramekins or small soufflé dishes, about 2 in/5 cm deep and 3 to 4 in/7.5 to 10 cm in diameter, with butter. Coat the sides and bottoms of the ramekins evenly with about one-quarter of the bread crumbs.

Beat the egg yolks, 6 Tbsp of the sugar (half of the 3/4 cup/150 g), and the grated lemon zest in a medium bowl with an electric mixer on medium speed until pale and frothy, about 2 minutes.

In another medium bowl, beat the egg whites until stuff peaks form, 3 to 4 minutes. Gradually add another 6 Tbsp of the sugar (the remaining half of the 3/4 cup/150 g) to the egg whites and beat for about 30 seconds. Add one-quarter of the egg whites to the egg yolk mixture and stir. Fold the remaining egg whites and the remaining bread crumbs into the egg yolk mixture and stir well.

Divide the batter evenly between ramekins and bake on a baking sheet for about 25 minutes, or until the puddings are cooked through and golden. Allow the puddings to cool in ramekins for about 5 minutes, then turn then out onto a rack and set aside to cool to room temperature.

Meanwhile, combine the wine, the remaining 2/3 cup/125 g of sugar, the lemon and orange juices and zests, cloves, and cinnamon in a medium saucepan and bring to a boil over medium-high heat, stirring occasionally. Reduce the heat to medium-low and simmer for about 10 minutes. Strain the wine into a medium bowl, discarding the solids, and set the wine aside to cool.

Arrange the puddings side by side in an 8-x-12-in/20-x-30-cm baking dish, drizzle with the mulled wine, cover with plastic wrap, and set aside for about 3 hours to allow the puddings to soak in some of the wine.

Serve the puddings in individual bowls, spooning some wine over each one and topping each with a spoonful of whipped cream.

Mary Cannon's Carrot Pudding

Serves 8

Between about 1700 and 1707, Mary Cannon, who lived with her husband, Patrick, at Tivoli House in Dun Laoghaire, County Dublin, wrote down household recipes in a "common book." The little volume disappeared for generations, resurfacing for a time in the late 1930s and then vanishing again. Cannon's great-great-great-great-granddaughter, writer Marjorie Quarton of Nenagh, County Tipperary, has all that remains of the recipes: a selection of them in her own mother's hand, copied verbatim out of the original during its brief twentieth-century reappearance. There are, notes Quarton, "quite a number of recipes for 'ffish' and 'ffleshe,' but not a single mention of potatoes."

One of the more intriguing recipes is for what Cannon called "a Carriott Pudding." Her version reads "Take a stale two penny Loafe & grate it; Mingle it well with half as much Raw Carriotts grated, 8 youlkes & 4 whits of Egges well beaten, Rose water, sug'r, 2 grated Nuttmeggs & Crame. When you put it in ye Dish you bake it in, put in half pound Melted Butter, sture well & soe bake it." This is my attempt at reconstructing the recipe (and adjusting quantities for modern tastes).

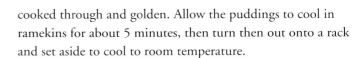

CHÂTEAU TIPPERARY?

Surprisingly, given their long and close association with ale and whiskey, the Irish have also been serious wine drinkers for more than a thousand years. Wine was first brought to the island by Viking traders as early as the eighth century. Ireland never had vineyards of its own, unlike England and Wales, perhaps because the Romans, who brought vine growing and wine making to Britain, never reached the island. But Ireland quickly became a thirsty market for vintages from the Continent, and as early as 1187, Gerald of Wales noted that the Irish imported large quantities of wine from Poitou, in the Loire Valley.

Traveling through Ireland in the late sixteenth and early seventeenth centuries, Fynes Moryson reported that Spanish and French wines were readily available in Irish taverns, adding that "when [Irish farmers] come to any market town to sell a cow or horse, they never return home till they have drunk the price in Spanish wine (which they call the King of Spain's daughter)." In 1745, Philip Dorner Stanhope, 4th Earl of Chesterfield, wrote home from a tour of Ireland that "Nine gentlemen out of ten are impoverished by the great quantity of claret which, from the mistaken notions of hospitality and dignity, they think it necessary to be drunk in their houses." And he notes that they are never able to improve their estates because the instant they're paid by their tenants, they settle up with their wine merchants.

A number of Irishmen did start making wine—and very good wine it turned out to be—but not at home. The so-called Wild Geese were well-to-do Catholic emigrés who fled Ireland after the Treaty of Limerick in 1691, becoming anti-English mercenaries in the armies of France and other European countries. Some eventually settled in Bordeaux, where they bought wine-growing properties. These men had names like Barton, known today through the châteaux Léoville- and Langoa-Barton (still owned by the Barton family), Lynch (Lynch-Bages), Phelan (Phélan-Ségur), Boyd (Boyd-Cantenac), and Clarke (Château Clarke). Another family, the Hennessys, ended up not far away in Cognac.

(The story that Château Haut-Brion was once owned by an Irishman named O'Brien is probably apocryphal.)

In recent decades, there have been a few ambitious attempts to make wine, from noble European grape varieties, on Irish soil. One pioneer was Michael O'Callaghan at the historic Longueville House in Mallow, County Cork, who grew the German cultivars Müller-Thurgau and Reichensteiner. His neighbor Billy Christopher tried making wines under the Blackwater Valley label. On the Cork coast at Kinsale, Thomas Walk has made wine from a hybrid red-wine variety called Rondo. (I tasted the 2004 vintage; it was bland and light, but could be drunk as a pleasant enough rosé if you chilled it.) To the best of my knowledge, the only Irish vigneron currently making grape wine on a regular basis for (highly limited) commercial sale is David Llewellyn, an apple farmer and artisanal cider maker in Lusk, in northern County Dublin. Llewellyn says that his region has the lowest winter rainfall in Ireland as well as good sunlight and frost-clearing ocean air, making it the most suitable terroir in Ireland for wine grapes (though most of his are protected by plastic tunnels). He makes two white wines and two reds, using Sauvignon Blanc, Chardonnay, some Gewürztraminer, and a German variety called Schönburger for the former, and Merlot, Cabernet Sauvignon, and some Rondo for the latter. The whites are aromatic and herbaceous and thoroughly drinkable; the reds are thus far stalky and light. (Llewellyn's bottlings, under the Luska label, are sold at a few wine and specialty shops around Ireland, including Country Choice in Nenagh, and are on the wine list at the elegant Merrion hotel in Dublin.)

The agricultural historian John Feehan has suggested that with global warming, the eastern and southeastern portions of the island may soon have a climate in which quality wine grapes could flourish. In his book *Farming in Ireland: History, Heritage and Environment*, he published a fanciful wine label for Wexford Fine Wines Chardonnay, 2035 vintage, above the caption "Tomorrow's world?" The European Commission has already listed Ireland as an official wine-producing country.

½ CUP/110 G BUTTER, MELTED,
PLUS MORE FOR GREASING

2 ½ CUPS/150 G DRY BREAD CRUMBS

1 ¼ CUPS/225 G GRATED RAW CARROT

1 CUP/200 G BROWN SUGAR

2 TSP GROUND NUTMEG

PINCH OF SALT

½ CUP/120 ML HEAVY CREAM

¼ TSP ROSEWATER

4 EGGS PLUS 4 EGG YOLKS

Preheat the oven to 400°F/200°C (Gas Mark 6). Grease a 1½-qt/1.5-L baking dish with butter.

In a large bowl, combine the bread crumbs, carrot, sugar, nutmeg, and salt, and set aside. In another large bowl, whisk together the heavy cream, butter, rosewater, and eggs and egg yolks. Add to the bread crumb mixture and stir until well combined.

Transfer the batter to the baking dish and smooth out the top with the back of a spoon. Bake until the pudding is set and the top is golden brown, about 45 minutes.

Peripatetic Pudding

Serves 4 to 6

Mary Rosse (1813–1885) of Birr Castle, County Offaly, was by all accounts a remarkable woman. She was not just a celebrated hostess, but also a pioneering photographer and an accomplished blacksmith, and she helped build the massive telescope for which Birr Castle became famous. This recipe, from the Birr Castle Archives, was found in Rosse's house-keeper's notebook. Alison Rosse, the modern-day Lady Rosse, notes "I am not sure why this is called peripatetic pudding, but I imagine it could be one of the puddings ending Mary Rosse's meals in her new dining room, with the astronomers by this stage anxious to go out and study the heavens through Lord Rosse's gigantic telescope." It should be noted that a

similar recipe, under the same name, appears in *The Godey's Lady's Book Receipts and Household Hints*, a collection from a popular American women's magazine of the time, published in Philadelphia in 1870.

½ CUP/100 G SUGAR

1 CUP/220 G BUTTER, MELTED,
PLUS MORE FOR GREASING

1 CUP/100 G ORANGE MARMALADE
[PAGE 327]

4 EGGS, BEATEN

1 TBSP SWEET SHERRY

6 LARGE SLICES SPONGE CAKE
[PAGE 299], WITHOUT THE WHIPPED
CREAM FILLING

Preheat the oven to 350°F/175°C (Gas Mark 4). Lightly grease a baking dish just large enough to fit the cake slices in a single layer.

In a medium bowl, mix the butter, marmalade, eggs, and sherry together well, then pour the mixture over the sponge cake. Bake for 1 hour or until the marmalade mixture is puffed up and golden brown.

CARRAGEEN LEMON PUDDING

Carrageen Lemon Pudding

Serves 6

Carrageen (*Chondrus crispus*), also known as Irish moss (see page 264), is used commercially today to thicken and stabilize all kinds of food products, from jellies and aspics to bologna to ice cream. Harvesting it at the seashore (or buying it at a shop), the Irish have a long tradition of eating it as it comes or employing it to add richness and texture to soups, desserts, and other foods. This recipe comes from Irish food writer Clodagh McKenna.

1/2 CUP/20 G DRIED CARRAGEEN MOSS
[SEE SOURCES, PAGE 369]

3 CUPS/720 ML MILK

3/4 CUP/175 ML HEAVY CREAM

I VANILLA BEAN

ZEST OF I LEMON, CUT INTO STRIPS

2 EGGS, SEPARATED

I TBSP SUGAR

Rinse the carrageen thoroughly; then put into a medium bowl, cover with lukewarm water, and set aside to soak for 15 minutes.

Drain the carrageen, and then put it into a small saucepan with the milk, cream, vanilla bean, and lemon zest. Bring to a boil over high heat; then reduce the heat to low and simmer, stirring occasionally, until the mixture thickens, about 30 minutes.

Strain the mixture through a fine sieve into a medium bowl, pushing the gelatin from the carrageen through with the back of a spoon. Put the egg yolks and sugar into a medium bowl and whisk until frothy, then slowly pour the carrageen mixture into the egg yolk mixture, whisking to combine.

In a clean medium bowl, whisk the egg whites until stiff peaks form; then fold the whites into the pudding, stirring gently.

Divide the pudding between 6 small bowls or glasses (¾ to 1 cup/175 to 240 ml in capacity). Cover with plastic wrap and refrigerate until set, at least 3 hours.

Steamed Syrup Sponge Pudding

Serves 6

The lineage of Ballyvolane, an estate and farm just outside Fermoy in northeastern County Cork, dates back at least to the sixteenth century, when it was the domain of the Coppingers (or Copingers), a prominent Cork family of Danish descent. In 1728, the property was purchased by Sir Richard Pyne, a onetime Lord Chancellor of Ireland (and briefly the owner of Blarney Castle, home of the Blarney Stone), who built a new house there. Jeremy Green acquired Ballyvolane from Pyne's descendants in 1955 and converted the mansion into a country guesthouse. His son, Justin, grew up on the property, then went off to learn the hotelier's trade in places like Hong Kong, Dubai, and Bali. Today, he's back home, with his wife, Jenny (whom he met while both were working at Hong Kong's Mandarin Oriental Hotel). The two run Ballyvolane House as an intimate inn, serving wonderful family-style dinners based largely on produce from the surrounding land. This is a version of one of their old house recipes.

1/2 CUP/110 G BUTTER, SOFTENED,
PLUS MORE FOR GREASING

1/4 CUP/60 ML LYLE'S GOLDEN SYRUP
[SEE SOURCES, PAGE 369], PLUS MORE FOR SERVING

1/2 CUP/100 G SUPERFINE SUGAR

2 EGGS

I 1/2 CUPS/150 G SELF-RISING WHITE FLOUR

WHIPPED CREAM FOR SERVING [OPTIONAL]

VANILLA ICE CREAM FOR SERVING [OPTIONAL]

Generously grease a 2-qt/2-L ovenproof pudding bowl. Pour the syrup into the bottom of the bowl and set it aside.

Put the sugar and butter into a large bowl and beat with an electric mixer on medium speed until well combined and fluffy, about 1 minute. Add the eggs one at a time, beating well after each addition. Add the flour and beat on low speed just until combined with the batter.

Spoon the batter into the pudding bowl on top of the syrup and smooth it out with the back of a spoon. Cover the bowl with 2 layers of foil and secure tightly with a rubber band or kitchen twine.

Put a rack in the bottom of a large pot and add 1 in/2.5 cm of water. Put the pudding bowl on the rack so that it sits just above the water. Cover the pot and bring to a boil. Immediately reduce the heat to low and steam until the pudding is just set and cooked through, about 1¾ hours. (Resist the urge to uncover the pot, since the steam escapes when you do.)

Carefully remove the pudding bowl from the pot, uncover, and set aside for 5 minutes to set. Use a rubber spatula or small knife to loosen the edges, then invert the pudding onto a large plate. Spoon any syrup remaining in the bowl over the pudding.

Serve with more syrup, heated, and with whipped cream and/or vanilla ice cream, if you like.

Christmas Pudding

Makes 2 puddings [*each serves 8 to 10*]

It's called a pudding, but it's really a kind of super–fruitcake cake, rich, moist, dense, and pretty much irresistible if you've got a sweet tooth. At Country Choice in Nenagh, County Tipperary, Peter and Mary Ward make about a thousand of these puddings for customers every year—"all by hand, and in the kitchen sink," says Peter Ward. The Wards usually end up consuming at least ten of them themselves before the season is over. Peter's mother believed that Christmas pudding should be made at least a month before it was eaten, to give the flavors time to marry. In fact, says Ward, it should keep for as long as two years.

1 CUP/150 G RAISINS

1 CUP/150 G SULTANAS [GOLDEN RAISINS]

2 CUPS/475 ML GOOD-QUALITY BRANDY

1/4 CUP/20 G ASSORTED CANDIED FRUIT [CHERRIES, MELON, CITRUS PEEL, ETC.], CUT INTO SHORT, THIN STRIPS

5 TBSP COLD BUTTER, CUT INTO 1/2-IN/1.25-CM CUBES, PLUS MORE FOR GREASING

1 3/4 CUPS/100 G FINE DRY OR DAY-OLD FRESH BREAD CRUMBS

1 CUP/85 G GROUND ALMONDS

1/4 CUP/50 G DARK BROWN SUGAR

3 TBSP WHITE FLOUR

2 TBSP SHREDDED UNSWEETENED COCONUT

2 TBSP FINELY GRATED CARROT

1/2 TSP FINELY GRATED LEMON ZEST

1/4 TSP FINELY GRATED ORANGE ZEST

PINCH OF CINNAMON

PINCH OF NUTMEG

1 EGG

1/2 TSP BLACK TREACLE OR MOLASSES

1/3 CUP/80 ML GUINNESS STOUT

2 TBSP FRESH ORANGE JUICE

3/4 TSP FRESH LEMON JUICE

WHISKEY BUTTER [PAGE 363] OR CLOTTED CREAM FOR SERVING [OPTIONAL]

Soak the raisins and sultanas in the brandy for 1 hour. Drain, reserving ⅓ cup/80 ml of the brandy for the recipe. (Save the rest for making egg nog or other holiday cocktails.)

Preheat the oven to 450°F/230°C (Gas Mark 8). Grease two 2½-cup/600-ml ovenproof glass or ceramic bowls.

Put the raisins, candied fruits, butter, bread crumbs, ground almonds, brown sugar, flour, coconut, carrot, lemon zest, orange zest, cinnamon, and nutmeg into a large bowl and stir well to combine.

Combine egg, treacle, Guinness, orange juice, lemon juice, and the reserved brandy in a medium bowl and stir well to combine, then stir into the fruit mixture.

Divide the batter equally between the prepared bowls. Cover each bowl with 2 sheets of waxed paper and 2 sheets of aluminum foil, then tie them into place with kitchen twine.

Put the bowls into a deep, wide baking pan with a cover. Pour boiling water into the pan to reach 2 in/5 cm up the sides of bowls. Cover the pan and steam the puddings in the oven for 4½ hours, adding more water as needed to maintain the same level.

Remove the bowls from the pan and let cool to room temperature. Replace the waxed paper and foil with fresh sheets, securing them again with twine. Refrigerate or store in a cool, dark place for at least 24 hours or up to 2 years.

To serve, reheat the puddings by steaming them as described above for 1 hour, then unmold onto serving plates. Serve with whiskey butter or clotted cream, if you like.

Burned Cream

Serves 4 to 6

Burned (or burnt) cream—*crème brûlée* to the French—is said to have been invented in the dining hall kitchen at Trinity College, Cambridge, as long ago as the early 1600s (though Catalan chefs also claim that their version, *crema catalana*, dates back to medieval times). The original version of this Irish recipe was written by Mrs. Creagh of Creagh Castle, County Cork, probably in the early to mid-nineteenth century. The sorrel or peach leaf was added for a touch of the acidity some recipes obtain with a few drops of lemon juice.

6 EGG YOLKS

9 TBSP SUGAR

1 TSP WHITE FLOUR

PINCH OF GROUND CINNAMON

3 CUPS/720 ML HEAVY CREAM

1 FRESH SORREL OR PEACH LEAF
[OPTIONAL]

Put the egg yolks into a heavy-bottomed, nonreactive saucepan, then whisk in 3 Tbsp of the sugar, the flour, and the cinnamon. Add the cream and whisk until it is well combined. Add the sorrel or peach leaf, if using.

Cook the cream mixture over medium heat, stirring constantly, until the custard is quite thick (don't let it boil, or it will curdle). Strain the custard through a sieve into a nonreactive bowl, cover with plastic wrap, and refrigerate until set.

In a small, heavy-bottomed saucepan, dissolve the remaining 6 Tbsp of sugar with 3 Tbsp of water and cook over low heat, swirling the pot over the heat frequently, until the sugar melts and caramelizes. Pour the caramelized sugar onto a cookie sheet and allow it to cool and harden, then break it into pieces and scatter it over the custard.

Brown Bread Ice Cream

Serves 10 to 12

The recipe for this no-stir ice cream, from the Blue Haven Hotel in Kinsale, County Cork, appeared in Georgina Campbell's 1995 book *Irish Country House Cooking*. Other versions of the recipe include eggs, but they're not necessary.

3 CUPS/180 G COARSE BREAD CRUMBS
FROM 2-DAY-OLD BROWN BREAD
[NOT SODA BREAD], SUCH AS BALLYMALOE
BROWN BREAD [PAGE 282]

1 1/2 CUPS/300 G DARK BROWN SUGAR

2 CUPS/475 ML HEAVY CREAM

3 TBSP SUGAR

1/4 TSP VANILLA EXTRACT

Position a rack in the oven about 6 in/15 cm from the heating element, then preheat the broiler.

Mix the brown sugar and bread crumbs together thoroughly in a large bowl. Spread out the mixture on a cookie sheet and broil for 3 to 4 minutes, or until caramelized, stirring well every 30 to 45 seconds. (Make sure the mixture doesn't burn.)

Return the mixture to the bowl, stir it well, and allow it to cool to room temperature, stirring frequently so that lumps don't form.

Pour the cream into a large stainless-steel or aluminum bowl and whisk it until soft peaks form. Gently fold in the sugar, stir in the vanilla extract, then fold in the caramelized bread crumbs until just combined (do not overmix). Press a piece of plastic wrap down firmly on the surface of the mixture, then cover the bowl tightly with a second layer of plastic wrap. Freeze the mixture for 8 hours or overnight.

THE WINE OF THE COUNTRY

Ireland actually does produce a few drops of grape wine (see page 312) and a few drops more of fruit wine, but the great Irish mealtime and pub-time beverage is ale, most often the rich variety known as stout. Ale, probably made mostly from barley at first (and later oats), dates back to prehistoric times in Ireland, and it figures in numerous legends and heroic tales, among them the famous "Vision of Mac Conglinne" (see page 175). Archeologist Caiman O'Brien says that in medieval times, "Every house had a vat of weak ale. It was probably the first thing people drank when they woke up in the morning. It was better than water, because bad water could kill you." Ale, in those days, was apt to be flavored, not with hops, but with various bitter herbs or with honey. An early connoisseur, Cano Mac Gartnáin, supposedly once declared, back in the seventh century A.D., "I have not tasted an ale to be preferred / to the ale of Cerna [probably in County Limerick]." In 1805, another connoisseur, English traveler John Carr, was already bemoaning the good old days of ale making, writing "The Irish ale is considered good, but it was much better when there were more private breweries."

This might have been in part a veiled reference to the massive brewery opened in Dublin by Arthur Guinness in 1759, on a plot of land at St. James's Gate that he leased for nine thousand years at a rent of forty-five pounds a year. (Needless to say, the brewery hasn't moved.) Porter was a rich, dark ale that had become popular in the early eighteenth century among street and river porters in London. Guinness began producing a potent "extra superior porter," and in 1840, the company changed its name to "extra stout porter." Soon only the "stout" part remained. English travel writer H. V. Morton visited the Guinness brewery in 1931. "Every visitor to the brewery ends up in the tasting-room," he wrote, "where the choicest vintage is ready for him. A wise man drinks only one tankard of that mysterious beverage known as 'foreign extra.' This is a stout of liqueur-like potency that has matured often for five or seven years. It is designed for foreign consumption, and is said that it reconciles exiles all over the world to the sadness of their fate. The kick of a full-grown mule is in each bottle. . . . The joke in this room is to give the visitor two bottles . . . and then watch him walk to the gate."

Guinness is ubiquitous in Ireland (in much of the world, for that matter), vastly preferred on draft. The Irish consider the serving, or pulling, of a pint to be an art, and will argue about which pub does it best. Down Cork way, though, stout-lovers tend to prefer the locally brewed Murphy's or Beamish, and there are partisans of Smithwick, made in Kilkenny. For a country that so obviously loves its beer, Ireland is surprisingly poor in brewpubs and microbreweries, with not more than a handful of the former and a dozen or so of the latter on the entire island. The small breweries that do exist often turn out pretty good stuff. Names to look for include Biddy Early in Inagh, County Clare; Carlow in the city and county of the same name; Kinsale Brewing Company, on the site of a three-hundred-year-old brewery in the County Cork seaside town of that name; Árainn Mhór on the island of the same name in Burtonport, County Donegal; Acton's in Macreddin, County Wicklow; Porterhouse in Blanchardstown, in suburban Dublin; Hilden in Lisburn, County Antrim; and Strangford Lough in Killyleagh, County Down. If only there were several dozen more of these. . . . Craft brewing, in any case, would seem to be a fertile field for would-be artisanal entrepreneurs in Ireland. Stout is useful to cook with, incidentally, and is called for in several recipes in this book; I've specified Guinness, which is the easiest Irish stout to find in America, but any good one will do.

Guinness and Ice Cream

Serves 2

I first heard of this surprisingly appealing concoction—sort of a root beer float for grown-ups—from my friend Belle Casares, née Holahan, a granddaughter of Irish-American writer John O'Hara, who was in turn descended from the Anglo-Norman Franeys of County Laois.

I PINT / 475 ML GOOD-QUALITY VANILLA
ICE CREAM, SOFTENED BUT NOT MELTED

I BOTTLE GUINNESS STOUT

Divide the ice cream equally between 2 tall, ice-cold, wide-mouthed glasses (soda fountain glasses) or glass beer mugs.

Divide the Guinness equally between the two, pouring it over the ice cream; then stir lightly.

Chocolate "Soufflé"

Serves 6

Alison, Lady Rosse, of Birr Castle in County Offaly, notes that this recipe, originally from prolific English food writer Ambrose Heath's 1937 book *Good Sweets*, was used regularly by her mother-in-law, Anne (Messel) Rosse. "Against it in her copy of the book," adds Lady Rosse, "she has written 'utterly lovely.'"

2 OZ / 60 G DARK CHOCOLATE

I TBSP MILK

I/3 CUP / 65 G SUGAR

I/2 CUP / 30 G FRESH BREAD CRUMBS

2 EGG YOLKS, BEATEN

I TBSP DARK RUM

I/2 CUP / 120 ML HEAVY CREAM, BEATEN

Put the chocolate and milk into a medium saucepan over low heat and stir until the chocolate melts. Stir in the sugar and bread crumbs. Mix well, then stir in the egg yolks and rum.

Remove the saucepan from the heat and whisk the ingredients until they cool to room temperature; then fold in the whipped cream.

Spoon the mixture into a large soufflé dish or 6 small ones, cover with plastic wrap, and refrigerate for 3 to 4 hours before serving.

Buttermilk Pancakes

Makes about twenty 3- to 4-in/7.5- to 10-cm pancakes
[serves 4 to 6]

In Catholic tradition, Shrove Tuesday, the day before Ash Wednesday and the beginning of Lent, has long been "pancake day." In earlier times, the observant abstained, for the forty days before Easter Sunday, not only from meat but also from butter, eggs, and milk. Making pancakes was a good way to use up these ingredients before the fast began. According to "Cookin' Woman" Florence Irwin, an old Shrove Tuesday practical joke, typically played on the new maid or some other gullible young lady, involved sending the victim to the neighbor's house to borrow a "pancake sieve." Arriving there, she'd be told that it had been lent to someone living near, so off she'd go to the next house—where of course she'd learn that it had been lent to yet another house. This went on until she at last returned home with the news that the sieve was nowhere to be found. At which point we can only hope that she was not sent out to borrow a left-handed monkey wrench.

3 1/2 CUPS/350 G WHITE FLOUR

I TSP BAKING SODA

1/3 CUP/65 G SUGAR

2 TBSP MELTED BUTTER

I EGG, BEATEN

I TBSP LYLE'S GOLDEN SYRUP
[SEE SOURCES, PAGE 369]

2 1/2 CUPS/600 ML BUTTERMILK

ABOUT 6 TBSP BUTTER, PLUS EXTRA
[OPTIONAL] FOR SERVING

HOMEMADE PRESERVES [PAGE 327] OR
MAPLE SYRUP FOR SERVING

Sift the flour, baking soda, and sugar together into a large bowl.

Make a well in the center of the flour mixture, and pour in the melted butter, egg, syrup, and buttermilk. Mix the ingredients together to form a batter that is thick but flows readily from a large spoon.

Heat a large cast-iron skillet or griddle or a nonstick skillet over medium heat and grease generously with some of the butter. Working in batches, spoon out circles of batter, being careful that they don't touch each other, and cook for 3 to 5 minutes or until bubbles appear on their surfaces. Turn and cook the other side until lightly browned. Repeat the process, adding more butter as needed.

Serve with butter and homemade preserves, or with maple syrup.

Yellowman

Makes about 1 lb/500 g

Yellowman (or yallaman) is a golden-hued toffee, so brittle that it must be broken into serving pieces with a hammer. It is traditionally a staple of country fairs, especially in Northern Ireland—most famously the Auld Lammas Fair, held the last Monday and Tuesday in August every year in Ballycastle, County Antrim. Florence Irwin's version of the recipe, published in her book *The Cookin' Woman*, is considered to be definitive. This is an adaptation of it.

2 TBSP BUTTER, PLUS MORE FOR GREASING

ONE I-LB/454-G TIN LYLE'S GOLDEN SYRUP
[SEE SOURCES, PAGE 369]

I 1/4 CUPS/250 G LIGHT BROWN SUGAR

2 TSP BAKING SODA

Grease a shallow rectangular baking dish and set aside.

Melt the butter in a medium saucepan over medium-high heat. Add the syrup, sugar, and 2 Tbsp of water and stir until the sugar dissolves. Continue cooking for 10 to 15 minutes without stirring until the mixture reaches 300°F/150°C on a candy thermometer.

Remove the saucepan from the heat and quickly sift in the baking soda; then whisk it vigorously for about 5 seconds (the syrup will bubble) and pour it into the greased baking dish.

Let the yellowman cool for at least 1 hour. Turn it out of the baking dish and break into pieces by gently tapping with a hammer.

SWEET SOMETHING

Beekeeping is an ancient art in Ireland. Before the introduction of cane sugar to the island in the sixteenth century, honey was used to flavor and sweeten foods (including milk), and also as a condiment and to make mead (see page 337). The importance of bees in Irish society may be seen from the fact that there's an entire tract on "Bee Judgments" in the Brehon Laws (see page 304). These dealt with ownership rights of hives, nests, and honey, and included a provision stating that if a bee from someone's hive stung a passerby, the victim was to be offered a meal of honey in recompense. Honey was also one of the substances considered an appropriate tribute to royalty.

The patron saint of Irish beekeepers is the sixth-century St. Gobnait of Ballyvourney, County Cork. It is said that when an invading army from another part of Ireland approached her town, she met them with a hive in her hand and let loose the bees—which stung the chieftain and his followers into retreat. Another tale from about the same era holds that the lad who was to become St. Ciarán, founder of the monastery of Clonmacnoise in County Offaly, was once scolded by his mother because he didn't bring home honey from the hives like the other boys did. He responded by going to the well and filling a bucket with water, then bringing it home and blessing it, at which point it turned into honey.

There are about two thousand small-scale honey producers in Ireland today, most of whom sell their wares at farmers' markets and in local shops. They don't make enough to meet demand in Ireland, though, so much of the honey you'll find there today is imported.

IRISH FEASTING

The quality, abundance, and variety of food and drink available to the wealthy in Ireland in the eighteenth and nineteenth centuries—not just to English landlords and the new Anglo-Irish gentry class, but also to the well-to-do Irish—was remarkable. Based on a wide array of imported foodstuffs (there are recipes for curries and chutneys in eighteenth-century manuscripts) as well as the bounty of their own estates, and often expressed with a French accent, the feasts enjoyed by the privileged few stand in marked contrast to the meager meals of the average Irish family, bereft of farmland to call their own, whose diet had grown steadily poorer and more monotonous.

Compared to some of the country-house repasts described in eighteenth-century manuscripts, the meal enjoyed by Edward Willes, an English judge and head of the Irish Exchequer, at a fortified house in Galway in 1755 sounds almost prosaic: "A bottle of Brandy was the wet before dinner, and the Entertainment was Half a Sheep Boiled at top, Half a sheep roasted at Bottom, broiled Fish on one side, a great wooden bowl of Potatoes on the other, and an heaped plate of salt in the middle." Considerably more elaborate was the lunch given to guests at 4:00 P.M. one fall day in 1764 by Dean Patrick Delany and his wife, Mary, at their house in Dublin. The meal included partridges, grouse, rabbits and onions, sweetbreads, boiled chicken, veal scallops and Veal Olives (page 181), chine of mutton, turkey in jelly, hare, lobster fricassée, and, for dessert, "nine things, six of them fruit out of our own garden, and a plate of fine Alpine strawberries." In 1812, at his Kilteeshan estate in Killbrine, County Roscommon, Dean French sat down to a scarcely less generous repast of soup, macaroni, stewed turkey, pâtés, lamb cutlets, wine coolers (!), ham, saddle of mutton, salmon ("almost out of season"), asparagus, shoulder of lamb, chancellor's pudding, and Flummery (page 334).

In the 1830s, in Callan, County Kilkenny, reports businessman and diarist Amhlaoibh Ó Súilleabháin, he dined frequently and well at the home of the local parish priest, Father Séamus Hennebry. Among the menus: "two fine sweet solid trout, one of which was the size of a small salmon, and hard-boiled hen eggs, boiled asparagus dipped in butter melted in hot milk, with salt"; "boiled leg of lamb, carrots and turnips, roast goose with green peas and stuffing, a dish of tripe boiled in fresh milk"; and "leg of lamb, bacon, pullets and white cabbage, two roast ducks and green peas; white wine and port, and plenty of punch." (Ó Súilleabháin subsequently reports, incidentally, that Father Hennebry died of a sudden attack of apoplexy.) In 1857, Lord Rosse (William Parsons), who had built what was then the largest telescope in the world on the grounds of his Birr Castle in County Offaly—it was known as the Parsonstown Leviathan—hosted a banquet for members of the British Association for the Advancement of Science, and served "turtle à l'Anglais, cucumber sauce, purée of spinach, veal with mushrooms, sole à la Normandy, whiting à la Mazarine, and deserts of a recherché character."

Though turkey in jelly and flummery aren't likely to be on the menu anymore, the modern-day visitor to Ireland can have a taste of the country-house dinner experience at properties all over the island. These grand old houses, restored or remodeled with skill and run with varying degrees of formality, are now open to the public as hotels with good dining rooms attached. These include Ballymaloe House (see page 242) and Ballyvolane House in County Cork, Glin Castle in County Limerick, Gregan's Castle in County Clare, Marlfield House in County Wexford, Ballyknocken House in County Wicklow, Bellinter House in County Meath, Castle Leslie in County Monaghan, Rathmullan House in County Donegal, and Beech Hill Country House in County Down, among many others.

FRUIT DESSERTS

and

PRESERVES

From Orchards and Fields

To Killaden then, to the place where / everything grows
that is best, / There are raspberries there and strawberries there /
and all that is good for men . . .

—James Stephens, "The County Mayo" [circa 1918]

I will eat good apples in the glen, and fragrant berries of rowan-tree.

— Aodh Ó Dochartaigh, *Dunaire Finn* [*The Poem Book of Finn*] [1627]

Parts of Ireland must have seemed like paradise to the island's early inhabitants, with their fields full of wild blackberry, bilberry, gooseberry, and raspberry bushes and their stands of crabapples

and other flowering trees and shrubs with edible berries—the elderberry; the rowan or mountain ash (a distant relative of the rose, of the genus *Sorbus*); the arbutus (genus *Arbutus*) or strawberry tree; the hawthorn (*Crataegus monogyna*), whose leaves as well as haws were edible; the blackthorn or sloe plum (*Prunus spinosa*), whose sturdy roots were the traditional raw material for the famous Irish walking-stick-cum-weapon called the *shillela*. Of course, not all of these grew in the country naturally—at least not according to the ancient lore. "Crimson nuts and arbutus apples and scarlet quicken berries [rowanberries]" came originally, according to the Fenian Cycle of Irish myths, from Tír-na-nÓg—the Land of the Ever-Young, the most important of the old Celtic netherworlds—and had special properties as a result. Hazelnuts, apples, and acorns (the fruit of the oak tree) were also thought to be magical—and it was said that a diet of all three would give one all the nutrients essential for a healthy life.

The historian Bríd Mahon writes that a ninth-century Irish hermit praised his diet of eggs, honey, apples, cranberries, strawberries, raspberries, hazelnuts, and blackberries, washed down with hazel mead. Cultivated apples date back at least to early Christian times in Ireland, and there is a tradition that St. Patrick himself once planted an apple tree. It was the Anglo-Normans in the twelfth and thirteenth centuries, though, who introduced large-scale apple orchards to the island, and these were said to flourish particularly in counties Armagh, Fermanagh, and Down. In the frequency of its mention in legend and early verse and its popularity in recipes from medieval times down the present, it may well be that the apple is the definitive Irish fruit. Nearly as popular are *fraughans*, as the Irish call bilberries, a fruit associated with the Celtic festival of Lughnasadh (see page 135). The Irish are fond of blackberries, as well. The best part of a group of things is sometimes called *an sméar mullach*, "the top blackberry" in Irish, and something very common might be said to be *chomh fairsing le sméara*, or "as plentiful as blackberries."

Many other kinds of fruit have been grown in Ireland for centuries, too, including both red and black currants, plums, peaches, pears, cherries, apricots, rhubarb, figs, and melons. The first pineapple grown in Ireland, in a nursery, dates from the early eighteenth century. In the nineteenth century, says chef and food scholar Máirtín Mac Con Iomaire, pineapple, oranges, lemons, and other exotic fruits would have been widely grown in Irish hothouses. "The idea of manipulating climate was very popular in those days," he says.

Recipe manuscripts from the eighteenth and nineteenth centuries are full of fruit recipes, including those for preserves and chutneys, fools, puddings, pies, and more. Often, though, fruit was simply stewed and served with honey and/or cream.

"Stewed fruit and custard or fresh fruit tarts were the 'old reliables' of my youth," wrote pioneering Irish food writer Monica Sheridan in the 1960s.

Orange Marmalade

Makes enough to fill 6 to 8 one-pint/475-ml jars

Orange marmalade is associated above all with Scotland, and especially with the town of Dundee, where—according to folklore—an eighteenth-century merchant named James Keiller ended up with a cargo of bitter oranges instead of sweet ones, and passed them on to his obviously industrious wife, who turned them into what must have been very many jars of bitter-sweet preserves. In fact, the word *marmalade*, from the Portuguese *marmelada*, "quince paste," has been used to describe fruit preserves in English since at least 1480, and has referred specifically to citrus preserves since the seventeenth century. Oranges, lemons, and other exotic fruits were being imported in considerable quantity into Ireland by then, and orange marmalade was almost certainly being made on the island, and in Scotland, before James Keiller was born. The addition of whiskey to marmalade is probably a more recent innovation.

2 LB/1 KG SEVILLE OR OTHER BITTER ORANGES,
HALVED CROSSWISE

8 CUPS/1.5 KG SUGAR

3 TBSP IRISH WHISKEY [OPTIONAL]

Squeeze the juice from the oranges into a large nonreactive bowl. With a sharp spoon or grapefruit knife, scrape out and discard the flesh, seeds, and pith from the peels.

Cut the orange peels into thin strips no more than 2 in/5 cm long and add to the bowl with the juice. Add 4 cups/1 L of water to the bowl and stir gently. Cover and refrigerate overnight.

Put the orange peels and liquid into a large nonreactive pot, and bring to a boil over high heat. Reduce the heat and simmer, uncovered, for 2 to 2½ hours or until the peel is soft enough to dissolve between your fingers and the liquid is reduced by about half.

Stir in the sugar a little at a time, making sure it is well dissolved. (If you add sugar before the orange peels are very soft, they will harden.) Increase the heat to medium-high and boil gently for 15 to 20 minutes, or until the temperature reaches 220°F/100°C on a candy thermometer, skimming any foam that rises to the surface. Reduce the heat and test to see if the marmalade has set by spooning a bit of the marmalade onto a chilled saucer. Allow the marmalade to cool slightly, then tilt the saucer to one side. If the marmalade remains in a blob with a few ripples, it's ready. If you wish to add whiskey, remove the pot from the heat and allow marmalade to cool for 10 to 15 minutes; then stir in the whiskey.

Divide the marmalade evenly between 6 to 8 sterilized 1-pint/475-ml jars; then seal with sterilized rings and lids. Transfer the filled jars to a canning rack, submerge in a pot of gently boiling water (make sure that jars are covered by at least 1 in/2.5 cm of water), and boil for 5 minutes. Carefully lift the jars from the water with jar tongs and place on a dish towel to cool, undisturbed, for 24 hours.

Fraughan Preserves

Makes enough to fill 3 to 4 one-pint/475-ml jars

Fraughan (or *frocken*) is the Irish name for the bilberry—which, next to the apple, notes Theodora FitzGibbon, is "perhaps . . . the most Irish of all fruits." A small bluish-black berry of the genus *Vaccinium*, the bilberry, also called the "whortleberry," is a sweet-tart relative of the American blueberry and huckleberry (either of which may be used in its place). The Irish traditionally gather bilberries (they tend to grow in bogs and sometimes under heather, and aren't always easy to find) on the last Sunday of July, known as Fraughan Sunday, and also on the ancient Celtic harvest holiday of Lughnasadh, which follows in the first few days of August. It was said that the quantity picked predicted the size of the harvest for other crops later in the season. Various medicinal properties are attributed to the bilberry, and during World War II, British aviators sometimes ate bilberry preserves before flying night missions, in the belief that it improved their night vision.

4 CUPS/600 G FRESH BILBERRIES, HUCKLEBERRIES,
OR BLUEBERRIES, STEMMED

4 CUPS/800 G SUGAR

CRABAPPLE JELLY

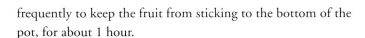

Put the berries into a medium heavy-bottomed pot. Crush the berries gently but firmly with a potato masher or fork to release their juice.

Add the sugar to the berries and juice and bring the mixture to a boil over medium heat. Cook at a boil, stirring frequently to keep the fruit from sticking to the bottom of the pot, for 30 to 45 minutes, or until the temperature reaches 220°F/100°C on a candy thermometer. Skim any foam that rises to the surface. Reduce the heat and test to see if the preserves have set by spooning a little onto a chilled saucer. Allow the preserves to cool slightly, then tilt the saucer to one side. If the preserves remain in a blob, they're ready.

Divide the preserves evenly between 3 to 4 sterilized 1-pint/475-ml jars; then seal with sterilized rings and lids. Transfer the filled jars to a canning rack, submerge in a pot of gently boiling water (make sure the jars are covered by at least 1 in/2.5 cm of water), and boil for 5 minutes. Carefully lift the jars from the water with jar tongs and place on a dish towel to cool, undisturbed, for 24 hours.

Crabapple Jelly

Makes enough to fill 6 to 8 one-pint/475-ml jars

"Collect wild crab apples after first frost," writes Mary Ward of Nenagh, County Tipperary, who likes to serve this jelly with cold roast lamb. "Check that the pips [seeds] are brown." If you've got a crabapple tree or two in the backyard (and it gets frosty in your neighborhood), you can follow her advice. Othewise, look for the fruit at farmers' markets.

IO LB/5 KG CRABAPPLES, CORED AND
COARSELY CHOPPED

I CUP/150 G BLACKBERRIES

6 WHOLE CLOVES

SUGAR AS NEEDED

Put the crabapples and blackberries into a large pot. Add the cloves and cover with enough water to come within 1 in/2.5 cm of the top of the fruit. Bring to a boil over medium-high heat, then reduce the heat to medium and allow to boil, stirring

frequently to keep the fruit from sticking to the bottom of the pot, for about 1 hour.

Choose a large bowl that will fit inside the pot with the crabapples. Set 8 layers of 20-in/50-cm square sheets of cheesecloth over the bowl letting the cheesecloth hang amply over the sides. Spoon the apple mixture and pot juices into the middle of the cheesecloth; then rinse out the cooking pot. Set the bowl down into the clean pot. Gather the opposing ends of the cheesecloth and tie securely to make a sack. Suspend the sack from a rolling pin or broom handle set across the edges of the pot and allow the fruit to drain into the bowl overnight.

Measure the juice that has drained into the bowl; then put into a medium saucepan with an equal amount of sugar. (Discard the solids.) Bring to a rolling boil over high heat. Boil until the temperature reaches 220°F/100°C on a candy thermometer, about 15 minutes, skimming any foam that rises to the surface. Reduce the heat and test to see if the jelly has set by spooning a bit onto a chilled saucer. Allow the jelly to cool slightly, then tilt the saucer to one side. If the jelly remains in a blob with a few ripples, it's ready.

Divide the jelly evenly between 6 to 8 sterilized 1-pint/475-ml jars, then seal with sterilized rings and lids. Transfer the filled jars to a canning rack, submerge in a pot of gently boiling water (make sure the jars are covered by at least 1 in/2.5 cm of water), and boil for 5 minutes. Carefully lift the jars from the water with jar tongs and place on a dish towel to cool, undisturbed, for 24 hours.

Damson Jam

Makes enough to fill 4 to 5 one-pint/475-ml jars

Seamus Heaney, the distinguished Irish poet, born and brought up in County Derry, memorably evokes "the wine-dark taste of home, / The smell of damsons simmering in a pot, / Jam ladled thick and steaming down the sunlight." Damsons are a purple-blue, acidic plum, well suited to jam making, not unlike the fruit sold seasonally in supermarkets as "prune plums."

3 POUNDS DAMSONS OR PRUNE PLUMS

6 CUPS/1.2 KG SUGAR

Put the damsons and 2 cups/475 ml of water into a large pot. Bring to a boil over medium heat, and continue to gently boil, stirring occasionally to keep the fruit from sticking to the bottom of the pot, for 45 to 60 minutes or until the skins of fruit break.

Stir the sugar into the pot. Increase the heat to high and continue boiling for 15 to 20 minutes, or until the temperature reaches 220°F/100°C on a candy thermometer, skimming the foam and plum pits as they rise to the surface. Reduce the heat and test to see if jelly has set by spooning a bit of jam onto a chilled saucer. Allow the jam to cool slightly, then tilt the saucer to one side. If the jam remains in a blob, it's ready.

Divide jam evenly between 4 to 5 sterilized 1-pint/475-ml jars; then seal with sterilized rings and lids. Transfer the filled jars to a canning rack, submerge in a pot of gently boiling water (make sure that jars are covered by at least 1 in/2.5 cm of water), and boil for 5 minutes. Carefully lift the jars from the water with jar tongs and place on a dish towel to cool, undisturbed, for 24 hours.

Marrow [Zucchini] Jam

Makes enough to fill 3 to 4 one-pint/475-ml jars

Northern Irish newspaper columnist and cookbook author Florence Irwin gives three different recipes for marrow jam, all flavored with "green root ginger" and "cayenne pods" (kept whole and removed before canning), suggesting that this unusual preserve could function as a substitute for chutney alongside cold roast meats and other appropriate preparations. It's also good on toast or crackers.

8 TO 10 MEDIUM GREEN OR YELLOW ZUCCHINI, OR A COMBINATION OF BOTH, PEELED, SEEDED, AND DICED

3 TBSP GRATED PEELED FRESH GINGER

JUICE OF 1 LEMON

1 TBSP SALT

1 TO 2 TBSP CRUSHED RED PEPPER FLAKES [OPTIONAL]

3 1/2 CUPS/700 G SUGAR

Mix the zucchini, ginger, lemon juice, salt, and pepper flakes (if using) together in a large nonreactive bowl. Cover and refrigerate overnight.

Put the zucchini mixture into a large pot, add about 1 cup/240 ml of water, and bring to a boil over high heat, stirring frequently to keep the fruit from sticking to the bottom of the pot. Cook until the liquid has reduced by half. Stir in the sugar and continue stirring until the sugar has completely dissolved. Continue cooking for another 5 minutes.

Divide the jam evenly between 3 to 4 sterilized 1-pint/475-ml jars, then seal with sterilized rings and lids. Transfer the filled jars to a canning rack, submerge in a pot of gently boiling water (make sure the jars are covered by at least 1 in/2.5 cm of water), and boil for 15 minutes. Carefully lift the jars from the water with jar tongs and place on a dish towel to cool, undisturbed, for 24 hours.

Canned Fruit Chutney

Makes enough to fill about 2 one-pint 475-ml jars

This versatile relish, made at the delightful Brocka on the Water restaurant in Ballinderry, on Lough Derg in County Tipperary, is a good example of the use-what's-in-the-larder school of cookery. It goes well with cold meats, poultry, and cheese.

3 TO 4 CUPS/450 TO 600 G DRAINED ASSORTED CANNED FRUIT, SUCH PINEAPPLE, PEARS, PEACHES, AND APRICOTS

1 SMALL ONION, MINCED

1 CUP/240 ML WHITE WINE VINEGAR

1 TSP SWEET ASIAN CHILE SAUCE

1/2 CUP/100 G SUGAR

1/4 CUP/40 G RAISINS

1/4 CUP/40 G SULTANAS [GOLDEN RAISINS]

1 TSP CURRY POWDER

1 TSP PICKLING SPICES

Combine all the ingredients in a medium nonreactive pot, and bring to a boil over medium-high heat. Reduce the heat to low and simmer, stirring occasionally, until the chutney thickens and the fruit is very soft, 1 to 1½ hours.

Set aside to cool; then transfer to a bowl or pot, cover tightly, and refrigerate for at least 6 hours before using. Bring to room temperature before serving.

Mint, Onion, and Apple Chutney

Makes about 1 cup / 250 g

Catherine Fulvio serves this simple chutney with various lamb dishes at her Ballyknocken House in Ashford, County Wicklow. She notes that, unlike traditional chutneys, this one is best used fresh, though it will keep for up to 2 days in the refrigerator.

3 CUPS / 50 G LOOSELY PACKED FRESH MINT LEAVES

I ONION, COARSELY CHOPPED

I LARGE COOKING APPLE, PEELED, CORED, AND SLICED

3 TBSP SUGAR

I/2 TSP SALT

Mix the mint leaves, onion, apple, sugar, and salt together in a small bowl; then transfer to a blender or the bowl of a food processor. Process at slow speed until the ingredients are finely chopped but not puréed. Adjust the sugar and/or salt if necessary.

Rhubarb Chutney

Makes about 3 pints / 1.5 kg

This recipe comes from West Cork food writer and TV personality Clodagh McKenna.

3/4 LB / 375 G RHUBARB, DICED

I COOKING APPLE, PEELED, CORED, AND CHOPPED

I/2 CUP / 100 G BROWN SUGAR

I/2 CUP / 120 ML CIDER VINEGAR

I CUP / 150 G RAISINS

I TBSP LEMON JUICE

I TSP GRATED FRESH GINGER

I/2 TSP GROUND CUMIN

Combine the rhubarb, apple, sugar, vinegar, raisins, lemon juice, ginger, and cumin in a medium heavy-bottomed saucepan. Bring to a boil over medium heat, then reduce the heat to low and simmer for about 10 minutes, or until the rhubarb and apple are very soft but still hold their shape. (Do not cook into a mush.)

Let the chutney cool to room temperature; then transfer to an airtight container and refrigerate. The chutney will keep for up to 1 week refrigerated.

THE LITTLE PEOPLE

Ireland was once a land of gods and it became a land of fairies. There's a connection between the two according to some scholars, who believe that fairies are known as "the little people" because they are shrunken or weakened versions of the Celtic deities who lost their power after the arrival of Christianity. The most famous Irish fairies of all, of course, are leprechauns, pint-sized green-clad fellows who always seem to have a pot of gold stashed somewhere. They are frequently depicted as shoemakers; Yeats wrote that the leprechaun's very name comes from the Irish *leíth bhrogan*, meaning "maker of one shoe." But leprechauns are also associated with Lugh, the sun god, honored by the feast of Lughnasadh in early August.

Many superstitions regarding fairies (beliefs known collectively in Irish as *piseogs*) link them with food and drink. They are frequently accused of stealing milk or butter and sometimes grain, and there are all manner of customs aimed at placating them—setting a saucer of milk out for them on the windowsill, for instance, or leaving crumbs from the evening meal on the dinner table (or in the westernmost room of the house, through which fairy paths run) so that they can have a late-night snack. Fairies are also said to be able to sour the milk at farms that have been unfriendly to them, and sometimes to steal not actual food but "the goodness" out of it. And if a man takes his pipe outside the house while his wife is churning butter, fairies will take the butter.

The pooka or *púca* is a mischievous fairy who often takes the shape of a horse to harry travelers. When berries on the bush are killed by a frost, it is said that the pooka has spit on them. And white puffball mushrooms, often found in Irish meadows, are called *cáise púca*, or pooka cheese. The *fear-gorta* or "famine man" roams the countryside in times of privation, begging food—and rewarding anyone who gives him some. The *cluricaun* is a party animal, always drunk (some believe that he's just a leprechaun on a bender). If you treat him well, he will protect your wine cellar, but if you abuse him, he'll sour your wine or steal it. Whiskey or poitín (see page 341) made with water from wells or springs associated with fairies was said to be particularly potent, and if a housewife with an ailing family member left cream or bread by the fairy mound at night, she often found a cup of fairy moonshine with curative powers on her doorstep the next morning.

Irish fairies are famously unpredictable, capable of great generosity and largesse if you stay on their good side, but vengeful if you wrong them. They are rarely downright evil, though. In an essay criticizing the Scots for having turned their own fairies into unpleasant creatures, Yeats defends his country's little people: "When a peasant strays into an enchanted hovel, and is made to turn a corpse all night on a spit before the fire, we do not feel anxious; we know he will wake up in the midst of a green field, the dew on his old coat."

Applesauce

Serves 8 to 10

This classic accompaniment to roast pork, pork chops, black pudding, or roast goose is very easy to make and tastes infinitely better than the commercial version. Darina Allen of the Ballymaloe Cooking School in Shanagarry, County Cork, has discovered that applesauce freezes well, so don't be reluctant to make a large batch.

2 POUNDS COOKING APPLES, PEELED, CORED,
AND COARSELY CHOPPED

1/2 TO 3/4 CUP/100 TO 150 G SUGAR
[DEPENDING ON THE SWEETNESS OF THE APPLES]

Combine the apples, sugar, and about ½ cup/120 ml of water in a large pot. Bring to a boil over high heat, then reduce the heat to low. Cover and simmer over low heat, stirring occasionally, for 20 to 30 minutes, or until the apples are broken down and very soft.

Beat the apples into a purée with a fork or whisk.

Compote of Blackberries and Apples

Serves 4

This recipe comes from Myrtle Allen at Ballymaloe House in Shanagarry, County Cork.

1 CUP/200 G SUGAR

2 COOKING APPLES, PEELED, CORED, AND CUT INTO
MATCHSTICKS 1/4 IN/6.5 MM THICK

1 CUP/150 G FRESH BLACKBERRIES

Bring 2 cups/475 ml water to a boil over high heat in a medium saucepan. Stir in the sugar and cook, continuing to stir, for about 1 minute to make a syrup.

Reduce the heat to low and add the apples, making sure they are all submerged. Cook for 10 to 15 minutes or until the apples are very soft but have not broken up. Add the blackberries and continue cooking for 5 to 6 minutes more, or until the blackberries are very soft.

To serve, divide the fruit evenly between 4 bowls and spoon a little syrup over each serving.

Dad's Amazing Baked Apples

Serves 4

In her *Irish Farmers' Market Cookbook*, Clodagh McKenna recalls, "When I was growing up [in County Cork], my dad would come home during his lunch break to prepare a three-course dinner for us, which would be served at 6 P.M. on the dot! With a meagre budget, he experimented with every type of apple dessert, but this was my favourite."

4 COOKING APPLES, CORED

1/2 CUP/100 G BROWN SUGAR

2 TSP HONEY [AS RUNNY AS POSSIBLE]

2 TSP GROUND CINNAMON

1 TBSP BUTTER

16 WHOLE CLOVES

FRESH WHIPPED CREAM FOR SERVING [OPTIONAL]

Preheat the oven to 350°F/175°C (Gas Mark 4).

With a teaspoon, enlarge the core cavity of each apple to twice its original size. Put the apples into a baking dish just big enough to hold them. Divide the brown sugar evenly between them, then do the same with the honey and the cinnamon. (If the honey is too thick to distribute it easily, warm it for 2 to 3 minutes over low heat in a small saucepan.) Put ¼ tsp of butter on top of the cinnamon in each apple. Stud each apple with 4 cloves, evenly spaced around the rim, about ½ in/1.25 cm from the cavity.

Bake the apples for 30 minutes or until they're soft. Serve hot, with freshly whipped cream, if you like.

Apple Barley Flummery

Serves 4

The dictionary defines *flummery*, from the Welsh *llymru* ("nonsense"), as mumbo jumbo, meaningless conversation, or empty flattery. In culinary terms, though, it is a pudding, typically rather bland in flavor, made with stewed fruit and thickened with cornstarch, oatmeal, or—as with this version, which appears in Norma and Gordon Latimer's little self-published booklet *Irish Country Cooking*—pearl barley.

1/4 CUP/50 G RAW PEARL BARLEY

1 1/2 LB/750 G SWEET EATING APPLES [NOT COOKING APPLES]

1/3 CUP/35 G SUGAR

JUICE OF 1 LEMON

1 TBSP HEAVY CREAM

Put the barley into a medium saucepan with 4½ cups/1 L of water and bring to a boil. Reduce the heat to low, add the apples, and simmer for about 20 minutes, or until the apples and barley are soft.

Purée mixture in a food processor or blender, then return to the pot. Add the sugar and lemon juice and bring to a boil, then remove from the heat and allow to cool.

When the mixture has cooled to room temperature, transfer it to a serving bowl, cover it, and chill it in the refrigerator for at least 3 hours. Stir the cream in just before serving.

Gooseberry Fool

Serves 4 to 6

Fools are simple desserts based on fresh seasonal fruit, crushed or puréed and mixed with cream. (The name comes from the French *fouler*, "to crush.") They have been known in Ireland at least since the mid-eighteenth century.

1 CUP/200 G SUGAR

1 LB/500 G GOOSEBERRIES

1 TO 2 CUPS/240 TO 475 ML HEAVY CREAM, LIGHTLY WHIPPED

Combine the sugar and 1 cup/240 ml of water into a medium saucepan and bring to a boil over medium-high heat, stirring constantly. Immediately reduce the heat to low and continue cooking, stirring constantly, for 2 minutes to make a syrup.

Add the gooseberries to the syrup and return to a boil over medium-high heat. Reduce the heat to medium and cook for 6 to 8 minutes or until the gooseberries begin to crack.

Purée the fruit with the syrup coarsely in a blender or food processor; then set aside to cool. When fruit has cooled to room temperature, measure it into a medium bowl and add half that volume in whipped cream. Stir together gently, then refrigerate for 1 to 2 hours before serving.

Rhubarb Tart

Serve 6 to 8

Rhubarb has grown wild in Ireland for centuries. In recent years, a variety of wild rhubarb from the Western Hemisphere (*Gunnera tinctoria*), sometimes called "elephant's loincloth" for its oversized foliage, has run rampant in the Irish countryside, especially in counties Mayo, Clare, and Galway, choking out native vegetation. A more benign European strain has long been cultivated around the island for its tart, flavorful stalks (the plant's leaves, extremely high in oxalic acid, are toxic), and its appearance each spring is eagerly anticipated.

FLOUR FOR DUSTING

BUTTER FOR GREASING

I LB/500 G PUFF PASTRY, HOMEMADE [PAGE 363], OR STORE-BOUGHT

I LB/500 G RHUBARB, FINELY CHOPPED

I CUP/200 G PLUS I TBSP SUGAR

I EGG, BEATEN

Preheat the oven to 475°F/250°C (Gas Mark 9).

On a floured board, roll out half the pastry into a disk 13 to 14 in/32 to 36 cm in diameter. Place in a lightly greased 10-in/25-cm pie pan. Leave about ½ in/1.25 cm overhanging the edge all around and trim off and set aside the excess pastry.

In a medium bowl, mix the rhubarb and 1 cup/200 g of the sugar, then spoon into the pie shell, gently evening it out with the back of a spoon.

Roll out the remaining pastry into a disk about 12 in/30 cm in diameter and lay it on top of the pie. Press the edges into the rim of the pie pan, then fold the pastry overhanging the dish from the bottom crust over the edges of the top crust. Crimp the edges with your fingers and cut a slash in the top of the pie.

Roll out the dough trimmings and cut them into strips. Arrange them on the top crust in a decorative pattern, pressing them down slightly. Brush the pastry with the beaten egg and sprinkle with the remaining 1 Tbsp of sugar.

Bake for about 15 minutes, then reduce the oven temperature to 375°F/190°C (Gas Mark 5) and bake for 45 minutes more.

Blackberry Mousse

Serves 4

Blackberries are mentioned in the medieval Irish epic tale *Buile Shuibhne* as one of the wild foods eaten by the mad king Sweeney, and they've been a favored field fruit in Ireland for many centuries. In his poem "Blackberry-picking," Seamus Heaney describes going out "with milk cans, pea tins, jampots / Where briars scratched and wet grass bleached our boots" to gather the fruit. And he summons up the memory of the first blackberry tasted each year: "its flesh was sweet / Like thickened wine: summer's blood was in it. . . ." This is a simple traditional blackberry dessert.

I LB/500 G BLACKBERRIES

I/2 CUP/100 G SUGAR

ONE I/4-OZ/7-G ENVELOPE UNFLAVORED POWDERED GELATIN

I CUP/240 ML MILK

I CUP/240 ML HEAVY CREAM

Combine the blackberries, sugar, and 1 cup/240 ml of water in a medium saucepan and bring to a boil over medium-high heat. Reduce the heat to medium-low and simmer until the berries are very soft, about 20 minutes. Drain through a sieve set over a large bowl. Set the berries aside and save the juice for another use (for instance, as pancake syrup or to mix into lemonade or cocktails).

Put the gelatin into a large heatproof bowl. Heat the milk in a small saucepan over medium heat until just boiling, then pour over the gelatin and stir until dissolved, 2 to 3 minutes. Stir in the blackberries and set aside.

Whisk the cream in a large bowl until stiff peaks form, then whisk half into the blackberry mixture. Spoon the remaining whipped cream on top and fold in gently to combine. Divide the mixture between 4 bowls, cover each with plastic wrap, and refrigerate until chilled and set, about 2 hours.

IRELAND'S GARDEN

County Wicklow, just south of Dublin, has been called "the last county," because it was carved out of parts of counties Dublin and Carlow in 1606, long after other county boundaries had been established (though in fact counties Tipperary and Dublin have been divided for administrative purposes, forming new counties, since then). It is also known as "the garden of Ireland," for the sheer abundance of its greenery, edible and otherwise. It is particularly attractive in this regard to citizens of Dublin, which is less than twenty miles/thirty kilometers from its northernmost border. Wicklow towns nearest to the capital, and those adjacent to the N-11 national road farther south, have become bedroom communities of a sort, and there are weekend houses everywhere. As one vaguely jaundiced observer said to me one day, "Dubliners come to Wicklow because they want to be able to say that they own five acres and a pony."

But Wicklow—the name comes from Vykinglo, which is what the Vikings called their original settlement there—is serious agricultural land, too, important for its cereal crops and dairy products, and famous for the lamb reared on its hill and mountain pastures. It is also important to food lovers for other reasons: It's home to Catherine Fulvio's Ballyknocken House, a small hotel with an excellent dining room, and the adjacent Ballyknocken Cookery School (there are several of Fulvio's recipes in these pages). Avoca Handweavers, the Irish clothing manufacturer and retailer whose shops are found all over the island (and in Annapolis, Maryland), dates its origins back to an early water-powered mill on the River Avoca, in the Wicklow town of that name. Today, in addition to clothing and gifts, many of the stores have full-fledged food departments; some have cafés serving fresh, simple fare; and several Avoca cookbooks have been best-sellers. And County Wicklow is the site of Ireland's only fully organic restaurant, the Strawberry Tree. Evan Doyle presciently announced a commitment to wild, organic, and free-range foods when he opened the original Strawberry Tree in Killarney, County Kerry, on the other side of Ireland from Wicklow, way back in 1992. In 1999, Doyle and his brothers moved the restaurant to a restored hamlet and residential community called Macreddin Village in Aughrim, and opened a hotel called BrookLodge to go with it. The Strawberry Tree sources local products almost exclusively, smokes its own salmon and beef, and in general serves simple but well-cooked food that honors the raw materials. More recently, Doyle and company have opened an Italian place on the site, Armento Taverna, with the same philosophy. There is also an organic farmers' market at Macreddin Village the first Sunday afternoon of every month from March through October.

OTHER THAN ALE

Possibly even before they figured out how to ferment malted grain and water into ale, the Irish discovered that the juice of various fruits, left unattended, would eventually begin to fizz and turn intoxicating. They almost certainly made cider from the juice of crabapples before the advent of large-scale apple cultivation, and once the Anglo-Normans began planting apple orchards around the island, cider making became common. By the seventeenth century, it had turned into a major agricultural occupation—especially in areas with large English populations, like the northern counties and Cork, Limerick, Wexford, and Waterford in the south. Margaret Johnson, an American authority on Irish food, calls that era "the First Golden Age of Cider" and reports that more than 250 named varieties of cider apples were cultivated in Ireland at the time. A late-eighteenth-century English visitor, Arthur Young, wrote that Irish orchards did something "very uncommon in the cider countries of England, yield a crop every year." English novelist William Makepeace Thackeray, after traveling in Ireland, called the beverage "obstreperous cider."

In 1937, in Clonmel, two commercial cider makers joined forces to establish Bulmer-Magner, Ltd., and that brand's ciders (under both the Bulmer and the Magner labels) are Ireland's most famous, and are sold all over the world. There are a few artisanal cider makers in various parts of the island, among them David Llewellyn (see page 312) of Lusk, County Dublin. They sell their ciders primarily at farmers' markets and local shops, and these are well worth looking for.

Mead is a fermented honey wine, another ancient tipple. It was associated with Ireland's monasteries (which usually kept beehives and thus had a ready source of honey) and with the Celtic aristocracy. (In "The Vision of Mac Conglinne," from the eleventh century or thereabouts, it is referred to as "the dainty of the nobles"; see page 175.) The Bunratty Mead and Liqueur Company in Bunratty, County Clare, is the only commercial-scale producer of the beverage in Ireland today.

Summer Pudding

Serves 8

Cookbook author and food historian Theodora FitzGibbon writes that "Summer pudding was often made in the past by people who didn't like pastry." I suspect that it would probably be more accurate to say "people who didn't like to [or know how to] *make* pastry." Some purists insist that summer pudding should be made only with raspberries and red currants, but I can't imagine why you wouldn't want to use an assortment of whatever berries are in season. In any case, though it is called a pudding, it is mostly pure fruit.

16 TO 20 SLICES DRY [BUT NOT TOO HARD] GOOD-QUALITY WHITE BREAD, CRUSTS TRIMMED

2 1/2 LB/1.25 KG ASSORTED SUMMER FRUIT, SUCH AS STRAWBERRIES, RASPBERRIES, BLACKBERRIES, BLUEBERRIES, RED CURRANTS, AND/OR BLACK CURRANTS, AT LEAST TWO KINDS, WITH LARGER FRUIT HALVED OR QUARTERED

1/4 TO 3/4 CUP/50 TO 150 G SUGAR, DEPENDING ON THE SWEETNESS OF THE BERRIES

CLOTTED OR WHIPPED CREAM FOR SERVING [OPTIONAL]

Line a 1-qt/1-L bowl or pudding basin with the bread slices, overlapping them slightly and cutting them as necessary to fit the bottom and sides. Leave aside enough slices to completely cover the top.

Combine the fruit, sugar, and ½ to 1 cup/120 to 240 ml of water (depending on the juiciness of the berries) in a medium saucepan over medium heat. Bring to a slow boil, stirring constantly and crushing the berries slightly with a wooden spoon. When the mixture boils, remove from the heat and set aside to cool for 10 minutes.

Spoon the fruit mixture into the bread-lined bowl, then fit the remaining slices on top. Cut a piece of wax paper to exactly cover the top layer of bread, put a plate or pie pan that fits the space exactly, then weigh the pudding down with with 1 or 2 heavy cans.

Refrigerate overnight, then remove the weights and plate and invert the pudding onto a serving platter.

Serve with clotted or whipped cream, if you like.

Rhubarb-Ginger Crumble

Serves 6 to 8

Crumble is served the year around at Country Choice in Nenagh, County Tipperary, with the fruit changing according to the season and the spice or flavoring changing according to the fruit: This is a springtime version; in the summer it might be made with plums poached with cinnamon. Crumble is particularly good served with clotted cream.

2 LB/1 KG RHUBARB STALKS, CUT INTO 1-IN/2.5-CM PIECES

2 TBSP MINCED FRESH GINGER

2 1/2 CUPS/500 G SUGAR

2 CUPS/200 G FLOUR

PINCH OF SALT

14 TBSPS COLD BUTTER, CUT INTO SMALL PIECES

Preheat the oven to 350°F/175°C (Gas Mark 4).

Combine the rhubarb and ginger in a medium bowl and mix well. Transfer to a large glass or ceramic baking dish. Sprinkle 2 cups/400 g of the sugar over the rhubarb and set aside.

Whisk the flour, salt, and the remaining ½ cup/100 g of the sugar together in a medium mixing bowl. Using a pastry cutter or 2 table knives, cut the butter into the flour mixture until it resembles coarse meal flecked with pea-size pieces of butter. Scatter the mixture evenly over the rhubarb.

Bake for about 1 hour and 15 minutes, or until the topping is golden brown and the rhubarb is soft. Set aside to cool slightly, and serve warm. Or allow to cool to room temperature before serving.

RHUBARB-GINGER CRUMBLE

Lemon Curd Tart

Serves 6 to 8

I had my first taste of real Irish food not in Ireland but in Santa Monica, where a young cooking teacher from Belfast, Gerri Gilliland, opened Gilliland's restaurant in 1984. Though her menu was multicultural Californian, it included such references to her native land as Irish stew, champ, potato-parsnip cakes with smoked salmon—and this addictive lemon curd tart. She learned how to make the tart, says Gilliland, when she went to school at the Dominican convent on Falls Road in Belfast in the 1960s. "The nuns there," she notes, "were well-known for their baking skills." The shortcrust pastry Gilliland uses is considerably sweeter than Myrtle Allen's version (see page 363), and it makes a nice counterbalance to the tartness of the filling. (Gilliland's closed in 1998, incidentally; Gilliland now runs a cooking school, a Mexican restaurant called Lula, and an Irish pub, Finn McCool's, at which this tart and other Irish specialties are still served.)

For the cake:

1 1/2 CUPS/150 G FLOUR, PLUS MORE FOR DUSTING

4 1/2 TBSP GROUND ALMONDS

4 1/2 TBSP POWDERED SUGAR

1/2 TSP VANILLA EXTRACT

PINCH OF SALT

9 TBSP COLD BUTTER, CUT INTO 1/2-IN/1.25 CM CUBES

1 EGG PLUS 1 EGG YOLK, LIGHTLY BEATEN

For the filling:

1/2 CUP/120 ML FRESH LEMON JUICE

1/2 CUP/100 G SUGAR

ZEST OF 2 LARGE LEMONS

2 TBSP BUTTER, SOFTENED

5 EGG YOLKS, LIGHTLY BEATEN AND STRAINED THROUGH A FINE SIEVE

1 TBSP SUGAR

To make the cake: Put the flour, ground almonds, powdered sugar, vanilla, and salt into a food processor and pulse until well combined. Add the cold butter and pulse just until the mixture resembles coarse bread crumbs. Drizzle in 1 Tbsp of the beaten egg mixture and pulse until combined. Cover and refrigerate the remaining beaten egg mixture.

Turn the dough out onto a floured board and knead briefly to bring the dough together. Form about one-third of the dough into a disk and wrap in plastic wrap. Form the remaining two-thirds of dough into a second disk and wrap with plastic wrap. Refrigerate both wrapped disks until the dough is just firm, about 1 hour.

To make the filling: Put the lemon juice, 1/2 cup/100 g sugar, and the lemon zest into a medium saucepan over medium-low heat. Add the softened butter and whisk until the butter melts. Add the strained egg yolks and cook, whisking constantly, until thickened, 6 to 8 minutes. (Do not allow to boil.) Transfer the mixture to a medium bowl and set aside to cool.

Preheat the oven to 350°F/175°C (Gas Mark 4).

On a floured board, roll out the larger disk of dough into a 12-in/30-cm circle. Fit the dough into a 10-in/25-cm tart pan, leaving some pastry overhanging the edges. Spoon the cooled lemon curd into the pastry shell and spread it out evenly.

On a floured board, roll out the remaining disk of dough into a 10-in/25-cm circle. Moisten the edges of the dough in the tart pan with some of the refrigerated beaten egg mixture, then top the pie with the remaining dough. Trim off any excess dough, and then crimp the edges. Brush the tart with the remaining beaten egg mixture; then sprinkle the 1 Tbsp of sugar over the top.

Bake until crisp and golden brown, 30 to 35 minutes. Set aside to let cool completely before serving.

THE CONNEMARA DOCTOR

I had my first taste of real poitín (also spelled "poteen" and "potcheen")—which is basically Irish moonshine, the original "mountain dew"—in, well, a town somewhere in the middle of Ireland, where the proprietor of a very nice restaurant (and I've absolutely forgotten the names of both person and place) offered me a bottle, after hours. The bottle itself said "Stolichnaya," but the clear liquid inside was not vodka (moonshiners recycle). I thought it was pretty good—undeniably fiery but clean-edged, with hints of elusive fruit and a tinge of smoke; I might have mistaken it for a very young artisanal Alsatian eau-de-vie. It had obviously been distilled by an expert, not some weekend hobbyist. But then the distillation of this illegal, well, call it proto-whiskey, is a craft at which the Irish have excelled for centuries.

Having invented whiskey, the Irish naturally felt free to produce it at will, and, being an independent race, were disinclined to accept its regulation by the government—any government—much less to pay taxes on it. When the British Crown introduced the first excise duty on distilled spirits in 1661, it was simply ignored in Ireland. Licensed, taxpaying distilleries did open, but as more and more rules were imposed and ever-higher taxes were collected, these often went underground. What legal spirits were still being made were often derided as "Parliament whiskey," and considered inferior. Tax rolls from 1782, for instance, show thirty-nine licensed distilleries in County Cavan; by 1796, it had only two—and it's a pretty safe bet that overall whiskey production in the region had not declined. Small-scale distillers around the island proliferated, if anything. In 1834, British tax officials seized 692 illegal stills in Scotland—and 8,192 in Ireland. Traveling in Ireland in the early part of the twentieth century, English travel writer H. V. Morton recounts his own experience with the illegal potion: "'If you want a taste of poteen,' said my friend, 'go to the place I'm telling you of and say "Mike O'Flaherty's black cow has died on him."'" Morton, though skeptical at first, delivers the catchphrase and is rewarded with a draught. "It was like fire with the smoke in it," he reports. "It was white in colour, it burned the throat, a crude, coarse, violent raw spirit." Today the governments of both Ireland and Northern Ireland strenuously enforce antimoonshine legislation. And at least some of their citizens continue to distill their own.

Poitín was widely considered an efficacious remedy for a variety of ills—one of its many nicknames was "the Connemara Doctor"—and obviously had psychological effects as well. Watching fishermen sharing a bottle of the stuff while mending their nets on the Aran Islands in the late nineteenth century, poet and playwright J. M. Synge noted that "their grey poteen, which brings a shock of joy to the blood, seems predestined to keep sanity in men who live forgotten in these worlds of mist." (It's not surprising to learn that poteen was distilled even by inmates at the infamous Long Kesh prison in Lisburn, County Antrim, during "the Troubles" in Northern Ireland.)

Two companies distill and sell what they describe as legal poitín in Ireland today: Bunratty Irish Potcheen is a 90-proof version made by Oliver Dillon, a well-known producer of mead in Bunratty, County Clare (home of the legendary Durty Nelly, who some credit with having concocted the original recipe for poitín). Knockeen Hills, bottled in Waterford (though with corporate headquarters in England) releases theirs in three strengths: 101, 140, and 180 proof. That last one is 90 percent alcohol—more than enough to kill O'Flaherty's black cow.

The Irish
Touch

[T]he ancient favourite aliment in Ireland is called stirabout,
a sort of hasty pudding made of oaten-meal.

—John Carr, esq., *The Stranger in Ireland; or, a Tour of the Southern and Western Parts of That Country, in the Year* 1805

I eat oatmeal seven mornings a week.

—Artisanal miller Donal Creedon of Macroom, County Cork, [2005]

Oats, better suited to Ireland's damp climate than wheat, have grown prolifically on the island for centuries. Probably precisely because they were so common, though, they weren't

always held in high regard. The Brehon Laws, 1,300 years ago or so, in listing seven Irish cereals in order of importance, place oats last (wheat is number one). In dictating what kind of porridge should be fed to children of different classes, one tract specifies wheaten meal with milk and honey for the sons of kings, barley with new milk and fresh butter for the sons of chieftains, and oatmeal seasoned with stale butter for the poor.

Oatcakes and oaten bread (in parts of Ireland where flat griddle breads are common, the distinction between the two is not always clear) appear frequently in Irish literature and in the accounts of visitors. The steed made of bacon in the eleventh-century "Vision of Mac Conglinne" (see page 175) has "four hooves of coarse oaten bread." A Catalan pilgrim in 1397 was served "two little oatcakes as thin as wafers and they bent like raw dough and they were of oats and earth as black as coal, although they were very tasty." Robert Ditty, the oatcake-making baker from Castledawson, County Derry, called my attention to a carving on an eighth-century "scripture cross" (one bearing illustrations of biblical scenes) in a monastery near Moone, County Kildare, in which the story of the loaves and fishes is illustrated by two river trout, two eels—and what are very clearly five oatcakes.

Oatmeal stirabout, or porridge, is to this day a popular breakfast in Ireland. The food writer Monica Sheridan remembers the breakfasts of her childhood on the family farm in County Tyrone in the early part of the twentieth century. These included milk "straight from the cow and still warm," boiled eggs, "a great cake of brown bread" with farm-made butter and honey, and "enormous draughts of strong, sweet tea." But, she adds, "[N]o matter what else we had the day

always started with porridge. We all firmly believed that porridge put the roses in our cheeks and the curls in our hair." It was eaten both sweetened and not, she says. "Some took their porridge straight, lightly salted as it came from the pot, some sprinkled soft brown sugar on it, while the smaller ones made a hole in the center and dropped a spoonful of honey into it."

Another approach to oatmeal was described by P. W. Joyce: In the early nineteenth century, he writes, "The carters who carried bags of oatmeal from Limerick to Cork (a two-day journey) usually rested for the night at Mick Lynch's public-house in Glenosheen. They often took lunch or dinner of porter-meal in this way: Opening the end of one of the bags, the man made a hollow in the oatmeal into which he poured a quart of porter, stirring it up with a spoon: then he ate an immense bellyful of the mixture. But those fellows could digest like an ostrich."

Good steel-cut Irish oatmeal, under the McCann's label, is available in America today, as are rolled Irish oats—flattened into flakes—from Flahavan's. The best oatmeal for Stirabout (page 349), though, is Macroom, milled by Donal Creedon in the town of that name in County Cork. His oatmeal—he also mills wheat, spelt, and rye flour—is stone-ground and kiln-toasted, and very coarse and full-flavored. He eats it daily himself, says Creedon, with "linseeds and sunflower seeds ground in one whip of the coffee grinder, brown sugar, and a drop of milk at the side." See Sources, page 369, to mail-order any of the aforementioned brands.

Mealie Greachie
[Toasted Oatmeal]

Serves 4

Florence Irwin, known in northern Ireland as "the Cookin' Woman," called this "a dish in North Antrim which has survived a couple of centuries' use," back in 1949, and noted that "it is one of the dinners expected by farm labourers at harvest time in North and North-East Antrim to this day."

8 SLICES IRISH BACON, PREFERABLY GALTEE'S SLICED CURED PORK LOIN, TOMMY MOLONEY'S MILD-CURED [NOT SMOKED OR BACK RASHERS], OR DONNELLY'S [SEE SOURCES, PAGE 369]

I TBSP BUTTER

I ONION, MINCED

I CUP/160 G IRISH ROLLED OATS

Fry the bacon in a large skillet over medium heat until it starts to brown. Remove from the heat, wrap in foil, and set aside to keep warm.

Add the butter to the pan; then fry the onion for 7 to 8 minutes or until it softens and begins to brown. Add the oatmeal, stir well, and continue cooking, stirring frequently, until the oatmeal has browned.

Serve with the reserved bacon.

Herring Fried in Oatmeal

Serves 2 to 4

Herring has historically been abundant in Irish waters, and thus cheap at the fishmonger's. Florence Irwin believed that of all the fish available on the island, "Perhaps the herring gives most recipes." They are invariably simple ones, using basic ingredients, like this.

2/3 CUP/100 G IRISH ROLLED OATS

SALT AND PEPPER

3 TBSP BUTTER OR BACON FAT

4 LARGE FRESH HERRING FILLETS

1/2 LEMON, HALVED

MUSTARD SAUCE [PAGE 360] OR HORSERADISH SAUCE [PAGE 358] FOR SERVING

Season the oatmeal generously with salt and pepper.

Melt the butter or heat the bacon fat over medium heat in a medium skillet.

Wash the herring, pat dry, then dip in oatmeal to coat well, pressing the flakes into the fish. Fry the herring in the butter or bacon fat until golden brown, 4 to 5 minutes per side.

Squeeze lemon juice over the herrings before serving. Serve with mustard sauce or horseradish sauce if you like.

STIRABOUT

Stirabout

Serves 4

Stirabout—which is simply the evocative Irish name for porridge—has been eaten in Ireland since at least the fifth century A.D. Over the years it has been made from many different kinds of grain, including barley, cornmeal, and wheatberries, but today, the term has become synonymous with oatmeal. Purists frown on the addition of anything sweet to their stirabout and grace it only with salt and butter or cream. Fair warning, incidentally: It is sometimes said in Northern Ireland that stirring porridge counterclockwise will summon up Satan. Serve with cream or butter, and (if you must) with white or brown sugar or honey to taste. Some stalwarts splash a little Irish whiskey in as well.

2 TSP SALT

I CUP/160 G IRISH STEEL-CUT, STONE-GROUND, OR ROLLED OATMEAL

Bring 3½ cups/850 ml of water to a boil in a medium saucepan. Add the salt, then remove from the heat, add the oatmeal, stir well, and cover the pot. Set aside for at least 6 hours or overnight.

Reheat the oatmeal over medium heat, stirring frequently. Add a bit more water if necessary to prevent sticking, and adjust the seasoning if necessary.

Pratie Oaten
[Potato-Oat Cakes]

Serves 4 to 6

Pratie oaten are basically Fadge (page 225) made with oatmeal instead of flour. They make a good breakfast dish, served with eggs and bacon or sausage. Florence Irwin, author of *The Cookin' Woman*, credits these to County Antrim, and notes tersely after giving her version of the recipe: "Not food for invalids."

2 CUPS/420 G FRESHLY MADE MASHED POTATOES [PAGE 223], WARM

I CUP/160 G IRISH ROLLED OATS, PLUS MORE FOR DUSTING

I/2 CUP/125 G BUTTER, SOFTENED, OR BACON FAT, PLUS MORE FOR FRYING

SALT

Work the potatoes and oatmeal together with your hands in a large bowl to form a soft dough. Mix in the butter or bacon fat and season to taste with salt.

Dust a board with oatmeal, then roll out the dough on it. Cut into 12 to 16 pieces of similar size and shape, or form into 2 or 3 flat rounds and cut each into quarters. Fry the cakes, a few at a time, in a nonstick skillet lightly greased with butter or bacon fat. Cook for about 3 minutes on each side, or until the cakes are golden brown.

Oatcakes

Makes 20 to 24

Griddle breads and flat cakes made of oatmeal have been eaten in Ireland for more than a thousand years, and all through the Middle Ages and into the modern era, almost every traveler to the island from elsewhere has mentioned these foods. Today, oatcakes are most popular in the north of Ireland, where a number of large commercial bakeries turn them out in great quantity. The best ones, though, are those made by celebrated baker Robert Ditty of Castledawson, County Derry (see page 276). He makes traditional oatcakes but also ones made with smoked flour or flavored with dulse and sesame, celery and black pepper, or Gubbeen cheese from County Cork. They're available in the United States (see Sources, page 369) and are well worth sampling.

I/2 CUP/IIO G BUTTER, PLUS MORE FOR GREASING

2 CUPS/320 G IRISH ROLLED OATS
[SEE SOURCES, PAGE 369]

I/2 CUP/50 G FLOUR, PLUS MORE FOR DUSTING

3/4 TSP SALT

I/2 TSP BAKING SODA

Preheat the oven to 350°F/175°C (Gas Mark 4).

Lightly grease a large baking sheet.

Melt the butter with 2 Tbsp of water in a small saucepan or skillet over low heat.

Mix the oatmeal, flour, salt, and baking soda together in a medium bowl. Make a well in the center of the mixture, then pour in the hot butter mixture and stir with a wooden spoon to form a crumbly dough.

Turn the dough out onto a floured board and firmly roll out the dough with a floured rolling pin (or press it with floured hands) into a rectangle about ¼ in/6.5 mm thick. Using a cookie cutter or the floured rim of a glass, cut the dough into circles 2 to 2½ in/5 to 6.5 cm in diameter. With a spatula, transfer the circles to the baking sheet, leaving about 1 in/2.5 cm between them.

Bake for 20 to 25 minutes or until nicely browned and firm. Carefully transfer the oatcakes to a wire rack and let them cool, uncovered, overnight to harden.

SCHOOL FOOD

Touring Ireland in 1842, English novelist William Makepeace Thackeray visited the Templemoyle Agricultural School in Derry, and made note of the weekly menu given to students. He reproduced it, in the form below, in an account he later wrote of his travels, originally published under the pseudonym Mr. A. M. Titmarsh.

Breakfast - Eleven ounces of oatmeal made in stirabout, one pint of sweet milk.

Dinner [i.e. the midday meal]

- Sunday - Three-quarters of a pound of beef stewed with pepper and onions, or one half-pound of corned beef with cabbage, and three and a half pounds of potatoes.
- Monday - One half-pound of pickled beef, three and a half pounds of potatoes, one pint of buttermilk.
- Tuesday - Broth made of one half-pound beef, with leeks, cabbage, and parsley, and three and a half pounds of potatoes.
- Wednesday - Two ounces of butter, eight ounces of oatmeal, made into bread, three and a half pounds of potatoes, and one pint of sweet milk.
- Thursday - Half a pound of pickled pork, with cabbages or turnips, and three and a half pounds of potatoes.
- Friday - Two ounces of butter, eight ounces wheat meal made into bread, one pint of sweet milk or fresh buttermilk.
- Saturday - Two ounces of butter, one pound of potatoes mashed, eight ounces of wheat meal made into bread, two and a half pounds of potatoes, one pint of buttermilk.

Supper - In summer, flummery made of one pound of oatmeal seeds, and one pint of sweet milk. In winter, three and a half pounds of potatoes, and one pint of buttermilk or sweet milk.

WHAT WE ATE IN COUNTY ANTRIM

One afternoon in Belfast, I had tea with quilt preservationist and collector Roselind Shaw and her mother, Kathleen McClintock. McClintock grew up near the city in Greenisland, County Antrim, near Carrickfergus—the town celebrated in one of the most famous of Irish ballads. I asked McClintock what she ate as a girl and young adult in the 1920s and 1930s, and this is what she told me:

We led a very plain life. Nowadays, a lot of the food, I wouldn't touch it. We were country folk. Everything we ate was plain, nothing artificial. The only thing we would have bought was salt. We reared chickens, and grew parsley, celery, carrots, parsnips, peas in the summer, turnips, big beautiful cabbages, potatoes of course, black and red currants, gooseberries, blackberries. We made potato bread, just potatoes cooked with flour and salt dry on the griddle. All the cooking was done on a big open fire with two hobs and a crane with a kettle on it. We drank buttermilk with dinner. Shortcrust apple cake was a specialty.

Our father had a razor strop cut into strips that was used for punishing us, and one day we buried it among the potatoes. Of course, he found it the next time he dug potatoes and it was put to use again. My grandmother Annie Campbell had the best garden. She coated eggs in isinglass [fish-bladder gelatin] to preserve them, and she had a goat. You always had to smell the jug at Granny's house to make sure you weren't getting goat's milk.

We had porridge every morning, with golden syrup. You would steep the oatmeal in water the night before, then heat it up in the morning. We say 'steep the oatmeal' but 'wet the tea.' We also made oatcakes, and dipped the potato bread into very fine oatmeal before frying it. We called it 'wheaten oaten,' and I didn't like it much.

During World War II, I worked in the American Red Cross. There was rationing, and you could only get one egg and two ounces of butter a week. My husband had a motor bike, and we'd go down south where they had no rationing, because they were neutral during the war, and we'd send home parcels of butter and sugar and ham. Of course, the country people made butter where we lived, but it was always too salty for me.

RESOURCES

Fish Stock

Makes 2 to 3 qt/2 to 3 L

Use only white-fleshed saltwater fish for this stock.

3 LB/1.5 KG FISH CARCASSES OR BONES,
WITH BITS OF MEAT AND SKIN ATTACHED

1 LARGE ONION, COARSELY CHOPPED

1 STALK CELERY, COARSELY CHOPPED

1 LEEK, WHITE PART ONLY, COARSELY CHOPPED

1 BAY LEAF

JUICE OF 1 LEMON

1/2 BOTTLE/375 ML DRY WHITE WINE

10 WHITE PEPPERCORNS

Put all the ingredients into a large pot and add enough cold water to cover completely. Cover the pot and bring to a boil over high heat. Uncover the pot, reduce the heat to low, and simmer for 30 minutes, skimming any foam that forms on the surface as needed.

Strain the stock, discarding the solids. Rinse out the pot, then return the stock to it and simmer for about 15 minutes longer. Cool to room temperature; then refrigerate or freeze in several containers.

Chicken Stock

Makes 2 to 3 qt/2 to 3 L

Substitute duck or rabbit bones for chicken bones, if you like. (Rabbit makes a particularly flavorful stock.)

3 LB/1.5 KG CHICKEN BONES WITH
BITS OF MEAT AND SKIN ATTACHED

1 LARGE ONION, COARSELY CHOPPED

2 CARROTS, COARSELY CHOPPED

1 STALK CELERY, COARSELY CHOPPED

1 LEEK, WHITE PART ONLY, COARSELY CHOPPED

1 BAY LEAF

Put all the ingredients into a large pot and add enough cold water to cover completely. Cover the pot and bring to a boil over high heat. Uncover the pot, reduce the heat to low, and simmer for 2½ hours, skimming any foam that forms on the surface.

Strain the stock, discarding the solids. Rinse out the pot, then return the stock to it and simmer for about 30 minutes longer. Cool to room temperature, then refrigerate or freeze in several containers. If desired, refrigerate for about 3 hours, until the fat rises to the top and solidifies, then remove the fat before freezing.

Beef or Lamb Stock

Makes about 3 qt/3 L

4 TO 5 LB/2 TO 2.5 KG BEEF OR LAMB BONES
WITH BITS OF MEAT ATTACHED

1 LARGE ONION, COARSELY CHOPPED

2 CARROTS, COARSELY CHOPPED

1 STALK CELERY, COARSELY CHOPPED

2 TO 3 LARGE SPRIGS PARSLEY

2 TO 3 LARGE SPRIGS THYME

2 BAY LEAVES

2 WHOLE CLOVES

3 CLOVES GARLIC, UNPEELED

2 TBSP TOMATO PASTE

Preheat the oven to 450°F/230°C (Gas Mark 8).

Spread the bones out in a roasting pan and roast for 30 minutes, then add the onion and carrots and continue roasting for 20 minutes more.

Transfer the bones to a large pot and add the celery, parsley, thyme, bay leaves, cloves, garlic, and tomato paste. Deglaze roasting pan on the stovetop over high heat with a little water, then add contents of pan to pot. Add 6 qt/6 L of water to the pot, or as much as you need to cover the ingredients completely. Cover the pot and bring to a boil over high heat. Uncover the pot, reduce the heat to low, and simmer until the stock has reduced by half, 4 to 6 hours. Skim any foam that forms on the surface.

Strain the stock, discarding the solids. Rinse out the pot, then return the stock to it and simmer over low heat for about 30 minutes longer. Cool to room temperature, then refrigerate or freeze in several containers. If desired, refrigerate for about 3 hours, until fat rises to the top and solidifies, then remove the fat before freezing.

Mayonnaise

Makes about 2 1/2 cups/600 ml

2 EGG YOLKS

1/4 CUP/60 ML LEMON JUICE

1 TSP DIJON MUSTARD

1 TSP SALT

1 CUP/240 ML CANOLA OIL

1 CUP/240 ML MILD EXTRA-VIRGIN OLIVE OIL

In a medium bowl, beat the yolks slowly but firmly with a whisk until they become creamy and light yellow in color. Add 2 Tbsp of the lemon juice, the mustard, and salt, and mix well.

In a small bowl, combine the canola and olive oils; then drizzle very slowly into the yolk mixture while whisking constantly. (Be careful not to overbeat.)

Stir the remaining 2 Tbsp of lemon juice into the mayonnaise; then cover and refrigerate for at least 2 hours before using.

(To make mayonnaise in a food processor, follow the instructions for Garlic Mayonnaise [Aïoli], page 358, omitting the garlic.)

Green Mayonnaise

Makes about 2 cups/475 ml

Serve with cold poached salmon, Dublin Bay prawns, and other fish and shellfish.

1 CUP/240 ML MAYONNAISE,
PREFERABLY HOMEMADE [THIS PAGE]

1 BUNCH WATERCRESS,
TRIMMED AND FINELY CHOPPED

6 TO 8 CHIVES, SNIPPED INTO SMALL PIECES

Put 2 Tbsp of the mayonnaise into the bowl of a food processor and add the watercress and chives. Pulse several times to obtain a rough purée.

Put the remaining mayonnaise in a small bowl, then mix the watercress mixture in well.

Garlic Mayonnaise [Aïoli]

Makes about 2 1/2 cups/600 ml

4 TO 5 CLOVES GARLIC

4 EGG YOLKS

JUICE OF 1/2 LEMON

SALT

2 CUPS/475 ML EXTRA-VIRGIN OLIVE OIL

Mix the garlic, egg yolks, lemon juice, and plenty of salt together in a small bowl, then transfer to a blender or the bowl of a food processor. Process at slow speed, while pouring the oil in a slow, steady stream. When the mayonnaise emulsifies, stop processing immediately.

Tartar Sauce

Makes about 1 1/2 cups/360 ml

1 CUP/240 ML MAYONNAISE,
PREFERABLY HOMEMADE [PAGE 357]

1 TSP DIJON MUSTARD

3 TO 4 CORNICHONS, MINCED

2 TBSP CAPERS, DRAINED AND MINCED

3 TO 4 CHIVES, SNIPPED INTO SMALL PIECES

2 TO 3 SPRIGS PARSLEY, TRIMMED AND MINCED

1 TBSP LEMON JUICE

Put the mayonnaise into a small bowl, then stir in the remaining ingredients, mixing well.

Maura Laverty's Onion and Apple Sauce

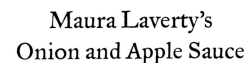

Makes about 1 1/4 cups/300 ml

Serve this with cold chicken or roast meat.

1 CUP/240 ML MAYONNAISE,
PREFERABLY HOMEMADE [PAGE 357]

1 TBSP CHOPPED ONION

1 TBSP CHOPPED GREEN APPLE

1 TBSP CHOPPED CELERY

SALT

Combine the ingredients in a small bowl and mix together well. Season to taste with salt.

Horseradish Sauce

Makes about 1 cup/240 ml

1 CUP/240 ML CREAM,
WHIPPED UNTIL SOFT PEAKS FORM

2 TBSP FRESHLY GRATED HORSERADISH

1 TSP SUPERFINE SUGAR

1/4 TSP POWDERED MUSTARD

1 TSP WHITE WINE OR CIDER VINEGAR

SALT AND PEPPER

Spoon the whipped cream into a medium bowl and gently fold in the horseradish, sugar, mustard, and vinegar into the cream, incorporating them well. Season to taste with salt and pepper.

Sorrel Sauce

Makes about 1 1/2 cups / 360 ml

This sauce is particularly good with simply cooked fish.

1/2 LB / 250 G SORREL LEAVES, FINELY CHOPPED
1/4 CUP / 60 ML DRY WHITE WINE
1/2 CUP / 125 G BUTTER, SOFTENED
PINCH OF GROUND MACE

Combine the ingredients in a medium saucepan. Bring to a boil, reduce the heat to low, and simmer for about 20 minutes.

Purée in a food processor or blender. Serve hot.

Mint Sauce

Makes about 1/2 cup / 120 ml

10 TO 12 MINT LEAVES, JULIENNED
1 TBSP SUGAR
1 TSP SALT
2 TBSP WHITE WINE VINEGAR

Combine the ingredients in a small bowl. Pour in ¼ cup/60 ml of boiling water and stir until the sugar dissolves.

Serve in a small bowl or sauceboat with a spoon so that diners may stir the sauce before using.

Michael Kelly's Sauce

Makes about 1 cup / 240 ml

Michael Kelly (1762–1826) was a Cork-born composer; actor; and operatic tenor who achieved celebrity in England, Austria, and Italy; and befriended Mozart. After ending his performing career, he ran a combination sheet-music store and wineshop in London (his father had been a Dublin wine merchant). Somewhere along the line, he invented what he called "Mr. Michael Kelly's sauce for boiled tripe, calf's-head, or cow-heel." His English contemporary William Kitchiner includes the recipe in his eccentric volume *Apicius Redivivus, or the Cook's Oracle*. In reviewing that book, Thomas Hood noted, "Gad-a-mecy, what a gullet must be in the possession of Mr. Michael Kelly!" The sauce does indeed liven up simply cooked tripe, but is also an appropriate condiment for Crubeens (pig's feet, page 203) or baked or boiled ham.

1 TSP BROWN SUGAR
1 TSP PEPPER
1 TSP POWDERED MUSTARD
1 TBSP GARLIC VINEGAR
1 CUP / 250 G BUTTER, MELTED

Mix the sugar, pepper, and mustard together in a medium bowl, then stir in the vinegar. When well blended, stir in the melted butter. Serve warm.

White Sauce

Makes about 1 1/2 cups / 360 ml

This sauce may be used on its own with chicken or fish, and serves as the base for numerous other sauces.

I SMALL ONION, PEELED AND STUCK WITH
2 CLOVES

I SMALL BAY LEAF

I CUP / 240 ML HEAVY CREAM

2 TBSP BUTTER

2 TBSP WHITE FLOUR

Put the onion and bay leaf into a small saucepan and add the cream. Bring to a boil over medium heat; then remove from the heat and set aside to infuse for 15 to 20 minutes.

Strain the infused cream into a small bowl and wipe out the pan. Melt the butter in the pan over low heat and whisk in the flour, stirring for about 1 minute to make a roux. Slowly pour the strained cream into the roux, and cook, stirring, for another minute or so.

Parsley Sauce

Makes about 2 1/2 cups / 600 ml

Theodora FitzGibbon calls this "perhaps the most widely used traditional sauce in Ireland." It is commonly served with corned beef, boiled ham, and poached salmon, but goes nicely with many other kinds of fish and meat, as well as poultry.

I CUP / 240 ML WHITE SAUCE [THIS PAGE]

I CUP / 240 ML BEEF, LAMB, FISH, RABBIT, OR
CHICKEN STOCK [PAGES 356 TO 357], OR ANOTHER
STOCK [SUCH AS HAM], DEPENDING ON WHAT THE
SAUCE IS TO BE SERVED WITH

1/2 CUP / 20 G MINCED FRESH PARSLEY

SALT AND PEPPER

Warm the white sauce in a medium saucepan, then stir in the stock and cook over medium heat, stirring frequently, for 3 to 4 minutes, or until the consistency is creamy. Stir in the parsley and season to taste with salt and pepper.

Watercress Sauce

Makes about 3 cups / 720 ml

This sauce goes well with salmon, eel, and various freshwater fish.

I 1/2 CUPS / 360 ML FISH STOCK [PAGE 356]

I LARGE BUNCH WATERCRESS,
TRIMMED AND STALKS RESERVED

1/2 CUP / 120 ML WHITE SAUCE [THIS PAGE]

SALT AND PEPPER

Bring the fish stock to a boil in a small saucepan, then cook the watercress stalks in the boiling stock for about 15 minutes, or until tender. Strain the stock, discarding the stalks.

Heat the white sauce in another small saucepan over low heat, then slowly add the strained stock, whisking gently to thoroughly combine the ingredients. Stir in the trimmed watercress leaves and season to taste with salt and pepper.

Mustard Sauce

Makes about 2 cups / 475 ml

This sauce goes well with grilled or fried fish.

2 CUPS / 475 ML WHITE SAUCE [THIS PAGE]

I TBSP PLUS I TSP GOOD-QUALITY FRENCH OR
ENGLISH MUSTARD

Heat the white sauce over low heat in a small saucepan, then stir in the mustard, mixing well.

Celery Sauce

Makes about 2¹⁄₂ cups / 600 ml

This sauce is a common accompaniment to roast goose or ham.

1 CUP / 240 ML CHICKEN STOCK [PAGE 356]
OR TURKEY STOCK

HEART OF 1 BUNCH CELERY, CHOPPED

PEPPER

1 CUP / 240 ML WHITE SAUCE [FACING PAGE],
WARMED

PINCH OF FRESHLY GRATED OR
GROUND NUTMEG

1⁄4 CUP / 60 ML CUP CREAM

SALT

Bring the stock to a boil in a small saucepan, add the celery, reduce the heat, and season with pepper. Cover and simmer for about 30 minutes.

Allow the celery and liquid to cool slightly, then transfer to a blender or the bowl of a food processor. Add the white sauce and purée.

Pour into a small bowl and whisk in the nutmeg, cream, and salt and pepper to taste.

Brine for Meats

Makes 2 gal / 8 L

Use this brine to cure pig's head and beef tongue for Collared Head (page 207) or to make your own corned beef, as for Corned Beef with Parsley Sauce (page 177). Prague Powder #1 is a mixture of salt and sodium nitrite commonly used in curing meats; it is not essential to this recipe but will give the meats an attractive rosy color.

5 CUPS / 1 KG KOSHER SALT

5 CUPS / 1 KG SUGAR

2 WHOLE STAR ANISE

2 STICKS CINNAMON

6 WHOLE CLOVES

12 BLACK PEPPERCORNS

1⁄2 CUP / 120 G PRAGUE POWDER #1
[OPTIONAL; SEE SOURCES, PAGE 369]

Combine the salt, sugar, star anise, cinnamon, cloves, and peppercorns in a large stockpot and add 1 gal/4 L of cold water. Bring to a boil, stirring to dissolve the salt and sugar thoroughly. Remove the pot from the heat and let the liquid cool to room temperature. Add 1 gal/4 L of cold water, then stir in the Prague Powder #1 (if using).

To brine meat, submerge the meat in the brine, weighing it down with a heavy nonreactive plate if necessary to keep it submerged. Set aside in a cool place (do not refrigerate) for 2 to 4 days.

Discard the brine after use.

Clarified Butter

Makes about 1 3/4 cups / 420 ml

1 LB / 500 G BUTTER

Melt the butter in a small saucepan over low heat. Remove from the heat and spoon off and discard any white solids that have risen to the top. Carefully pour off the butter into a glass jar or bowl, stopping before you reach the cloudy liquid at the bottom of the pan. Discard the cloudy liquid, or add to cream sauces. Clarified butter will keep, tightly covered in the refrigerator, for up to 1 month.

Bread Sauce

Makes about 3 cups / 720 ml

An old-fashioned condiment, this was once considered an essential accompaniment to roast turkey or game birds.

2 CUPS / 475 ML MILK

1 ONION, STUCK WITH 4 WHOLE CLOVES

PINCH OF NUTMEG

10 OR 12 WHOLE WHITE PEPPERCORNS

1 BAY LEAF

1 CUP / 60 G WHITE BREAD CRUMBS
[PREFERABLY GRATED FRESH FROM A
2-DAY-OLD LOAF WITH CRUSTS REMOVED]

SALT AND GROUND WHITE PEPPER

1 TBSP BUTTER, SOFTENED

1 TBSP HEAVY CREAM

Pour the milk into a small saucepan and add the onion, nutmeg, peppercorns, and bay leaf. Bring to a boil; then remove the pan from the heat, cover, and let steep for 30 minutes.

Strain the milk into another small saucepan, then stir in bread crumbs. Season to taste, then stir in the butter and cream.

Red Currant Sauce

Makes about 2 cups / 475 ml

This is a classic accompaniment to venison, wild boar, or other hooved game, but it is also good with duck (both wild and domestic) or chicken.

2 CUPS / 475 G FRESH OR
THAWED FROZEN RED CURRANTS

1/2 CUP / 100 G SUGAR

Put the currants into a medium saucepan with 1 cup/240 ml of water and bring to a boil over high heat. Reduce the heat to medium-low, cover the saucepan, and simmer for 5 minutes or until the currants are very soft.

Drain the currants and press them through a food mill or medium sieve into a medium bowl to remove the stems and seeds.

Return the currants to the saucepan, stir in the sugar, and add 1 cup/240 ml of water. Simmer over low heat for 10 to 12 minutes, or until the purée thickens slightly.

Custard Sauce

Makes about 3 cups / 720 ml

2 1/2 CUPS / 600 ML MILK

1/2 VANILLA BEAN

6 EGG YOLKS

1/4 CUP / 50 G SUGAR

Combine the milk and vanilla bean in a medium saucepan and bring almost to a boil over medium-high heat. Reduce the heat and simmer for 2 minutes. Remove and discard the vanilla bean.

In a medium bowl, beat the egg yolks and sugar together until thick. Whisk in half the hot milk, then whisk the mixture back into the milk remaining in the saucepan. Cook over low heat, stirring constantly, until the custard thickens and coats the back of a spoon.

Strain into a small bowl, then cover and refrigerate. The sauce will keep for about 2 days in the refrigerator.

Whiskey Butter

Makes about 1 1/2 cups/360 g

3/4 CUP/190 G BUTTER, SOFTENED

3/4 CUP/150 G SUGAR

1/4 CUP/60 ML IRISH WHISKEY

Beat the butter and sugar together in a medium bowl with an electric beater (or a whisk and plenty of elbow grease) until light and fluffy. Add the whiskey and beat until thoroughly combined.

Refrigerate until firm.

Puff Pastry

Makes 2 to 2 1/2 lb/1 to 1.25 kg

3 1/2 CUPS/350 G WHITE PASTRY FLOUR, CHILLED, PLUS MORE FOR DUSTING

PINCH OF SALT

1 LB/500 G BUTTER, SLIGHTLY SOFTENED

Sift the flour and salt into a large bowl. Drizzle in enough cold water (1 to 1½ cups/240 to 360 ml), stirring constantly with a floured wooden spoon, to form a firm dough.

Shape the dough into a ball, return the dough to the bowl, cover, and refrigerate for about 1 hour.

Roll the dough out on a floured board to form a square about ½ in/1.25 cm thick. With your hands, shape the butter into a square about ⅛ in/3 mm thick and place it in the center of the dough square. Fold the dough over the butter to form a packet.

Roll out the dough into a rectangle about 6 x 18 in/15 x 45 cm. Next fold in the two narrow ends of the dough, as neatly as possible, to meet in the center and form a 6-in/15-cm square packet 1 in/2.5 cm thick. Seal the edges of the packet with a rolling pin.

Repeat the process, rolling out the dough into a rectangle again, then folding in the two ends and sealing the edges. Wrap in plastic wrap and refrigerate for 30 minutes.

Repeat process 4 more times, wrapping and refrigerating the dough for 30 minutes between the first 2 and last 2 times.

Chill the dough for at least 30 minutes before using.

Myrtle Allen's Shortcrust Pastry

Makes about 1 lb/500 g

For use with savory pies, leave out the sugar.

2 CUPS/200 G WHITE PASTRY FLOUR, PLUS MORE FOR DUSTING

1/2 TSP SALT

1 TBSP POWDERED SUGAR [OPTIONAL]

3/4 CUP/170 G COLD BUTTER, CUT INTO SMALL PIECES

1 EGG YOLK, BEATEN WITH 2 TBSP COLD WATER

Combine the flour, salt, and sugar (if using) in a large bowl and rub in the butter until the mixture resembles coarse meal. Add the beaten egg and toss with a fork, gradually adding 1 to 3 Tbsp more of cold water, until the dough can be gathered into a ball.

Halve the dough on a board lightly dusted with flour, and pat each half into a 4- to 5-in/10- to 12-cm disk. Wrap each disk separately in plastic wrap and chill for at least 1 hour or as long as 24 hours before using.

Roasted Hazelnuts

Makes 4 cups

These make a good snack.

2 TBSP BUTTER, MELTED

2 TBSP VEGETABLE OIL

4 CUPS/675 G SHELLED RAW HAZELNUTS

SALT

Preheat the oven to 275°F/135°C (Gas Mark 1).

Combine the butter and oil in a rimmed baking sheet. Add the hazelnuts and toss in the butter and oil so that they are well coated. Roast in the oven until the nuts are golden, about 20 minutes.

Drain on paper towels and season to taste with salt.

Cool slightly before serving, or store at room temperature in a covered container for up to 2 weeks.

Irish Tea

Serves 1

"[T]here are only two requirements," writes John Long in his book *Johnny Barleycorn*, "for a good cup of Irish tea: strong and hot. If it doesn't burn your tongue on the first sip, send it back. And if it's not as black as Guinness in your cup, it's not strong enough. If your teaspoon will stand up straight in it and is hot enough to blister your fingers, you've got yourself a good cup." There's an old Irish expression that tea should be so dense that "you could trot a mouse on it." Some old-timers claim that it's best made with lake water boiled over a wood fire, and strained through a sprig of gorse stuck down the spout of the kettle. That may be going a little far in the quest for authenticity.

1 HEAPING TSP LOOSE BLACK TEA,
PREFERABLY AN IRISH-STYLE BLEND, FOR
INSTANCE, MALACHI McCORMICK'S DECENT TEA OR
BELFAST BREW FAIRTRADE IRISH BREAKFAST TEA
[SEE SOURCES, PAGE 369]

Bring 1 cup/240 ml of cold filtered fresh water to a boil over high heat in a teakettle, then pour into a small teapot (emptying the kettle). Let sit for 1 minute to warm the pot, then empty out the water.

Bring slightly more than 1 cup/240 ml of cold filtered fresh water to a boil over high heat in the same teakettle. When the water is about to boil, put the tea leaves into the teapot, then immediately pour in the boiling water. Let the tea infuse in a warm spot (in a sunny window frame, on top of the stove, or under a tea cosy) for 5 to 6 minutes (or longer if you plan on trotting a mouse), then strain into a warmed teacup and serve with room-temperature milk and sugar on the side.

BIBLIOGRAPHY

BOOKS CONSULTED

(Those I have particularly relied on are marked with an asterisk.)

[Allen, Robert] A Cosmopolite. *The Sportsman in Ireland.* London: Edward Arnold, 1897.

Allen, Darina. *Darina Allen's Ballymaloe Cooking School Cookbook.* Gretna, LA: Pelican Publishing Company, 2002.

(*) ———. *The Complete Book of Irish Country Cooking: Traditional and Wholesome Recipes from Ireland.* New York: Penguin Studio, 1996.

(*) ———. *The Festive Food of Ireland.* West Cork: Roberts Rinehart, 1992.

(*) Allen, Myrtle. *The Ballymaloe Cookbook,* revised and extended edition. Dublin: Gill & Macmillan, 1987.

——— and Fawn Allen. *Local Producers of Good Food in Cork.* Cork: Cork Free Choice Consumer Group, 2004.

Arensberg, Conrad. *The Irish Countryman: An Anthropological Study.* Garden City, NY: The Natural History Press, 1968.

Bates, Margaret. *A Belfast Cookery Book.* Belfast: The Blackstaff Press, 1993.

Belfast Women's Institute Club. *Ulster Fare,* 3rd ed. Belfast: Graham and Heslip Ltd., 1948.

Bell, Jonathan, and Mervyn Watson of the Ulster Folk and Transport Museum. *Farming in Ulster.* Belfast: Friars Bush Press, 1988.

———. *Irish Farming: Implements and Techniques 1750–1900.* Edinburgh: John Donald Publishers Ltd., 1986.

Bellew, Lady Ellinor [compiled by]. *Ellinor, Lady Bellew's Collection of 18th and 19th Century Recipes of Ireland.* Atlanta: The Bellew Family Association of America, 1989.

Bladey, Conrad. *Irish Teatime Companion,* 2nd ed. Linthicum, MD: Hutman Productions, 2000.

(*) Bunn, Mike. *Ireland: The Taste & the Country.* London: Anaya Publishers Ltd., 1991.

Bury, J.B. *Ireland's Saint: The Essential Biography of St. Patrick.* Edited with an introduction and annotations by Jon M. Sweeney. Brewster, MA; Paraclete Press, 2008.

(*) Caherty, Mary. *Real Irish Cookery.* London: Robert Hale Ltd., 1987.

Cahill, Katherine. *Mrs. Delany's Menus, Medicines and Manners.* Dublin: New Island, 2005.

Campbell, Georgina. *Irish Country House Cooking: The Blue Book Recipe Collection.* Dublin: Wolfhound Press, 1995.

Carberry, Mary. *West Cork Journal 1898–1901 or "From the Back of Beyond."* Edited by Jeremy Sandford. Dublin: The Lilliput Press, 1998.

Carr, John, esq. *The Stranger in Ireland: or, a Tour of the Southern and Western Parts of That Country, in the Year 1805.* London: Richard Phillips, 1806.

(*) Clarkson, L.A., and E. Margaret Crawford. *Feast and Famine: A History of Food and Nutrition in Ireland 1500–1920.* Oxford and New York: Oxford University Press, 2001.

Conaghan, Pat. *The Zulu Fishermen: Forgotten Pioneers of Donegal's First Fishing Industry.* Donegal: Bygones Enterprise, 2003.

Connery, Clare. *Irish Food & Folklore: A Guide to the Cooking, Myths, and History of Ireland.* San Diego: Laurel Glen Publishing, 1997.

(*) Cowan, Cathal, and Regina Sexton. *Ireland's Traditional Foods: An Exploration of Irish Local & Typical Foods & Drinks.* Dublin: Teagasc, The National Food Center, 1997.

Davidson, Alan. *The Oxford Companion to Food.* Oxford and New York: Oxford University Press, 1999.

Davidson, James. *Our Daily Bread: A Look at Ulster Bakeries.* Newtownards: Colourpoint Books, 2004.

(*) De Bhaldraithe, Tomás, ed. and trans. *The Diary of an Irish Countryman 1927–1835: A Translation of Humphrey O'Sullivan's* Cín Lae Amhlaoibh. Cork: Mercier Press, 1979.

Donnelly, Nell. *Pot Luck: Potato Recipes from Ireland.* Dublin: Wolfhound Press, 1987.

Dowling, Mary, ed. *The Kylemore Abbey Cookbook.* Dublin: Gill & Macmillan, 1997.

Dundon, Kevin. *Full on Irish: Creative Contemporary Cooking.* Dublin: Epicure Press, 2005.

Feehan, John. *Farming in Ireland: History, Heritage and Environment.* Dublin: University College Dublin Faculty of Agriculture, 2003.

FitzGibbon, Theodora. *A Taste of Ireland: Irish Traditional Food.* New York: Avnel Books, 1968.

(*) ———. *Irish Traditional Food.* Dublin: Gill and MacMillan, 1983.

Flynn, Paul, and Sally McKenna. *Irish Food Fast & Modern.* Durrus: Estragon Press, 2005.

(*) Galvin, Gerry. *The Drimcong Food Affair.* Moycullen: McDonald Publishing, 1992.

Giraldus Cambrensis (Gerald of Wales). *The Historical Works of Giraldus Cambrensis: Containing the Topography of Ireland, and the History of the Conquest of Ireland,* trans. Thomas Forester; *The Itinerary Through Wales, and The Description Of Wales,* trans. Sir Richard Colt Hoare; revised and edited with additional notes by Thomas Wright (Bohn's Antiquarian Library). London: G. Bell, 1913.

Gravette, Andy Gerald. *A Taste of Old Ireland.* London: Caxton Editions, 2002.

Heaney, Seamus. *Opened Ground: Selected Poems 1966–1996.* New York: Farrar, Straus & Giroux, 1998.

Hill, Ian. *The Fish of Ireland.* Belfast: Appletree Press Ltd., 1992.

Hill, Jacqueline, and Colm Lennon, eds. *Luxury and Austerity: Historical Studies XXI.* Dublin: University College Dublin Press, 1999.

Holohan, Renagh. *The Irish Châteaux: In Search of Descendants of the Wild Geese.* Dublin: The Lilliput Press, 1989.

(*) Irwin, Florence. *The Cookin' Woman: Irish Country Recipes.* Belfast: Blackstaff Press, 1986.

Johnson, Margaret M. *Irish Puddings, Tarts, Crumbles, and Fools.* San Francisco: Chronicle Books, 2004.

(*) ———. *The Irish Heritage Cookbook.* San Francisco: Chronicle Books, 1999.

———. *The Irish Pub Cookbook.* San Francisco: Chronicle Books, 2006.

Joyce, P.W. *A Smaller Social History of Ancient Ireland.* London: Longmans, Green & Co., 1908.

———. *English As We Speak It in Ireland.* Dublin: Merlin Publishing, 1988.

(*) Keane, Molly. *Molly Keane's Nursery Cooking: Well-Loved Recipes from Childhood.* London: Macdonald & Co., 1985.

Kelly, Bill, and Vonnie Kelly. *The Book of Kelly's.* Compiled by Ronan Foster. Dublin: Zeus Publishing, 1995.

Kennedy, Brian P., and Raymond Gillespie, eds. *Ireland: Art into History.* Dublin: Town House; and Niwot, CO: Roberts Rinehard Publishers, 1994.

Kinsella, Mary. *An Irish Farmhouse Cookbook.* Belfast: Appletree Press, 1983.

Klein, Betsy. *Cottage Industry: Portraits of Irish Artisans.* Dublin: New Island Books, 2006.

Latimer, Norma, and Gordon Latimer. *Irish Country Cooking.* Los Angeles: Norma and Gordon Latimer, 1985.

(*) Laverty, Maura. *Feasting Galore: Recipes and Food Lore from Ireland.* New York: Holt, Rinehart and Winston, 1961.

———. *Full & Plenty. Vol. 1, Breads and Cakes.* Dublin: Anvil Books, 1960.

———. *Maura Laverty's Cookbook.* London: Longmans, Green & Co., 1947.

(*) Lennon, Biddy White and Georgina Campbell. *The Irish Heritage Cookbook.* London: Lorenz Books, 2004.

Ligoniel Local History Group. *Ligoniel–Ballysillan "Memories."* Belfast: Ligoniel Local History Group, 1999.

Long, John. *Johnny Barleycorn.* College Station, TX: Virtualbookworm Publishing, 2004.

(*) Lucas, A.T. *Irish Food Before the Potato, Gwerin Vol. III, 1960–62.* Denbigh: Gee & Son Limited, 1962.

MacBain, Alexander. *An Etymological Dictionary of the Gaelic Language,* facsimile of the 1911 edition. Glasgow: Garim Publications, 1982.

Mac Coitir, Niall. *Irish Wild Plants: Myths, Legends & Folklore.* Cork: The Collins Press, 2008.

Madden, Lucy. *The Potato Year: 365 Ways of Cooking Potatoes.* Monaghan: Milu Press, 1997.

Magee, Malachy. *Irish Whiskey: A 1000 Year Tradition.* Dublin: The O'Brien Press, 1991.

(*) Mahon, Bríd. *Land of Milk and Honey: The Story of Traditional Irish Food and Drink.* Dublin: Poolbeg Press, 1991.

Marnell, Josephine B., Nora M. Breathnach, et al. *All in the Cooking. Book I, Coláiste Mhuire Book of Household Cookery.* Dublin: The Educational Company of Ireland, Limited, n.d.

McCarthy, Thomas. *Mr. Dineen's Careful Parade: New & Selected Poems.* London: Anvil Press, 1999.

———. *Merchant Prince.* London: Anvil Press Poetry Ltd., 2005.

McCormick, Malachi. *Colum Cille: His Life & Times.* New York: The Stone Street Press, 1996.

———. *A Decent Cup of Tea.* New York: Clarkson Potter, 1991.

———. *In Praise of Irish Breakfasts.* New York: The Stone Street Press, 1991.

(*) ———. *Irish Country Cooking.* New York: Clarkson Potter, 1988.

———. *Irish Traditional Cooking* [boxed set]: *Irish Festive Fare* (1984), *Irish Traditional Soups* (1984), and *Irish Bread & Cake* (1991). New York: The Stone Street Press, 1984–1991.

McGuffin, John. *In Praise of Poteen.* Belfast: The Appletree Press, Ltd., 1978.

(*) McKenna, Clodagh. *The Irish Farmers' Market Cookbook.* London: Collins, 2006.

McQuillan, Deirdre. *Irish Country House Cooking.* New York and Avenel, NJ.: Crescent Books, 1994.

Montgomery-Massingberd, Hugh, editor-in-chief. *Burkes Irish Family Records: Burkes Landed Gentry of Ireland*, 5th ed. Reprint of the 1976 edition. Buckingham: Burkes Peerage & Gentry, 2008.

Morton, H.V. *In Search of Ireland.* London: Methuen & Co., Ltd., 1930.

Moryson, Fynes. *A History of Ireland, from the year 1599 to 1603 with a short Narration of the State of the Kingdom of Ireland from the year 1169. To which is added, a description of Ireland*, Vol. 1 and 2. Dublin: S. Powell for George Ewing, 1735.

O'Connor, Patrick J. *Fairs and Markets of Ireland: A Cultural Geography.* Coolanoran, Newcastle West: Oìreacht na Mumhan Books, n.d.

(*) Ó Crohan, Tomás. *The Islandman.* Translated by Robin Flower. New York: Charles Scribner's Sons, 1935.

O'Curry, Eugene. *On the Manners and Customs of the Ancient Irish.* Edited by W. K. Sullivan. Dublin: Williams and Norgate, 1873.

O'Doherty, Pat. *Fermanagh Black Bacon Cookbook.* Enniskillen: O'Doherty's Fine Meats, 2007.

Ó Drisceoil, Diarmuid, and Donal Ó Drisceoil. *Serving a City: The Story of Cork's English Market.* Cork: The Collins Press, 2005.

O'Mahony, John, and R. Lloyd Praeger. *The Sunny Side of Ireland: How To See It by the Great Southern and Western Railway*, 2nd ed. Dublin: Alex. Thom & Co., n.d. [c. 1900].

O'Mara, Veronica Jane, and Fionnuala O'Reilly. *An Irish Literary Cookbook.* Dublin: Town House, 1991.

O'Shea, Bernadette. *Pizza Defined.* Durrus: Estragon Press, 1997.

Pim, Lady, collector and compiler. *Further Culinary Adventures . . .* Belfast: Northern Whig Ltd., 1947.

Quarton, Marjorie. *Breakfast the Night Before: Recollections of an Irish Horse Dealer.* Dublin: The Lilliput Press, 2000.

———. *Saturday's Child.* London: André Deutsch, 1993.

Reynolds, Bruce. *A Cocktail Continentale.* New York: George Sully & Company, 1926.

Romans, Alan. *The Potato Book.* London: Frances Lincoln Limited, 2005.

Ross, Ruth Isabel. *Irish Family Food.* Dublin: Gill & Macmillan, 1996.

(*) Sexton, Regina. *A Little History of Irish Food.* London: Kyle Cathie Ltd., 1998.

(*) Sheridan, Monica. *The Art of Irish Cooking.* New York: Gramercy, 1965.

Some Bakers Past and Present with Helen McAlister and Fionnuala Carragher. *Fadge Farls and Oven Pots: Glens of Antrim Traditional Breads.* Ballycastle: Feís na nGleann, 2005.

Squire, John, ed. *Cheddar Gorge: A Book of English Cheeses.* London: Collins, 1937.

Stevenson, John. *A Boy in the Country: An Antrim Peat Bog.* London: Edward Arnold, 1912.

———. *Pat M'Carty, Farmer, of Antrim: His Rhymes, with a Setting.* London: Edward Arnold, 1903.

———. *Two Centuries of Life in Down 1600–1800.* Belfast: McCaw, Stevenson & Orr, 1920.

Synge, J.M. *The Aran Islands.* Edited with an introduction by Tim Robinson. London: Penguin Books, 1992.

Thackeray, William Makepeace. *The Irish Sketch-Book.* 1843. Reprint, Charleston, SC: Forgotten Books, 2007.

Tinne, Rosie, compiled by. *Irish Countryhouse Cooking.* New York: Weathervane Books, 1974.

250 Irish Recipes Traditional & Modern. Dublin: Mount Salus Press, n.d.

Uí Chomáin, Máirín. *Irish Oyster Cuisine.* Dublin: A. & A. Farmar, 2004.

Wilkins, Noël P. *Alive Alive O: The Shellfish and Shellfisheries of Ireland.* Galway: Tír Eolads, 2004.

Wilmot, Catherine. *An Irish Peer on the Continent, Being a Narrative of the Tour of Stephen, 2nd Earl Mount Cashel, Through France, Italy, etc. (1801–1803).* London: Williams and Norgate, 1920.

Wilson, Anne C. *Food & Drink in Britain from the Stone Age to the 19th Century.* Chicago: Academy Chicago Publishers, 1991.

———, ed. *Traditional Country House Cooking.* London: Wieidenfeld and Nicolson, 1993.

Yeats, W.B. *The Celtic Twilight: Faerie and Folklore.* Mineola, NY: Dover Publications, 2004.

Zuckerman, Larry. *The Potato: How the Humble Spud Rescued the Western World.* Boston and London: Faber & Faber, 1998.

WEBSITES

A number of websites have been very useful to me in writing this book, and are recommended to those who wish to further investigate Irish food and its cultural and historical underpinnings. Most of the country house hotels and restaurants mentioned in the preceding pages have their own sites, too.

Tourism (including food) in Ireland and Northern Ireland

Georgina Campbell's Ireland:
www.ireland-guide.com

Vacation in Ireland (Official Website of Tourism Ireland):
www.discoverireland.com/us

Eating and Drinking Guides

Bridgestone Guides:
www.bestofbridgestone.com

Good Food Ireland:
www.goodfoodireland.ie

Artisanal and Regional Foods

Country Choice:
www.countrychoice.ie

Ditty's Home Bakery:
www.dittysbakery.com

Food Culture West Cork:
foodculturewestcork.wordpress.com

McGeough's Connemara Fine Foods:
www.connemarafinefoods.ie

Slow Food Ireland:
www.slowfoodireland.com

Taste of Ulster:
www.tasteofulster.org

Food History and Culture

A History of Irish Cuisine:
www.ravensgard.org/prdunham/irishfood.html

Irish Culture and Customs:
www.irishcultureandcustoms.com

Real Traditional Irish Cooking:
www.realirishfood.blogspot.com

Miscellaneous

Ballymaloe Cookery School: www.cookingisfun.ie
The site for Darina Allen's acclaimed school in Shanagarry, County Cork

Clodagh McKenna: www.clodaghmckenna.com
A lively site, filled with recipes, event listings, and more, by a prominent young Irish food writer, television personality, farmers' market advocate, and Slow Food activist

Corpus of Electronic Texts from University College Cork: www.ucc.ie:8080/cocoon/celt/index
Translations of a great deal of early Irish literature, some with food references

Kerrygold: www.kerrygold.com/usa
The official website of the Irish Dairy Board

Wikipedia.org
Includes an astonishing number of well-researched entries on Irish historical figures, towns and villages, literature, etc.

◦ SOURCES ◦

Many Irish or Irish-style products are available in specialty shops and/or by mail order in the United States. Some Irish artisanal producers (for instance, fish smokers) will ship directly from Ireland. Express shipping costs are high (usually more than the cost of the merchandise), so it makes sense to order larger rather than smaller quantities and avoid importing from Ireland what can be found here. In addition, import regulations, especially for perishables like smoked fish and meat, tend to be enforced erratically, and most purveyors ship at the customer's risk. In other words, if your order gets delayed on a loading dock or seized by customs, you pay for it anyway. The sources listed here are all U.S.-based except where otherwise noted.

Various Products

FoodIreland.com: www.foodireland.com
The best all-around source for Irish foods, including a number recommended in this book: Galtee and Donnelly brands of Irish bacon and white pudding, Galtee brand of sausage and black pudding, Winston's sausages, Burren Smokehouse smoked salmon, Odlums Irish flours and bread mixes, and Kerrygold butter in bulk. The site also sells some Irish cheeses, marrowfat peas, and such pantry items as Bisto and Chef and YR sauces.

LittleShamrocks.com
An affiliate of FoodIreland.com that carries many of the same products and also Cashel Blue cheese and Kinvara smoked salmon

Tommy Moloney's: www.tommymoloneys.com
A variety of Irish products, including Kerrygold butter in bulk, Tommy Moloney's own brand of bacon (recommended), and other cured meats, among them chef Kevin Dundon's Dunbrody specialty sausages

Smoked Fish

Ducktrap River of Maine: www.ducktrap.com
Excellent smoked mackerel fillets and also smoked salmon

Frank Hederman: www.frankhederman.com
Hederman's Belvelly Smoke House in Cobh, County Cork, is not currently shipping his excellent smoked products, including salmon, eel, and mackerel, but it's worth checking in occasionally to see if the situation has changed.

Nantucket Wild Gourmet & Smokehouse: www.nantucketwildgourmet.com
An American source of good Irish-style smoked salmon, made by Irish-born Peter O'Donovan, who learned the art from Sally Barnes at Woodcock Smokery

Ummera Smoked Products: www.ummera.com
Smoked organically farmed salmon and smoked eel, as well as smoked chicken and Irish bacon, shipped directly from Ireland

Woodcock Smokery: www.woodcocksmokery.com
Smoked wild salmon and a variety of other smoked fish from one of the best producers in Ireland

Cheese

Artisanal Cheese: www.artisanalcheese.com
Some Irish cheeses

Cowgirl Creamery: www.cowgirlcreamery.com
Some Irish cheeses

Di Bruno Bros.: www.dibruno.com
Some Irish cheeses

Meat and Fish

Browne Trading Company: www.brownetrading.com
Finnan haddie, and also an excellent source for fresh fish and shellfish of all kinds, including organically farmed trout from Ireland

D'Artagnan: www.dartagnan.com
Venison loin and other cuts, plus artisanal-quality chicken, duck, and goose

Scottish Gourmet USA: scottishgourmetusa.gourmetfoodmall.com
Dublin Bay prawns (sold as "Scottish langoustines") and finnan haddie

Miscellaneous

Chelsea Market Baskets: www.chelseamarketbaskets.com
A source for Ditty's oatcakes; if these aren't listed on the website, call 212-727-1111 for information.

Harney and Son Fine Teas: www.harney.com
Malachi McCormick's Decent Tea

Irlonline: www.irlonline.com/carrageen
Carrageen

King Arthur Flour: www.kingarthurflour.com
Irish-style organic whole wheat flour and other high-quality flours, as well as baking utensils

Maine Coast Sea Vegetables: www.seaveg.com
Dulse and laver

Sausage Source: www.sausagesource.com/catalog
Prague Powder #1

Suki Tea: www.suki-tea.com
Belfast Brew Fairtrade Irish Breakfast Tea

Wilderness Family Naturals: www.wildernessfamilynaturals.com
Freeze-dried elderberries

❖ INDEX ❖